P(

Aspe
majc
clear

- In
- C
- A
- G
- D
  cc
- C
- W
- Il

Step
publ
The
1918

Aspe
Step
grad
inter
Brita

ASPECTS OF BRITISH POLITICAL HISTORY, 1815–1914

Stephen J. Lee

London and New York

For Margaret and Charlotte

First published 1994
by Routledge
11 New Fetter Lane, London EC4P 4EE

Simultaneously published in the USA and Canada
by Routledge
29 West 35th Street, New York, NY 10001

Reprinted 1995, 1996, 1999, 2000, 2002

Routledge is an imprint of the Taylor & Francis Group

Typeset in Garamond by
Florencetype Ltd, Stoodleigh, Devon
Printed and bound in Great Britain by
TJ International Ltd, Padstow, Cornwall

British Library Cataloguing in Publication Data
Lee, Stephen J.
Aspects of British Political History,
1815–1914. – (Aspects of History)
I. Title II. Series
941

Library of Congress Cataloguing in Publication Data
Lee, Stephen J.
Aspects of British political history, 1815–1914 / Stephen J. Lee.
p. cm. – (Aspects of history)
Includes bibliographical references (p.) and index.
1. Great Britain – Politics and government – 19th century. 2. Great
Britain – Politics and government – 1901–1910. I. Title.
II Series: Lee, Stephen J. Aspects of history.
DA530.L44 1994
941.081–dc20   94–432

ISBN 0–415–09007–5

CONTENTS

ILLUSTRATIONS

Figures

ILLUSTRATIONS

Plates

1

AN INTRODUCTION TO BRITISH POLITICAL HISTORY 1815–1914

This book is intended to introduce the reader to a range of interpretations on nineteenth- and early twentieth-century British political history. It is designed to act as a basic text for the sixth-form student and to introduce the undergraduate to the wide range of ideas and research relating to the period. I hope it will also capture the imagination of the general reader who likes to go beyond narrative into the realm of debate.

Why *political* history? And what does it mean? During the 1970s and 1980s there was an outpouring of books specifically on social and economic history, a departure from the older type of text which aimed to cover all areas but within the broad context of political history. To some extent the focus on social and economic history is part of a process of establishing a new balance. In the words of G.R. Elton, the reaction against political history, 'although often ill-informed and sometimes silly, has its virtues. These arise less from the benefits conferred upon other ways of looking at the past than from the stimulus given to political history to improve itself.'[1]

Political history now seems to be making a determined come-back, although in a more eclectic guise, covering a wider spectrum and drawing from social, economic and intellectual issues. It is also based more on controversy and debate and less on straight narrative.

Political history may be defined as 'the study of the organisation and operation of power in past societies'.[2] It focuses on people in positions of power and authority; on the impact of this power on various levels of society; on the response of people in power to pressures from below; and on relationships with power bases in other countries. The study of political history fulfils three functions. One is the specific analysis of the acquisition, use and loss of

1

power by individuals, parties and institutions. A second is more generally to provide a meeting point for all other components: social, economic, intellectual, religious – these can all be brought into the arena of political history. But above all, political history offers the greatest potential for controversy and debate. As Hutton maintains, 'More than any other species of history, it involves the destruction of myths, often carefully conceived and propagated. No other variety of historian experiences to such a constant, and awesome, extent, the responsibility of doing justice to the dead.'[3]

The rest of this chapter will outline the main political issues covered in this book. It will also introduce a range of general themes which appear in chapters 2–19 and, finally, look at three broad historiographical frameworks for historical analysis.

THE MAIN POLITICAL ISSUES 1815–1914

In the first two decades of the nineteenth century Britain was at war with France and confronted by the threat of internal revolution (*Chapter 2*). This did not, however, materialise – partly because of the relative weakness of those radicals who wanted violent change and partly because of the effective counter-revolutionary measures taken by Lord Liverpool's government, especially after the end of the French wars in 1815. These, in turn, have been the subject of considerable controversy among historians (*Chapter 3*). The usual interpretation is that the Tories pursued a reactionary course between 1815 and 1821 – the chief advocates of which were Sidmouth and Castlereagh – while from 1822 more enlightened ministers such as Huskisson, Robinson, Canning and Peel introduced a series of reforms which transformed reaction into a period of 'liberal Toryism'. A similar divergence has been claimed in Tory foreign policy (*Chapter 4*) between the measures of Castlereagh and Canning. The former is often strongly associated with the Congress System and with a closer working relationship with the autocratic powers, especially Austria, while Canning is usually held to have followed a more independent line, pursuing British interests which were often in tune with liberal movements in Europe and elsewhere. In both domestic and foreign policy, however, there are strong arguments in favour of an underlying continuity.

It is certainly true that the major change of the first three decades of the nineteenth century was the reform of Parliament by the 1832 Reform Act (*Chapter 5*), and this was introduced by the Whigs in

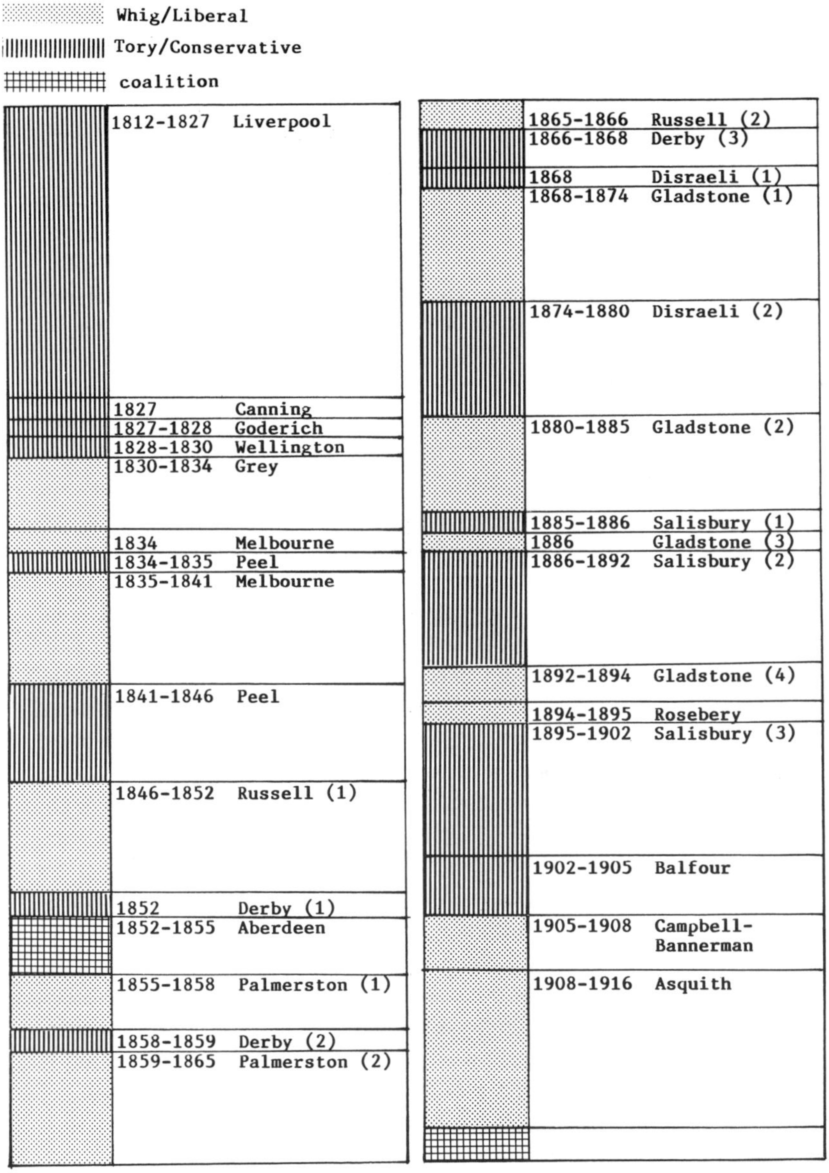

INTRODUCTION

▒▒▒▒▒▒▒	Whig/Liberal
‖‖‖‖‖‖‖‖‖	Tory/Conservative
▥▥▥▥▥	coalition

1812-1827	Liverpool

1865-1866	Russell (2)
1866-1868	Derby (3)
1868	Disraeli (1)
1868-1874	Gladstone (1)

1874-1880	Disraeli (2)

1827	Canning
1827-1828	Goderich
1828-1830	Wellington
1830-1834	Grey

1880-1885	Gladstone (2)

1834	Melbourne
1834-1835	Peel
1835-1841	Melbourne

1885-1886	Salisbury (1)
1886	Gladstone (3)
1886-1892	Salisbury (2)

1892-1894	Gladstone (4)

1841-1846	Peel

1894-1895	Rosebery
1895-1902	Salisbury (3)

1846-1852	Russell (1)

1902-1905	Balfour

1852	Derby (1)
1852-1855	Aberdeen

1905-1908	Campbell-Bannerman

1855-1858	Palmerston (1)

1908-1916	Asquith

1858-1859	Derby (2)
1859-1865	Palmerston (2)

Figure 1 Prime Ministers 1812–1916

3

the teeth of Tory opposition. To some extent, the Whigs saw this as a measure to stave off any future threat of revolution by extending the franchise to the middle classes. Although its political effects were disappointingly limited, the Reform Act did make possible a decade of political domination by the Whigs, which was used to introduce a series of social reforms (*Chapter 6*). These were motivated partly by pressure groups and partly by a genuine desire by the Whig leaders to improve conditions and bring about a more efficient administration at local level. There were, however, deficiencies in these measures, and the overall reforming programme ran out of steam after 1835; hence in 1841 the Whigs lost a crucial general election to the Tories.

Another reason for the political change-over after ten years of Whig power was the revival of the Tories and their transformation into the Conservative party. Largely responsible for this was Sir Robert Peel (*Chapter 7*) whose reputation rests on two bases: his leadership of the Tory party and his national statesmanship. During the 1830s, the two combined very effectively to make Peel a successful leader of a revived and reinvigorated opposition and, at the same time, a much respected national figure. As Prime Minister between 1841 and 1846 he secured a large measure of economic reform, all very much in the national interest, but with the dwindling enthusiasm of the party. In 1846 he quite deliberately put the national interest first and his battle to secure the repeal of the Corn Laws split his party and brought about his own fall.

Meanwhile, two movements had come into existence to campaign in different ways for quite different objectives. One of these was Chartism (*Chapter 8*) which aimed to remedy the gaps left by the 1832 Reform Act and achieve universal suffrage. This was justified partly as an inherent political right and partly as a device to ensure the type of parliament which would best be able to secure the extensive social reforms still needed by the working classes. Because of its diverse origins, membership and measures, and because Peel's economic measures ensured a fairly steady period of economic growth, Chartism never really stood much chance, and the movement folded up in 1848. The other pressure group, the Anti-Corn Law League, was more successful. Set up with the specific purpose of persuading the government to repeal the Corn Laws of 1815 and 1828 (*Chapter 9*), the League eventually won Peel over to its cause. The repeal of the Corn Laws in 1846 more or less completed Peel's policy of free trade and probably contributed to the period of agricultural prosperity in the 1850s and 1860s generally known as the 'golden age of agriculture'. The political impact, however, was the more substantial. The Conservative party split on the issue, the minority joining Peel in the political wilderness. The Peelites, after some years' existence as a separate party between the Conservatives and the Whigs, eventually joined the latter.

A divided Conservative party gave the Whigs a new lease on life for twenty years after 1846. It was no coincidence that this period was dominated by Lord Palmerston (*Chapter 10*), probably the most influential politician of the entire century. Usually associated by historians with an aggressive, individualistic and eccentric foreign policy, Palmerston was also a highly successful Home Secretary and, during the years 1855–8 and 1859–65, a popular Prime Minister. Although a traditionalist Whig (despite his Tory origins), Palmerston was instrumental in bringing together a new political coalition of Whigs, radicals and Peelites, which was already during his lifetime being called the Liberal party. Nevertheless, Palmerston was in many ways an obstacle to further political change and progressives welcomed the end of the 'age of Palmerston' in 1865.

An immediate development was the further extension of the suffrage in 1867 (*Chapter 11*). This came about, curiously, as a result of direct competition between the Liberal and Conservative parties to enfranchise the upper levels of the working class. A further instalment occurred with the 1884 Reform Act. These and other measures greatly broadened the base of party politics. The era when the Whigs and Palmerston had dominated now gave way to an alternation of Conservative and Liberal governments led respectively by Disraeli and Gladstone.

Disraeli (*Chapter 12*) had developed his ideas long before he became prime minister. He had provided the Conservative party with new principles during its period in political exile, although he was unable to give effect to what became known as Disraelian Conservatism until his two ministries of 1867–8 and 1874–80. The reforms of his second government, in particular, showed a combination of progressive aims and pragmatic methods, the precise proportions of which have been the subject of extensive historical debate. The career of his political opponent, Gladstone (*Chapter 13*), followed a very different course. He, too, had been a member of the Tory party but, unlike Disraeli, had been strongly influenced by Peel's economic ideas and followed him into political exile before eventually joining the Whigs and assuming the leadership of the new Liberal party after the death of Palmerston. Gladstonian Liberalism showed influences which were both progressive and traditionalist, the uneasy compromise between the two being all too apparent in his domestic policies. But his major priority after 1880 was to settle the Irish problem. His decision to adopt Home Rule may have been based on genuine altruism, or it may have been an attempt to provide the Liberal party with a single, predominant issue to prevent it from becoming divided on the question of the pace of domestic reform, which the more radical members such as Joseph Chamberlain wanted to accelerate. Whatever the truth, Gladstone's Irish policy split the Liberal party and gravely weakened its electoral performance against the Conservatives between 1885 and 1905.

Meanwhile, British foreign policy had entered a particularly difficult period in the post-Palmerston era (*Chapter 14*). Gladstone and Disraeli advanced different solutions. The former favoured a revival of multilateral co-operation and respecting the nationalist aspirations of the peoples of the Balkans, now Europe's major trouble spot; in the process, however, it cannot be claimed that he achieved very much in any specific sense. Disraeli, on the other hand, applied more pragmatic solutions – based on the balance of power – which often cut through the claims for national self-determination and, while solving immediate diplomatic crises, stored up problems for the future. Another development after 1870 was the revival of British imperialism after a comparative lull for three quarters of a century and its focus especially on the continent of Africa (*Chapter 15*). A variety of reasons have been given for this, including economic rivalries, complications in European diplomacy and the expression of strategic interest. There was also a change in party perceptions: the Conservatives were transformed under Disraeli into the party of Empire. Gladstone, although unenthusiastic in principle, found himself drawn in by local crises. By the end of the century there was, on the one hand, a broad inter-party consensus and, on the other, differences within parties, especially between Liberal Imperialists like Rosebery and little Englanders like Lloyd George.

Dramatic events in the Empire had some impact on the twists and changes in party politics at home. Between 1885 and 1905 the Conservative party dominated the political scene (*Chapter 16*), winning three out of the four general elections of this period. This was due partly to internal crisis within the Liberal party, especially the split over Home Rule for Ireland, and partly to the growing support for the Conservatives brought about by an effective party organisation and by Lord Salisbury's leadership. All of this, however, was changed by the traumatic experience of the Boer War, which shattered Conservative dominance and set the charges for the Liberal landslide of 1906.

The next eight years saw a government which was prepared to commit itself to a more intensive programme of legislation than had ever been seen before (*Chapter 17*). Edwardian Liberalism, under Campbell-Bannerman, Lloyd George and Asquith, aimed at extending the role of the state to secure social reform; this reversed the more traditional emphasis on 'self-help' which had been a feature of Gladstonian Liberalism. In the process, Asquith came into direct confrontation with the Conservative-dominated House of Lords. But although the Liberals won this particular contest, the years 1911–14 saw a slowing of their reforming impetus because of their preoccupation with three further crises, which proved even more destabilising: the opposition of the suffragettes, a resurgence of particularly violent industrial unrest, and the revival of the Irish question. By 1914 the future of Liberal power was very much at issue. A potential threat had also emerged from the left – in the form of a new Labour party (*Chapter 18*). At first Labour MPs had been elected, during the 1870s and 1880s *within* the Liberal party as so-called 'Lib-Labs'. In 1900, however, a new party was established, comprising several Labour groups. But although Labour had separated from the Liberal party, having to some extent grown out of it, it was not yet strong enough to compete with it. Hence, in 1903 an electoral pact was drawn up between the two parties, and Labour managed to exert at least some influence on the domestic policies of Campbell-Bannerman and Asquith. By 1914, however, it had become clear that such co-operation was wearing extremely thin. But what could the next stage be? Direct competition would damage both, to the benefit of the Conservatives.

Another theme of the period is the transformation of Britain's relations with the other powers of Europe between 1895 and 1914 (*Chapter 19*). During the latter half of the 1890s Britain experienced self-imposed isolation in international diplomacy; although contemporaries referred to this as 'splendid' isolation, it is a term which has attracted much controversy. After the turn of the century, this isolation was gradually undermined by a series of agreements although, again, there are disagreements as to whether these meant that Britain was deliberately refocusing her attention away from the Empire and back towards Europe. A probable explanation is that the agreements with France and Russia were conceived as the settlement of imperial rivalries but that they increasingly acquired European commitments, especially as German naval-building was seen as a mounting threat. In 1914 the Liberal government had to decide whether or not to support France against Germany in the crisis following the assassination at Sarajevo and the precise motive for Britain's entry into the First World War is still the subject of historical debate.

The next two chapters provide a more general economic and social focus on the period as a whole. *Chapter 20* examines the process by which mercantilism and protection were gradually replaced during the first half of the nineteenth century by *laissez-faire*; this was due partly to government policy, partly to objective conditions. Despite an obvious slowing down of Britain's economic growth by comparison with other industrial countries after 1870, official policies remained committed to free trade and successive governments refused to introduce the sort of protection applied elsewhere. Virtually the reverse process was apparent in social policies (*Chapter 21*). The side-effects of industrial growth were so serious that governments became more and more inclined after 1815 to intervene in social issues. The result was legislation on factory conditions and public health. Between1870 and 1906 the scope of collectivism was greatly expanded until, with the Liberal reforms between 1906 and 1914, the welfare state was born. As yet, however, there was no attempt to develop macro-economic policies to engineer social change; this was very much a consequence of the world wars of the twentieth century.

Throughout the period 1800–1921 Ireland was a constant theme in British political history. *Chapter 22* provides an overall survey, with the basic argument that long-term trends do not always lead to the apparently logical outcome. Throughout the nineteenth century there was a sustained movement towards breaking the close connection established with Britain by the Act of Union (1800). At first the impetus was O'Connell's radicalism which, in turn, gave way to the nationalism of Parnell and Butt. After the frustration of Gladstone's failure to introduce Home Rule in the 1880s and 1890s, the relationship between the two countries was apparently on the point of a moderate redefinition in 1914. What happened next was a distortion of the previous long-term trends as Ireland moved rapidly towards republicanism in the south and partition in the north: an open acknowledgement of Britain's greatest political failure.

THE MAJOR THEMES OF THE PERIOD

In the course of covering such topics, these chapters will also provide plenty of examples to illustrate a range of terms of particular interest to the political historian; examination of specific issues will at times therefore include comments on more general themes.

The most obvious of these can be referred to collectively as 'dynamics'. Within this category will be found references to 'development', examples being the formation of the political ideas and methods of parliamentarians like Gladstone and Disraeli (*Chapters 12 and 13*). Frequent references are made also to 'change'; this can be either gradual and cautious, as during the Liverpool administration (*Chapter 3*) or aimed more deliberately at pushing back existing political constraints, as occurred after 1905 (*Chapter 17*). 'Evolution' tends to be the keynote of most government policy, although there are instances of pressure being brought to bear by 'protest' and the threat of 'revolution' (*Chapters 2, 3, 5 and 8*). There are several instances of 'transformation' and 'metamorphosis', perhaps the best examples being the reversal of the fortunes of the Liberal and Conservative parties between 1885 and 1906 (*Chapter 16*) and the gradual emergence from an isolationist foreign policy (*Chapter 19*). In the case of every topic there is scope for studying the influences behind change within the context of 'subjective' and 'objective' (or 'internal' and 'external') factors. In *Chapter 15* these can be used literally as well as metaphorically.

Dynamics are usually activated by 'catalysts', events which have a significance far beyond their immediate context. *Chapter 3*, for example, deals with the Catholic Emancipation Act, which set in motion a series of political changes leading eventually to the victory of the Whigs in 1830 and the Great Reform Act of 1832. *Chapter 9* covers the repeal of the Corn Laws which completely altered the political balance in mid-Victorian Britain, just as the Crimean War (*Chapter 10*) changed the shape of British foreign policy for the next thirty years. The Great Depression of the 1870s won and lost elections (*Chapters 12 and 13*) and greatly assisted the rise of Labour (*Chapter 18*). Above all, the Irish situation had a profound impact on British politics, Peel's response in 1846 splitting the

Conservative party (*Chapter 7*) and Gladstone's from 1885 doing the same to the Liberals (*Chapters 13 and 16*).

The interaction of dynamics and catalysts sometimes produces a general trend identifiable as an 'era', although these are often of questionable validity. One was the era of Tory domination, extending through the first two decades of the nineteenth century (*Chapters 2, 3 and 4*). This is often considered to have been followed by an age of reform (*Chapter 6*), a term used by Halévy and Woodward.[4] The middle of the century was controlled by the Whigs – the so-called era of Palmerston (*Chapter 10*), who exerted a greater personal dominance over the political scene than any other Prime Minister of the entire century. A fourth example was the age of imperial expansion (*Chapter 15*), which followed a long period of comparative indifference to colonial acquisitions.

Many of these developments were initiated, or at least affected, by a political decision, usually associated with a particular government or individual. This brings into play the theme of 'motivation'. Why did Peel decide between 1845 and 1846 to repeal the Corn Laws permanently, when suspending them temporarily might have alleviated more quickly the Irish famine (*Chapter 7*)? Why did Disraeli, having led the Conservative opposition to a Liberal measure for parliamentary reform in 1866, introduce the following year a bill which went much further (*Chapter 11*)? And why did Gladstone adopt the policy of Home Rule for Ireland (*Chapter 13*)? Was it through personal conviction that it was an essential means of fulfilling Irish needs? Or was it expediency, an attempt to keep the Liberal party from dividing by focusing its attention on a single great issue?

In dealing with any of these areas, the historian is bound to come across instances of 'stereotyping', the acceptance of a particular place or role for an individual. Castlereagh, for example, is generally labelled a reactionary, Canning a progressive (*Chapters 3 and 4*). Palmerston is considered to have been a great Foreign Secretary but to have offered very little in the domestic field (*Chapter 10*). Gladstone is seen as an idealist, basing his policies on moral principle and Christian ethics, whereas Disraeli was a pragmatist, responding to the demands and opportunities of the moment (*Chapters 11 to 14*). At one extreme, stereotyping may be the result of oversimplification, selection or distortion; as such it is easy to detect. At the other, it is open to historical debate; what to one historian is stereotyping might to another be using a particular

10

historical method for analysis. This brings us to the final subject of the present chapter.

'WHIG', 'TORY' AND 'MARXIST' HISTORY

In addition to specific dynamics there are also broader styles of historical interpretation which apply as much to the nineteenth and early twentieth centuries as to any other period. Three are especially significant: the 'Whig' interpretation, the 'Tory' reaction against this, and the 'Marxist' view.

So-called 'Whig' interpretations focus on British history as a *process*. This involves the gradual evolution of institutions and society through stages which are all integral links in a chain of development. An underlying assumption is the triumph of progress. The nineteenth-century historian, Macaulay, maintained that 'The history of our country during the last hundred and sixty years is evidently the history of physical, of moral and of intellectual improvement'.[5] J.R. Green, a near-contemporary of Macaulay, went a stage further by assuming that this capacity for progress was unique to the English-speaking peoples. It was a result of their predominantly beneficial historical experiences which had fostered toleration and liberty via landmarks like Magna Carta, the 'Glorious Revolution' of 1689, and the 1832 Reform Act. It was common to all 'Whig' historians to make value judgements, to see history as the triumph of progress over stagnation, of reform over reaction. Fundamental to this was the intervention of benevolent influences aiming consciously at reform; these, whether individuals or political parties, were driven as much by altruism as by self-interest.

Against all this is the so-called 'Tory' reaction, a development which is exclusively of the twentieth century and which owes much to the meticulous and detailed research of Sir Lewis Namier. The 'Tory' method reverses the 'Whig' approach in two ways. First, it attaches much less importance to the influence and ideas of individuals, whether politicians or theorists, and sees changes or reforms occurring in a more impersonal manner. Second, 'Tory' history stresses the multiplicity of the influences on any one period or sequence of events. Causation therefore becomes more unpredictable and complex. This is partly because it depends upon more detailed research. According to Namier, 'One has to steep oneself in the political life of a period before one can safely speak, or be sure of understanding its language'.[6] The 'Tory' approach therefore produces an intricate patchwork of more detailed studies rather than the more easily identifiable line favoured by the 'Whigs'. The 'Tories' emphasise depth of study, with the method seen as of equal importance to the deduction, while to the Whigs the deduction is the *rationale* and the revelation. 'Tory' history explains, 'Whig' history justifies.

A third approach to historical study is the 'Marxist' interpretation. In their *Communist Manifesto* of 1848, Marx and Engels wrote that 'The history of all hitherto existing society is the history of class struggles'.[7] The original Marxist argument was that by the nineteenth century History had developed through three phases, each being transformed as a result of an underlying conflict between the class or group in power and a class which was in the ascendant. During the first period, the rivalry had been between ancient monarchies and the nobility. This had produced a synthesis in the second period, in the form of feudalism which, in turn, had been gradually eroded by the bourgeoisie to form capitalism, the system in operation in Britain during the nineteenth century. This third phase, Marx predicted, would eventually be succeeded by a fourth as the working class replaced capitalism with socialism.

As a political analysis this provided a structured rationale for radical, even revolutionary, change. As an historical method, however, it is highly deterministic. History is seen in terms of an inexorable movement towards the replacement of one class by another, with the underlying assumption that this is a positive change. 'Marxist' theory therefore shares with the 'Whig' interpretation a belief that history is the record of progressive development, the triumph of positive forces over negative, although the two approaches had very different notions as to what *was* positive and negative. It should perhaps be pointed out that modern Marxist historians have come a long way since the initial highly structured approach, to which they now refer as 'vulgar Marxism'. They tend to play down the long-term view and focus instead on the complex economic and social issues contributing to particular situations. Perhaps 'Marxist' history has, like 'Whig' history, experienced a 'Tory' reaction.

This book contains many references to historical debates on issues concerning nineteenth-century Britain. The reader will be able to detect several fertile areas for 'Whig', 'Tory' and 'Marxist' controversy. Two might be mentioned here as examples.

The first concerns the period of Lord Liverpool's administration,

INTRODUCTION

especially the years 1815–27 (*Chapter 3*). 'Whig' history would
divide this into two distinct phases: the first as a period of unrelieved reaction, the second of more progressive reform as the
administration began to see the light. Indeed, this was Macaulay's
view during the 1830s. His legacy has only recently been questioned
– by the 'Tory' school, which maintains that a detailed study of the
entire period shows much continuity between the two periods and
that the apparent contrast between 'reaction' and 'reform' is based
on the selection of facts to fit a theory of progress. 'Marxist' history
would emphasise continuity for a different reason: there was no
change at this stage in the social and economic base of the political
support for the Tory government – so why should that government
suddenly introduce a programme of reform?

The second example concerns the reforms of the Whig governments during the 1830s (*Chapter 6*). 'Whig' historians put these
down to a combination of altruism, a desire for greater efficiency,
the influence of philosophers like Bentham, and the political
energies of the Whigs themselves; all of these left a milestone in the
progression of nineteenth-century social reform. 'Tory' historians
query the extent of the changes made or, indeed, their intention:
politicians were influenced more by pragmatic aims, dictated by the
needs of the moment, than by an altruistic search for improvement.
They also dispute the likelihood of Benthamite influences on
nineteenth-century reform. Historians like MacDonagh[8] argue, for
example, that the pattern for reform owed very little to Bentham,
but should rather be seen as 'natural' solutions which would have
occurred to contemporaries anyway. 'Marxist' historians would
again query the actual effectiveness of such reforms in any meaningful social context. Where there was a major departure from past
practice, as with the abolition of the slave trade (1807) and of slavery
in the British Empire (1833), there must have been some change in
Britain's economic base. Slavery, which had helped finance the
Industrial Revolution, had outlived its usefulness and therefore had
to go. What was presented as a humanitarian reform was in reality
an economic adjustment.

The terms 'Whig', 'Tory' and 'Marxist' history describe styles of
historical interpretation rather than *political* viewpoints. But do the
latter in practice exert some influence on the former? This is more
likely to apply to 'Whig' and 'Marxist' than to 'Tory' historians.
Since 'Whig' history sees individual statesmen or parties as the main
influences behind progress, it could easily be inferred that the

Whigs, as reformers, were the positive pole of nineteenth-century British history, while the Tories were the negative, because they invariably defended existing institutions. Similarly, 'Marxist' history might well overemphasise the element of economic or class-based interest when dealing with political or social reform, assuming that the aims of all Whig-Liberal and Tory-Conservative governments were fundamentally the same: that is, to uphold an economic system based on exploitation of cheap labour. Since 'Tory' history is largely a reaction against the earlier habit of drawing out long-term trends and focusing instead on detailed study, it is more likely to be politically neutral and to avoid any tendency to polemicise.

On the other hand, few historians would now wish to be labelled within any one of the three schools. Even the most self-conscious of the three, the 'Marxist' historians, make great play out of the difficulty of defining modern 'Marxist' – rather than 'vulgar Marxist' – history. In any case, few western historians would *wish* to show political bias, aiming quite deliberately at rising above it. Perhaps, therefore, it makes sense to select the most constructive components of all three approaches and thereby achieve a synthesis between them. This might include an awareness of progress (but also of regress), an ability to relate political developments to social and economic influences, and a willingness to search in depth for an understanding of a particular period in the past without the intrusion of some ulterior motive dictated by the present.

2

BRITAIN AND THE THREAT OF REVOLUTION 1789–1832

The opening of the nineteenth century saw Britain at war with France and in the throes of social and economic change. But was she also vulnerable to revolution? The French historian E. Halévy argued in 1922 that she was. That she escaped it was more by luck than through any inherent stability; indeed, the whole country 'might easily have lapsed into anarchy had there existed in England a bourgeoisie animated by the spirit of revolution'.[1] The British economic historian E. Hobsbawm subsequently provided the motive. At no time since the seventeenth century, he wrote in 1968, had the common people been 'so persistently, profoundly, and often desperately dissatisfied'.[2]

This chapter will examine three specific periods in the light of these arguments. The first is the period of Britain's struggle with Revolutionary and Napoleonic France; the second is the turbulent years immediately following the 1815 peace settlement; and the third is the much shorter but more acute crisis over the passing of the Reform Bill between 1831 and 1832. In each case it will examine the nature of radical and revolutionary activity, assess the extent of any threat, and explain how it was overcome.

1793–1815

At first sight it would appear that the period between 1793 and 1815 provided a unique opportunity for a sudden change of regime. An essential prerequisite for revolution is economic upheaval, usually exacerbated by war. Between 1793 and 1815, Britain's period of accelerated industrial change had been interrupted and retarded by the struggle with France; according to J. and B. Hammond, 'the poverty and misery it caused are incalculable'.[3] Annual government

15

expenditure rose from £20 million per annum to £106 million, financed partly by heavy increases in taxation on essential items such as salt, soap, leather, sugar, tea and candles. More serious still was the impact of Napoleon's attempted economic blockade; the Berlin Decrees of 1806 closed European markets to British wool and cotton exports, with a consequent effect on unemployment. The overall economic situation was so serious that it seemed for a while that all the recent advances of the Industrial Revolution had been suddenly checked.[4] During the 1790s an extra dimension was added by a series of disastrous harvests which drove up food prices and created severe shortages. Overall, distress was widespread, acting, in the view of H.T. Dickinson, as 'a major recruiting agent for the radical cause'.[5]

This cause was given impetus after 1789 by the French Revolution. The ideas of liberty and equality, developed by Rousseau and enacted by the National Assembly, were initially widely welcomed. Even more influential was Thomas Paine's *Rights of Man* which adapted the principle of popular sovereignty to British conditions and advocated extensive reform introduced by 'a general convention elected for the purpose'.[6] A variety of groups sprang up, including the Friends of the People, the Society for Constitutional Information (1791), the London Corresponding Society (1792), the Friends of Universal Peace and Rights of Man (1792), and the Sheffield Association (1792). Even after the outbreak of war with France in 1793, there was sympathy for the French Republic. In 1795, for example, the London Corresponding Society's anti-war protest in Copenhagen Fields attracted 150,000 supporters. Even religious groups were suspect. The Bishop of Rochester, for example, attacked the Methodists as being the 'tool' of the Jacobins.[7]

But did economic distress and the growth of radical ideas necessarily mean that there was a threat of revolution in Britain? There were certainly sporadic threats to government security in England, which were influenced by Republican ideas; these included the naval mutinies at Nore and Spithead in 1797 and the activities of the United Englishmen societies in Cheshire, West Yorkshire and the Midlands. Rumours of uprisings persisted throughout the War. In 1812 they were taken so seriously by the government that 12,000 troops were allocated to quell disturbances. There was also a latent menace in Scotland. Mob riots were widespread in August and September 1797 in an area extending from Perthshire to the

Borders, largely in response to the government's decision to extend conscription. It was from Ireland, however, that the real threat emanated. There was considerable scope for this resentful colony to undermine the war effort against France. It had a population of 4 million (compared with a mere 10 million in Britain itself), much of it Catholic and radicalised by religious and political grievances and by nationalist opposition to British rule. Both the French Republic and Napoleon's Empire realised the potential offered by Ireland for chaos; they therefore financed disturbances wherever possible and on occasion resorted to direct intervention, as for example an attempt to land an invasion force in 1796. In 1798 there were no fewer than three uprisings in Ireland. The first, in May, occurred in the south, to be followed, in June, by a rebellion in the north-east, and in the autumn by two invasions. In 1803 Emmett's rising in Dublin again stretched British defences. There was also the possibility of raids on the north-western coasts of England. Indeed, according to H.T. Dickinson, there was a real attempt at 'a union of revolutionary forces in Ireland, France and Britain'.[8]

Despite these manifestations of unrest, most historians now accept that there was relatively little threat of general insurrection, at least on the British mainland.[9] A variety of reasons can be advanced for this.

In the first place, the ideology of Revolutionary France exercised only a limited influence on Britain. With the exception of idealists like Paine and Godwin, most English theorists related less to French developments than to the 'Glorious Revolution' in Britain: less to 1789 than to 1689. This meant that their emphasis was not so much on starting again and constructing a new political system as on reforming the existing one to revive the spirit of an earlier age. Most were therefore inspired more by Locke than by Rousseau. In any case, the disturbances which occurred before and after 1800 had precedents in the eighteenth century; there had been serious rioting long before the outbreak of the French Revolution, together with campaigns for constitutional reform led by the likes of Wilkes and Wyvill. There was therefore already a tradition of radicalism within Britain. The French Revolution revived enthusiasm for it but did not, except for a minority of activists, provide a blueprint for change. Besides, the societies with the widest appeal were usually those which were the least explicitly revolutionary. They existed more as discussion groups, with an overtly educational purpose.

Second, those organisations which did aim consciously at

insurrection had serious organisational deficiencies. They showed little understanding of how to plan a concerted campaign involving several areas simultaneously or of the need to secure the full involvement of labour combinations. This was partly because the organisers themselves tended not to come from these levels of society and showed little understanding of them. Even in Ireland, always the most unstable part of the British Isles, the opportunities for insurrection were often missed through problems of direction and of liaison with France. After the disaster of 1796 the French were unwilling to act without previous evidence of full-scale Irish rebellion; the Irish were reluctant to risk this without a guarantee of French intervention.

Third, various forms of Protestantism acted as a restraining influence. It was originally thought that Methodism played an active role in inciting revolution in Britain. Canning, for example, denounced all Dissenters in 1792 and the Bishop of Rochester considered that the French Jacobins were 'making a tool of Methodism'. Twentieth-century historians, however, have tended to reverse the argument, and to see Methodism as a major factor preventing political upheaval, although there has been considerable disagreement as to how this worked in practice. Halévy found in Methodism the explanation he needed for middle-class quiescence. 'From the beginning', he argued, 'Nonconformity had been the religion of the middle class and particularly of the lower middle class'.[10] As such it had denounced political activism. In 1792, for example, the Statutes of the Wesleyan body emphasised loyalty and obedience to King and government. 'None of us shall either in writing or in conversation speak lightly or irreverently of the Government. We are to observe that the oracles of God caused us to be subject to the higher powers; and that honour to the King is there connected with the fear of God.'[11] E.P. Thompson also made a case for Methodism stressing political conformity, but argued that this affected the working rather than the middle class. This was largely because Methodism believed fervently in hard work, which tended to favour industrial obedience rather than radical syndicalism. Hence, according to Thompson, the Methodist leaders 'weakened the poor from within, by adding to them the active ingredient of submission; and they fostered within the Methodist Church those elements most suited to make up the psychic component of the work-discipline of which the manufacturers stood most in need'.[12] The arguments of Halévy and Thompson may be overstated and place insufficient emphasis on the contributions of Methodism to parliamentary and social reform. But they do demonstrate that even the non-established religious sects in mainland Britain acted as a stabilising force. They had no reason to undermine the existing regime or to question its legitimacy, even though many of their members were experiencing hardship and distress.

Revolutions normally break out when governments lose control and fail to take effective measures to deal with disturbances, whether organised or spontaneous. There is no evidence that the administrations of Pitt and his successors ever lost the initiative, even when they admitted that they were hard pressed. Severe penal measures were introduced, including the prosecution of Thomas Paine and the transportation of activists such as Palmer and Muir. The government also established the Committee of Secrecy in 1794, which provided information on plots and attempted uprisings. Legislation included the Treasonable Practices Bill 1795, the Seditious Meetings Bill 1795, the Corresponding Act 1799 banning Corresponding Societies, and the Combination Acts of 1799 and 1800 which prohibited organisations of workmen. According to Gregg,[13] reformers stood little chance against such a battery of measures. Although there were instances of violence and attempted uprisings, these were isolated and had no support from a broader reforming movement, since the latter had been effectively silenced. 'In this respect Pitt's Government had done its work well.'[14]

The British government in any case had a broader base of stability than mere repression. Revolutions do not usually occur when this base exists or, in the words of H. Arendt, 'where the authority of the body politic is truly intact'.[15] Despite Halévy's reservations about them, British institutions were in fact fundamentally stable. All the problems leading to the collapse of the *ancien régime* in France had been at least partially addressed in Britain. Arbitrary royal power had been checked by the Revolution of 1688-9; the executive was rooted firmly in the legislature, ministers being drawn from both Houses; financial responsibility rested unequivocally with the Commons, a principle which had been won at the expense of the Stuart dynasty in the seventeenth century; and governments functioned more or less efficiently as a result of the evolution of the cabinet system during the eighteenth century. The whole system was lubricated by a rudimentary party system which allowed for the controlled expression of political opposition.

The *status quo* also possessed powerful ideological backing.

A regime is especially vulnerable to radical change when it provokes the unanimous opposition of the intellectuals. The writers in eighteenth-century France had been devastating in their criticism of French institutions. The same, however, did not apply to the writers of the British Enlightenment. In Edmund Burke the British establishment found its greatest defender and advocate. His *Reflections on the Revolution in France* and his *Appeal from the New to the Old Whigs* attacked the abstract constitutional prescriptions devised in the minds of philosophers as the 'nakedness and solitude of metaphysical abstraction'; these could result only in 'artificial contrivances' of government. A country's political system was a living organism which benefited from evolutionary growth but would be killed by a sudden and violent change. Revolution could only produce chaos, with a broad-based government narrowing rapidly to tyranny. In his view, 'Neither the few nor the many have the right merely to act by their Will'.[16] Other writers included Robert Nares, William Cusac Smith, Francis Plowden, Samuel Horsley, John Reeves, Samuel Cooper and William Paley. Their ideas underpinned the British parliamentary system, providing a powerful antidote to the democratic principles of Rousseau.

There is one possible scenario in which political stability *might* have degenerated overnight into chaos. What if Britain had been invaded and defeated in the French Wars? The whole regime would have been destabilised through the cumulative pressures of financial collapse, the disintegration of the army and of the secondary forces of law and order, and the psychological impact on the population. This, of course, did not happen. Secure behind the wooden battlements of the Royal Navy, Britain avoided the bruising encounters with Napoleon experienced by Russia, Prussia and Austria. Instead, the British government was able to select the points of confrontation: hence the naval victories at Cape St Vincent, the Nile and Trafalgar, and the military successes of the Peninsular War. Virtually the only engagement actually forced upon the British was the last: Waterloo in 1815. Throughout the War the government remained fully in control and could rely on an incipient patriotism felt by most of the population. It also retained the economic initiative. Although short of essential supplies and unable to avoid a major trade depression, Britain was able to win the economic war started by Napoleon. Finally, the army and navy were far from disintegration and there was to be no repetition of the mutinies of 1797.

1815-22

It would seem a reasonable deduction that the return to peace in 1815 would lift from Britain all threats of insurrection. But, if anything, the situation deteriorated – initially for economic reasons. Over a period of twenty-two years the British economy had adjusted itself to the distortions imposed by perpetual warfare. The government had become the major customer of the Industrial Revolution, stimulating certain selective industries and compensating, to some extent, for the closure of overseas markets. Orders had been placed to supply the Royal Navy, and the troops fighting Napoleon in the Peninsular War, with uniforms from Lancashire and Yorkshire and arms from Sheffield and Birmingham. This artificial stimulus suddenly ceased in 1815, to be replaced by a huge gap in the domestic market. This was not yet filled by demand for British goods by the rest of Europe which was, of course, experiencing its own post-war crisis. Since manufacturers could not take immediate advantage of the lifting of the Continental System, their only solution was to reduce production. In many instances this meant closure, a typical example being the loss of twenty-four out of Shropshire's thirty-four blast furnaces. The result was a sharp increase in unemployment, exacerbated in turn by the demobilisation of 300,000 men from the armed services. The labour market was therefore flooded at the very time that industrial production was contracting. The only way out of this vicious circle was expansion, but this was delayed immediately after the War by a major, world-wide trade depression.

For a while most of the population at least benefited from low corn prices, the result partly of good harvests in 1813 and 1814 and partly of the resumption of imports of corn from Europe. Bread prices actually dropped by 50 per cent between 1813 and 1815. Unfortunately this had a serious impact on the producers. The government reacted with a round of fierce protectionism in the form of the 1815 Corn Law, which prevented the import of foreign corn into Britain until the price of domestic supplies had reached 80 shillings per quarter. The basic problem confronting Liverpool's administration was that action to help one part of the population adversely affected another, thereby increasing the likelihood of violent opposition.

With this background it is not surprising that radicalism continued after 1815, even attaining a new momentum. After 1815 three trends were apparent. The first was peaceful radicalism advocating parliamentary reform and based on campaigns by Major John Cartwright, Henry 'Orator' Hunt, Francis Place and William Cobbett. As in the case of the meeting at St Peter's Fields in 1819, their motives were frequently misinterpreted by the authorities, resulting in tragedy. The second trend was a more spontaneous expression of grievances, often without concerted leadership. The Luddites, for example, went in for widespread machine-wrecking in the West Riding of Yorkshire, Lancashire and the Midlands until 1817; in that year also occurred the March of the Blanketeers, a peaceful campaign intended to bring to the attention of government authorities the plight of northern workers. Third, there were organisations which were more directly committed to subversion and revolution. The two main instances of this were the Derbyshire Insurrection (Pentridge Uprising) of 1817 and the Cato Street Conspiracy of 1820 which aimed to assassinate Lord Liverpool's entire cabinet. Similar plots were uncovered in the same year in Glasgow, Huddersfield, Sheffield and Barnsley. Sometimes the three levels of radicalism overlapped. Perhaps the best example of this was the Spa Fields Riots of 1816; a reform rally convened by 'Orator' Hunt degenerated into a more spontaneous eruption of grievances among the crowd, a section of which came under the influence of revolutionary Spenceans and broke into gunsmith shops to arm themselves for an attack on the Tower. The authorities were inevitably confused in their interpretation of this type of incident, a problem exacerbated by the absence of regular law enforcement machinery.

Contemporaries were in no doubt about the threat posed by such outbreaks or about the extent of disillusionment and hatred. Henry Cockburn, for example, said 'I have never known a period at which the people's hatred of the government was so general and so fierce'.[17] Modern authorities also state that it would be unwise to 'deny that a revolutionary underground existed in Britain'.[18] They stress, too, the limitations of the law enforcement machinery, which was equivalent in 1820 only to that in 1588.[19] Had there been revolutionary outbreaks, the authorities would not have been able to deal with them. F.O. Darvall, in particular, focuses on 1816-17, along with 1811-12; 'there occurred during those years the most widespread, persistent, and dangerous disturbances, short of actual revolution or civil war, that England has ever known in modern times'. He adds: 'Then, if ever, the seeds of a revolutionary situation existed. Then, if ever, a revolutionary attempt would have had a real chance of success'.[20]

Darvall admits that this can be no more than speculation. The fact is that revolution did *not* occur after 1815, largely because the majority of the radicals did not consider it a serious option. Those who were most influential in their demands for change in England were radicals like Cobbett, whose *Letter to the Luddites* in 1816 actually deprecated the use of violence and argued the case for reform. N. Gash goes so far as to say that 'Cobbett was a tory radical rather than a doctrinaire democrat'.[21] The genuine revolutionaries, such as the Spenceans or the colleagues of Arthur Thistlewood or Doctor Watson, were always on the fringes of radicalism, never part of its mainstream. They had no national organisation to promote subversion and no means of linking together the individual conspiracies which occurred in isolation in separate parts of the country. There were no consistent concentrations of discontented mobs, no mass migrations to the capital, and there was no scope for direct participation in national events. All this was in marked contrast to the history of France between 1789 and 1792 which, as historians like R. Cobb and G. Lefebvre have demonstrated, was heavily influenced by the 'crowd'.

It could also be argued that any possibility of insurrection was nipped in the bud by a government which recognised the threat to the extent of exaggerating it. Liverpool's responses were no less decisive than those of Pitt which, according to E.J. Evans, they 'exactly mirrored'.[22] At first the government concentrated on gathering information by using spies who, like Oliver, provided vital warning of the Derbyshire Insurrection. Then, in 1817, the government suspended habeas corpus and imposed a ban on 'seditious meetings'. These measures were followed in 1819 by Sidmouth's Six Acts, which empowered magistrates to search houses for firearms and seditious literature; prohibited military drilling by civilians; imposed restrictions on political meetings; enabled trials to take place without juries; and increased stamp duties on pamphlets and newspapers. The effects of the Six Acts have been hotly debated. N. Gash, for instance, considers that they were never fully enforced, while J. Marlow argues that they were 'a virtually watertight blanket over the Radical activities'.[23] Either way, the government can be considered to have come out on top. If, as Gash believes, the powers allowed to the authorities went by default, the reason must have been the declining threat posed to them. Alternatively, as Marlow maintains, the Six Acts may have had a direct bearing on the bankruptcy of radicalism, reducing the movements from a peak in 1818 and 1819 to 'next to nothing – a most spectacular collapse'.[24]

1831–2

We have seen Darvall's view that the periods immediately before and after 1815 were potentially the most dangerous in recent British history. Thomis and Holt, however, put forward a different case, arguing that the crisis over the Reform Bill between 1831 and 1832 enabled activists to 'produce a better scheme for accomplishing revolution than anything previously devised'.[25]

The background was a period of sustained pressure and discontent. The first threat came from Ireland with Daniel O'Connell's election to Westminster, despite a legal ban on Catholic representation. The Duke of Wellington made a sensible tactical withdrawal, acceding to Catholic emancipation in 1829. In the process, however, he provided ammunition for those who argued that the reform of the House of Commons needed to be more extensive still (see Chapter 5). The lobby to extend the franchise was by this stage more extensive than it had ever been before, and included a wide range of opinion from the official Whig opposition, through the lower middle-class radicals, to the more militant sectors of the urban and rural working classes. It was rendered the more effective because of two crises lurking in the background. One was the agricultural distress of 1830, which precipitated the Swing riots in the south-eastern counties. The other was the outbreak of the French Revolution in the same year, which overthrew Charles X. The latter particularly worried the Tory Home Secretary, Peel, who complained:

> The success of the Mobs and either the unwillingness or inability of the soldiers to cope with them in Paris and Brussels is producing its natural effect in the Manufacturing districts, calling into action the almost forgotten Radicals of 1817 and 1819, and provoking a discussion upon the probable results of insurrectionary movements in this country.[26]

Peel had cause to be concerned, although the actual disturbances in Britain occurred during the troubled passage of the parliamentary Reform Bill during the administration of the Whig leader, Grey.

There were two particular periods in which revolution was more than just a theoretical possibility. The first was October 1831. Grey requested and secured a general election on the issue of parliamentary reform. Since this resulted in an increased majority for the Whigs, Grey took it as a mandate to proceed. But the House of Lords refused the Commons Bill on 7 October. Widespread disturbances followed in different parts of the country. In Bristol, especially, mobs rioted for several days, in the process committing considerable destruction. Much the same happened in the West Country, including Sherborne, Tiverton and Yeovil. Worse was to follow in May 1832 when the Lords again rejected the government's proposals. Grey resigned in disgust and the King invited Wellington to take his place. In the renewed rioting which ensued, the normally non-violent radicalism of men such as Francis Place and William Attwood gave way to dark threats. 'Let the Duke take office as Premier', warned Place, 'and we shall have a commotion in the nature of civil war'.[27] In the event, this resolve was not tested. Wellington failed to form a government, Grey returned, and the Lords bowed to the Commons under the threat of being flooded with newly created Whig peers.

There are two ways of looking at the threats underlying these events. One is to see in them a real danger of revolution. It could be argued, for example, that the forces of law and order would have been impossibly stretched had the crisis over the Reform Bill continued through 1832 into 1833. Policing difficulties had been painfully exposed by the disturbances of 1831 and 1832; how could a total of 11,000 men hope to cover the entire country in the event of a more concerted campaign? Ranged against them would have been more carefully prepared groups which had been collecting arms at a rate which was 'far more extensive than it had been during any previous crisis'.[28] Revolution did not, of course, materialise. But this was because the passing of the First Reform Act removed the immediate source of aggravation and neutralised the arguments for violent action. In other words, the threat of revolution was sufficient; further action was unnecessary.

There is an alternative perspective. The situation in 1832 was altogether different from that in the 1790s or 1815–20. A reforming government had been elected on a mandate to change the electoral system but had been stopped in its tracks by a reactionary response from the House of Lords. The popular response was one of outrage against the obstacle, not against the government – in clear contrast to the demonstrations against the earlier Tory administration. The Whig government actually benefited from the demonstrations and threats of instability, although there is no evidence that it encouraged them. It was unlikely to be harmed directly by them as long as their motivation remained political and did not adopt a more radical motive of social change. The great Whig historian, Macaulay, who was then a young idealist, argued that the best prophylactic against revolution was reform, which would produce 'a complete reconciliation between the aristocracy and the people'. In particular, he was concerned about 'a narrow oligarchy above; an infuriated multitude below. That government is attacked is a reason for making the foundations of government broader, and deeper, and more solid'.[29] This approach produced a temporary identity of interest between the Whigs and the radicals, who vented their resentment instead against the typical view of the House of Lords expressed by the Tory, Eldon: 'sacrifice one atom of our glorious constitution and all the rest is gone'.[30] This situation was certainly confusing and disconcerting; but did it amount in any way to a threat of revolution?

COMMON FEATURES

Although differing in many repects, the three periods of instability had a common link. Radical activity aimed at achieving political reform and rarely strayed into the area of social transformation. During the 1790s, many societies actually warned against attempting to achieve greater social equality by revolutionary action. The Sheffield Society for Constitutional Information, for example, stated: 'We are not speaking of that visionary equality of property, the practical assertion of which would desolate the world, and replunge it into the darkest and wildest barbarism'.[31] Of all the radical leaders throughout the period only Thomas Spence included landed property as one of his targets.[32] Why was this?

The main reason was that radical social movements were not within the recent British experience. There had been no ideologist to argue that change should have economic roots. Transformation was seen as political first and foremost, with the cause of universal suffrage the best means of dealing with the 'bread and butter' question. Throughout the first half of the nineteenth century there had also been a reluctance for tactical reasons to encumber a campaign for political reform by a demand for direct social action. This could well explain why 'The popular movements never became revolutionary and the revolutionary movements never became popular'.[33]

3

TORY RULE 1812–30

Lord Liverpool succeeded Spencer Perceval as Prime Minister in 1812 and governed Britain until incapacitated by a stroke in 1827. With the exception of Sir Robert Walpole's term (1721–41), this was the longest continuous service given by any prime minister in British history. In complete contrast, the next three years saw a rapid succession of three ministries: Canning (1827), Goderich (1827–8) and Wellington (1828–30).

These contrasting timespans suggest two issues for analysis. First, did the long administration of Liverpool divide into distinct phases, or did it experience overall continuity? And second, why did the Tory party fall into rapid decline after 1827, enabling the Whigs to form a government in 1830?

'REACTIONARY' AND 'LIBERAL' TORYISM

One of the major debates on early nineteenth-century Britain concerns the nature of Toryism between 1815 and 1830.

The traditional view is that Liverpool's administration experienced a change of heart half-way through, shifting from reaction to reform. E. Halévy, for example, contrasted 'the counter-revolutionary terror'[1] initiated in December 1816 with the 'first victories of British Liberalism'[2] won in the early 1820s. Sir L. Woodward maintained that the watershed was the suicide of Castlereagh, which 'marked the end of the old toryism because the leadership of the House of Commons passed to Canning'.[3] W.R. Brock, too, emphasised the importance of ministerial changes enabling Liverpool 'to gather round him a group of liberal-minded men ready to take whatever opportunities were offered for economic reform'.[4] More recently this line has also been followed by

D. Beales, who refers to a distinctive period of 'Liberal Toryism', [5] and by A. Wood, who considered Canning, Peel and Huskisson as 'the main force in the new policy that is so striking in the last years of the Tory reign'.[6] This interpretation is really a refinement of the older view of the nineteenth-century Whig historians. Spencer Walpole, for example, argued that before 1822 men like Eldon 'withstood all reform' and that 'Englishmen enjoyed less real liberty than at any time since the Revolution of 1688'. That was until 'the Tory Party, under new guidance . . . deserted its old colours' and for 'the first time in its history . . . had the courage to pass over to the popular cause'.[7]

This seems an attractive thesis. The main features of the period 1815–20 had apparently been disturbances alternating with government repression. Hence the Spa Field Riots (1816), the March of the Blanketeers (1817) and the Pentridge Uprising (1817) were followed by the suspension of habeas corpus, while the more comprehensive measures included in the Six Acts were the immediate reaction to the Peterloo massacre of 1819. After 1822 there was a striking change as the pattern of distress, demonstrations and reaction gave way to a more or less sustained impetus of reform. The economic measures of Huskisson and Robinson included the reduction of import duties on a variety of materials and the relaxation of the Navigation Acts to promote trade reciprocity agreements with other countries. Attempts were also made to alleviate the effects of the 1815 Corn Law by the introduction in 1828 of a more flexible sliding scale. Meanwhile, working-class organisation was legalised in 1824 by the repeal of the Combination Acts in 1824 and by the 1825 Amending Act. Law and order were substantially affected by Peel's reforms at the Home Office; these included the revision of the penal code to reduce the number of capital offences, the partial reform of the prisons through the Gaols Act (1823), and the introduction of a new system of law and order for London in the Metropolitan Police Act of 1829. Finally, the period saw two important religious reforms; Dissenters benefited from the repeal of the Test and Corporation Acts in 1828 and Catholics from the Emancipation Act of 1829.

The consensus of recent experts, however, is that the contrast between the periods before and after 1822 has been overdrawn. J.E. Cookson, for example, argues that Liverpool's administration was 'neither reactionary nor suddenly reformist in 1822'.[8] N. Gash, too, presses the case that 'the mythical transformation of the ministry from "reactionary tory" before 1822 to "liberal tory" afterwards was the invention of subsequent historians. Liverpool's object was not to alter course but to reorganise his crew for a voyage that had already started'.[9]

There are three possible ways in which such continuity can be established between the two periods. In the first place, it can be argued that the government's reputation for unrelieved repression before 1822 is undeserved. Liverpool's early measures hardly amounted to a reign of terror, as Halévy claimed. The suspension of habeas corpus in 1817 was intended to be temporary, lasting from June 1817 until January 1818 and altogether affecting forty-four people. It was designed as a specific instrument to deal with a specific threat – revolutionary subversion such as the attempted Pentrich Uprising. Peterloo was, of course, a disaster for the government's public image. But it was also uncharacteristic in its bloodshed and violence; it was for this reason, according to Gash, that it 'achieved notoriety'.[10] The scope of the Six Acts has also been exaggerated. Powers given to the magistracy to search for arms and prevent mass meetings were strictly temporary, while the other measures plugged loopholes in laws which already existed. Throughout this troubled period the government resorted to legal measures when it had to, but preferred to conciliate when it could. Occasionally it was even prepared to reprimand hardline employers. Sidmouth, for example, criticised magistrates and ship-owners for being excessively harsh and for provoking Tyneside disturbances of 1815. And, during a weavers' strike in 1818, the government accused Manchester manufacturers of 'relying on the support of the law instead of considering the justice of the demands made on them'.[11]

Second, the reforms introduced after 1822 were preceded by others during the so-called 'reactionary' period; in many instances the latter were actually the foundations of the former. This was partly because of a basic continuity in the personnel of Liverpool's administration, despite the attention given to cabinet changes. Most of the supposedly new and progressive ministers had in fact already served 'lengthy and generally dutiful apprenticeships before 1822'.[12] Robinson, for example, had been in government since 1809, while Huskisson had been attached to Liverpool's team of economic advisers. Early reforms of intrinsic importance included the legislation of 1817 alleviating the truck system in coal mines and iron and steel industries; the promotion of savings banks; and a government scheme for sponsoring employment of the poor through loans for fisheries and public works.[13] Even more important were the 1819 Factory Act, which regulated the employment of children in the mills, and the promotion of Friendly Societies to encourage self-help. Such reforms were accompanied by a series of blueprints for future changes. The budgets of Vansittart and Wallace established the basic principles of free trade which were to be developed more fully after 1822 by Huskisson and Robinson.[14] Similarly, Sidmouth had already prepared the groundwork and even a first draft for some of Peel's reforms of the criminal code. Even in foreign policy there was more continuity than has generally been recognised. Castlereagh's death did not necessarily mark a major break or usher in a new direction based on the withdrawal of Britain from conti-nental commitments: to some extent this had already been fore-shadowed in Castlereagh's State Paper of 1820.

The balance between the periods before and after 1822 can be reset in a third way. Just as the early years of Liverpool's adminis-tration were not as repressive as was once thought, so the period 1822–30 was less progressive. The extent of the Tory government's reforms should not be exaggerated. There were limits beyond which none of the Tory ministries were prepared to go. There was, for example, permanent and sustained opposition to the possibility of parliamentary reform, in direct contrast to the Whigs who had espoused it as an integral part of their party policy. Social and religious reforms were safer and less radical, but even these were tactical concessions to prevent the build-up of intolerable pressures, rather than the proof of a change of heart. For example, the repeal of the Combination Acts was in part a means of neutralising working-class subversion by legitimising organisation and preventing it from going underground again. The grant of Catholic emancipation in 1829 was due at least in part to the potentially dangerous situation in Ireland. Wellington's solution was to concede the religious prin-ciple without acknowledging that it had any relevance to the consti-tution. It was left to the Whigs after 1830 to draw the connection between the two and adopt a more comprehensive approach to reform.

THE DECLINE OF THE TORIES 1827–30

After 1827 the grip held until then by the Tories gradually loosened until, in 1830, the Whigs were able to form their first government since their brief spell in power between 1806 and 1807. A variety of factors contributed to this political transformation.

The most immediate was the vacuum left by the sudden resignation of Liverpool himself. His leadership proved impossible to replace and the personal deficiencies of his successors – Canning, Goderich and Wellington – seemed all the more obvious by comparison. Liverpool had been renowned as an efficient administrator and had been the only Tory statesman capable of holding together the former supporters of the Younger Pitt and maintaining the unity of the party, despite the existence of contrasting personalities and viewpoints. Although a strong and dominant cabinet leader, he had lacked personal charisma. This, however, had actually been an advantage. He had, for example, been able to reconcile differences between strong personalities and to encourage individual members of the team to maximise their own strengths. He had always been careful, therefore, to maintain a balance between self-projection and self-effacement. Liverpool's approach had suited the Tories at a time when party unity was far from complete. The problem was that his successors were by temperament unable to sustain Liverpool's style of leadership. The balance was to tip towards either too much or too little authority, while the party began to come apart under the growing pressure of personal antagonisms.

These soon became apparent during the ministry of Canning (1827). He was thoroughly disliked by many of his contemporaries, who found him self-centred, authoritarian, vain and overbearing. According to E.J. Evans, he inspired 'fission, distrust, envy and hatred'.[15] No fewer than six ministers refused to join Canning's government: Wellington, Peel, Westmorland, Bathurst, Eldon and Melville. To compensate for this, Canning was obliged to manufacture a majority by forming a coalition with three Whigs – Lansdowne, Tierney and the Earl of Carlisle. In one respect, this drew the sting from the problem. Canning may have incurred the disapproval of members of his own party, but his coalition was also opposed by the opposition leader, Grey. Hence, in the words of a contemporary, 'Canning has dissected both Whigs and Tories'.[16] On the other hand, the whole episode was to prove ultimately more serious for Tories than for Whigs, who were at least given a taste of political responsibility after two decades of political exile.

Given time, Canning might have learned to rein his overbearing manner; he might have grown into statesmanship and learned how to emulate internally the evident successes of his foreign policy. But all this was prevented by his premature death in July 1827 and a further succession crisis which resulted in a swing in the opposite direction to weak personal leadership. Robinson, now elevated to Lord Goderich, made a promising start by keeping intact the Canningite coalition. Unfortunately, he was unable to prevent royal interference in cabinet decisions and appointments, now the more unwelcome because it was so unusual. This was taken as a reflection on Goderich himself; according to Huskisson, 'Never surely was there a man at the head of affairs so weak, undecided, and utterly helpless!'[17] It therefore came as no surprise to anyone when the ministry collapsed in January 1828.

The time had now surely come for the party to rally round its elder statesman, the man who had forged a formidable military reputation during the latter phase of the Napoleonic Wars. As is often the case, however, military qualities did not translate readily into political success. In fact, the Duke of Wellington has earned widespread criticism from historians, Gash, for example, describing him as 'a disastrous leader'.[18]

It is possible to divide the administration of Wellington into two phases, however, and to reserve the full weight of this censure for the second. Between 1828 and 1830 Wellington struggled genuinely to tackle the most contentious problems of the day. He succeeded temporarily in reuniting the party on his assumption of power in 1828 and managed to hold on to the Canningites in the process. But he was unable to avoid splitting the party anew over two new issues. The first was his proposed disenfranchisement of Penryn and East Retford in 1828, over which Huskisson and several other leading Canningites resigned. Thus was lost the more progressive wing of the party, which crossed permanently to the Whigs. He did, however, retain the support of the right wing of the party (known as 'Ultras') who considered the Canningite defection no great loss. More serious was the second issue – Catholic emancipation – over which Wellington and Peel lost at a stroke the confidence of the ultras. Wellington's decision to introduce the measure was a sensible, even statesmanlike, step to prevent a potential crisis and it is difficult to see how he could have avoided incurring the wrath of the party die-hards. Principle and national safety were placed above party unity over an issue which even Liverpool had ducked. The real test of Wellington's leadership was whether he could heal the rift he had caused. Otherwise his ministry could do no more than limp on with minimal parliamentary support.

Here Wellington was deficient as a party leader and mismanaged the whole situation in 1830. The Tories were not at the time in imminent danger. After the 1830 election (called on the accession of the new King, William IV), the opposition had not significantly increased its representation in the Commons. The Whigs were prepared to bide their time, preferring a lame government under Wellington to a reactivated Tory ministry influenced by the ultras. They therefore gave him a breathing space and refrained from taking the offensive. Wellington, however, did not take advantage of this, showing, in the words of A. Briggs, 'no signs of political mastery'.[19]

His first priority was to reunite the party, but in this he signally failed. This was partly because he was over-confident and lacked the subtlety necessary to negotiate between the complex shades of Toryism. He tried to reclaim both individuals and groups. His negotiations with the Canningites foundered, partly because of the untimely death of Huskisson at the opening of the Liverpool to Manchester railway line, but largely because of a major clash with Palmerston over policy. Turning to the Ultras, Wellington then attempted, then made, one of the major errors of his career. The Ultras had strangely espoused the cause of parliamentary reform, largely because they wanted to reduce the number of seats available through patronage and thus hit back at the government power held by Wellington and Peel. This showed that the ultras were concerned less about the prospect of parliamentary reform than about the implications of religious changes. Wellington failed to see this and made an ill-advised speech against parliamentary reform, in which he affirmed that 'the legislature and the system of representation possessed the full and entire confidence of the country'.[20] This permanently alienated the Canningites, to the extent that four of them were to serve in Grey's cabinet in 1830. It also failed to convince the ultras and therefore undo the damage caused by Catholic emancipation.[21] By this stage Wellington appeared to have lost his grip altogether and resigned over a defeat on the civil list vote in 1830. This indicated that he had given up; the issue was not one on which a government's future depended, and Liverpool had survived a number of such defeats.

To what extent was the end of Tory rule due to the resurgence of the Whigs? It is tempting to see the reunification of the Whigs under Grey and Althorp as a counterpart to the disintegration of the Tories under Wellington. This would, of course, be an oversimplification. The Whigs themselves had split over the decision by a minority of their ranks to join Canning's administration in 1827. This disunity actually increased between 1829 and 1830,[22] when, for a period of eighteen months or so, English parties appeared to be dissolving into the more traditional pattern of factions. Yet the events of 1830 showed a remarkable recovery by the Whigs which was entirely absent among the Tories. The former had long since adopted parliamentary reform as their main cause and they were given a unique opportunity by Wellington's unfortunate speech in parliament on the issue. They sank their own differences and launched an offensive against the common enemy, able now to give effect to Althorp's earlier warning that 'We shall feel it our duty not to allow the country any longer to remain in such inefficient hands if we can prevent it'.[23] At the same time, they were also willing to exploit the disintegration of the Tories and to foster a temporary alliance with such strange bedfellows as the ultras; this was of vital importance during the 1830 civil list vote, which provided the means of levering the Tories out of power.

If by 1830 the Tories appeared to have lost the will to govern, the Whigs were at last able to take their place. They now had coherent aims and were able increasingly to project themselves as the party of reform, contrasting themselves with the Tories, from whom only limited concessions had been extorted and who were now bankrupt of ideas and initiatives. Above all it was they, and not the Tories, who benefited from the turbulent period at the beginning of the 1830s which affected both Britain and the Continent, and who publicised their strategy of preventing revolution from below by introducing reform from above.

4

THE FOREIGN POLICY OF CASTLEREAGH AND CANNING

Tory foreign policy between 1815 and 1830 was dominated by Lord Castlereagh, Foreign Secretary between 1814 and 1822, and his successor, George Canning, who occupied the same post between 1822 and 1827. The first and third sections of the chapter will assess their priorities and the degree to which they were successful. The middle section will reconsider the longstanding debate as to whether there was an underlying continuity or contrast between the two administrations.

CASTLEREAGH

Castlereagh had served his political apprenticeship under the Younger Pitt. He had been especially influenced by the latter's Memorandum of 19 January 1805 which had defined the British government's underlying aim once it had concluded the apparently interminable struggle with Revolutionary and Napoleonic France. This was to establish 'a general agreement and guarantee for the mutual protection and security of the different powers, and for re-establishing a general system of public law in Europe'.[1] Pitt died in 1806 but Castlereagh had the chance to implement this long-term objective. From 1814 onwards, his main priority was to establish in Europe an underlying equilibrium. This had a number of manifestations: an appropriate settlement for France combining firmness and conciliation; the proper balancing of the territorial interests of the major powers; and the formation of a system of regular consultation to deal with disputes between them.

Effective control over France was the immediate priority since, even after the defeat of Napoleon, she was potentially the greatest of all the powers. France was still the most populous state in Europe

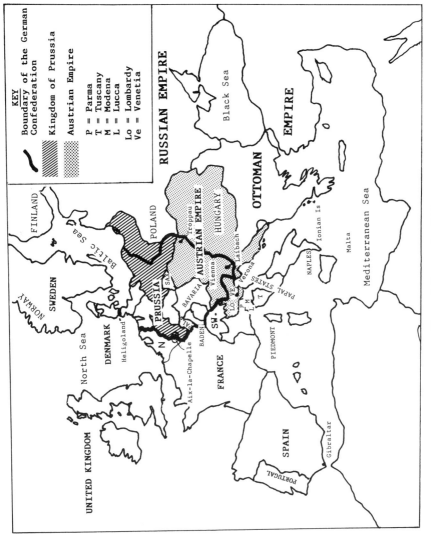

Figure 2 Europe in 1815

and possessed the resources and manpower to undertake renewed conquests given the right circumstances. But control had to be accomplished by a carefully judged balance between containment on the one hand and conciliation on the other; conscious equilibrium like this was one of the more positive hallmarks of Castlereagh's approach to the peace settlement.

Castlereagh played a significant part in assembling a convincing package of containment. One of the components was ideological. The second restoration of the Bourbon monarchy was considered an essential prerequisite for future stability and as a means of breaking the cycle of revolution, military dictatorship and conquest. Another element of containment was financial: France was expected to pay an indemnity and to support an army of occupation in the meantime. But the third was the most significant. This involved pulling the French frontiers back to those of 1790 and strengthening the states on the other side. Hence the United Netherlands were created by combining the former Austrian Netherlands, or Belgium, with Holland; much of the Rhineland was transferred to Prussia; the Palatinate was united with Bavaria, the largest state in southern Germany; Baden and Switzerland were both enlarged; and Piedmont was more than doubled in area and resources by the addition of Savoy, Genoa and Sardinia. Clearly Castlereagh hoped that such changes would prevent France from expanding in future into the relative power vacuum of central Europe.

In this he succeeded. With the exception of Savoy and Nice, ceded by Piedmont in 1859, France made no territorial acquisitions in the nineteenth century and the expansion of the frontier over four centuries was halted for good. In creating the various constraints, however, the statesmen of 1815 were storing up a number of problems for the future, for which Castlereagh must take his share of the responsibility. The restored Bourbons were overthrown in 1830 and France experienced a period of internal instability which took her through Orleanist monarchy and revolutionary republic before finally arriving in 1852 at the rule of another Napoleon. The frontier also looked precarious for a while as, in 1830, Belgium broke away from the Netherlands and precipitated a diplomatic crisis involving Britain and France. Also, in his anxiety to contain France, Castlereagh helped deliver the prosperous Rhineland to Prussia. This established the key connection between industrial and military strength which underlay the eventual unification of Germany and saw the displacement of one major power by another.

It was due largely to Castlereagh's influence that containment of France was modified by a parallel policy of conciliation. He believed in particular that France not be crushed since 'The prosperity of France was the essential prerequisite for the security of Europe'.[2] As he informed Lord Liverpool, 'it is not our business to collect trophies, but to try if we can to bring the world back to peaceful habits'.[3] He therefore collaborated as closely with the French delegate, Talleyrand, as with the Allies in his search for a settlement which would avoid the taint of vindictiveness and hence remove the longer-term threat of revanchism. He was certainly more successful here than Lloyd George in 1919. All his actions from 1818 show a genuine desire to rehabilitate France and allow her to play a full part in the international order – but under close Allied supervision. He believed that the expedient was 'to give France her concert, but to keep our security'.[4] Hence he supported a reduction of the indemnity, the early withdrawal of the army of occupation and the representation of France at the Congress of Aix-la-Chapelle in 1818.

A second manifestation of equilibrium was a territorial settlement which would satisfy all the major powers, remove any foreseeable cause of contention between them and convince them that their interests would be best served by a lasting peace. Castlereagh aimed to reconcile conflicting territorial interests while ensuring that no power excited the animosity of the others through acquiring too much. The gains were therefore moderate and balanced. Britain kept essential naval bases and staging posts such as Trinidad, Tobago, St Lucia, Ceylon, Mauritius, the Cape of Good Hope, Heligoland, Malta and the Ionian Islands. Russia was ceded Finland by Sweden and also incorporated the lion's share of Poland. Prussia received the Rhineland, about two-fifths of Saxony, Western Pomerania, Pozen and Danzig. Austria was rewarded with Lombardy, Venetia and the Adriatic coastline for being one of the most consistent of all of Napoleon's enemies. Such arrangements inevitably involved some hard bargaining over differing claims. One example was Castlereagh's successful collaboration with Metternich to resist Prussia's claim for the whole of Saxony.

Castlereagh was criticised by some of his contemporaries on the grounds that he acted fundamentally against British interests by making too many concessions to the continental powers in his pursuit of the principle of the balance of power. For example, he restored the Dutch East Indies, even though these might have become a vital economic component of the British Empire. It was also argued that equilibrium meant the undue involvement of Britain in European affairs, at a considerable financial cost which worked its way through into export duties and hence damaged commercial relations with other states. In other words, he should have pursued Britain's own interests on the periphery instead of placing her in the continental balance. Castlereagh might be defended, however, on the grounds that he had a realistic understanding of Britain's interests. He knew that British isolation from Europe could never be more than a temporary expedient and that any continental conflict over territorial issues would sooner rather than later involve British resources and lives. It therefore made sense for Britain to influence a settlement which might prevent this and, in the process, for Britain to give up those gains which were not essential to her own military and naval security. Unless Castlereagh showed willingness to do this, how could he expect Prussia, Russia and Austria to do likewise?

Third, Castlereagh proposed to sustain the newly created equilibrium through a series of international congresses which would be convened to settle controversial issues. This was a laudable aim. During the eighteenth century warfare had become the accepted means of seeking adjustments in dynastic frontiers, while the Napoleonic era had added the ingredient of ideology to conflicts between states. It was hardly surprising that the military theorist, von Clausewitz, should have considered that war was 'the continuation of policy by other means'.[5] There was thus a greater need than ever before to break the cycle of diplomacy and military conflict through the establishment of institutions specifically intended to maintain the peace. It has been argued that Castlereagh looked beyond the framework of diplomacy to the principle of internationalism itself. He observed in 1818: 'It really appears to me to be a new discovery in the European Government, at once extinguishing the cobwebs with which diplomacy obscures the horizon . . . and giving to the counsels of the great powers the efficiency and almost the simplicity of a single State'.[6] If his intention was to set up a permanent international system with regularly functioning congresses, then he clearly failed. The so-called Congress System was limited to four such meetings: Aix-la-Chapelle, Troppau, Laibach and Verona, the last two of which were not even attended by a fully accredited British representative. But it would be an anachronism to assume that Castlereagh sought to establish an incipient European

Community with its own network of governing institutions. As Derry maintains, 'He was not trying to unify Europe. He was attempting to minimize the inevitable tensions between the Powers.'[7]

In any case, Castlereagh was operating on a fourth principle: that European equilibrium could best be maintained with the very minimum of interference in the internal affairs of individual states. The question of intervention was most likely to arrive when revolutionary activity threatened to change the political complexion of a particular state and to spread radical ideologies to its neighbours. Castlereagh was not in principle a sympathiser with such movements. Quite the contrary. Although he respected representative government as it had evolved in Britain, he was deeply suspicious of any theoretical attempt to give it universal validity – as had been shown by the French Revolution. He was therefore not averse to internal action like the Carlsbad Decrees in 1819 against what he considered the 'germs' of radicalism. At the same time, he was very much against the use of new international bodies to eradicate revolution on a wide scale. He did not want to freeze Europe into a condition of extreme reaction, nor did he want to involve Britain in the sort of ideological crusade which the Younger Pitt, for all his determination to resist French expansion, had always opposed. Hence he wrote in his memorandum on the Spanish Question: 'We shall be found in our place when actual danger menaces the system of Europe; but this country cannot and will not act upon abstract and speculative principles of precaution'.[8] Did Castlereagh succeed in holding the Congress System to this limited perception of intervention?

At first the main ideological threat to Castlereagh's emphasis on equilibrium came from Tsar Alexander I, in the form of the Holy Alliance established in 1815. Between 1818 and 1820, however, Britain managed, through a special relationship with Austria, to apply a counterbalance to Russia and the latter's growing *rapprochement* with France. Castlereagh and Metternich were, for example, in agreement on the issue of joint intervention to suppress the Spanish revolution of 1820. The State Paper of 1820 emphasised that the basic principle of British foreign policy was non-intervention and that such action was well outside the purpose of the Congress System. Metternich had his own reasons for welcoming Castlereagh's view over Spain, since he had no wish to see Russian armies in western Europe. This joint resistance ensured that the whole issue was postponed and that the Holy Alliance was not invoked.

In the longer term Metternich moved away from the pragmatic response of Castlereagh and towards the ideological opposition to revolution expressed by Alexander. The catalyst for this change was the revolt in Naples, which Metternich perceived as a direct threat to the stability of the new Italian state system. Castlereagh was ambivalent. On the one hand, he was prepared to countenance unilateral Austrian intervention in Naples to protect Austrian interests. On the other hand, he could not be seen as supporting this action within any international context; while conceding that Metternich had a job to do, he emphasised that this had nothing to do with the Congress System. Castlereagh was particularly averse to the Troppau Protocol drawn up in 1820 by Russia, Prussia and Austria to justify intervention by the major powers against any revolution which they considered a threat to European stability. His response was the 1820 State Circular, which stated that the British government 'do not regard the Alliance as entitled, under existing Treaties, to assume, in their character as allies, any such general powers'. He also refused to attend the next Congress at Laibach, downgrading British representation to an official observer.

The loss of Britain's connection with Austria seemed to presage the collapse of Castlereagh's diplomacy. Yet Castlereagh managed to hold this off. The occasion was the Greek issue. Worried about the possibility of Russian intervention, he once again worked with Metternich, not to suppress the revolt but to try to prevent Russian involvement. Distrust of Russian motives therefore temporarily restored the convergence of British and Austrian policies. It is even possible that Castlereagh might have restored more permanently his own limited vision of the purpose of the Congress System. By 1822 he had rediscovered some of his earlier enthusiasm and was preparing for full British representation at the Congress of Verona. But the whole prospect was ruined by the tragic circumstances of Castlereagh's suicide in 1822 and his replacement by George Canning who showed no such willingness to perform a last-minute rescue operation.

Castlereagh was also weighing up proposals for restoring equilibrium between Europe and the Americas. This had been disrupted by the success of the liberation movements, under Bolivar and O'Higgins, in shaking off colonial rule, and by the intention of Spain and Portugal to reimpose it. Again Castlereagh was ambivalent. As a staunch monarchist he had little sympathy for republican rebels. On the other hand, he was concerned that British interests in the New World, greatly enhanced since the ejection of Spanish and Portuguese rule, should not be jeopardised by their return. There was also the possibility that an unsympathetic attitude might increase the involvement of the United States in the area and lead to the latter's total domination of the New World. He therefore hoped to use the Congress System to reach a balanced settlement in which Spain and Portugal would be persuaded to come to terms with their ex-colonists, who might in their turn instal new monarchies closely attached to the old. Castlereagh intended to put this solution to the Congress of Verona.

Another element of Castlereagh's policy towards the New World was more bilateral and was deliberately excluded from the scope of the Congress system; this was the volatile relationship between Britain and the United States. Castlereagh was fully aware that Britain's real interest lay in reconciliation: 'there are no two states whose friendly relations are of more practical value to each other, or whose hostility so inevitably entails upon both the most serious mischiefs'.[9] His main emphasis had to be on long-term healing, since 'Time will do more than we can'.[10] But he was also prepared to make certain short-term concessions. In 1814, for example, he dropped the Foreign Office's insistence on Britain's right to search foreign ships, a move which accelerated the signing of the Treaty of Ghent. He also intervened to prevent a wave of anti-American hysteria following President Jackson's confirmation in 1818 that two British subjects should be executed for allegedly taking part in raids from Florida into United States territory. Although several points of contention remained, including the delineation of the frontier between the United States and Canada, Castlereagh should be given credit for his intelligent and restrained policies. When added to his handling of central and south American issues, these deserve Derry's conclusion that 'The image of the icy apostle of universal reaction is nowhere more false, more shamelessly inaccurate or more wilfully misleading than when applied to Castlereagh's sophisticated and judicious attitude towards American questions'.[11]

Overall, Castlereagh faced an immensely complex task which Clarke has likened to 'walking an uncomfortable tightrope'.[12] He had been instrumental in creating a new international system in 1815 and had, somehow, to maintain it without allowing it to distort Britain's interests. He also had to educate British parliamentary opinion about the advantages of maintaining co-operation with continental regimes which many MPs instinctively disliked while, at the same time, spelling out to continental leaders the sort of use Britain was not prepared to make of the Congress System. This meant that 'in England he appeared very reactionary whilst on the Continent he looked dangerously liberal'.[13] Whether, given time, he could have succeeded in dragging the Congress System back from the brink of interventionism is a more open question than most historians seem prepared to acknowledge. It is true that the Holy Alliance assumed from 1820 more and more the characteristics of an international police force which was using the Congresses to articulate its aims. On the other hand, Castlereagh showed considerable skill in restraining Metternich and might, had he lived, have ensured that the Congress System went on beyond Verona in 1822. Castlereagh's personal tragedy in 1822 may therefore have had a greater impact on foreign policy than it did on home affairs.

CONTINUITY AND CHANGE

A key issue in British foreign policy between 1815 and 1830 is the connection between Castlereagh and Canning. Although the earlier controversy about them seems to have reached a consensus, there is still scope for a revised interpretation.

It was once believed that 1822 represented a strong dividing line between two contrasting periods of foreign policy. The first, under Castlereagh, was perceived as negative and reactionary, the second, under Canning, as positive and progressive. Castlereagh had a poor image throughout the nineteenth century. Whig historians like Macaulay demolished his reputation, seeing him as a reactionary influence holding back the tide of progress. In her *History of the Thirty Years' Peace*, Harriet Martineau described Castlereagh as 'the screw by which England had riveted the chains of nations', asserting that his death was 'a ray of hope in the midst of thickest darkness'.[14] The Romantic poets also had their say. Shelley, for example, in 'The Mask of Anarchy' wrote:

> I met Murder on the way –
> He had a mask like Castlereagh.

Byron's language in *Don Juan* was even more intemperate:

States to be curbed, and thought to be confined,
Conspiracy or Congress to be made –
Cobbling at manacles for all mankind –
A tinkering slave-maker, who mends old chains.

Two influences combined to turn the most sensitive of poets into crude polemicists. One was Castlereagh's association with the union of Ireland with Britain in 1800; the other his outspoken support for the domestic policies of Sidmouth at the time of the Peterloo Massacre in 1819. Castlereagh was remembered above all for these, rather than for his complex international diplomacy, about which the British public were ill-informed. Canning, by contrast, had no such connections with domestic reaction; if anything, he was associated with an apparent surge of liberal Toryism after 1822 and given full credit for the application of liberal principles in his foreign policy.

It was once thought that Castlereagh and Canning both inherited the policies and attitudes of the Younger Pitt: Castlereagh the negative and reactionary, Canning the positive and progressive. This whole approach is now usually seen as simplistic and inaccurate, largely as a result of the work of historians such as Webster and Kissinger, who have pointed to an underlying continuity in their foreign policy. They, and others, provide alternative explanations for any differences. According to Southgate, for example, differences of policy were due to personality rather than to party ideology,[15] while Ward[16] points to the greater flamboyance of Canning. Derry considers the key factor to have been the importance attached by Canning to popularity and public image, something which Castlereagh neglected 'to his ultimate cost'.[17] Canning therefore had the greater concern for how he would be judged by posterity. He realised that real popularity came from outside the precincts of the House of Commons, in which Castlereagh performed most convincingly, and from the public at large. For this reason he avoided the sort of vitriol which was meted out to Castlereagh.

But there was more, surely, to the differences between Castlereagh and Canning than their personalities and their public image. Another crucial factor was the contrast in the *momentum* of their policies. Castlereagh's particular concern after 1815 was to establish and maintain a state of equilibrium – to set the balance. Canning, by contrast, was determined to reset the balance, even if this should mean the partial destruction of the original equilibrium. It is true that problems were already beginning to emerge before Castlereagh's death in 1822 and that the latter's State Paper of 1820 did envisage an adjustment in British policy. To this extent it might be argued that Canning followed the course which Castlereagh might have been forced along had he lived longer. He endeavoured to retain some of the key points of equilibrium in so far as they were salvageable but was prepared to kill off the rest, especially the regular system of congresses, which he had opposed at the outset. In this sense equilibrium was at least partially replaced by movement. Canning was less committed than Castlereagh to an international system which he had had no hand in creating and was therefore understandably less reluctant to destroy it if he had to. This can certainly be seen in his policies towards the Congress System, Spain, Portugal, South America and Greece. To these we now turn.

CANNING

Canning had a conception of the purpose of international congresses which differed fundamentally from that of his predecessor. He was certainly less inclined than Castlereagh to participate in a 'system' of any kind. He had strongly opposed any regular commitments for Britain, preferring instead to think in terms of periodic involvement to deal with specific emergencies. Nor did he have the sort of personal connections which Castlereagh had built up with the continental leaders. Because he was widely known and respected, Castlereagh had been able to work with the likes of Metternich, whereas Canning could not. Canning considered such close connections a sign of weakness and deliberately aimed to increase the distance between himself and European politicians.

There was an almost immediate side-effect. When Castlereagh committed suicide in 1822, Metternich was deprived of his main ally: Canning, it was widely known, could not abide him, referring to him as 'the greatest rogue and liar on the continent, perhaps in the civilized world'.[18] As a result, Metternich had no incentive to work closely with Britain. He preferred instead to move closer to the other continental leaders, even though this meant withdrawing his objections to French intervention against the Spanish Revolution, and had no option but to agree to French intervention in Spain. This measure, in turn, intensified Canning's desire to be done with the Congress System. In contrast to Castlereagh, who had consistently placed the pursuit of British interest within an international context, Canning dispensed altogether with the international superstructure. It is true that difficulties after 1820 had forced Castlereagh to move Britain towards the periphery of the Congress System; he nevertheless retained the option of rejoining it fully once the intervention issue had been resolved: he had hoped that the Congress of Verona would prove to be the turning point and that the regular Congress System would reassert its primacy over the Holy Alliance. Canning's perspective was entirely different. From the start he actively pursued a policy of disengagement from the System, which he associated directly with the machinations of the Holy Alliance. Hence, as Rolo states, 'his road to the destruction of the . . . Holy Alliance lay through the ruins of the Congress System'.[19]

This was illustrated by the Spanish crisis. Ever since the 1820 revolution had installed a constitutional regime in Spain, Russia, Prussia and France had favoured external intervention to restore full royal authority to Ferdinand VII. Castlereagh had put this down to the influence of the Holy Alliance and had tried to use what was left of the Congress System to prevent it through an understanding between Austria and Britain. Canning made no such distinction and was not prepared to salvage the Congress of Verona in 1822. Losing the support of Austria, Britain had to try to prevent intervention unilaterally. But Canning's efforts behind the diplomatic scenes to maintain the peace were unsuccessful and, since he had unwisely signalled in advance Britain's unwillingness to prevent intervention, he had to watch, helpless, as French armies invaded Spain in 1823. Britain therefore came closer to humiliation than at any other time between 1815 and 1830.

Canning was sufficiently affected by this experience to break with Castlereagh's emphasis on equilibrium. He was determined that Britain would never again be outwitted by the continental powers and was prepared to take a strong stand on future issues, even if this should suggest open defiance. During the Spanish crisis he had fulminated in parliament against France and he now replaced Castlereagh's internationalism with his well-known maxim 'every nation for itself and God for us all'. The occasion for demonstrating this arose immediately, indeed in the wake of the Spanish problem. Canning was determined that the conquest of Spain should not mean the acquisition also of Spain's overseas possessions; as he said in parliament, 'if France had Spain it should not be Spain with the Indies';[20] this meant, in his grandiose phrase, that he 'called the New World into existence to redress the balance of the Old'.

A key element in British policy towards Latin America was the nation's economic and commercial interest. During the Napoleonic Wars Spanish and Portuguese colonies in central and south America managed to liberate themselves from colonial rule. In the process they built up a substantial trade with Britain which accounted for 5 per cent of the latter's exports by 1815 and nearly 10 per cent by 1825. There was every prospect of a further build-up of new markets to absorb the products of Britain's accelerating Industrial Revolution, in exchange for a wide range of valuable raw materials and bullion. The threat to this attractive scenario was the attitude of the continental powers, all of which intended in the name of the Congress System to restore Spanish and Portuguese rule to the Americas. Canning's response was openly abrasive. He refused to have anything to do with proposals – never implemented – to call a fifth congress in Paris to discuss the American issue. He pursued, instead, a strictly unilateral approach. He tried first, although not overhard, to mediate between Spain and the colonies, before resorting instead to the policy he clearly preferred. This was direct diplomatic recognition in 1824 of the independence of several new states – Mexico, Buenos Aires and Colombia. He was able to write to the merchants of Glasgow: 'The fight has been hard, but it is won. The deed is done. The nail is driven. Spanish America is free; and if we do not mismanage our matters sadly, she is English.'[21]

Was Canning exaggerating his success? Not according to the new republics themselves, who regarded him as a major influence in the liberation process. Most modern historians also give him his due. It has, for example, been argued that

> It is to Canning's credit that in the crisis over Latin America he was prepared to reconcile himself more quickly than any others to a wholly new *status quo*. In addition, it must be said underlying his own policies was a highly realistic assessment of Britain's political and commercial advantage yet combined with appreciation of the reaction of others.[22]

On the other hand, Canning's contribution was largely indirect. He was given much publicity for his rhetoric and for his deliberate obstruction which brought the Congress System to its knees. But there was never any real threat of intervention by the continental powers against the new republics. The logistical problems would have been colossal and it is unlikely in the extreme that Austria, Russia and France would have been prepared to make sacrifices merely to reimpose the monarchical principle. Canning may even have overstated his own role in 'driving the nail'; possibly the most important factor discouraging the Holy Alliance was the 1823 Monroe Doctrine, in which the United States warned off any would-be attempts from Europe to reimpose its influence on the New World. It could be argued that Canning hastened to recognise the new republics in the wake of the Monroe Doctrine in order to prevent the United States from receiving the bulk of the credit.

Meanwhile, Canning had also made his point forcibly and successfully in another issue affecting the Iberian Peninsula. Portugal had also experienced a transition to a liberal constitution, but the government showed an understandable reluctance to go the same way as Spain and experience French occupation in the name of the interventionist principles of the Holy Alliance. The Portuguese Foreign Minister therefore requested British aid. Canning used the occasion to recover British prestige after the Spanish fiasco and to demonstrate Britain's antipathy to the Congress System. He advised the Prime Minister in 1824 that 'Portugal appears to be the chosen ground on which the Continental Alliance have resolved to fight England hand to hand, and we must be prepared to meet and defeat them, under every imaginable form of intrigue and intimidation, or be driven from the field'.[23] In the process of intensifying the confrontation with the Continent, Canning demonstrated to the Commons some of his most impressive powers of oratory, winning for himself considerable popularity and public support. He urged:

> Let us fly to the aid of Portugal by whomsoever attacked, because it is our duty to do so; and let us cease our interference where that duty ends. We go to Portugal, not to rule, not to dictate, not to prescribe constitutions, but to defend and to preserve the independence of an ally.[24]

This was followed by the despatch to Lisbon of a naval squadron and 5,000 marines to defend Lisbon against a possible attack by the French or by the newly restored Spanish autocracy.

Canning's Portuguese policy was perceived in Britain as a notable success. France and the other continental powers were warned off further intervention and the liberal regime in Lisbon survived for the time being. There was also a beneficial side-effect. The transition to independence of Portuguese Brazil was much easier than had been the case with the Spanish colonies; under Canning's influence, the son of John VI of Portugal, Pedro, was appointed viceroy of Brazil, thus retaining the monarchical principle which had disappeared elsewhere in Latin America. This was more acceptable both to aristocratic England and to autocratic Europe.

Relations between Britain and the United States provided Canning with a particular problem. As we have seen, one of Castlereagh's priorities had been to improve these and he had been prepared to make some major concessions. Canning was less amenable to this course, for three reasons. First, according to Dixon, he had 'a fairly large degree of disdain for the Americans, mainly because their diplomatic brashness offended his sense of how things ought to be done'; he also considered them too susceptible to 'popular pressure' and saw them as 'unreasonable people with whom to negotiate'.[25] Second, he was concerned about the potential threat posed by the United States as an expansionist power, following the Louisiana Purchase from France and the collapse of the Spanish presence in North America. Canning feared that the new Latin American republics might soon fall under the influence of the United States, a key factor in his early recognition of their independence. And third, he was convinced that the United States would seek to destroy Britain's new trading interests in the region. He therefore reversed Castlereagh's careful efforts to foster commercial co-existence so that, by 1825, the complex negotiations on mercantile controls had all but collapsed.

It might, therefore, be argued that Canning destroyed the equilibrium established by Castlereagh. Or, if this seems to be going too far, he could be seen as having set a new balance based on different principles. Castlereagh had encouraged a three-cornered *co-operation* between Britain, the United States and Europe. Canning resorted instead to balancing their *antagonisms*, adding to his diplomacy a strong element of deterrence. The Monroe Doctrine was especially useful here. It is true that it was seen as a latent threat to British interests in the New World. But this disadvantage was more than outweighed by the use Canning could make of Monroe's stand as a means of preventing the continental powers from pursuing their policies of intervention in the New World. Even the ideological divisions could be exploited; in 1824 Canning wrote: 'The effect of the ultra-liberalism of our Yankee co-operators, on the ultra-despotism of our Aix-la-Chapelle allies, gives me just the balance I wanted'.[26]

The most complex problem with which Canning had to deal was the Greek Revolt against Turkish rule. This was less cut and dried than the other issues of the 1820s, involving a clash of Britain's own interests. On the one hand, there was much public sympathy within Britain for the Greeks, promoted by an influential philhellenic movement and by the heroic exploits of the poet Byron. Canning was hardly immune to this pressure, especially since he was himself a classical scholar. On the other hand, the revolt threatened Britain's strategic interest in the Near East. Russia had taken a strong interest in the Greek cause, making an exception to her general antipathy to revolutionary movements. The reason was partly that the Greeks were fellow-Christians involved in a struggle against an Islamic regime, and partly that Russia stood to make territorial gains in any war against Turkey. This was precisely what Canning wanted to avoid; he had come to regard Russia as potentially the largest threat to Britain on the Continent, now that France had been cut down to size, and an important way of preventing her expansion into the eastern Mediterranean was by bolstering up the Ottoman Empire.

Canning's priority, therefore, was to restrain Russia. To do this he first tried to revive the understanding between Britain and Austria, which had been one of Castlereagh's hallmarks. In 1825, however, he had to switch to an entirely different approach since the new Tsar, Nicholas I, was clearly bent on immediate intervention. Now Prime Minister, Canning decided that the only feasible option was to go along with Russia in order to exert whatever restraint was possible, in particular preventing Russia from gaining territorially. In 1827, therefore, he negotiated with Russia and France the Treaty of London which undertook to support Greek independence, if necessary by the use of force.

Did this work? Canning did not live long enough to find out. In 1827, two months after his death, a combined British, Russian and French fleet defeated the Turkish and Egyptian navies at Navarino. This seemed sufficient to guarantee Greek independence and Canning's policy appeared to have been fulfilled. Indeed, Dixon argues that

> Canning deserves congratulation on his handling of the Eastern Question. By playing the straight role of honest broker he had ensured a central role for Britain in the

settlement of the various issues involved. He had outwitted Metternich and made France play second fiddle. He had, for the moment, avoided a Russo-Turkish war and at the same time secured Greek independence.[27]

The long-term outcome was less happy, although part of the responsibility for this must lie with Canning's successors. Wellington withdrew Britain from her alliance with Russia and apologised to the Turks. Released from all constraints, Russia promptly declared war on Turkey and, by the Treaty of Adrianople (1829), secured control over the mouth of the Danube. Russia was now in a position to put pressure in the future on Moldavia and Wallachia. The whole process ended, as Evans points out, 'with an enhanced Russian presence in South-east Europe'.[28] Canning had therefore inherited an 'Eastern question' and, although unintentionally, bequeathed an Eastern problem.

Was Canning a great statesman? His time at the Foreign Office was certainly eventful. More than anyone else, he contributed to the demise of the Congress System which, arguably, Castlereagh had been trying to salvage. He recovered British prestige after the Spanish fiasco by preventing French intervention in Portugal. He ensured that there would be no intervention against the Latin American republics, for which he secured British recognition in 1824 and 1825. Everywhere, it seemed, British interests were being aggressively pursued. On the other hand, Rolo argues that Canning was never fully tested, since times were relatively quiet.[29] Canning's task was hardly monumental, although it suited him to project it as such. At no time were Britain's fundamental interests seriously threatened; at no time did Britain face a serious prospect of war. In the case of the South American colonies, recognition would have come eventually anyway and Canning's policy here was largely a matter of personal image. Overall, therefore, Canning deserves to be praised for his foreign policy – but faintly.

5

THE 1832 REFORM ACT

The period between 1830 and 1832 was one of political and constitutional change. In the first place, the long period of Tory rule ended in the autumn of 1830 when Earl Grey replaced the Duke of Wellington as Prime Minister. His main commitment was now to secure the reform of the electoral system for the House of Commons. A Reform Bill, introduced by Lord John Russell in March 1831, passed the second reading in the Commons, but was defeated in committee. Grey obtained a dissolution from William IV and, in the general election of April 1831, secured an increased majority for the Whigs; this was widely seen as a mandate to press the issue to its conclusion. A second Bill passed all stages in the Commons in September, only to be rejected in the Lords. A third Bill fared little better, being substantially amended by the Lords in committee. Grey's request for the creation of fifty new Whig peers was at first refused by William IV, until the King found it impossible to appoint an alternative government. When he finally agreed to comply, the Lords gave way and in June 1832 passed the Bill in the third reading.

This chapter concentrates on four major issues connected with the Act which finally emerged from this tortuous process. What arguments were advanced for and against parliamentary reform? Why, despite the extensive obstacles placed in its way, had the impetus for reforming legislation succeeded by 1832? How extensively did the Act change the franchise and distribution of seats? And what was the impact on key institutions outside the House of Commons?

ARGUMENTS FOR AND AGAINST
PARLIAMENTARY REFORM

During the eighteenth century, it has been said, the system to elect the House of Commons 'worked not unsuccessfully' and could be seen as 'providing a parliament which reflected the leading interests of the nation'.[1]

Several factors had already rendered it obsolete, however, by the beginning of the nineteenth century. One was the transformation of society as a result of industrial growth which reduced the comparative economic importance of agriculture and the land. As yet, however, there was no means of increasing the political influence of industrial and commercial interests or of enfranchising the majority of those involved in them. Industrialisation in the North, with its consequent urbanisation, had also created serious distortions in the distribution of parliamentary seats. Lancashire in 1831 had a population of 1,337,000 but had only two MPs, in contrast with Cornwall which, with 300,000 inhabitants, returned forty-two members. Manchester, Birmingham, Leeds and Sheffield, with a combined population of over half a million, were entirely unrepresented, while twelve seats were available for six Cornish coastal boroughs with less than 6,000 people in total. A large proportion of such seats were 'pocket', 'rotten', or, in political parlance, 'nomination' boroughs. These were a means whereby an MP could enter Westminster without having to fight an election. Indeed, where constituencies *were* contested, crippling expense could be incurred by the candidates. In an election in Yorkshire in 1807, for example, Fitzwilliam spent £97,000, Harewood £94,000 and Wilberforce £30,000.

Pressure to reform the system came both from below and from above. The former was strongly influenced by the French Revolution and its English connection, especially by the ideas of Thomas Paine's *The Rights of Man*, published between 1791 and 1792. The French Revolution has, in fact, been called a 'watershed' which popularised the cause of parliamentary reform,[2] particularly in the hands of individuals like Hardy and organisations such as the London Corresponding Society. Although they found their cause inhibited during the French Wars by government repression, they took up the cause again from 1815; Cobbett, Hunt, Cartwright and the Hampden Clubs now aimed to transform society and economic conditions by achieving a more representative political balance in parliament.

54

Meanwhile, reformist arguments were also being put by a group already strongly based in parliament, the Whigs. Their intentions were less sweeping than those of the radicals, but as longstanding. Grey, for example, had shown interest in the 1790s, sponsoring unsuccessfully a parliamentary Reform Bill in 1797 to enfranchise all householders and increase county representation. The interest of the Whigs declined over the next twenty years, to revive in 1822 with Russell's proposal to provide representatives for some of the larger towns by removing one MP from the smallest boroughs.[3] Some Whigs were never entirely convinced about the need for such changes, but most were gradually won over by a variety of arguments.

These did not, of course, include a case for democracy. The emphasis was on bringing other groups into the arena of power, not on handing power over to them. Above all, the Whigs did not intend to destroy the base of aristocratic control. Grey stated, at the height of the Reform Bill crisis in November 1831, 'There is no-one more decided against annual parliaments, universal suffrage and the ballot, than I am. My object is not to favour, but to put an end to such hopes and projects'.[4] Their conception of the need for and role of reform was more limited; basically they aimed to save the constitution by making it work more effectively. They considered this to be directly in line with the argument of Edmund Burke that, although drastic changes were always to be avoided, any political system had occasional need for a sharp corrective in order to ensure its survival. Hence Grey always maintained that 'The principle of my reform is to prevent the necessity for revolution' and that he was 'reforming to preserve and not to overthrow'.[5]

At the same time, any measure introduced to prevent revolution had also to be worthwhile in its own right. That is why Grey warned the king that 'not to do enough to satisfy public expectation would be worse than to do nothing'.[6] He was referring specifically to the 'satisfaction of the rational public', or the productive middle classes. The Whigs advanced two arguments for giving them the vote. One was to detach them from radicalism and thereby provide a guarantee against the sort of revolutionary activity which was affecting the Continent. Macaulay argued for bringing the middle classes into parliament to strengthen the *status quo*. 'At present', he said, 'we oppose the schemes of revolutionists with only one half, with only one quarter of our proper force'.[7] Equally important, however, was the acknowledgement that the new wealthy fully merited inclusion within the electoral system. Grey wrote that they had made 'wonderful advances in both property and intelligence',[8] while Brougham considered them 'the genuine depositories of sober, rational, intelligent and honest English feeling'.[9] Why should it not be acknowledged that their proper link was with the aristocracy?

Needless to say, a different set of arguments was advanced by the Tories, this time in opposition to parliamentary reform. They also took their stand on Burke, but interpreted his ideas as being anti-reformist as well as anti-revolutionary; this is a good example of how two conflicting meanings can be read into the writings of one philosopher. The Tories considered that the Whig remedy against revolution was essentially concession and retreat, although the Whigs had wrapped this up in terms of strengthening the defensive basis of power. The Tories recognised only one form of defence: not to give ground and to stand firm against demands for reform. To do otherwise would be to risk opening the floodgates and bring upon Britain the deluge which had already affected the Continent. Britain's power base was firmly set in the constitutional settlement of 1689 and any attempts to meddle with it now would be to inflict serious damage. Croker was particularly disgusted by what he regarded as the 'levelling' effects of the Great Reform Act and, after its successful passage in 1832, withdrew from the Commons because he wanted nothing more to do with a House which was prepared to 'subvert the Church, the Peerage and the Throne'.[10]

The Tories had three specific objections to parliamentary reform. First, the end of nomination boroughs would have serious political implications, making ministers and MPs more dependent on popular opinion and without the safeguard of a secure seat. It would also accelerate the declining influence of the Crown and destroy any residual influence of patronage. According to Peel, reform would mean that 'flexibility in the working of the constitution would be lost' and the 'provision of an executive to carry on the King's government would be frustrated'. It would, above all, become next to impossible for the king to 'change a ministry'.[11] Second, the Whig argument for seat redistribution meant an attack on the small boroughs; this, in turn, would become a wider onslaught on private property. In a debate on 6 July 1831, Peel argued that the Bill 'subverts a system of government which has combined security to personal liberty, and protection to property, with vigour in the executive power of the State, in a more perfect degree than ever existed in any age, or in any country in the world'.[12] And third, the Tories defended as inevitable the absence of uniformity in seat distribution. What really counted, they maintained, was not the rapid increase in population in some areas but the pattern of property ownership, which was less likely to change.

It would be naive not to see behind both sets of arguments a strong degree of self-interest. The Whigs, out of office for so long, urgently needed to change the political system more in their favour and to enfranchise a section of the population from which they could expect substantial support in the future. The Tories, by contrast, were bound to remain wedded to a system which had for so long operated in their favour. After all, the existing electorate had consistently returned them to power for three decades and, in any case, the base of their position in the House of Commons rested on about two hundred nomination boroughs, compared with the seventy or so held by the Whigs. Peel expressed himself 'unwilling to open a door which [he] saw no prospect of being able to close'.[13] The unspoken corollary was that he also had no desire to see the Whigs pass through it.

THE OVERCOMING OF OBSTACLES TO PARLIAMENTARY REFORM

Time, however, favoured the Whig rather than the Tory analysis of the needs of the constitution; it proved easier to expand the base of power than to try to restrict it. Before 1829 there was very little prospect of the Whigs being able to form a government, let alone carry a highly contentious piece of legislation on parliamentary reform. Yet, within a year Grey had replaced Wellington as Prime Minister, within two he had won a general election on a mandate for reform, and within three he had overcome the mountainous obstacle of the House of Lords. All of this was in the teeth of Tory opposition with its dire warnings of revolution and upheaval.

The main reason for this remarkable transformation was the sudden collapse of the Tory monopoly of political power. Chapter 2 dealt with the end of the Liverpool era of stability; the subsequent instability under Canning, Goderich and Wellington; the contrasting styles of leadership; and the release of conflicting tendencies which tore apart the previous consensus which had more or less

57

passed for party unity. Wellington's fall in 1830 has been seen by C. Flick as 'one of the turning points in modern British history'.[14] Underlying this catastrophe for the Tories was the Catholic Emancipation Act, which has received increased attention from modern historians for its political rather than religious impact. According to R.W. Davies, Catholic Emancipation 'broke up the old Tory party of Pitt and Liverpool that had so long dominated the political life of the country'.[15] The Ultra Tories, who bitterly resented the measure, gave the Whigs the extra support they required – both in bringing down the Tory government and in securing the passage of the Reform Bill through the Commons.

It could also be argued that Catholic Emancipation was a watershed in a more constructive sense, by removing the absolute veto on all alterations to the constitution. In 1829 Wellington had adopted a position on Catholic Emancipation not too dissimilar to the Whig argument on parliamentary reform, namely that reform was necessary as a concession to prevent revolution. When the Tories revived their opposition to parliamentary change on the grounds that revolution might be encouraged, they appeared for the first time inconsistent. Catholic Emancipation had therefore blown a hole in Tory ideology as well as in Tory party unity. The Whigs were able to manoeuvre themselves through both, to achieve power and then to secure the passage of the Reform Act. The Tories did the Whigs another favour. By tackling the problem of Emancipation themselves, they removed from the Whigs the burden of being associated with this particular reformist cause. The Whigs, in other words, could concentrate on parliamentary reform and not have to divert part of their energy to pressing for the removal of an obvious injustice to a religious minority.

The Whigs also benefited from a combination of objective factors, not an experience familiar to them over the past few decades. In the early 1830s things moved more obviously in their favour. One example was the death of George IV, which meant the removal of a major obstacle to a Whig ministry. George IV's dislike of the Whigs in general and of Grey in particular had been reinforced by a royal veto on the whole issue of parliamentary reform. William IV was altogether a different proposition; he had no such prejudices and was willing to work with the Whigs provided, of course, that they could establish a stable government and present a proper case for reform. At the same time, another set of circumstances intervened to add a sense of urgency to what the Whigs were demanding.

Popular pressure and the disturbances analysed in Chapter 1 worked in favour of the Whigs between 1830 and 1832. The agricultural disturbances of 1830, especially the Swing Riots, favoured the Whigs by exposing the insensitivity of Wellington's policies and demonstrating that the Tories were no longer capable of governing effectively. Then the riots which accompanied the crisis of the Reform Bill in 1831 and 1832 added weight to the demands of the Whigs. This proved to be one of the few cases in modern British history where the threat of revolution promoted rather than inhibited the progress of reform.

CHANGES TO THE FRANCHISE AND SEAT DISTRIBUTION

The Reform Act received royal assent in June 1832, to be followed by provision for Scotland and Ireland in July and August. In England the county franchise now included 40 shilling freeholders, £10 copyholders and £50 leaseholders, while eligibility was extended in the boroughs to £10 householders. The total number of seats remained unchanged at 658, but 143 of these were redistributed. Fifty-six boroughs with less than 2,000 voters lost two members, while thirty-one boroughs with between 2,000 and 4,000 lost one member. Sixty-five seats were provided for previously unenfranchised boroughs, and a further sixty-five for the counties. Finally, the other two kingdoms also benefited from the redistribution – Scotland receiving six extra and Ireland five.

These measures went some way towards dealing with the previous problems and anomalies of the electoral system. In the first place, they brought unrepresented areas and individuals within the system for the first time and partially redressed the geographical imbalance between the North and South – at the expense of the rotten boroughs, which all but disappeared. Of the 143 seats reallocated, for example, 65 went to substantial centres of population such as Birmingham, Manchester, Sheffield, Leeds, Oldham, Bradford and Bolton. Second, the £10 householder qualification meant that a large proportion of the middle class living in enfranchised boroughs now had the vote, raising the total electorate from 478,000 to 813,000. Third, Scotland was particularly affected by the Act. Before 1832 she had possessed a total electorate of only 4,500, thinly spread across ninety-six constituencies which were, in effect, little more than a system of pocket boroughs.[16] After the new franchise, Scottish boroughs had an average of 1,300 voters and counties an average of 1,100, providing a fifteen-fold increase altogether.[17] Ireland also benefited, although for the most part the Act supplemented changes already made by the Act of Union in 1800 or by Catholic Emancipation in 1829.

On the other hand, the Reform Act clearly had its limitations. The vast majority of the total population of 24 million remained unenfranchised, including part of the lower middle class and the entire working class; this appeared to undermine somewhat the assertion of Lord Durham that 'to property and good order we attach numbers'.[18] Second, the redistribution of seats was by no means complete. Only the worst anomalies, the 'rotten' boroughs, were actually disenfranchised. Over 123 constituencies still had populations of less than 1,000.[19] This meant that patronage might continue a little longer into the future in elections, even if it no longer had the same influence on the making of governments. Third, there remained a fundamental imbalance between the North of England, which had the majority of the population but only 120 MPs, and the South, which still had 370 constituencies. There was a similar distortion between the boroughs and the counties, which had to be redressed by subsequent Reform Acts in 1867 and 1884. Finally, in the absence of any measure to introduce the secret ballot, there could be no effective control over electioneering methods. In fact, according to Gash the increased number of contested constituencies after 1832 may actually have increased the incidence of bribery and corruption.[20] The problem was not fully addressed until the passing of the Ballot Act (1872) and the Corrupt and Illegal Practices Act (1883).

The overall balance between what the Whigs changed and what they left alone has been aptly summarised by Finlayson. 'If, then, the electoral system after 1832 recognised new elements in the country and society, these had to exist within a framework which still gave scope to many of the older elements.'[21]

THE IMPACT ON INSTITUTIONS OUTSIDE THE COMMONS

Any analysis of the Reform Act would be incomplete without a brief consideration of its impact on institutions outside the House of Commons: the Lords, the Crown and the parties.

No reform of the House of Lords had been envisaged in the bills of 1831 and 1832. But the manner in which these bills eventually became the 1832 Act involved a change in the role of the Lords. For the first time they had been forced, very much against their will, to concede legislation with which they profoundly disagreed under the threat of being swamped with new Whig peers. This was an important precedent for the future and marked a vital stage in the transfer of real legislative power to the Commons. In his nineteenth-century survey *The British Constitution*, Walter Bagehot argued that the role of the Lords had significantly changed. 'The House has ceased to be one of latent directors, and has become one of temporary rejectors and palpable alterers.'[22] On the other hand this transition should not be painted too strongly. It was essentially a long-term and delayed by-product of the reform of the Commons. Any reform aimed explicitly at the Lords was unlikely at this stage, largely because of the difficulty of arriving at a consensus on an alternative composition. In any case, the Tories had a strong vested interest in keeping the Lords unchanged to counteract some of the damage done to them by the 1832 Reform Act, and to use the delaying powers to curb what they regarded as Whig excesses in the area of social reform. Indeed, it could be argued that the Lords emerged from the Reform Bill crisis temporarily strengthened, precisely because they were more than ever a repository of Tory influence and power acting to counterbalance the revival of the Whigs in the Commons.

As regards the power of the Crown, the 1832 Reform Act accelerated a decline already under way. It further reduced the scope for the operation of patronage, which had already been significantly undermined by the financial reforms of the 1780s. In disenfranchising the nomination boroughs, the 1832 Reform Act made it virtually impossible for the monarch actually to select a ministry; for example, there was no repetition of George IV's interference in the government of Goderich (see Chapter 3). Royal authority was also affected by the rise of political parties, which virtually replaced the Crown as the main channel for the flow of executive power from the legislature.

It is here that the Reform Act had its most important impact outside the House of Commons. The extension of the franchise meant a larger electorate to be won over, and the reduction of the nomination boroughs increased the number of constituencies where genuine elections would have to be held.[23] These two changes forced the parties to organise themselves more effectively and to compete more openly against each other to register the new voters. This resulted in the evolution of more effective management. For the Tories an important stage in this development was the establishment of the Carlton Club (1832), the purpose of which was to try to pull the party together after its period of humiliation and disintegration. For the Whigs, the equivalent was the Reform Club, set up in 1836. Influence radiated outwards from the centre and, under the guidance of managers like the Tory F.R. Bonham, built up a network of local party associations. The Act also brought a regional dimension to party support. The enlarged electorate in Scotland and Ireland meant that the Tories lost a significant number of nomination boroughs which, now that they were contested, tended to go to the Whigs. As a result, the Whigs and their successors – the Liberals – gradually built up a powerful basis of support in the Celtic fringe to offset the predominance of the Tories in the English heartland.

A 'WHIG' PROCESS?

There is a tendency to see reform as a self-sustaining momentum, with each individual achievement leading inexorably to the next stage in an unfolding pattern of progress. This was certainly the view of nineteenth-century Whig historians and their twentieth-century successor, G.M. Trevelyan. But such an analysis relies essentially on retrospection and reads too much into the motives of reformers at the time. The 1832 Act did not lead inevitably to those of 1867 and 1884. Nor was it the first step towards parliamentary democracy. Its essence was really to preserve and strengthen aristocracy by removing from it the taint of oligarchy.

This is not to say that the Whigs succeeded in this objective in the long term, or even that they continued to hold to it after 1832. The First Reform Act was followed by changes which were far more rapid than those which had preceded it. But, because the Act was primarily a defensive measure, these changes were brought about not directly through its clauses, but indirectly through its impact on those areas it was never intended to cover. As we have seen, the Act was a catalyst for the development of party organisation, which encouraged the formulation of more explicit party programmes to compete for the support of the electorate. The Whigs made the first adjustment to life after the 1832 Act, not by planning further constitutional changes, but by using what they had already accomplished as the means to secure social and economic improvements. Peel, in turn, had to adjust the priorities of the Tory party to enable it to compete. The result was the reforming ministries of the 1830s and 1840s.

6

WHIG REFORMS
IN THE 1830s

The Whigs were in power between 1830 and 1841, interrupted briefly by the Tories under Peel (1834–5). The first ministry (1830–4) was led by Grey, the second by Melbourne. During the period a considerable amount of legislation was passed. This included, in 1833, the abolition of slavery in the British Empire, Althorp's Factory Act, and the first education grant; the Poor Law Amendment Act (1834); the Municipal Corporations Act of 1835; in 1836, the compulsory registration of births, marriages and deaths, the Marriage Act, and the Tithe Commutation Act; and the introduction of the Penny Post in 1840.

This chapter will examine three key issues. First, what were the motives behind the Whig reforms? Were the Whigs legislating on the basis of deeply held convictions, or were they simply responding to the demands of those pressure groups they could not ignore? Second, how effective were the reforms once they had been passed? Did they constitute an 'administrative revolution', as has sometimes been claimed? And third, why, despite their apparently impressive achievements, did the Whigs lose to the Tories in the 1841 general election?

THE MOTIVES FOR REFORM

The Whigs thought of reform as the manifestation of benevolence to the majority by an enlightened aristocratic minority. This elite had already been prepared to extend its political power base and was now willing to confer social improvements on the people at large, no matter how humble they might be. Power, in other words, brought responsibility which transcended selfish interest. According to Kriegel, 'That the aristocracy should be benevolent agents of reform was an assumption whose validity the Whigs hardly questioned'.[1] It was partly a matter of conscience. The Whigs had a genuine belief in the importance of generosity, derived partly from the influence of eighteenth-century moralists, and they often called their reforms 'boons'.[2] Another motive might well have been the search for posterity, the importance of which had once been encapsulated by Fox: 'The truth is that all men when they are no longer young must look forward to something they expect to last beyond themselves'.[3] A Whig lawyer, Romilly, considered that 'generations yet unborn will bless our memories as the authors of their liberty and happiness'.[4] In return for their generosity, therefore, the Whigs expected gratitude. This would take the form of a proper deference from the lower orders, which would serve to strengthen the whole social fabric against popular resentment and radicalism.

Whig reformism was also pragmatic. Grey, Russell, Brougham and others continued to see in reform the best safeguard against revolution and therefore applied the same defensive arguments used to justify the parliamentary change (see Chapter 5). In addition, it is possible to see the strong influence of party interest. According to Fraser's Magazine in 1835, the Municipal Corporations Act was introduced 'simply and solely from party motives and as a party manoeuvre; in the hope that it would utterly destroy the Conservative party's hold on all the leading boroughs'.[5] Peel also accused the Whigs of pursuing partisan advantage. Although he favoured a measure of reform, he wanted a 'bona fide Reform' and 'not a mere pretext for transferring power from one party to another'.[6]

Whatever its motives for following a reforming programme, any government will, to some extent, be influenced by pressure groups outside its ranks. Between the two there is usually an ambivalent relationship.

On the one hand, no government is likely to take a reforming initiative unless it is under sustained pressure to do so. This is because the absence of such pressure would indicate general satisfaction with existing conditions which, in turn, would preclude the necessity for change. The Whigs were no revolutionaries. They did not propose to create new social or economic systems, only to strengthen existing ones by means of what had once been referred to by Edmund Burke as 'correctives'. To this end, the Whigs found pressure groups useful for two reasons. On occasion they could portray pressure as potentially dangerous, likely to bring about revolution if the reforming impetus faltered. This had applied especially to the events surrounding the passage of the Reform Bills between 1831 and 1832. Usually, however, the Whigs saw pressure groups during the rest of the 1830s in a more positive light – to provide both evidence of existing anomalies and suggestions for improvements. They were thus the first of the nineteenth-century governments to make systematic use of the administrative cycle of commission, enactment and inspection.

On the other hand, a reforming government is unlikely to see itself as in any way dependent on external pressure. This would be a virtual admission that it was not really in control: that it lacked an overall policy and that its whole approach was reactive rather than projective. The Whigs always claimed the credit for initiating change, and liked to think that they retained ultimate control by adapting the ideas of the various groups to their own purpose. This frequently alienated the members of pressure groups who had provided the ideas in the first place, thus ensuring that pressure gradually turned into opposition.

What were these groups? Generally, they were not as sharply focused as they were to become in the 1840s with, for example, the Anti-Corn Law League. Although there were clearly identifiable influences, these often merged with others. At the same time, there was sometimes a distinct lack of homogeneity, as one category might contain a dozen different viewpoints on a specific issue.

Probably the most influential of all the pressure groups were the Benthamites. This label covers a wide range of theorists, economists and active politicians, who used the ideas of Jeremy Bentham as the basis for their vision of change. The most fundamental of these was that 'the measure of right and wrong' was 'the greatest happiness of the greatest number'.[7] Related to this was the belief that institutions, which were entrusted with carrying out the common good, were only of value if they were efficient and useful. This emphasis on 'Utilitarianism' was apparent in nearly all the changes introduced by the Whigs in the 1830s. It was present in the Poor Law Amendment Act which, according to J.W. Hunt, was 'designed on a Utilitarian pattern of the purest kind'.[8] It underlay the legislation introduced by Brougham to reform the legal system, while the Municipal Corporations Act was virtually engineered by another Benthamite, Parkes.[9] Utilitarianism was influential also as a method of reforming procedure, which involved the collection and collation of information by means of Commissions, and the enforcement of subsequent legislative provisions through inspection and audit. Benthamites comprised the core of all the main enquiries. For example, Chadwick, Bishop Sumner, Bishop Blomfield, Bourne, Lewis and Nassau Senior were present on the 1832 Poor Law Commission. M. Bruce goes so far as to say that Benthamism gave 'a philosophical and schematic unity to the reforming urge of the day'.[10]

Another prominent group were the Evangelicals. The most obvious connection is between William Wilberforce (actually an Evangelical but a Tory by political persuasion) and the abolition of slavery in 1833. The influence of the Evangelical crusaders and the aristocratic Whigs has been analysed by A.D. Kriegel. Some of the younger Whigs, like Lord Howick, Lord Morpeth and Lord Milton, were very much under their influence and regretted that politics were serving 'to diminish religious feelings'.[11] At the same time, the Evangelicals were accepted by the older Whigs, like Grey, Russell and Brougham, who were impressed less by their religious fervour than by their belief that social hierarchy and aristocracy were divinely ordained. Wilberforce, for example, stressed the grand law of 'subordination' and of the 'inequalities of social' scale.

The third influence came from the Humanitarians. Often Evangelicals, but rarely Benthamites, they focused on improving conditions of child labour, arguing that the conditions of children in factories were analogous to those of slaves overseas. A significant number also became involved in the Ten Hour Movement, which aimed at reducing the number of hours worked by adults. Some Humanitarians, like Ashley and Sadler, were Tory MPs or, like Oastler, Tory land agents; others, such as Bull, Stephens and Fergus O'Connor, were of more radical persuasion. The impact of the Humanitarians was less consistent than that of the Benthamites or Evangelicals. On the one hand, they were influential in alleviating the conditions of child labour, by serving on the 1832 Select Committee and the 1833 Commission for Inquiring into the Employment of Children in Factories. On the other hand, they managed very little for adult workers, partly because their pressure was perceived as being directed against Whig manufacturing interests. To those in power, therefore, the Humanitarians were much more suspect than either of the other main pressure groups. They were also the first to express disillusionment with the limitations of Whig legislation and to look to the Tories to implement their ideas.

ANALYSIS OF THE REFORMS

Apart from the Great Reform Act, which has received separate treatment (see Chapter 5), the first major reform of Grey's administration was the long overdue Act abolishing slavery in the British Empire. Freedom was conferred on slaves within twelve months on condition that they served a seven-year apprenticeship to their masters who, in turn, received compensation from the government amounting to a total of £20 million.

The positive effects of this reform hardly need stating. The Act ended a major moral evil and cleared up the anomaly which had existed since the abolition of the slave trade in 1807. Now that slavery had been abolished at source it was no longer profitable for ruthless entrepreneurs to break the 1807 Act by transporting slaves from Africa illegally. Opposition arguments in parliament that slavery was a vehicle for civilisation and Christianity were confined to a small minority of Tories who embarrassed the rest of the party. On the other hand, the process of abolition could not be complete until the end of slavery in the United States which was not accomplished until the end of the American Civil War three decades later. Necessary though it was, abolition also brought certain problems to the British in the future, especially in South Africa. Here the immediate reaction of the Cape Boers was the Great Trek, which in turn saw the establishment of the independent republics of the Transvaal and the Orange Free State.

The year 1833 also saw the passing of the Factory Act, which prevented the employment of children below the age of 9 and restricted to eight hours the labour of children between the ages of 9 and 13, a provision which was to be enforced by inspectors. In addition, child workers were to receive two hours of education each day.

In some ways these measures were obviously deficient. They covered a fairly narrow definition of factories and excluded certain categories like lace mills. There were too few inspectors to enforce the proper working of the Act and, in any case, they were unable to prevent factory owners from evading the terms of the Act by using shift systems which could not be monitored easily. Until the compulsory registration of births, introduced in 1836, it was also difficult to establish precisely the age of individual child workers – and the onus to do so generally fell on the inspectors rather than on the mill owners. Little co-operation with the inspectors could be expected from parents, many of whom were desperate for the extra earnings provided by their children. Nevertheless, the Act had made a start. Its deficiencies were steadily dealt with over the rest of the century as successive regulations tightened the conditions of child labour, shortened the hours worked by adults and increased monitoring through the appointment of assistant inspectors.

Perhaps the most contentious piece of legislation passed during the whole era of Whig rule was the Poor Law Amendment Act of 1834. This was passed because the Whigs agreed with the Benthamite view that the Old Poor Law, especially the 1795 Speenhamland System, had broken down irrevocably. The New Poor Law, introduced by the 1834 Act, abolished outdoor relief and hardship allowances and substituted the 'less eligibility' principle by which the only alternative to employment in the case of the able-bodied was the workhouse, the conditions of which were made deliberately unattractive.

It has been argued that some of the results of this Act were beneficial. For example, the traditionally inefficient Roundsman system and the Labour Rate, props of the Old Poor Law, were ended. Similarly, farmers were obliged to increase the wages of agricultural labourers. There were also considerable administrative changes which set a precedent for the future: these included the election of local authorities, starting with the Board of Guardians. There is even a case for speaking of an 'administrative revolution'. The new system comprised 600 unions instead of the previous 15,000 parishes and underlay later changes in the public health system. There was also a financial saving. In 1834 poor relief cost 9 shillings per head, falling to 6 shillings by 1854. R.H. Tawney maintained that it was 'one of the pillars of social policy in the nineteenth century'.[12] Finally, harsh as it was, the New Poor Law has been directly connected with promoting the work ethic of Victorian England.

It is, however, easier to find defects with the Poor Law Amendment Act. The most devastating criticism has come from M. Blaug,[13] who questions the whole basis of the 1832 Commission's attack on the Old Poor Law and therefore the basic principle underlying the New Poor Law. He points especially to the unsatisfactory nature of the evidence provided to the Commission and argues that the rapid inflation of relief figures around 1830 was due not to any abuse of the system but to an increase in distress which the Old Poor Law was actually able to alleviate. Other critics of the

New Poor Law have emphasised the lack of harmony between those who administered the system. The Unions also had problems in setting up and controlling the workhouses. 'Some of them', according to U. Henriques, 'were geographical and administrative nonsenses'.[14] Above all, the very harshness of the new system reflected the hard edge of Benthamite principles, which showed a very narrow conception of the causes of poverty. As a result, private charities had increasingly to fill the gap left by the contraction of relief provided by the authorities. For example, the annual poor law rates in the 1830s in London amounted to £4.5 million; by the 1860s the amount provided annually by charities in the same area was up to £7 million.

It is hardly surprising that there was strong opposition to the Act in general and the workhouses in particular. J.R. Stephens, for example, reflected much contemporary opinion in calling the measure 'the law of devils'.[15] According to Oastler, 'it lays the axe to the root of the social compact: it must break up society and make England a wilderness'.[16] Another contemporary view was that the Act 'did more to sour the hearts of the labouring population than did the privations consequent on all the actual poverty of the land'.[17] As a direct result of the establishment of workhouses there were also public disturbances in the North and the Rebecca riots in Wales, while much of the early support for Chartism started as a backlash against the Act. There is some justification, therefore, in the view that 'The 1834 Act, in short, was one of the most lamentable pieces of social legislation devised in the nineteenth century.'[18]

The Whigs often regarded the Poor Law Amendment Act as their major achievement. More deserving of this description was the Municipal Corporations Act of 1835. It certainly impressed Halévy, who referred to 'a social revolution' and to the arrival of 'islands of representative democracy'.[19] There is more to be said for his latter comment, however, than for his former. On the one hand, there was a considerable improvement. The previous system had been thoroughly anachronistic, especially in view of recent reform of parliament. The franchise had been very restricted, nepotism had led to self-perpetuating oligarchies and finances had frequently been misdirected. The Act replaced corporations by elected councils, as all ratepayers were enfranchised for local elections, subject to a three-year residence qualification. The result was the gradual replacement of aristocratic control over local government by the upper middle classes, a process which was more obviously apparent here than in parliament. Continuity in the composition of corporations was guaranteed by allowing for elections to be staggered, one-third of councillors being elected at a time. Finally, control over the finances was considerably tightened by the auditing of accounts.

But problems remained. Local political changes did not necessarily mean social reform. The new bodies had very little willingness at first to go beyond cleaning up financial irregularities. The Act did provide enabling clauses allowing boroughs to take over key functions, but these were not yet compulsory. As yet there was little improvement in health or sanitary conditions, as was displayed only too clearly by the cholera epidemic between 1831 and 1833. Few of the corporations showed any inclination to assume the responsibilities of the Improvement Commissions; only twenty-nine boroughs had actually done this by 1848. Any improvements which did occur were confined mainly to urban areas; rural local government was hardly affected. Overall, therefore, the Act provided a potential rather than actual structure of local government and a whole series of further reforms was needed later in the century.

How should the reforms be assessed overall? Bentham had once stated that 'A reform which is not radical is a moderate reform; and a reform which is moderate is a Whig reform'.[20] It could certainly be argued that the Whig achievements were actually very limited (as in the case of the Poor Law Amendment Act), usually incomplete (as with the Factory Act) and grudging in their motivation. They were also very slow to develop in areas such as education; here the only positive action was an annual grant of £20,000 for two religious societies. Elsewhere, education policy was disappointing, and the attempt to integrate education into factory reform was a complete failure.

Alternatively, there was, according to Brasher, 'a legislative and administrative revolution. The means used by the Whigs to put into effect the social reforms of the decade marked the most important administrative advance since the Domesday Book'.[21] If this is going a little over the top, there is much to be said for Hunt's considered assessment: that 'these aristocrats had in two respects transcended the limitations natural to their class'. The first was the prevention of revolution by parliamentary reform. The second was the direction of the country 'towards a process of peaceful adjustment' against 'the stresses of change' more rapid than any known before.[22]

THE DECLINE OF THE WHIGS

The Tories had found it increasingly difficult after 1827 to hold on to power and had eventually given it up in 1830. This had been a protracted case of terminal illness. The subsequent Whig decline was more sporadic. They lost office temporarily between 1834 and 1835. But this was very different from what eventually happened in 1841. In the former case they were dismissed by the king, the last attempt to do so by a British monarch in the teeth of a parliamentary majority.[23] But the king's support was not sufficient to sustain the other party in power, as Peel disovered when he led a short-lived Tory ministry without the support of the Commons. The Whigs therefore had a second chance but, between 1835 and 1841, their electoral support began to drain away, enabling the Tories to win the 1841 general election with a majority of over seventy. This result can be ascribed partly to the weaknesses and vulnerability of the Whig governments and partly to the strengths and recovery of the Tory opposition.

The most serious problem confronting the Whig governments was the volatilty of their support, both within parliament and among the electorate at large. The general elections of the period showed a progressive loss of popular support; in 1835 the Whigs were no longer in control of the counties, in 1837 they lost England to the Tories, and in 1841 they surrendered the United Kingdom.[24] This meant that the parliamentary majority of Melbourne's government was extremely slender and, ultimately, depended on the unpredictable support of the Irish MPs. To make matters worse, the Whigs began to fray at the edges, losing a number of more radical members who were disillusioned with the limitations of some of the social legislation. The seriousness of the internal divisions was summarised at the time by the Duke of Bedford who referred to the difficulties of keeping in order 'a noisy and turbulent pack of hounds . . . of all descriptions of parties, and shades of parties, Whigs, moderates, ultra Whigs, Radicals and ultra Radicals etc. etc. etc'.[25]

To some extent, the Whigs projected a negative image which, after 1837, began to tell against them. There was considerable disappointment with the limited nature of the reforms concerned with factories and with the lack of any real attempt to deal with the problem of squalor in the towns. The Whig authorities also acquired a reputation for being willing at times to endorse repressive measures, as in the case of the Tolpuddle Martyrs in 1834. The Whigs actually succeeded in provoking working-class hostility in the late 1830s, a period which saw the growth of Chartism and a repetition of the threats of violence which had occurred at the beginning of the decade. They also alienated many elements of the pressure groups which had originally co-operated with the reforming legislation, especially Dissenters and Evangelicals, Radicals and Benthamites. Many decided to vote Conservative in 1841.

Underlying all these problems was the basic dilemma which confronted the Whigs. They had projected themselves as reformers and won the day over the 1832 Reform Act as a result of a nationwide confrontation with the Tories and the House of Lords. But this high level of activity and publicity could not be sustained indefinitely, especially in the arena of social and administrative reform. Under Grey reform still appeared to be the order of the day, but this was largely by comparison with a Tory opposition which still tended to be reactionary. Under Melbourne the impetus slowed somewhat. The result has been effectively summarised by Llewellyn: 'When, in the early 1830s, they were a genuinely reforming party, the Whigs were in the ascendant in the country; when after 1835 they were merely learning to live with the reforms that they had effected, they were in decline'.[26]

This was part of a complex process of change which was occurring from the mid-1830s. As the reforming impetus of the Whigs began to slow down, the Tories, under the leadership of Robert Peel, were experiencing a major revival. An essential part of this was the deliberate movement of the Tories into the reforming ground previously regarded as the preserve of the Whigs. Thus, according to Llewellyn, it must have seemed by 1837 that 'the Whigs were becoming less Radical and more "conservative" and that the Conservatives under Peel were becoming more "liberal" '.[27] To this theme we now turn.

7

SIR ROBERT PEEL AS PARTY LEADER AND NATIONAL STATESMAN

Sir Robert Peel entered parliament in 1809, serving Perceval's government as Under-Secretary at the Colonial Office (1810–12) and then Liverpool as Chief Secretary for Ireland (1812–18). His major responsibilities in this earlier period were as Home Secretary (1822–30) and as Leader of the House of Commons (1828–30). After replacing Wellington as leader of the Tory party in 1834, he served briefly as Prime Minister between 1834 and 1835. He then led the Opposition for the next six years until his victory in the 1841 general election gave him a second term of power until 1846. In the last phase of his life, between the repeal of the Corn Laws in 1846 and his death in 1850, he headed a splinter group of free traders, known as 'Peelites'.

Peel's career after 1834 therefore comprised two roles: party leader and national statesman. This chapter will examine the relationship between them: in the 1830s, when he was primarily in opposition, and in the 1840s when he headed a government.

During the 1830s, party leadership and national statesmanship converged. Peel was able, through the Tamworth Manifesto, to revive his party while, at the same time, being in opposition meant that he had little difficulty in putting national interests first. During the 1840s, the two roles diverged. Because he was now able as Prime Minister to formulate and implement policy, he could choose more directly between national statesmanship and party leadership. For almost the whole of his 1841–6 ministry he placed particular emphasis on the national interest, even where this conflicted fundamentally with his party's unity. Since he did not give a high priority to bridging the gap between the two, his legacy was, on the one hand, a series of measures which helped steer Britain towards economic primacy and, on the other, a badly split party.

Plate 1 Sir Robert Peel Bt, 1788–1850. Oil on panel, 45.5 × 37.8 (17 × 14). By John Linnell, signed and dated 1838. By courtesy of the Mary Evans Picture Library, London

The present chapter will explore this theme in three sections. The first will focus on Peel's reconstruction of the Tory party in the 1830s, the second on his policies as Prime Minister in the 1840s, the third on his leadership of the party in the same period.

PEEL'S RECONSTRUCTION OF THE PARTY IN THE 1830s

Most modern historians consider the decade between 1830 and 1841 one of major achievement for Peel. Their view is typified by two examples. N. Gash, for one, maintains that Peel was the 'outstanding parliamentarian of his age', that he provided 'unrivalled leadership' and a 'non-partisan intellect', together with a skill in politics which gave Conservatism 'a cohesion and purpose which no party in opposition had ever had before'.[1] Second, E.J. Evans considers that during this period the old Tory party was 'subsumed within a broader Conservatism under the guidance of its leader, Sir Robert Peel, whose achievement both in opposition and in government is such that he has a strong claim to be considered the supreme statesman of the nineteenth century'.[2]

Peel's task at the beginning of the decade must have appeared mountainous. According to a Tory supporter in 1832, 'No smash given by Napoleon in the midst of his greatest successes was more complete and terrific than the overthrow which has struck our party to the ground'.[3] The party had lost heart and direction after the death of Liverpool. It had split disastrously over Catholic Emancipation, lost to the Whigs the debate over parliamentary reform and been resoundingly defeated in the general election of December 1832, being reduced to only 175 seats. It had not been well led, especially during the period of Wellington's domination, and there had been comparatively little direct contact between the party in the Lords under Wellington and that in the Commons under Peel.

The extent of the subsequent Tory revival was impressive, as is shown by the number of seats won in successive general elections:

	1832	1835	1837	1841
Whigs	483	385	345	291
Tories/Conservatives	175	273	313	367

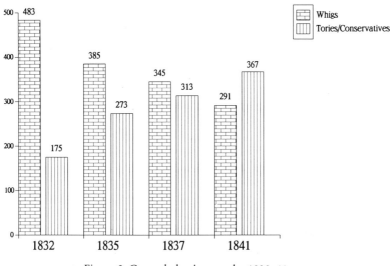

Figure 3 General election results 1832–41

What were Peel's contributions to this? To some extent, the Tories benefited from the growing difficulties experienced by the Whig governments in sustaining the reforming momentum (see Chapter 6). Most historians, however, are quick to give Peel personal credit for the transformation. For one thing, Peel had certain valuable personal qualities; according to Adelman he was 'a man, who in terms of intellect, experience and national influence, stood head and shoulders above any other member of the party or of the House of Commons'.[4] This is very much in line with the view of Peel's contemporary, Greville, that 'His great merit consists in his judgement, tact and discretion, his facility, promptitude, thorough knowledge of the assembly he addresses, familiarity with the details of every sort of Parliamentary business, and the great command he has over himself'.[5]

Of particular importance, however, was Peel's flexibility. His willingness to adapt to a new situation or to go with an irrestisible trend is what mainly distinguished him from Wellington. The major change was his acceptance of the basic principles contained within the Great Reform Act after he had initially opposed them. He also succeeded in converting the Tories to accepting the need to be open-minded about reform and saw the advantage here of moving closer to the Whigs and of contesting with them the reforming ground.

Peel found a new formula for Toryism, which gradually, and more appropriately, came to be known as Conservatism: he grafted reform on to tradition and justified it in the name of continuity. He also emphasised the reforming history within the Tory party, especially his own achievements as Home Secretary in the 1820s: this did away with any impression that Toryism had become Conservatism merely as a tactical conversion to change in the wake of the Whigs.

Peel also realised that he needed to rival the Whig conception of the alliance between the aristocracy and the middle class which had been embodied in the struggle for the Reform Act. Peel's counterpart to this was to extend the Tory party's social base. At present this was confined to the aristocracy, the country gentry and the Church. Peel now aimed to 'conciliate the goodwill of the sober-minded and well disposed portions of the community'[6] and to attract support from the middle classes and those who wanted moderate reform. In addition, he filled the gap left by the Whigs, who had never succeeded in winning over middle-class business-men; part of his appeal was that he himself was of middle-class origins.

The Tamworth Manifesto (1834) was symbolic of the new approach the Tory party adopted to the issue of reform. It started with a statement that Peel felt it essential 'to enter into a declaration of my view of public policy'. He went on to say that he had never 'been the defender of abuses, or the enemy of judicious reforms' and that he had already given an indication of this in his own reforms in the 1820s. The Reform Act itself must now be seen as 'a final and irrevocable settlement of a great Constitutional question'. The spirit of the Reform Bill, furthermore, allowed 'a careful review of institutions, civil and ecclesiastical, undertaken in a friendly temper, combining, with the firm maintenance of established rights, the correction of proved abuses and the redress of real grievances'.[7] The Tamworth Manifesto projected a much more modern and positive party image. According to Greville it was 'a prodigious sensation, and nobody talks of anything else'.[8]

On the other hand, the Manifesto was incomplete in two respects. In the first place, it made no reference to the term Conservative, which came into common usage more informally. And second, it soon became dated. Although it stood Peel in good stead for the next two general elections, which steadily eroded Whig support, Peel did not envisage a party manifesto as a means of preparing a specific statement of party policy for each election. In this respect, Peel only partially anticipated later party leaders like Gladstone and Disraeli.

Peel's party leadership in the 1830s is open to another criticism. In one respect the Tory party prospered irrespective of his actions: the central and local organisation, which followed the provision in the 1832 Reform Act for the registration of voters. The main initiative here was taken by F.R. Bonham and the Carlton Club. The new organisation also chose candidates, arranged and financed party canvassing, contributing in no small measure to the party's election victory in 1841.

For all that, it was without question Peel who reunited the Tory party, and in a way no one else in the 1830s could have done. The Ultras, who had defected to the Whigs after Catholic Emancipation, now returned to the fold and for a while submerged their separate identity. If anything, it was the Whigs who began to fragment, as has been seen in the previous chapter. It was now the turn of the Tories to benefit as in 1834 four members of the Whig government resigned over the Irish Church Bill; of these, Graham and Stanley were eventually to join the Conservatives. During the 1830s Peel experienced less embarrassment from his back-benchers than did Melbourne with his front-benchers; the three Tory revolts of the period, all concerning the issue of Ireland, were effectively neutralised. The process of Tory recovery and healing was completed by Peel's brief spell as Prime Minister between 1834 and 1835 after the dismissal of the Whigs by William IV. Although Peel's hold on power at this stage was tenuous and had to be returned to the Whigs within 100 days, the experience of office was vital to the party and definitely helped boost the Tory vote in the 1835 election. A similar, but briefer experience in 1839 probably helped consolidate the Tory vote in 1841.

One final point needs to be considered. After becoming Prime Minister in 1841, Peel soon acquired the reputation for putting nation above party. Does this also apply to the period he spent in opposition? In some respects it does. Peel was prepared to work for the benefit of the nation outside the narrow confines of party interest. For example, he frequently co-operated with the Whig governments over the social and economic reforms. Examples included the Poor Law Amendment Act of 1834 and the Municipal Corporations Act of 1835. Peel's main priority in the late 1830s appeared not to be to bring down the Whigs but, on occasion, actually to keep them in office. This could certainly be seen as a desire to uphold the integrity of a reforming government and maintain respect for the constitution. N. Gash considers that Peel was guided mainly by the 'governmental ethic'[9] in which the main duty of a parliamentary party was to sustain a government, not to try to remove it. The strong implication here was that the national interest came above that of the party, a position that Peel was again to demonstrate in 1846.

Yet there was also an element of party political wisdom here. If Peel had combined with the radicals to unseat the Whigs the Tories could easily have been projected in an ensuing general election campaign as the party which had undermined reform. Peel realised that the Conservatives had to develop an appropriate image as a government in waiting and that a premature grab for power might serve only to rescue the Whigs from their predicament. Much the same line had been taken in 1829 and 1830 by Grey when it appeared that the Tories were almost – but not quite – ready to fall to the Whigs. Peel was therefore very much in the line of opposition leaders who waited for governments to lose power rather than actively campaigned to win it. This restraint of the nineteenth century sometimes appears incongruous to the more aggressive style of party leadership of the twentieth.

PEEL AS PRIME MINISTER 1841-6

Peel's cabinet in 1841 signalled a very promising start to the new ministry; according to E.J. Evans, it ranks, along with Gladstone's 1868 government, 'as the ablest in the nineteenth century'. Peel was 'supremely confident of his own abilities and of the direction he must follow'. He also 'dominated the Commons by knowledge and brainpower'.[10] The potential was considerable; did Peel's achievement for the nation reflect it?

Peel's main perspective during this period was economic. He inherited finances which were in heavy deficit as well as a slump which served to accentuate the threat of radical movements like Chartism. It was apparent that the Whigs, for all their interest in social reform and their intentions to improve administrative efficiency, had let the economy slide.

His basic principles were ambitious. He envisaged a gradual economic improvement which would, in turn, bring about social change and complete Britain's adjustment to an urban and industrialised society. But the country would have to be steered in this direction by the government. Peel's chosen method was by tariff adjustments, and his budgets of 1842 and 1845 completely removed duties on 600 articles and reduced duties on 500 others. These certainly fostered the expansion of exports, which, in turn, contributed to a trade revival. It was no coincidence that the eventual failure of Chartism overlapped the decrease in unemployment and gradual reduction of food prices as Britain moved out of the slump of the early 1840s. Peel was also able to convert a government deficit of £7.5 million, which he inherited from the Whigs, into a surplus of £2.5 million.. This was due in part to the reintroduction of income tax at 7d (old pence) in the pound on annual incomes of over £150; although it was originally intended as a temporary measure to tide the finances over until the trade expansion would be able to sustain an increase in revenues, it proved sufficiently reliable to convince Peel and his successors that it should not be abandoned too readily. 'In all', says Gash, 'between 1842 and 1846, the work of transforming Britain into a free-trade country was largely accomplished, leaving only a remnant to be done by Gladstone in 1853 and 1860.'[11]

Peel was also conscious of two specific problems which disrupted the efficient running of the economy and were likely to inhibit the effectiveness of his other reforms. These were the absence of adequate controls over the issue of notes by private banks and over the formation of companies. The Bank Charter Act of 1844 has generally been praised for introducing a period of financial stability by reasserting the primacy of the Bank of England and, through pound-for-pound backing in gold for sums above £14 million, preventing overissue of notes in the future. This undoubtedly prevented a repetition of the all too common collapse of the more vulnerable smaller banks during a financial slump. Confidence was inevitably promoted in the whole system, and London soon emerged as the world's leading financial centre. On the other hand, the role of the Bank of England was still very limited and it was not until the 1860s that it began to influence the total level of credit and interest rates. In the meantime, there were further financial crises, although, it has to be said, not as serious as those of the early 1840s. Meanwhile, the Companies Act of 1844 provided for the compulsory registration of companies, the issue of prospectuses and the provision of regular accounts. The majority of companies were therefore brought under tighter controls, although the main culprits

– the railway companies – were for the time being exempt since they had been established by private bills in parliament.

The limitations of Peel's policies during the period 1841–5 were mainly apparent in his attitude to social problems, in which he showed little interest for their own sake. His view was that working conditions in factories would gradually improve with the increase of prosperity as a result of overall changes in the economy. For this reason, he was not receptive to the pressure of Shaftesbury and the Ten Hour Committee, and even voted against Shaftesbury's motion for a ten-hour working day. Shaftesbury's frustration with Peel's whole emphasis was apparent when he complained, in September 1842: 'Imports and exports, here is Peel's philosophy! There it begins and there it ends'. He added later 'All Peel's affinities are towards wealth and capital. What has he ever proposed for the working classes?'[12] Peel showed similar reticence in dealing with public health; although he formed a commission to examine the problem in the towns and cities, he took no further action. It was left to Russell's Governmment to secure a Public Health Act in 1848.

Allowing for these shortcomings, however, Peel's achievements for the nation had, by 1845, been considerable. He had unquestionably improved the finances and helped create an economic climate which was discouraging social and political radicalism. Furthermore, he had achieved all this while remaining personally scrupulous and bringing a new level of openness and honesty to British politics.

The climax of Peel's career came in 1846 with the repeal of the Corn Laws. Here historical judgement tends to be more ambivalent, although the overall balance settles eventually in Peel's favour.

On the positive side, Peel acted from the deeply held conviction that the Corn Laws were an anachronism which needed to be removed if economic growth were to experience a sustained increase. His argument was logical enough. To continue to protect the agricultural interest with artificially high tariffs would be entirely inconsistent with the free trade principle of his 1842 and 1845 budgets. Why should one sector of the economy receive preferential treatment merely because it was dominated by the landed aristocracy? It was not as if Peel was intending to sacrifice agriculture for the sake of industry and commerce. On the contrary, he always maintained that agricultural productivity would increase, since the removal of protection would force more farmers to use the scientific methods and agricultural improvements in which Britain already led the world. As a result, Britain's agricultural produce would, like her industrial goods, become increasingly competitive. It is possible to argue that Peel exaggerated the beneficial effect of repeal. Nevertheless, his measure did help stimulate the subsequent 'Golden age of British agriculture' and stabilise wheat prices at a level lower than that which would have resulted from the continuation of agricultural tariffs.

The timing of the repeal was dictated by the Irish crisis. Peel's handling of this was in many ways remarkably positive. He had, of course, already been converted to the need to end the Corn Laws long before the Irish potato famine of 1845–6. However, he brought forward, for humanitarian reasons, a measure he proposed in any case to submit to the electorate in 1847 or 1848. Recalling the famine in 1817, when he had been Secretary for Ireland, Peel was convinced that starvation would occur on a massive scale if urgent action were not taken. But relief could not be provided while the Corn Laws kept the price of bread artificially high. Having made his decision, he carried it through with total determination. He argued the case strongly to his cabinet in a series of specially convened meetings at the end of 1845. When he received the support of only three – Graham, Aberdeen and Herbert – Peel resigned on 6 December 1845, but was prepared to take up the struggle again when Russell proved unable to form a Whig government. Succeeding after 20 December in converting most of his cabinet, Peel battled for the next five months to carry repeal in the Commons against the combined weight of over two-thirds of the Conservative party. His singlemindedness eventually paid off and the Repeal Bill was carried, with the help of the Whigs, in May 1846. In doing this he exposed himself to his party's revenge a few weeks later as Tory dissidents helped turn him out of office over the Coercion Bill.

There is, however, one very awkward question about Peel's conduct during these months of crisis. If the Irish famine could really have been alleviated by lifting tariffs on corn, why did he not do so while the famine lasted, rather than fight a six-month campaign to secure their *permanent* removal? As A.J.B. Hilton maintains, 'If he had truly felt that the corn laws were practically deleterious, then he ought to have suspended them at once'.[13]

Three different explanations can be advanced for his not having done so, none of which reflect much to Peel's credit. First, he realised that suspending the Corn Laws would be followed by a bitter conflict within the party over their reinstatement once the Irish famine had passed; it was therefore preferable to complete the whole process at once. If this was the case, then Peel was putting his longer-term economic strategy of free trade before the immediate humanitarian argument for saving lives in Ireland. Or, second, he privately accepted the view of the Conservative protectionists that repealing the Corn Laws would make little difference to levels of grain supply in Ireland, despite his rejection of this view in the Commons. Peel would have realised, therefore, that delays over repeal would not have to be paid for with Irish lives. On the other hand, he would be open to the charge that he was justifying an economic policy by a specious humanitarian argument, and raising false hopes in the process. The third, and most likely, explanation is that Peel completely underestimated the degree of opposition and the timescale involved. He did not suspend the Corn Laws because he had made other contingency measures in the autumn of 1845, including imports from the United States of maize worth £150,000 for distribution in Ireland at 1d per pound. He expected the repeal to have been accomplished by the time the effects of this emergency provision had worn off. The subsequent delays he found particularly exasperating, with the result that his performance in the Commons became increasingly volatile. By this analysis, his fault was neither cynicism nor hypocrisy, but miscalculation, something to which all statesmen are susceptible.

PEEL AS PARTY LEADER 1841–6

If the balance is generally in favour of Peel in terms of the national interest, the same can hardly be said of his leadership of the Conservatives between 1841 and 1846. Indeed, this period saw the party he had so recently re-created torn asunder. This was not due to any Whig revival; in fact, the latter seemed to have given up the will to govern and were even prepared to co-operate to keep Peel in office in times of difficulty. The destruction of Conservative primacy was entirely self-inflicted. In 1846 the leader and a minority of the party went one way. The remainder went the other.

There had already been rumblings within the party, which indicated a clear difference of opinion between various groups and their leader. These manifested themselves in the form of open revolt in the House of Commons over the Factory Act of 1844, the bill on sugar duties, and the proposed Maynooth grant. In each case, Peel had to rely on Whig support to steer the legislation through against a tough and determined Tory opposition.

To some extent this conflict was unavoidable. Peel was pursuing a policy which was primarily economic and which had edges which cut into different Tory elements. One of these was the Tory radicals, such as Shaftesbury, who felt that Peel's economic policies precluded necessary intervention to improve social conditions. They considered Peel hard-headed, as did a second section, a group of Tory MPs known as Young England. Led by Smythe and Manners, they produced a romantic type of Toryism which, in the words of Adelman, 'stressed the traditional links between aristocracy and people in opposition to the harsh materialism of the commercial and manufacturing middle classes'.[14] The group was sharpened by the membership of Disraeli, who immediately launched a series of attacks on Peel's government as comprising 'Tory men and Whig measures'.[15]

The largest opposition group to Peel, however, was the agricultural interest, much of which had swung from the Whigs to the Tories in 1841 because they suspected that the Whigs were intending to do away with the Corn Laws. When Peel reduced the duties on corn in 1842 under the provisions allowed in the 1828 sliding scale, the protectionists grudgingly accepted what they hoped would be a final settlement. But Peel became increasingly unpopular with the county MPs as his free trade policy unfolded in his 1842 and 1845 budgets. One Lincolnshire farmer wrote 'The stream of our fortunes is careering away in an impetuous torrent towards the open gulf of Free Trade'. He added: 'we must stem it, quickly and with energy, or we are lost'.[16]

Finally, there was a substantial section within the party which strongly opposed any further concessions to the Catholic Church in Ireland and failed to appreciate Peel's attempt to act with moderation in increasing the annual grant to the Maynooth College, a Catholic training seminary, to £26,000. They also opposed his attempts to secure the appointment of a Catholic Under-Secretary of State for Ireland. Peel found himself confronting the same accusations of betraying the Established Church that he had already experienced after the Catholic Emancipation Act of 1829.

Between 1841 and 1845 these groups were vociferous in their opposition but, as yet, unconnected. The repeal of the Corn Laws, however, brought them together in bitter and united condemnation of Peel's free trade policies. The attack was led by Bentinck,

Stafford, Miles and, above all, Disraeli, who accused Peel in parliament of having betrayed the party by trading 'on the ideas and intelligence of others'. Peel's life, he said, had been 'a great appropriation clause'; indeed, 'From the days of the Conqueror to the termination of the last reign, there is no statesman who has committed political petty larceny on so great a scale'.[17] The very ferocity of Disraeli's attack on his leader and the enthusiasm with which Disraeli's words were received by Tory back-benchers show that fissures had been opening up within the party for some time. What the repeal of the Corn Laws did was to split the party open along the line of these faults.

Why was Peel unable to deal with this antagonism from within the party? The confrontation of 1846 showed that Peel had not been entirely successful in converting Toryism into Conservatism via the Tamworth Manifesto and that, lurking beneath the surface, were influences which sought any opportunity to prevent adaptation and change. The strongest statement of this view is provided by I. Newbould, who considers that Peel's problems in the 1840s were due at least in part to the limited nature of the changes actually effected by Peel within the party in the 1830s; many of Peel's policies, he argues, were aimed at strengthening his own position within the party at the expense of the Ultra Tories, while his eventual victory in the 1841 general election was the reassertion of all the traditional Tory values and strengths and not those of the new party Peel had tried to make.[18] This does, of course, go directly against the broader stream of interpretation, already examined, which gives Peel credit for transforming the party in the 1830s. At the same time, it indicates that between 1841 and 1846 Peel was struggling against internal opposition which was all the more formidable because it represented attitudes which were deeply ingrained. In the light of this, we should not be surprised that he failed to take most of the party with him in 1846.

Acknowledging the difficulty of his task should not, however, lead us to minimise his own contributions to the party split. Peel did. He always considered himself blameless in all his confrontations with the party, emphasising as he had done in the 1830s that his higher duty was to the state; when compared with the national interest the views of the party were incidental. He felt that his main task within the party was to educate it into accepting the permanence of change, and was interested less in the confidence of the party than in the authority and efficiency of his government. There are, of course, times when any party leader needs to take this line. But Peel signally failed to *persuade*. One Tory MP, generally sympathetic to Peel, complained 'He is asking from his party all the blind confidence the country gentlemen placed in Mr Pitt . . . without himself fulfilling any of the engagements on his side'.[19] Worse, he often showed a degree of contempt, especially for the county MPs: 'How can those who spend their time in hunting and shooting and eating and drinking know what were the motives of those who are responsible for the public security . . . ?'[20] He became increasingly autocratic, as was shown in the debate over the Maynooth Bill: here Peel argued that his government had the right to take whatever action it considered appropriate. This raised a storm 'at which', he said, 'I look with much indifference, being resolved on carrying the Bill, and being very careless as to the consequences which may follow its passing, so far as they may concern me'.[21] Or, he might have added, so far as they concerned the party.

Peel's deficiencies as a party leader were most apparent at the time of the crisis over the repeal of the Corn Laws, when he proceeded by ultimatum rather than persuasion. He was hard and unforgiving to the opposition he received from colleagues and subordinates, regarding it as blatant ingratitude for all that he had previously achieved as Prime Minister.[22] He did nothing to avoid the confrontation he was clearly expecting. Nor did he try to achieve his aim through the back door and thereby avoid a crisis. R. Blake[23] asks why, after his resignation on 6 December 1845, Peel was so willing to resume office a fortnight later when Russell failed to form a government. If, as there is no reason to dispute, his priority was really to secure the repeal of the Corn Laws, why could he not have insisted on letting his resignation stand and, instead, have supported a Whig bill from the opposition benches? The end result would have been the same for the nation, but the party might well have survived intact, although with a different leader; there were, after all, precedents for Tory minorities supporting the legislation of Whig governments in the 1830s.

But would this have been enough? That Peel considered himself the indispensable fulcrum of the whole issue is attested by two fellow Tories. One, Gladstone, supported him throughout the crisis, following him into political exile after 1846 and eventually emerging as leader of a reconstituted Liberal party. His view was that Peel was so far convinced that the national interest demanded repeal that he alone could be entrusted with seeing it through. Gladstone said in later life: 'From the language he held to me in December 1845 I think he expected to carry the repeal of the Corn Laws without breaking up his party. But meant at all hazards to carry it.'[24] Gladstone understood Peel's dilemma; indeed he eventually found himself in a comparable position in placing a national issue – Irish Home Rule – above the unity of the Liberal party. Peel's other subordinate, Disraeli, had a different perspective. He always felt that what motivated Peel was personal arrogance rather than high principle. As he said in December 1845, Peel 'is so vain that he wants to figure in history as the settler of all great questions; but a Parliamentary constitution is not favourable to such ambitions: things must be done by parties, not by persons using parties as tools'.[25] In Peel's defence, however, it could be argued that this view on the primacy of party was still very much in its infancy,[26] and that it was Disraeli himself who showed the way to reconciling party unity with national interest.

8

CHARTISM

In 1839 Thomas Carlyle stated, in his pamphlet on *Chartism*, that 'A feeling very generally exists that the condition and disposition of the Working Classes is a rather ominous matter at present; that something ought to be said, something ought to be done in regard to it.'[1] Carlyle hoped that action would come, as reform, from above. What actually happened betweeen 1836 and 1848 was concerted pressure from below, in the form of Chartism.

The People's Charter was drawn up in 1837. Its Six Points demanded universal male suffrage, annual parliaments, equal electoral districts, the abolition of property qualifications for MPs, voting by secret ballot and the payment of MPs. The movement behind this programme actually comprised three separate strands: the London Working Men's Association (LWMA) under Lovett, Netherington, O'Brien and Watson; the Birmingham Political Union under Attwood; and the Northern movement, inspired initially by Oastler and Stephens but led after 1836 by O'Connor. The Charter was presented to parliament by means of three petitions in 1839, 1842 and 1848, each of which was resoundingly defeated.

Other objectives were also expressed, although they have commanded less detailed attention. The LWMA aimed in 1836 to draw the working classes into 'one bond of unity'; to ensure for all classes their 'equal political and social rights'; to guarantee 'the free circulation of thought through the medium of a cheap and honest press'; to promote education; and to 'lead to a gradual improvement in the condition of the working classes without violence or commotion'.[2]

Chartism has been given a variety of emphases by different historians. According to A. Briggs, it was 'a snowball movement which gathered together local grievances and sought to give them common expression in a nationwide agitation';[3] Hopkins calls it 'the most striking and widespread working class movement for political reform in the nineteenth century';[4] while P. Gregg maintains that 'Chartism was a political movement based on economic grievances'.[5] A synthesis, as a starting point for analysis, might be that Chartism was a movement which had both local and national interests and structure. It sought political reform, partly for its own sake, partly as the most effective means of addressing social and economic problems. It employed a variety of strategies, which included both 'moral force' and 'physical force'[6] and was primarily working class in orientation and support.

THE REASONS FOR CHARTISM

What were the basic reasons for the emergence of Chartism? The movement's impetus was in part political, part social, part economic.

The *political* motivation was, of course, central. Recent historians have tended to see Chartism as flowing within the mainstream of political radicalism already represented in the eighteenth century by John Wilkes and Tom Paine and, in the early nineteenth, by 'Orator' Hunt, William Cobbett and Major Cartwright. H. Cunningham goes much further back, arguing that Chartist aspirations to restore the principle of liberty after prolonged erosion by corruption were also in the tradition of Magna Carta.[7] Their focus in the 1830s was the 1832 Reform Act, which had left intact many of the deficiencies of the electoral system. They were particularly aggrieved by the apparent selfishness of the newly enfranchised sections of the middle class. These had depended on radical agitation from the working classes between 1831 and 1832 for the passage of the Reform Bill but were now unwilling to broaden the franchise further. The Chartists therefore aimed at removing the cut-off point which each social class seemed bent on applying against the class immediately below itself.

The political emphasis of Chartism was also seen as an *enabling* process. Chartists were disillusioned not only with the limitations of the new parliament after 1832 but also with the social and economic legislation which the Whig governments pushed through it during the 1830s, especially the 1833 Factory Act and the Poor Law Amendment Act of 1834. The working classes were exploited precisely because they lacked the political power to end that exploitation; as Julian Harney said in 1839, 'The want of universal

CHARTISM

suffrage has allowed the horrors of the factory system so long to continue.'[8] It followed, therefore, that economic and social reform could best be accomplished by political action. This is what J.R. Stephens meant when he stated that universal suffrage was the means of securing every working man's 'right to a good coat on his back, a good roof over his head and a good dinner on his table'. He also believed that 'The question of universal suffrage is a knife and fork question . . . a bread and cheese question'.[9]

The key problem, of course, was how to secure the necessary political change: how to persuade a barely reformed House of Commons to reform itself still further. The Chartists placed their early hopes in the radicals then in parliament – Grote, Roebuck, Buller, and John and Edward Romilly – in the belief that these would spearhead a campaign from within the precincts of power. This, however, yielded nothing since most of the radical MPs preferred to identify with the policies of the Whigs. From 1838 onwards, therefore, Chartism distanced itself from all existing political groupings within the House of Commons and aimed instead at applying pressure on the system from without.

In the process, Chartism also took on board a range of social issues which dominated the period. In some areas, especially the North, Chartists became caught up in the popular protest against the operation of the New Poor Law. This was largely because the attempt to enforce the 1834 Act coincided with a prolonged business depression which in any case pushed up unemployment and brought the threat of starvation to handloom weavers. According to Stedman Jones, 'The great strength of the Charter in 1838–9, therefore, lay in its identification of political power as the source of social oppression, and thus, its ability to concentrate the discontent of the unrepresented working classes upon one common aim'.[10] This is very much reflected in contemporary opinion: Harney, for example, maintained that 'The Charter was a means to an end – the means was their political rights, and the end was social equality'.[11] There was also a strong element of desperation and bitterness, the harshness of factory conditions and of measures to deal with poverty both interacting with political disillusionment. This point is pressed by G.D.H. Cole: 'Hunger and hatred – these were the forces that made Chartism a mass movement of the British working class.'[12]

It has been argued that, throughout its course, Chartism was directly influenced by prevailing *economic* circumstances. W.W.

91

Rostow has shown that 'Intervals of high social tension' bred unrest, including Chartism, while 'low social tension' saw this fade. Specifically, Rostow produced a 'social tension chart' based on bread prices and the general state of the economy. 'High tension' was apparent in the periods 1837–42 and 1847–8, which corresponded with the peaks of Chartist activity, while 'low tension' existed in 1834–6, 1843–6 and 1850.[13] A local example of how closely Chartism was linked throughout its course with economic conditions was the depression in Manchester. There the boom of 1836 collapsed, causing immense hardship especially to the hand-loom weavers. The cotton manufacturers, influenced as they were by the policy of *laissez-faire*, made no effort to alleviate this. After the rejection of the second Chartist petition, the depression also interacted with the movement, the result of a further decline in trade and fall in wages. In 1842 there was a strike at Stalybridge which spread throughout the Manchester area. Much the same occurred in Yorkshire, Staffordshire, the Potteries, Warwickshire and Wales.

It is also possible to see a pattern in the progress made during this period by working-class movements as a whole. Trade unions, which concentrated on economic action, tended to flourish in prosperous times, while political activism, especially in the form of Chartism, came to the fore in bad times. The slump of 1837 reduced the attractions of trade unionism and provided Chartism with a sudden injection of popular support. In the same year John Bray launched a vitriolic attack on trade unions, arguing that 'The capitalist and the employer have ultimately been too strong for them' and that trade unions had become 'amongst the enemies of the working class, a bye word of caution or contempt'.[14] Indeed, by the late 1830s, many of the leading figures of the Chartist movement were disillusioned trade unionists who decided to switch to political action. During the mid-1840s and after 1849, however, trade unions recovered most of their former membership – at the expense of the Chartist movement.

THE CHARTISTS AND THEIR MEASURES

Who were the Chartists, and what measures did they take to achieve their objectives?

The classification used for Chartism has varied considerably. It is, however, possible to subdivide the movement into four main sections. One comprised the factory operatives in the West Riding of

Yorkshire, in Derbyshire, Lancashire, Scotland, Wales and the West country. London and Birmingham were not really represented here because in these cities the factory system had not taken root to anything like the same extent. The second group was the middle-class members of the Chartist movement, under the leadership of Thomas Attwood, an MP and prominent campaigner for the extension of the suffrage in 1832. They believed that what was really needed was monetary reform to relieve the adverse economic conditions which, in turn, would reduce unemployment and improve working conditions; this, however, could be implemented only by a reformed House of Commons. A third section was the skilled craftsmen, such as Lovett's London Working Men's Association, who were according to Lovett 'the intelligent and influential portion of the working classes'.[15] They were convinced of the need to acquire the vote for its own sake. They also placed a stronger belief in the moral influence of Chartism; Lovett hoped that the workmen would give up 'their various hobbies of anti-poor laws, factory bills, wages protection laws, and various others, for the purpose of jointly contending for the Charter'.[16]

Fourth, a significant part of the Chartist movement was made up of domestic outworkers – such as handloom weavers, nailers and stockingers – in Birmingham and the West Midlands, Lancashire, the West country, the West Riding of Yorkshire and Scotland. In these areas the impetus was quite often against the machinery which was perceived as the cause of unemployment and hardship. In fact, those who were suspicious of the motives and methods of Chartism often accused it of being a retrogressive force, as a reaction against industrialisation akin to Luddism. This is not, however, a supportable generalisation. Not all outworkers opposed industrialisation and, in any case, they were outnumbered by factory operatives who depended on the 'great changes' and by skilled workers, such as carpenters, shoemakers and tailors, who had as yet scarcely been affected by them. Hence, as Hopkins argues, 'it can hardly be argued that Chartism as a whole was a revolt against the Industrial Revolution'.[17]

These different groupings meant that behind the superficial appearance of unity there were deep divisions and disagreements over what were the main grievances to be addressed. This inevitably meant that there were different strategies.

It has been pointed out that the North provided the most radical contingents, Birmingham the most constitutional and opposed to violence, and London somewhere in between – also opposed to violence, but more sympathetic to the grievances expressed by the North.[18] Each of these influenced the measures which were attempted and the divergence between the groups meant that there was little chance of the measures being brought into full harmony.

The frontispiece of the whole movement was, of course, the Charter, conceived in London and accepted by Chartists everywhere – although for different reasons; the Birmingham and London sections considered that political reform was an end in itself, whereas the North regarded this as a necessary step to economic and social transformation. The Charter was given publicity by conventions and presented to parliament by means of petitions. As the situation became increasingly tense the central Convention was switched from London to Birmingham and proceeded from 1839 to consider, in the Committee of Ulterior Measures, special action to be taken should the petition be rejected by parliament.

Unfortunately, these measures were not realistic and the Committee was on to a loser at the outset. One was the threat of a general strike: but the main problem here was that most trade unionists were not within the Chartist movement. Another was the more traditional threat of a 'run on the banks' through the withdrawal of deposits. This, however, would scarcely have the government quaking, as the sums involved were small. Alternatively, support for the use of force was strictly limited. Eventually the Chartist movement divided along the seam of approbation for the use of violence. The North, especially O'Connor and the National Charter Association, became increasingly contemptuous of the Complete Suffrage Union which represented the more moderate and peaceful aspirations of Chartism for political reform. O'Connor said that, although he was for peace, 'if peace giveth not law, I am for war to the knife'.[19] A Manchester poster urged supporters: 'be sure you do not neglect your arms, and when you do strike . . . let the blood of all you suspect moisten the soil of your native land'.[20] There was, of course, one other device used by a minority of Chartists: O'Connor's Land Scheme, devised after the rejection of the second petition. This did not, however, command much support and was strongly opposed by moderates like Lovett and O'Brien who still hoped to win through by presenting a third and even larger petition.

A CLASS-BASED MOVEMENT?

Was Chartism a class-based movement which, during the 1830s and 1840s, represented the working class? The conventional Marxist view is that Chartism was the expression of working-class militancy and self-consciousness. Lenin, for example, called the movement 'the first broad and politically organised proletarian-revolutionary movement of the masses'.[21] This analysis has its limitations. It clearly fails to take into account the considerable effect of middle-class influences such as Attwood's Birmingham Political Union and their constitutional aims. Engels advanced the slightly more sophisticated argument that Chartism became a working-class movement after the breakdown of an initial alliance with the middle class. Chartism lost its middle-class adherents to the Anti-Corn Law League, from which moment 'Chartism was purely a working-man's cause freed from all bourgeois elements . . . The Radical bourgeoisie joined hands with the Liberals against the working-man in every collision'.[22]

There has been some disagreement over the basic assumption behind Engels' analysis – that there was such a thing as working-class self-consciousness. This has been questioned by R. Soffer, who argued in 1965 that 'the mass of working men, particularly in the industrial North, were not class conscious, and throughout the thirties and forties they remained uneducated, inarticulate, unskilled and unaware of any "identity of interests as between themselves"'.[23] On the other hand, D. Thompson maintains that 'The working classes . . . showed a strong inclination to follow leaders who preached a very simple doctrine of class hostility';[24] this applied especially to O'Connor. Both middle and working classes, indeed, had a 'strong sense of identity'.

Thompson and others have also argued that class identity soon became class antipathy. 'The years after 1832 saw the heightening of hostility between the middle and lower classes.'[25] There were several grounds for this. First, the middle classes were considered by O'Connor as the exploiters of labour and therefore as most unlikely to take any action in their interest. Second, middle-class manufacturers were resistant to any pressure to reduce working hours or improve working conditions. Third, unemployment was being used deliberately as a device to create a 'reserve army' of labour intended to weaken the position of newly developing trade unionism. Fourth, the middle classes were closing off to the working class any form of political redress since they had been 'bought off' by the provisions of the 1832 Reform Act. For these reasons, therefore, Chartism gradually became more conscious of itself as a movement which had to exist with minimal support from other classes even if, at the outset, it was not geared up to be antagonistic towards them. The vitriol came later. The *Poor Man's Guardian* believed that 'The middle classes are the real tyrants of the country. Disguise it as they may, they are the authors of our slavery . . . Government is but a tool in their hands.'[26] R.C. Gammage maintained that 'the aristocracy had availed themselves of the aid of that class to crush Democracy',[27] while even the Charter itself accused the middle classes of inciting the government to 'make war on the Chartists'.[28]

The Chartist movement was particularly antagonistic to the Anti-Corn Law League which it regarded as the manifestation of middle-class self-interest. Lovett considered the activities of the League to be potentially damaging because it drew attention away from the real issue. According to a Birmingham Chartist, J. Mason, 'Not that Corn Law Repeal is wrong; when we get the Charter we will repeal the Corn Laws and all other bad laws. But if you give up your agitation for the Charter to help the Free Traders, they will not help you to get the Charter.' He therefore urged Chartists not to be 'deceived by the middle classes again. You helped them to get their votes . . . But they and the rotten Whigs have never remembered you'.[29] Leaguers and Chartists often came to blows at meetings, as for example in Manchester in 1842, when a Leaguer described 'a tremendous fight' in which 'all the furniture was smashed to atoms'.[30]

There is a good case, therefore, for stating that Chartism gradually became conscious of itself as a class organisation and increasingly identified and targeted enemies from other classes. This is not, however, the same as saying that Chartism *represented* the working class, many members of which preferred to associate their grievances and aspirations with trade union activity; with this, of course, the Chartists never established a lasting connection. Often there was direct rivalry between local trade union branches and local Chartist organisations; in 1842, for example, the call of the Sheffield Chartists for a general strike caused seven local trade union branches to distance themselves immediately.[31] In the final analysis, Engels may have been right about the emergence of a class base within Chartism, but he ignored the development of very different organisations within the same class. The Marxist analysis of conflict between cohesive classes is difficult to reconcile with the existence of a fragmented proletariat.

WHY DID CHARTISM FAIL?

Chartism appeared to have reached its peak in 1848 with the presentation of the Third Petition and the hope that MPs would have swung behind it in the time that had elapsed since the Second. The rejection of this petition was a profound psychological blow from which it never recovered. Why did Chartism fail to achieve its political, social and economic objectives? Some of the answers have already been implicit in the previous sections, but can now be drawn out as follows.

In the first place there was a serious lack of unity. Chartism lacked a clear and specific direction and policy, being unable to agree on whether the priority was political, social or economic. Another centrifugal force was regionalism. The North was far more radical in its attitude and leadership than Birmingham or London, while the Scottish variant was initially closely associated with the churches to form 'Christian Chartism'. Later Scottish Chartism came under the control of Glasgow moderates who had more in common with middle-class radicals in England than with their fellows in the North of England.

Chartism also contained a variety of leaders, often discordant in their views and aspirations. Some, like Stephens and O'Connor, were crowd stirrers who were inclined to violence. Others, including Harney and O'Brien, were more intellectual and were clearly influenced by the French Revolution. According to Gash, there was a combination of 'genuine idealists, ambitious intellectuals and rootless demagogues'.[32] Compared with these, Thompson maintains, 'William Lovett and the London Working Men's Association represented not so much an alternative leadership to the Chartist movement, as a different sort of movement altogether'.[33] Lovett and Place were certainly profoundly hostile to O'Connor, whom they saw as a profoundly destabilising influence, 'the most restless of them all, who, by his volubility, his recklessness of truth, his newspaper, his unparalleled impudence . . . triumphed over every other agitator'.[34]

External factors weighed heavily on Chartism, particularly the economic cycle of depression and prosperity; as we have seen, support for Chartism tended to be directly in proportion to the extent of suffering. The middle of the 1840s saw a return to prosperity which considerably reduced the popularity of Chartism. The calculated reforms of the governments of Peel and his successors also helped undercut some of the social appeal which the Chartists had previously exercised. These included the 1842 Mines Act, the repeal of the Corn Laws in 1846 and the Ten Hours Act in 1847. It is true that there was a sudden reversion to depression in 1847, which affected the whole of Europe and helped precipitate a series of revolutions on the Continent. Chartism experienced a temporary revival during this period but this was dashed by the rejection of the Third Petition. During the 1850s, however, there was again a trade recovery and the general increase in prosperity meant that Chartism never again had a residue of discontent on which to call.

Some within the movement hoped that Chartism would join the mainstream of revolution sweeping across Europe in 1848. But it was here that the movement had least chance of success. Violence was never likely to meet with much success in Britain in the 1830s or 1840s. The greatest threat of revolution had already passed. As Evans states, 'The Chartists menaced the authorities less in 1839, 1842 and 1848 than had the radical reformers in 1831–32.'[35] Certainly insurrection was tried: arms were collected, handbills issued, and an Italian treatise on street fighting studied.[36] But there was little evidence of concerted planning except on a local scale – such as the Newport Rising of 1839. There was never a real possibility of collating such incidents elsewhere in the country, although the government worked on the assumption that this would be attempted. Violence in any case was self-defeating. It could hardly be justified in advancing the cause of constitutional reform and where it occurred it succeeded only in alienating the moderates and the middle-class supporters. Alternatively, it split those who remained faithful to the movement into 'physical force' and 'moral force' Chartists. The threat of violence in 1848 had a strong Irish connection. O'Brien, for example, hoped that the preoccupation of the British government would mean the reduction of the British presence in Ireland and hence increase the likelihood of a successful rebellion there. This hope was not, of course, shared by the majority of Chartist sympathisers who were at best embarrassed, at worst outraged, by the Irish link.

For violence to have stood any real chance of success it needed to have been endemic in the capital. The various French revolutions

(1789, 1830 and 1848) would have been inconceivable without the initial impetus of radicalism and street fighting in Paris. London was not, however, particularly affected by Chartism – largely because it was not a new centre of industrialisation; nor had it experienced the violent opposition to the introduction and spread of workhouses under the New Poor Law that had occurred in the North. London was merely the stage on which Chartism acted out its major role; but the response of parliament to the Charter showed how hostile this was to prove.

The government's response was also more measured than usual, calculated to avoid inflaming the situation and inciting further support for the movement. General Napier, responsible for the preservation of law and order, was particularly careful not to repeat the mistake of precipitate military action seen at Peterloo in 1819. He kept his troops out of sight most of the time, but was careful to publicise precisely how he could contain outbursts of violence, even going to the extent of saying what military dispositions he would make if threatened. Overall he achieved a rare balance between moderation and effective deterrence. In any case, the government had more advantages at its disposal than before, including the more rapid deployment of troops as a result of the building of railways and the more efficient collection of information through the use of the telegraph. The forces of law and order therefore mobilised the latest technology against isolated manifestations of insurrection.

DID CHARTISM FAIL?

Chartism did not, in the short term, achieve any of its objectives. But can it also be considered a failure in the longer timescale?

As is often the case with radical movements, time has given justification and effect to the demands of the Chartists. All but one of their points were eventually conceded by the British establishment. In chronological order, the property qualifications for MPs were scrapped in 1859, secret ballot was introduced in 1872, MPs were paid from 1911, and the franchise acts of 1918 and 1928 introduced universal suffrage and made adjustments for more equal electoral districts. In each case, however, more sustained pressure was necessary and the connections with Chartism were tenuous. Nevertheless, the long-term outcome has done much to restore the credibility of Chartism as a far-sighted and progressive movement, albeit torn by internal dissension, and not as the lunatic fringe organisation which was the perception of many contemporaries.

One of the Six Points was never implemented – annual parliaments. The Charter had argued that this step would present 'the most effectual check to bribery and intimidation' and would ensure that MPs 'would not be able to defy and betray their constituents as now'. The intention was clearly to prevent the growth of executive power, perhaps because governments would still be dominated by Whigs or Conservatives and therefore by aristocratic and middle-class interests. Chartists could not have foreseen that the type of reforming programme introduced by the Liberals after 1906 or Labour after 1945 (both largely on behalf of the working classes) would require up to five years of guaranteed power. It was, therefore, the one part of their programme which proved entirely impractical, based on the only assumption which became obsolete.

In the long time lag between the collapse of the movement and the fulfilment of five of the Six Points, Chartism was not without a certain residual influence, especially in the political sphere. Through the Chartist experience, the working classes gained valuable knowledge of the art of organisation, even if this was partly in the negative form of how to avoid the repetition of basic mistakes. More positively, Chartism provided a powerful psychological influence on working-class consciousness and movements in the future. Chartism also provided a link between the Reform Acts of 1832 and 1867 by keeping alive the pressure and agitation for parliamentary reform. During the 1860s conditions proved more favourable than in the 1850s for the further extension of the franchise and a number of former Chartists played an important role in the newly established Reform League. Many former activists moved into mainstream political organisations. One example was the penetration of the left wing of the Liberal party under Gladstone, thus providing the early Liberal party with a strong working-class element and ethos. Others resisted this temptation and were numbered among the founders of the Independent Labour party in 1893.

Did Chartism have much of an impact on mid-century social developments? Not according to Thompson, who maintains that two of the original aims of the LWMA were achieved in spite of, not because of, the Chartists. One was the reform of the Poor Law. Although the 1834 Act was partially modified, this was because of the inefficiency and expense of its operation; on the other hand, workhouses remained in existence even after the First World War.[37]

Second, the Chartists had aimed at free and universal education controlled by the community. But in practice early initiatives passed to the factory schools and even the 1870 Act fell far short of Chartist aspirations. More significant perhaps was the influence of Chartism on increasing the confidence and tenacity of working-class organisations in negotiating on working conditions. In this respect, it had a lasting psychological impact, as was pointed out in 1920 by J. West:

> The Chartist movement was the first organised effort to stir up class consciousness on a national scale. Judged by its crop of statutes and statues, Chartism was a failure. Judged by its essential and generally overlooked purpose, Chartism was a success. It achieved not the Six Points, but a state of mind.[38]

9

THE CORN LAWS
AND THEIR REPEAL

One of the dominant issues of the period between 1815 and 1846 was protection and the campaign for free trade, the focus of which was the future of the Corn Laws.

During much of the eighteenth century so-called 'corn laws' had been used mainly to prevent wild fluctuations in the price of grain; this had been done by promoting the export of grain by a bounty in years of surplus and, conversely, reducing import duties on imports of foreign corn when domestic prices increased after a bad harvest.[1] Some historians, like D.G Barnes[2] and C.R. Fay,[3] have argued that this procedure did encourage more stable prices and promoted a genuine balance between the interests of producers and consumers.

But this did not last. The Corn Laws which were rushed through parliament in 1791 and 1804 had an altogether different purpose. The emphasis was now very much on higher protection against foreign competition, which meant positive discrimination in favour of producers at the expense of consumers. This could be partially explained by the special conditions of war in which Britain was placed at the turn of the century, but the new approach was continued and intensified after the arrival of peace.

THE CORN LAWS AND THEIR OPERATION

The terms of the 1815 Corn Law were very much within this revised approach. They stipulated that foreign corn could be imported and warehoused free at all times but that it could be released for sale only when the home price had reached 80 shillings per quarter for wheat, 53 shillings for rye, 40 shillings for barley and 26 shillings for oats. What was the reasoning behind this legislation?

The producers, who had applied strong pressure to the predominantly agricultural interest in parliament, were not entirely without a case. They were seriously concerned about the immediate impact of peace after the country had accustomed itself to prolonged warfare with France. During the French Wars, the price of corn had remained at a consistently high level: 90 shillings (s) per quarter in 1795, 113s 10d in 1800, 119s 6d in 1801, and 126s 6d in 1812. A foretaste of change was provided in 1814, when the price dropped to 75 shillings per quarter and there were indications that it would go down still further. Farmers argued that they would be ruined by the anticipated influx of cheap imports from the Continent, where corn could be grown more cheaply. This would be a poor return indeed for the heavy capital investment made by the larger British farmers, who had also paid dearly through soaring cultivation costs.

Their ruin could, in turn, lead to the destruction of Britain's agricultural base. Some theorists, including Malthus, believed that protection was necessary to keep agriculture profitable. Agriculture, he argued, was not just a sectional interest but was vital for the prosperity of the whole country, contributing as it did one-third to the total national income and giving employment to one-third of the working population. Clearly it would be unrealistic for farmers to expect wartime prices to be sustained, but a guaranteed price of 80 shillings per quarter was seen as a reasonable compromise. It should even be possible to achieve the dual objective of ensuring good prices for the producer while, at the same time, preventing the wilder excesses which had previously hit the consumer.

The 1815 Corn Law did not, however, work well. There were inconsistencies and wild fluctuations in price levels. These at first rose above 85 shillings because of poor harvests in 1817 and 1818. Although this was the point at which imports might have come in, they did not because the Continent had been similarly affected. Then continental production recovered and large imports came into England which reduced the price to 44s 7d in 1822; this was followed by exceptionally favourable harvests in 1821 and 1822. The problem was that the Corn Law accentuated fluctuation rather than controlled it; according to Chambers and Mingay, 'the sudden turning on and off of the import tap as prices fluctuated above and below 80s added to the instability of the grain market'.[4]

As prices reached exceptionally low levels in 1821–2 there was pressure on parliament to take action. Hence two further measures were passed to modify the 1815 legislation. The first was the Corn

Law of 1822 which reduced the limits at which corn could be released from the Continent to 70 shillings and to 50 shillings for British North America; the corresponding levels were 35 shillings for barley and 25 shillings for oats. Import duties were to slide up and down according to prices: for example, when the price of wheat was 70 shillings, the duty was 17 shillings, when the price was 85 shillings, the duty was 10 shillings. But this change meant very little in practice since the graduated scales did not come into operation until the price of wheat had reached 80 shillings.[5] The second measure was the Corn Law of 1828, which discarded the concept of the fixed ceiling embodied in the 1815 Corn Law. It replaced the fixed scale by a sliding scale, with the duties falling as the home prices increased. Absolute protection was still applied when the average price was below 52 shillings, after which foreign wheat could be released with a duty of 34s 8d. There would then be a gradual reduction in duty until, when the home price had reached 73 shillings, it was a nominal 1 shilling.

The Corn Laws, as the measures of 1815, 1822 and 1828 were now collectively known, had thus become more and more complex. It is hardly surprising that they were also subject to increasing controversy, with arguments being marshalled both in support and in opposition. According to Deane, 'The debate over the Corn Laws ebbed and flowed in the 1820s and 1830s and flared up in the 'forties'.[6]

THE CAMPAIGN AGAINST THE CORN LAWS

The attack was launched by the manufacturers, merchants and traders, and free trade theorists like Bentham and Ricardo. The arguments were varied and related to the sectional interests of those involved. A particularly strong case, however, was articulated by the Anti-Corn Law League, formed in 1838 with the specific purpose of putting pressure on the government of the day to repeal the Corn Laws.

One of the League's strongest arguments was economic. The English agricultural interest would have to be forced to recognise that the greater economic good could be served only by the full introduction of free trade, which would promote the long-term expansion of industry and commerce. The end of restrictions on foreign corn would encourage the exporting countries to reciprocate by increasing their imports of British manufactured goods. Dr

Bowring, a speaker at one of the League's meetings, claimed that French farmers were saying: 'Admit our corn and then we'll see whether anybody can prevent the importation of your manufactures into France. We are millions willing to clothe ourselves in the garments you send us, and you have millions of hungry mouths to take our corn.'[7] Foreign corn producers would have much larger incomes at their disposal which they would be likely to use for buying British manufactured goods. This would boost production in Britain which, in turn, would lead to greater demand for labour, resulting in improved wages. The working classes, meanwhile, would be doubly better off because cheaper bread would bring a reduction in the cost of living. But if this opportunity were not seized immediately, continental countries would begin to rival Britain as industrial economies, since funds would be diverted from agriculture into manufactures. The best way of ensuring a permanent British lead in industry was to gain access to foreign markets; this, in turn, could be done by offering to foreign farmers the prospect of open access to Britain.

The League also had a number of political arguments, although these were less forcibly stated than the economic. Since many of the League activists were radicals it is hardly surprising that they were dissatisfied with the limited changes introduced by the 1832 Reform Act. It was also hoped that following the cause of repeal would serve to bring together the radicals who were in a state of disarray while, at the same time, driving a wedge into the more united ranks of the Conservatives under Peel. Perhaps this might be a way of breaking the fabric of British politics, something which 1832 had failed to bring about. According to Bright, the League was deeply involved in a struggle of 'the commercial and industrial classes against the lords and the great proprietors of the soil'.[8] The battleground was the House of Commons, the prize an expanded electorate. In this way, the Corn Laws were presented as the spectre of reaction; protection was seen to guarantee the parliamentary seats of the landed gentry just as much as their profits.

There was even a humanitarian and religious dimension to the League's case against the Corn Laws, strongly supported by the Evangelicals, especially the Dissenters. Bright stirred this up when, in 1842, he attacked the Anglican Church, declaring that the clergy were 'almost to a man guilty of causing the present distress by upholding the Corn Law – they having themselves an interest in the high price of bread'.[9] The repeal of the Corn Laws would, in the course of promoting the 'free flow' of trade, greatly increase the economic value of the worker and, in turn, a consciousness of his own worth. At times the League acquired a quasi-religious fervour and the Corn Laws were described as 'blasphemous' and 'unnatural'.[10] Repeal would, in the League's view, confer a universal benefit since it would 'knit nations together in bonds of fellowship too strong to be broken'.[11] All reasons for war would disappear as the aggressive and military nobility would eventually be superseded by the more peaceful and productive middle classes, especially manufacturers and traders, whose interests would be served only by the absence of conflict.

How effectively was the Anti-Corn Law League organised? After initial difficulties it became the most successful pressure group of the whole of the nineteenth century. *The Times* in 1843 was aware of something momentous, saying that a new power had arisen in the state and referring to the League as 'a great fact'.[12] In some respects, the League was even more efficient than the political parties. The basic organisation was the work of J.B. Smith and Joseph Hickin; the structure comprised the Council, or governing body, and a series of specialist committees. Although the League's headquarters were in London, the nerve centre was to be found in Newall's Buildings in Manchester, England's second city. The local organisation comprised twelve districts which were further subdivided; each district had a League agent who received instructions either from London or from Manchester. It is significant that the work of the League was highly specialised and carefully broken down into departments responsible for publication, sorting, elections and others.

The activities of the League were immensely varied. Funds were raised in bazaars, public meetings, subscriptions and donations from manufacturers who stood to benefit from the repeal of the Corn Laws. These contributions were put to good use. Halls were hired all over the country for public meetings which aimed at maximum publicity and used packed audiences to create a positive impression. Electors in all constituencies were sent packages of free trade leaflets, and newpapers were also founded, including the *Anti-Corn Law Circular*, and the *League*, along with pamphlets and magazines like the *Economist*. Above all, the League went in for all forms of electoral manipulation which were not actually banned by law. For example, the credentials of known protectionist candidates in constituencies were systematically challenged, an unwelcome form of attention which actually persuaded a number of candidates to keep a low profile on the issue of the Corn Laws, especially if these candidates happened to be Conservatives. By 1846 the League had developed a mastery over propaganda and a familiarity with the techniques of electoral manipulation which even the mainstream political parties could not rival. It was hardly surprising that MPs unsympathetic to its aims came to see it as subversive and unconstitutional.

THE CAMPAIGN TO RETAIN THE CORN LAWS

Meanwhile, an equally active – if less well organised – campaign was being conducted by those who were committed to upholding protection and retaining the Corn Laws.

The original argument of the agriculturalists had a certain logic. Why should they not have at least as much protection as manufacturers from imports? After all, during the French Wars import duties on industrial goods had been increased far more extensively than those on agricultural merchandise; the duty on glass, for example, had been increased to 114 per cent, on cotton goods to 85 per cent.[13] Gradually, however, the emphasis changed. Manufacturers came to accept that lower import duties on raw materials and manufactured goods would not necessarily threaten their prosperity and many swung behind the tariff reductions of Huskisson and Robinson in the early 1820s and Peel in the 1840s. Their conversion to free trade left the farmers isolated in their demand for continued protection and with the problem of justifying their opposition to the flood tide of *laissez-faire*.

Some at first did not feel impelled to try. After all, the landowners continued to control parliament. Even after the 1832 Reform Act they still possessed two-thirds of the seats in the House of Commons and, provided they kept together on this issue, they had little to fear. Such a view, however, proved simplistic. Many wavered, some even joined Peel in his conversion to free trade, accepting his reassurance that agricultural improvements at home would minimise the impact of competition from abroad. The remainder, a hard core within the Conservative party, had to try to stem the flow to free trade and stiffen the resistance within the House of Commons. They had to find a means, above all, of combatting the ideas and methods of the Anti-Corn Law League.

Accordingly, the tenant farmers of Essex set up the Anti-League in 1844. This was intended specifically to fight against free trade propaganda and to bring pressure to bear on MPs to vote against any attempt to repeal the Corn Laws. From local groups of country gentlemen and farmers there quickly developed a national association, supported by large landowners like the Duke of Richmond and publicising its views in the *Farmers' Magazine*. The main leaders were O'Brien, Miles, Newdigate amd Heathcote, MPs respectively for Northamptonshire, Somerset, Warwickshire and Rutland.

A key argument of the Anti-League was that there had to be a permanent and reliable source of grain. This could only be Britain herself, since the Continent was destabilised by periodic political convulsions. The British farmer had to be protected from undue competition in times of peace to prevent him from being put out of business, an eventuality which would prevent Britain being self-sufficient in time of war. It was worth paying the price of short-term oscillations to avoid a longer-term crisis and vulnerability to countries with a still strong agricultural base, such as France, Russia, Prussia and the United States. J.W. Croker therefore wrote in 1845 that 'we cannot believe that any compensation would or ought to reconcile the agricultural interests of England to the abandonment of all protection'.[14]

The Anti-League also advanced a political case. It urged Peel not to bow to the growing pressure of the Anti-Corn Law League, which was, after all, an unelected extra-parliamentary group which was blatantly manipulating the electoral system for its own ends. The Anti-League considered itself duty-bound to make it clear to Peel and his ministers that 'the most influential and powerful body of men, viz: the agriculturalists of this country are determined to support them against the machinations of a conspiracy and that the farmers of England are determined to act against it as one man'.[15] The impression given was that the government needed stiffening in its resolve and to be reminded of its obligation to uphold a constitution which was coming under sustained pressure. Any further advance towards free trade would be the clearest signal that the programme of an elected government could be subverted by a pressure group. The retention of the Corn Laws was therefore more than an economic necessity; upon it rested the safety of the constitution itself.

THE CAMPAIGNS COMPARED

How effective were the Anti-Corn Law League and the Anti-League in influencing the government and the Conservative party during the repeal crisis of 1845–6?

There is a strong case for arguing that the Anti-Corn Law League increased support for repeal within parliament by raising the temperature of debate and by publicising all the arguments in favour. It may even have helped Peel come to a decision, although it is unlikely that it converted him completely from an opposite stance: it is more likely to have articulated more clearly the arguments which Peel was already in the process of developing. On the other hand, how much longer would Peel have taken to come to his decision without the pressure applied on him? Admittedly most of this came from the conversion of Russell and the Whigs to repeal in 1845, but this was, in turn, undoubtedly accelerated by the arguments of the League through its parliamentary spokesman, Bright. By all accounts the articulate and eloquent MPs which the League was fortunate enough to possess also had a direct impact on Peel himself. This would explain the incident in the House of Commons on 13 March 1845 when Peel, after hearing Cobden's speech, declined to reply, crumpled his notes and said to Sidney Herbert, a fellow front-bencher, 'You must answer this, for I cannot'. It could also be argued that the League helped create throughout the country the sort of tension and passion which persuaded the House of Lords, mindful of the threat of violence in 1831, to confirm the Commons' decision. In this case, it would seem that Wellington learned from history, or rather that he was reminded of it by the activities of the League.

The Anti-League faced a much greater problem than the Anti-Corn Law League. Its ultimate aim was, of course, to prevent repeal from being carried through the Commons. Since the Whigs had already been converted to free trade in agricultural produce, this meant that the Conservative party had to remain united against it. The uncertain factor was Peel's attitude. For a while, in 1845, the Anti-League was hopeful that Peel was trying to find a way between his own preferences for *laissez-faire* and the protectionist stance of most of the Conservative party. During this delicate phase the Anti-League tried to avoid embarrassing Peel by not applying pressure directly on him; this was in contrast to the Anti-Corn Law League which, sensing that he was yielding, was pushing as hard as it could for him to introduce repeal. The Anti-League had to pursue a more devious strategy. Its main objective was to prevent Peel from bringing any such measure before parliament; hence it preferred to concentrate its attack on the Anti-Corn Law League and to persuade Peel not to yield to 'unconstitutional' pressure. At the same time, the Anti-League could not afford to take any chances and had to prepare for the possibility that repeal would be introduced despite its efforts. This meant that it also had to put the strongest economic arguments before Tory MPs to convince them that they should not support such a move.

Thus the Anti-League tried, by one strategy, to persuade Peel not to be pushed into taking the fateful step which would split the Conservative party; at the same time, by the other, it was setting up the opposition which would guarantee that split should Peel decide to go ahead. How much simpler and more direct appeared the objectives and methods of the Anti-Corn Law League – and how much more successful. For in 1846 the Anti-Corn Law League saw the accomplishment of its economic aim, with the attractive prospect of a period of political change to follow. By contrast, the Anti-League could not save for the farmers the legislation which protected them or the party which represented them.

EFFECTS OF THE REPEAL OF THE CORN LAWS

Economic

Peel's act of 1846 introduced a temporary sliding scale. When the price of wheat fell below 48 shillings a duty of 10 shillings would be imposed; this would be reduced to 4 shillings as the price of wheat rose to 54 shillings. After 1 February 1849 this sliding scale would be replaced by a nominal duty of 1 shilling on wheat, barley and oats, irrespective of price levels. This amounted, in effect, to the total removal of the Corn Laws of 1815, 1822 and 1828. What were the effects?

The strongest arguments against repeal had been that there would be economic disaster. The farming interest would be ruined and prices would never again achieve any stability. It is true that there were temporary problems as prices fell between 1848 and 1852. But, as P. Deane argues, 'to a large extent this was a consequence of speculative activities which Protection had encouraged. There had been speculation in land, rents had risen to extravagant levels, and it was these extravagances which came to grief with Repeal'.[16] Quite simply, the doom forecast by the protectionists did not occur. The 1850s and 1860s experienced what has often been called a 'golden age of agriculture' and it seemed that protection had been a 'spurious issue' and that its importance had been greatly exaggerated.[17] Grain prices achieved a remarkable degree of consistency. Between 1846 and 1876 they averaged 53 shillings per quarter, compared with 58 shillings between 1820 and 1846. What happened, according to Chambers and Mingay, was that the world price of wheat was brought up to the British level, rather than British prices plummeting to foreign levels.[18]

Britain was not flooded with cheap corn during the 1850s and 1860s partly because of favourable circumstances not immediately within her control. One was an accelerating population growth everywhere in Europe, which meant that many countries had to cater for increased home consumption. A second was the sheer expense of moving and shipping grain in large quantities during a period when improvements in transport infrastructure were far from complete. A third was the intervention of two major wars. The Crimean War (1854–6) severely disrupted the supplies of grain from the great plains of eastern Europe and closed the Baltic to Russian traffic, while the American Civil War (1861–5) greatly reduced the exports of the world's largest grain producer.

It has also been argued that the potentially damaging effects of repeal were cushioned by a series of agricultural improvements introduced by the more progressive British farmers. These included the foundation of agricultural colleges, the publication of Liebig's *Organic Chemistry in its Applications in Agriculture and Physiology* and a range of agricultural journals (including *Practical Agriculture*), and a host of technical improvements in farm machinery and in land drainage. It has even been suggested that Peel actually intended the repeal of the Corn Laws to accelerate this trend which had already become apparent by 1846. D.C. Moore, for example, maintained that, as a member of the English Agricultural Society, Peel was using free-trade arguments to 'encourage the adoption of high farming techniques by those agriculturalists who either still resisted the blandishments of science or could not afford to hear them'.[19]

What of the longer term? By the late 1870s British agriculture had entered a depression which brought the 'golden age' to an ignominious close. This was due in part to the reversal of the role of objective factors: favourable during the 1850s and 1860s, these became hostile during the 1870s and 1880s. For example, the United States re-established and intensified its role as the world's granary now that it had emerged from civil war and cut production and transportation costs by developing combine harvesters and constructing rail links between the prairies and the ports. To make matters worse, there was also a run of bad harvests in Britain, caused mainly by adverse weather.

It is, of course, difficult to attribute these developments to the repeal of the Corn Laws. The time-lag between the end of protection in 1846 and the onset of depression in the late 1870s is just too great to establish any direct connection. In any case, had protection remained in force, it is arguable that agriculture would have been in an even more parlous state in the 1870s, since it is unlikely that farmers would have had quite the same incentive during the intervening period to make technical improvements and provide more advanced methods of drainage. On the other hand, there was a revival in the demand for protection and by the 1880s some were arguing that the Corn Laws could have provided at least some form of buffer against the flood of cheaper grain from the United States. There was also some concern that too much faith had been placed during the 1850s and 1860s in 'improvements'. As Chambers and Mingay point out:

> In retrospect much of what came to be known as 'high farming' was a strategic miscalculation, a misdirection of resources. Landlords sank capital in drainage and buildings, and farmers devoted much time and money to developing advanced systems of cultivation, neither of which could pay at the prices which ruled in the last decades of the century and for long after.[20]

EFFECTS OF THE REPEAL OF THE CORN LAWS

Political and social

If the full economic impact of the repeal of the Corn Laws was delayed for three decades, the political effects were felt immediately. Peel predicted in his resignation speech in 1846: 'In relinquishing power I shall leave a name severely censured I fear by many who on public grounds regret the severance of party ties.'[21]

He was right. Those Conservatives who had supported the repeal of the Corn Laws became in effect a new political party, known as the Peelites. They separated from the Conservatives in parliament, contested constituencies against them, and appointed their own party whips and election managers. This gravely weakened the Conservative party, which lost a series of general elections in 1847, 1852, 1857, 1859 and 1865. In the first of these Conservatives managed to hold only fourteen out of the forty-one counties which normally provided their safest seats and were forced back on the bedrock of their support in Berkshire, Buckinghamshire, Cambridge, Huntingdonshire, Leicestershire and Worcestershire. They failed to win an election outright until 1874, a lapse of thirty-three years since Peel's famous victory over the Whigs in 1841. During this period they were in power, as minority governments, for only five years: under the Earl of Derby in 1852, 1858–9 and 1866–8, and under Disraeli in 1868. These were inevitably inexperienced, especially the 'Who? Who?' government of 1852.

The Conservatives could not, therefore, govern alone. Nor could they reunite with the Peelites, although Derby did try this after Peel's death in 1850. The two parties were kept apart by the issue of protectionism, which remained an issue for some time to come. The Peelites would not retract, and the Conservatives could hardly accept them back unless they did. As Stewart put it: 'Having branded Peel a traitor, they could not themselves slough off the corn laws in a day.'[22] Even when, during the 1850s, the Conservatives no longer felt obliged to reintroduce the Corn Laws at the first opportunity that arose, they nevertheless antagonised the Peelites by seeking to load any taxation reliefs in favour of the agricultural interest; this applied especially to Disraeli's 1852 budget, which reduced the malt tax while increasing the house tax.[23]

In addition to contrasting points of principle, the Conservatives and Peelites also had lying between them a coil of bitterness, especially in the vital period when Peel was still alive. The latter never forgave the bulk of the Conservatives for having opposed him in 1846. He had no intention of seeking reconciliation with them, and was not in favour of anyone else doing so. He was, indeed, thoroughly disillusioned. He had already recaptured moderation for the party after Wellington had lost it from Canning and Liverpool. But why should he now have to do it a second time because of the likes of Bentinck and Disraeli? In any case, as Blake maintains, 'the Derbyites, though not Derby, became less and less ready to receive them back even if they had wished to be received'.[24]

The crisis of the Conservatives gave rise to two other political developments. First, their split made possible the mid-century revival of the Whigs, with whom, second, the Peelite offshoot eventually coalesced to form the Liberal party. The Whigs and Liberals ruled for twenty-eight out of the thirty-three years between Peel's resignation and Disraeli's first majority government, in the periods 1846–52, 1852–8, 1859–66 and 1868–74. Under Russell (1846–52 and 1865–6) and Palmerston (1855–8 and 1859–65) the Whigs had a tighter grip on power than at any time since the eighteenth century. The Whigs were fortunate in having in Palmerston the most popular (although not the most accomplished) statesman of the entire century, precisely when they could use him to the best effect. And through Gladstone the Peelites were able to accomplish the transition from Whiggery into Liberalism. Instrumental in this was a series of budgets introduced while Gladstone was Chancellor of the Exchequer (1853–5 and 1859–65) which completed the free trade policies initiated by Peel and espoused by the Whigs.

The connection between the Peelites and Whigs was therefore a permanent effect of the repeal of the Corn laws. But the decline of the Conservative party was only temporary. By the 1870s the political effects of the repeal of the Corn Laws had worked their way through, in contrast to the economic impact, which had, as we have seen, been disguised. The two-party system had now fully re-emerged, as it had done in the past after the Whig supremacy in the eighteenth century and the Tory domination of the early nineteenth. One factor in this was the death of Palmerston in 1865. Another was the reorientation of the Conservatives. Disraeli finally showed the Corn Laws to be a dead issue when, during the 1860s, he abandoned protection and made a determined effort to contest the middle ground, even to the extent of 'dishing the Whigs' in securing the passage of the second Reform Act in 1867.

Finally, what was the social significance of the repeal of the Corn Laws? The landed classes certainly experienced a decline in economic importance by comparison with the commercial middle classes and it used to be thought that the natural corollary to this was a rapid reduction of their political status as well. The latter point, however, has been denied by recent historians, who have argued that the landed classes continued for some years to come to dominate parliament. According to Chambers and Mingay, 'The gentry . . . although not making large territorial acquisitions, seem to have been holding their own with fair success'.[25] Stewart goes further, showing that 'For another generation and more the membership of the House of Commons and of cabinets continued to reflect the staying power of the landed class'.[26] This applied as much to the Liberal party, with its Whig element, as to the Conservatives. Thus the reward for adjusting – whether willingly or unwillingly – to the new economic reality was continued political predominance well into the twentieth century. This would have disappointed the activists of the Anti-Corn Law League, who won all the economic arguments, while giving a wry satisfaction to the Anti-League, who lost them.

10

PALMERSTON'S FOREIGN AND DOMESTIC POLICIES

Henry John Temple, later Lord Palmerston, became a Tory MP in 1807 and served his nation continuously until his death fifty-eight years later. Although he did not come immediately to high office, this was his own choice: he declined the Chancellorship of the Exchequer in 1809, opting instead to be Secretary at War – an administrative post which hardly stretched his political abilities. One of the so-called 'liberal Tories' of the 1820s, he served under Canning but crossed over to the Whigs after the latter's death. He became a powerful influence in his newly adopted party, serving as Foreign Secretary in the years 1830–4, 1835–41 and 1846–51 under Grey, Melbourne and Russell respectively. He experienced a change of role, between 1852 and 1855, as Home Secretary, before becoming Prime Minister from 1855 to 1858 and from 1859 to 1865.

What sort of politician was Palmerston? According to A.J.P. Taylor, 'he served a more prolonged apprenticeship in administration than any other Prime Minister has ever done'.[1] He had an apparently inexhaustible capacity for hard work, spending at least eight hours each day standing at a high-desk, in addition to the normal parliamentary commitments and official functions. He was, however, no faceless bureaucrat. He was an effective parliamentarian who made up for a lack of instinctive brilliance in oratory by a powerful presence, an unprecedented knowledge of his subject gleaned from civil service files, and a mastery of quotable one-liners. He knew how to cultivate popularity and to build up a political image: more than any other nineteenth-century statesman, he developed an immense appeal and to the man in the street personified British patriotism. According to the nineteenth-century constitutional expert, Walter Bagehot, Palmerston 'was not a common man, but a common man might have been cut out of him. He had in him

Plate 2 Viscount Palmerston, G.C.B., 1784–1865. Drawn and engraved by D.J. Pound. By courtesy of the Mary Evans Picture Library, London.

all that a common man has, and something more'.[2] His bluntness and arrogance were greatly admired by those who did not have to endure them, provided of course that they were directed against foreigners and were justified by frequent references to British interest. Palmerston had little difficulty in enlisting the help of the press. He had contacts with the *Globe* and benefited from the support of the Tory-inclined *Times*. In the words of D. Judd, he was also 'one of the first Cabinet ministers to make a careful study of the art of propaganda and to appeal to the public as a whole over the heads of the political establishment'.[3]

Palmerston had a natural aptitude for foreign policy, which was always his preferred area of political activity. It would be a mistake, however, to focus on this at the expense of home affairs, over which he also had a considerable influence. This chapter will therefore cover a range of issues, including the general characteristics of his foreign policy; the successes and failures of specific enterprises all over the world; his contributions to change at home; and his importance in transforming the Whigs into the Liberals.

THE PRINCIPLES OF PALMERSTON'S FOREIGN POLICY

Was Palmerston's foreign policy based on any underlying principles? It would be difficult to find an ideological basis for his actions. No principle was immutable, apart from the pursuit of what was of benefit to Britain. In a speech in parliament in 1848 Palmerston said that 'We have no eternal allies, and we have no perpetual enemies. Our interests are eternal and perpetual, and those interests it is our duty to follow.'[4]

These interests would best be fulfilled by the achievement of certain objectives. The first was the containment of Russia which Palmerston saw as the greatest threat on the European Continent as well as to British interests in the Indian sub-continent. It was therefore considered necessary to bolster up two autocracies which acted as a bulwark against further Russian expansion: Turkey and Austria. The latter was also pivotal to Palmerston's second aim – to maintain a balance of power in Europe. He told parliament in 1849:

Austria stands in the centre of Europe, a barrier against encroachment on the one side, and against intervention on the other. The political independence and liberties of Europe are bound up, in my opinion, with the maintenance and integrity of Austria as a great European Power.[5]

Third, Palmerston aimed to extend British prestige abroad. In his most famous oration to parliament, occasioned by the Don Pacifico incident in 1850, he claimed that just as the Roman,

> in days of old, held himself free from indignity, when he could say 'Civis Romanus sum'; so also a British subject, in whatever land he may be, shall feel confident that the watchful eye and strong arm of England will protect him against injustice and wrong.[6]

Such activism was designed to promote the expansion of British trade in a period when Britain was unquestionably the world's greatest economic power. Palmerston did not favour going beyond this into the acquisition of more colonies but, at the same time, intended that no other power should expand its empire either, whether it should be France in the Pacific or Russia in China. 'Let us all', he urged, 'abstain from a crusade of conquest.'[7]

But the absence of an underlying ideology to his policies does not mean that Palmerston necessarily lacked political sympathies or preferences. He simply learned to keep these subordinate to his perception of the national interest. A case in point was his attitude to liberal movements on the Continent, a recurrent theme throughout his time in office. Instinctively more progressive than Castlereagh, he possessed the general Whig preference for regimes which emphasised constitutionalism rather than legitimism; this was given a certain logic by the extension of the franchise in Britain by the 1832 Reform Act. On one occasion he affirmed 'Constitutional states I consider to be the natural allies of this country', while he openly expressed his approval for the constitutional changes in France in 1830, adding that 'we shall drink the cause of Liberalism all over the world'.[8] Eighteen years later he was widely condemned by the European autocracies for apparently meddling in their internal affairs. And yet he was also very cautious, since the occasions were few when British intervention on behalf of a liberal cause happened to coincide with the defence of a British interest. He was generally sympathetic to Italian nationalism, since the Austrian presence in Lombardy and Venetia was of no direct use to British security or the balance of power. He was more ambivalent, however, about the aspirations of the Hungarians. On the one hand, he sympathised with the aristocratic nature of the revolt and the aim to revive an ancient kingdom with its own identity. On the other, he was concerned about the possible impact on the Austrian Empire, which he saw as part of the European equipoise which was so important to Britain.

Did the selectiveness of Palmerston's sympathies apply also to his moral scruples? It would certainly seem that he attached far less importance to moral principles in his foreign policy than, for example, did Gladstone. The latter was especially critical of Palmerston's involvement in the Opium War, accusing him in 1840 of indifference to the damage inflicted on China by the deliberate protection of the Bengal opium traffic. He pointed out that the British flag 'has always been associated with the cause of justice, the opposition to oppression, with respect for national rights, with honourable commercial enterprise, but now, under the auspices of the noble Lord, that flag is hoisted to protect an infamous contraband trade.'[9] Palmerston contemptuously dismissed any moral arguments about the affair, claiming that 'There is an opium-growing interest in China as there is a corn-growing interest in England'.[10] It would be untrue, however, to say that he had no issue for which he was prepared to crusade. He had a particular aversion to the slave trade which, although abolished in 1807, was conducted illicitly throughout the first half of the nineteenth century. He worked hard for a series of agreements with a range of countries in Europe and Latin America to secure its effective suppression. It could, of course, be argued that the slave trade was both a moral issue and a threat to attempts being made by British merchants to establish an alternative commerce, such as the extraction of palm oil from West Africa. In this case, therefore, Palmerston gave a moral dimension to the threat of an old British interest to a new one. This is not to deny that he meant it, but he could afford it.

Palmerston became Foreign Secretary at a time when the regular multilateral diplomacy between the European states had collapsed, along with the formal Congress System. Canning had been content to see this replaced with bilateral diplomacy which involved Britain and the country concerned with a specific crisis. Palmerston adopted a more diverse approach.

On occasion, he maintained Canning's policy of bilateralism. This worked as follows. When a power appeared as a major threat to British interests, Palmerston avoided, where possible, direct confrontation. Instead, he acted to restrain that power through a temporary alliance with it. There were several examples of this. In 1832 he managed to overcome the threat of French expansion into the Low Countries by arranging joint Anglo-French action to liberate Belgium from the Dutch. Second, in 1838, Palmerston sought to influence the French government which was veering towards supporting Mehemet Ali's rebellion against the Turkish Sultan.[11] He proposed joint Anglo-French action against Mehemet Ali: Britain would send a fleet to support the Sultan against his rebellious vassal, and 'We should like the French squadron to go there too at the same time, if the French are willing to do so.'

At other times a multilateral approach seemed more appropriate. This took the form of the 'concert of Europe', a looser and irregular replacement for the Congress System. In 1834, for example, he was instrumental in forming the Quadruple Alliance, comprising Britain, France, Spain and Portugal. This was intended partly as a counterbalance to the Treaty of Münchengratz signed by Austria, Russia and Prussia in 1833, which he interpreted as a latter-day Holy Alliance. Palmerston's answer had two objectives. The first was to 'settle Portugal' and to 'go some way to settle Spain'. Second, 'it establishes a quadruple alliance among the constitutional states of the west, which will serve as a powerful counterpoise to the Holy Alliance of the east.'[12] On the other hand, Palmerston strongly opposed any attempt to revive the more formal system once favoured by Castlereagh. In 1863 he wrote:

> The truth is that the assembling of a Congress is not a measure applicable to the present state of Europe. In 1815 a Congress was a necessity. France had overrun all Europe, had overthrown almost all the former territorial arrangements, and had established a new order of things . . . Nothing of this kind exists in the present state of Europe.[13]

He added that any new Congress System would incite 'squabbles and animosities' as all the European powers would attempt to unpick the various treaties which had gradually established international security during the nineteenth century.

There has inevitably been some debate as to whether Palmerston was influenced by any of his predecessors. Some historians consider that in many respects he was the pupil of Canning. Bell argues that 'In his desire that England should stand upon her own feet, his appreciation of the great force of public sentiment, and his taste for constitutional government as the proper medium between autocracy and democracy, he was a natural-born Canningite',[14] while P. Guedalla considers him to have been 'the last of the Canningites'.[15] There were certainly similarities in style. Palmerston had Canning's appreciation of the importance of public opinion and of the effect of rhetoric. He was probably influenced by Canning in his policy of allying with a potential rival in order to influence it, a device used by Canning in handling Russia during the crisis concerning Greek independence. Other historians put an alternative case. Webster, for example, argues that Palmerston's approach to Europe was 'more that of Castlereagh than of Canning'.[16] It could certainly be argued that Palmerston was closer to Castlereagh than to Canning in his emphasis on the balance of power in Europe, in his belief in maintaining the integrity of Austria, and in his use of multilateral diplomacy. Above all, he did everything possible to contain France and to prevent a possible Franco-Russian alliance, both of which had been priorities of Castlereagh.

Palmerston was too individiualistic to have owed his precepts in foreign policy to a single source. It is most likely that he was influenced by both Canning and Castlereagh, but that he adapted their ideas in a way which he considered appropriate to the changing conditions of international diplomacy after 1830. The result was a Palmerstonian synthesis which cannot be identified specifically with either of his predecessors. Like Castlereagh he considered multilateral diplomacy important, but without the superstructure of the Congress System, which had been swept away by Canning. Like Canning, his focus was often on bilateral diplomacy, but he was more willing to switch, if necessary, to agreements involving several powers. The style and public image of his policies owed much to Canning and he was much given to quoting Canning in times of crisis. The focus on British interest was also distinctively Canningite. But in those areas of foreign policy where he was less iconoclastic, he returned to the more patient and complex methods of Castlereagh.

THE PHASES OF PALMERSTON'S FOREIGN POLICY

It is possible to see British foreign policy unfolding in three distinct phases during the decades in which it was under Palmerston's direction. The first, a period of adjustment during the 1830s, saw considerable success. The second, between 1848 and 1860, has been described as 'playing to the gallery' and as 'the era of gunboat diplomacy *par excellence*'.[17] During the third phase (1860–5), Palmerston's policies became less and less effective and, in the words of Clark, his bluff was finally exposed.[18]

Palmerston's two great successes during the 1830s concerned Belgium and the Eastern Question. The Belgian revolt against union with Holland was the first direct challenge to the Vienna Settlement and was immediately complicated by France's determination to profit from assisting the Belgians. According to M.E. Chamberlain, 'The situation was perilous. If the French intervened on the Belgian side, the Austrians, Prussians and Russians would probably intervene on the Dutch side.'[19] The result would be a major European confrontation which would inevitably involve Britain. Palmerston's response to the crisis was clear and unmuddled. He immediately declared British support for Belgian independence, thus reversing the previous hopes of Britain and Prussia that the united Netherlands would work:

His Majesty's Government consider the absolute and entire separation of Belgium and Holland to be no longer a matter for discussion, but to have become, by the course of events, an established, and as far as at present can be foreseen, an irreversible fact.[20]

His priority now was to prevent French annexation or, alternatively, the spread of French influence through the candidature of the Duc de Nemours for the Belgian throne. He did this by associating Britain closely with every action taken by France, a device used on a number of occasions. Hence the French were authorised to remove the Dutch from Antwerp, while at the same time there was joint Anglo-French naval action against the coast and at the mouth of the Scheldt.

The result was highly satisfactory to Britain. France gained neither territory nor a puppet king; indeed the new Belgian state, formally established in 1839 by the Treaty of London, remained permanently pro-British. The settlement also brought stability to a region previously known as the 'cockpit of Europe' for the incessant attention it had received from the major powers. Chamberlain advances the generally accepted argument that the Belgian issue was 'an example of Palmerstonian policy at its best, when he showed not only firmness and decisiveness but also the tact and patience which he so often lacked'.[21] It might be argued that he was helped by factors beyond his immediate control. The eastern powers were preoccupied by revolutions elsewhere, especially in Italy and Poland, which tied down both Austria and Russia. On the other hand, this situation was more likely to work in favour of France than of Britain. The former had a much larger regular army and it was a tribute to Palmerston's statesmanship that this ultimately counted for nothing. Talleyrand, the elder French statesman and chief French plenipotentiary at the time of the Congress of Vienna, described Palmerston as 'the most able man of business whom I have met in my career'.[22]

Overlapping the Belgian issue was an even more complex crisis, this time concerning the Eastern Question and involving a potential threat not from one power, but from two – France and Russia. Again, Palmerston proved resolute but flexible, knowing when to stand firm and when to shift from one tack to another.

A cardinal feature of British foreign policy was to constrain Russia by upholding the integrity of Turkey. This was threatened when, in 1832, the Sultan's Egyptian governor, Mehemet Ali, invaded the province of Syria and defeated the Turkish armies sent against him. Both Russia and France became actively involved, the former signing with Turkey an alliance at Unkiar Skelessi (1833), the latter after 1839 providing assistance for Mehemet Ali. Clearly Russia hoped to be given control over access to the Straits by a grateful Sultan, while France intended to add Egypt to the list of the dependencies she had already acquired along the coast of North Africa. Either way, Britain's long-standing influence in the eastern Mediterranean would be severely curtailed. In Palmerston's words, part of the Ottoman Empire 'will be the dependency of France, and the other a satellite of Russia; and in both of which our political influence will be annulled, and our commercial interests will be sacrificed'.[23]

Palmerston reasoned that the priority must be to keep the Sultan's dominions intact. This made his fixed target the defeat of the Egyptian rebellion, an objective sharpened by the personal antipathy he had conceived for its author: 'I hate Mehemet Ali, whom I consider as nothing better than a barbarian . . . I look upon this boasted civilisation of Egypt as the arrantest humbug'.[24] Relations with France and Russia were adjustable to the needs of the moment. Palmerston had initially tried – but failed – to enlist the help of France in defeating Mehemet Ali. He then switched to a policy of co-operation with Russia. This was placed firmly, however, within the multilateral Treaty of London (1840), which also included Austria and Prussia. This provoked a violent upsurge of anglophobia in France, but Palmerston was convinced that this would not result in war; after all, he argued, 'France now is a very different thing from the France of the empire'.[25] The four powers put pressure on Mehemet Ali to withdraw from northern Syria. When he ignored this, expecting an increase in French aid, British and Austrian troops landed at Acre and Beirut and the Royal Navy bombarded the Egyptian port of Alexandria.

The result was a marked success for Palmerston. The Sultan had the whole of Syria restored, thus ensuring that his empire remained intact. French backing for Mehemet Ali counted for nothing and the Straits Convention of 1841 also neutralised Russia, ending her special relationship with Turkey and guaranteeing that the Straits should be closed to all warships. In the words of Judd, 'Palmerston had won a tricky game hands down'.[26]

At the peak of his success, Palmerston was forced out of office by the Conservative victory in the 1841 general election. He returned as Foreign Secretary in 1846, when Russell headed another Whig government. The next fourteen years brought a mixture of success and failure, culminating in 1855 with a display of effective wartime leadership. Throughout the period Palmerston placed particular importance on his image at home and abroad; at times this resulted in displays of arrogance which enhanced his popularity with the British public, although not with the government.

The first problem, the Spanish marriages of 1846, was inherited from his predecessor at the Foreign Office, Lord Aberdeen. The French king, Louis Philippe, had intended his younger son, the Duc de Montpensier, to be betrothed to the Spanish queen, Isabella. Since this presented the unwelcome prospect of a future union between France and Spain, the British government proposed that Isabella should marry the Duke of Cadiz and that Montpensier should marry Isabella's younger sister instead. Aberdeen was working towards an agreement that Montpensier would marry only after Cadiz and Isabella had produced a Spanish heir. As soon as Palmerston returned to power, statements were immediately made to parliament about the desirability of thwarting French plans; Palmerston's object was, in his own words, to ensure that 'for the future there should be neither an Austrian Spain nor a French Spain, but a Spain that should be Spanish'.[27] The French government now contrived to get one over on Palmerston and to achieve at least a modicum of revenge for the Mehemet Ali affair. Louis Philippe managed to have the two marriages arranged for the same day and, to make matters worse, Cadiz was subsequently discovered to be impotent.

The outcome was Palmerston's first humiliation. His own analysis was characteristic. 'We have', he said, 'been defeated by our own timidity, hesitation and delay.'[28] If anything, the reverse is probably true. Palmerston was too forthright and his lack of subtlety completely destroyed the chance of resolving a sensitive problem. According to Brasher, 'Palmerston can hardly be said to have negotiated on this matter at all. He dictated his views with the utmost tactlessness to the French and Spanish governments.'[29] Palmerston had, in effect, destroyed the chance of an acceptable agreement. He ignored the briefing given to him by Aberdeen and assumed that he could simply revert to the style of diplomacy to which he had become accustomed.

The fiasco of 1846 was followed by a more cautious period. Palmerston had comparatively little direct influence on the course or outcome of the 1848 Revolutions in Europe; he was, after all, anxious to convey that British interest demanded detachment from the chaos on the Continent. On the other hand, Palmerston lost no opportunity to seek self-publicity and to promote a progressive image. Hence he entertained the Hungarian revolutionary leader, Kossuth, and urged the Austrian government to relinquish its Italian provinces. He was particularly outspoken in 1850 over an incident at a London brewery involving General Haynau, the key figure in the re-establishment of Austrian control over Hungary. Applauding the rough treatment given by the draymen, Palmerston stated that they should have 'tossed him in a blanket, rolled him in a barrel, and sent him home in a cab'.[30] Although such outbursts echoed public opinion as no Foreign Secretary had done before, they were hardly statesmanlike and did much to undermine his credibility with foreign governments.

Palmerston was much more at home in 1850 in his handling of an affair involving Don Pacifico, a moneylender born in Gibraltar (and therefore claiming British citizenship), whose house in Athens was burned down by a mob. Palmerston sent part of the Royal Navy to blockade Piraeus to force the Greek government to pay £27,000 in compensation. He defended his action in parliament in a very long speech, in which he argued that a British citizen in any part of the world 'shall feel confident that the watchful eye and the strong arm of England will protect him against injustice and wrong'.[31] This was a triumph for Palmerston's own public image and it engendered, even if only for a short time, the belief that Britain was able to assert herself anywhere as the world's unquestioned premier power. On the other hand, Palmerston acted without concessions to diplomacy. He failed to consult France and Russia, who had also been instrumental in securing Greek independence, while his stance provoked much opposition within Britain, not least within his own party. It was only a matter of time before his actions became unacceptable to the government. This occurred in 1851, when he was dismissed for recognising the new regime of Louis Napoleon without consulting either the Prime Minister or the Queen.

Palmerston was not, therefore, involved in the build-up to the Crimean War, but the disasters experienced in the early stages of the conflict precipitated him into the premiership at the expense of Aberdeen. He took over the administration of the war effort, especially the details of the Sevastopol campaign, and was also closely involved in drawing up the Peace of Paris in 1856. His role in this period has attracted a greater diversity of viewpoints than any other phase of his career. The positive side is put by A.J.P. Taylor, who considers that the Crimean War showed Palmerston at his best. 'Again and again in modern history, Great Britain has drifted unprepared into war; then, after early failures, has discovered an inspired war-leader.'[32] Taylor therefore places Palmerston on a par with Chatham, Lloyd George and Churchill as the nation's rescuers in times of need. An alternative point of view is put by L.C.B. Seaman. He considers that the impression that Palmerston alone 'could have turned, and might yet turn, the Crimean War into a brilliantly prosecuted triumph of British arms, was wholly without foundation'. He further argues that it is untrue that Palmerston revived British performance in the latter stages of the Crimean War. 'The new men he put into responsible positions in the military sphere were worse than those he replaced.'[33] He did not change the composition of the army and refused to countenance the abolition of flogging. N. Brasher goes so far as to say that 'The major effect of the Crimean War was not to strengthen Britain's position in the Near East but to make it infinitely more vulnerable to the bitter resentment roused in Russia against the British and French'.[34]

Whether or not Palmerston merits the harsh judgements of Seaman and Brasher, there can be little doubt that the Crimean War once again boosted his prestige after a period of comparatively indifferent performances between 1846 and 1851. He gained further credit for his action over the *Arrow* incident of 1857, when he supported the bombardment of Canton by British warships following the Chinese seizure of a British-registered merchant vessel suspected of piracy. The incident escalated into a war with China as Palmerston used it as an excuse to press the Chinese government to open more ports to foreign trade, an objective accomplished by 1860.

This was the last occasion, however, on which Palmerston was able to exert the full force of British retribution – or, to put it more bluntly, to coerce a weaker power. Three separate issues from 1860 onwards showed Palmerston in a more negative light, as the British threat became less and less convincing.

The first was Palmerston's handling of relations with the two sides in the American Civil War. His initial attitude was restrained support for the Southern states. This was based on the mistaken assumption that they would succeed in their secession from the Union and that Britain's moral support would eventually be rewarded by an expansion in trade. This predilection for the Confederacy led to two incidents which caused a crisis with the Northern states. In 1861 two Southern agents were seized by a Northern cruiser from a British ship. Palmerston's protest was so strongly worded that it risked conflict with the Union along the Canadian frontier. The no-nonsense approach he was inclined to adopt on these occasions was therefore potentially dangerous, and it took the intervention of the Prince Consort, who toned down the message, to defuse the crisis. The other incident showed clumsiness of a different type. The government failed in 1862 to prevent the sailing of the *Alabama*, a warship built on Merseyside for the Southern states, despite an embargo placed on armaments to both sides. The *Alabama* subsequently sank a large amount of Northern shipping with the result that the Northern government claimed compensation. Since it had been forewarned the British government was clearly culpable, although the charge of negligence is perhaps more appropriately applied to the Foreign Secretary, Russell, than to the Prime Minister. Even so, Palmerston came out of the period of the American Civil War with very little credit. He was even obliged to recognise that he had backed the wrong side. After the Union victory at Gettysburg, he suddenly established diplomatic relations with the North; in the words of Seaman, 'it was

Palmerston's principle only to bully the weak, and the Federal government had proved after all to be strong'.[35]

Palmerston also proved unable to protect the weak against the strong, even when it suited his purposes to project the latter as a bully. This was clearly shown by Polish revolt against Russian rule in 1863. Palmerston's immediate response was enthusiastic support for the Polish cause and strongly worded complaints to St Petersburg, together with implied threats of retaliation. This proved to be empty rhetoric. The Poles intensified their struggle, doubtless remembering Anglo-French intervention less than ten years earlier over the Balkan principalities and the integrity of Turkey. This time, however, the British government had no intention of becoming involved since no territorial or strategic interests were involved. Palmerston even refused to support a proposal by Napoleon III to convene a European Congress on Poland, fearing that France might, in the process, seize the diplomatic initiative and use the Congress for other purposes. The results were the brutal suppression of the revolt by the Russian army and subsequent attempts by Alexander II to eradicate Polish culture. Palmerston emerged with little credit from a sorry episode in British diplomacy. He had misled the Poles, made pointless threats to the Russians, and antagonised the French by rejecting the solidarity offered by Napoleon III.

Worse was to follow. Between 1863 and 1864 Palmerston became entangled in a humiliating dispute over Schleswig-Holstein. Christian of Denmark proposed to incorporate these Duchies, already under his sovereignty, into the Danish state. This was contested by the Prussian Chancellor, Bismarck, who clearly intended to add them to Prussia at a time of his own choosing. Palmerston believed firmly in the importance of Danish integrity and was reluctant to see the area come under Prussian influence, not least because the construction of a canal through Holstein would give Prussia direct access to the North Sea. He therefore announced to parliament that 'those who made the attempt [to attack Denmark] would find that it would not be Denmark alone with which they would have to contend'.[36] Bismarck contemptuously dismissed this threat and, jointly with Austria, invaded the Duchies in 1864. Denmark immediately appealed for British support. This now had to be refused by an emergency meeting of Palmerston's cabinet.

Palmerston had blundered badly. Without learning from the lesson of the Polish revolt the year before, he had glibly undertaken to defend Denmark. His assumption, as in earlier – and happier – years, was that the threat would be sufficient to deter what he regarded as an inexperienced politician running a second-rate power. He did not reckon on Bismarck's astute diplomacy in involving Austria on a joint invasion of the Duchies in 1864 which resulted in their detachment from Denmark. He also missed the opportunity to enlist the aid of France. Here, Palmerston's reasoning was especially defective. He concluded that France would easily defeat Prussia and would subsequently expand into the Rhineland, thus reversing all the policies of containment pursued by Britain since 1815. In this he overrated the military strength of France as much as he underrated that of Prussia, in the process destroying any last chance of decisive action. He was forced to the unpalatable, if sensible, conclusion that the British army was too run down to be able to play anything like a continental role.

When Palmerston died, in 1865, Britain was weaker and more isolated in relation to the other European powers than at any other time since the eighteenth century. This should not be laid entirely at Palmerston's door. Conditions were changing rapidly in Europe, favouring the rise of a German state with which Britain could not reasonably have been expected to compete. Russia had pulled back into isolation after the Crimean War, while defeat in the wars for Italian unification had diverted Austrian ambitions away from central Europe into the Balkans. It is true that Palmerston could not have done very much – even then he performed the best possible service to Britain by keeping her out of an increasingly dangerous series of crises. On the other hand, this was an achievement by default, the unintended result of a series of miscalculations which had to be unpicked at the last minute. This was in contrast to the 1830s when he had more obviously been in control of the situation.

PALMERSTON'S DOMESTIC POLICIES

Palmerston's domestic record was sidelined by his foreign policy. It has, nevertheless, been much understated, and formed a vital part of his overall political development.

Throughout his career, Palmerston showed an underlying respect for stability, combined with a dislike of injustice. There is some question, however, as to how progressive he really was. On the one hand, A.J.P. Taylor believes that 'he hated tyranny and oppression wherever it occurred'.[37] On the other, Judd argues that 'it should not be supposed that Palmerston was an earnest philanthropist and humanitarian'.[38] It is perhaps most realistic to see in him a tendency both to uphold tradition and to initiate reform. The extent to which either predominated varied at each stage in his career. There appears to be no gradual or consistent development from one to the other, possibly because, as in his foreign policy, Palmerston disliked ideological labels and acted with a large measure of pragmatism.

At the outset, Palmerston was indistinguishable from the law-and-order Tories. He was firmly behind Castlereagh and Sidmouth and supported the Six Acts of 1819; if anything, he thought that the measures dealing with the press were too lenient. He regretted the death of Castlereagh, whom he had supported. He was also a firm estate owner: one of his employees, who wounded his gamekeeper while poaching, was hanged – largely because Palmerston intervened belatedly and very reluctantly on his behalf. During the 1820s, however, he gradually moved towards the more progressive wing of the Tory party and won his new seat at Cambridge in the 1826 general election largely with the support of Canningites, with whom he now identified, and of the Whigs, who saw him as a potential political convert. The issue which made all the difference was Catholic emancipation. He was firmly wedded to this even while the majority of the Tory party, including the leadership, still opposed it. He said: 'It is strange that in this enlightened age and civilised country people should still be debating whether it is wise to convert four or five millions of men from enemies to friends and whether it is *safe* to give peace to Ireland'.[39] He went so far as to resign his post as Secretary at War in 1828 in protest against the delay of Wellington's government in dealing with the issue.

But why did Palmerston subsequently find it necessary to join the Whigs? After all, Peel, who was also on the progressive wing of the Tory party and was himself instrumental in getting Catholic emancipation through parliament, made no such switch. Nor was Palmerston particularly sympathetic to the main component of Whig policy at this time – parliamentary reform. He had become impatient, it is true, with the Tory establishment, but then the Whigs scarcely excited his admiration; he had once called them that 'stupid old Tory party, who bawl out the memory and praises of Pitt while they are opposing all the measures and principles which he held most important'.[40] The main reason for his switch is probably that Palmerston was a member of a faction rather than a party.

As a Canningite after the death of Canning he was a member of a splinter group which found it impossible to collaborate with Wellington and Peel. Hence he moved with that group into the party which accepted it, a process which happened several times in nineteenth-century British politics. In any case, he stood a much better chance of achieving political prominence with the Whigs. After 1828 it was only a matter of time before they came to power and they would be more inclined to make use of his experience by offering him high office, especially his preferred post of Foreign Secretary. If, on the other hand, he remained with the Tories, he would have to compete with Peel and Wellington, both of whom he disliked.

During the period 1830–41 Palmerston was involved in foreign affairs. His interest in domestic issues developed in two stages. The first was in opposition between 1841 and 1846, when he found himself increasingly sympathetic to the plight of the working man; persuaded by the arguments of Shaftesbury, he voted in 1844 for the Ten Hours Bill. The second was as Home Secretary between 1852 and 1855. It is often thought that Palmerston, having been dismissed from the Foreign Office in 1851, was brought back into the cabinet in a role where he could cause least damage. In fact, Palmerston actually chose his new post. 'It does not do', he said, 'for a man to pass his whole life in one department.'[41]

There is virtual unanimity that Palmerston made a good job of the opportunity offered. P. Guedalla considers him 'one of the most reforming of the Home Secretaries',[42] a view echoed by Judd: 'On the whole Palmerston's tenure at the Home Office was astonishingly progressive for a man nearing seventy with no previous experience of domestic administration. His readiness to increase government interference in a wide range of fields was particularly surprising.'[43] Shaftesbury provided the ultimate eulogy – that Palmerston accomplished 'more than ten of his predecessors'. He added: 'I have never known any Home Secretary equal to Palmerston for readiness to undertake every good work of kindness, humanity, and social good, especially to the child and the working class.'[44] This is praise indeed when compared with his view of Peel (see Chapter 7).

As Home Secretary, Palmerston was concerned primarily with four main areas. He addressed working conditions by the 1853 Factory Act, which limited work for women and children from 6 a.m. to 6 p.m., allowing one-and-a-half hours for meals. Second, he introduced one of the earliest environmental measures; the 1853 Smoke Abatement Bill was intended to control air pollution in the cities and hence reduce the incidence of smog. More extensive was his commitment to public health measures. He sponsored a private members' bill for compulsory vaccination and introduced legislation to remove the automatic right of burial within churches. He also produced extensive plans, some of which were implemented, to extend the size and range of London's sewer network and to ensure that the main discharge was downstream of the population centres. Finally, he undertook the first significant measures for some thirty years to improve prison conditions. These reduced maximum periods of solitary confinement from eighteen months to nine; abolished transportation through the 1853 Penal Servitude Bill; introduced an early form of probation for good conduct; and, through the 1854 Reformatory Schools Act, greatly improved the lot of young offenders.

This is a significant list of achievements for someone who, in the 1830s, had not been an enthusiastic supporter of the domestic measures of the Whigs. There are two possible explanations for this apparent change. One is that social reforms had become a matter of common sense. Palmerston, like many other Whigs and progressive Conservatives, believed that the state should gradually withdraw from directing the economy, but that it should become more involved in remedying social abuses. *Laissez-faire* in the economy could only be fully effective if it were accompanied by a measure of social reform. He was convinced by the reports of Chadwick and Shaftesbury on sanitary conditions and mines that poor health and unregulated working conditions actually reduced efficiency and wasted human potential. A second reason for Palmerston's apparent burst of reforming zeal was that he was actually part of a reforming ministry which, according to M.E. Chamberlain, contained 'almost every first-rate political talent of the period'. He was part of 'a remarkably homogeneous team' who acted together on domestic issues. He was not, as is often said, 'ploughing a lonely reforming furrow'.[45]

Palmerston's record of domestic achievement as Prime Minister was, by contrast, very disappointing. The obvious reason was that he was concerned primarily with a series of complex issues in foreign policy. There is, however, another explanation. By the late 1850s and the 1860s the focus had shifted to areas of reform with which Palmerston had little sympathy. He was happy enough to take up the cause of an oppressed minority, such as Catholics or child workers, but was less sanguine about introducing measures to raise the consciousness and influence of the working class. As Home Secretary, he had already opposed an attempt to legalise peaceful picketing. As Prime Minister he gave a very low priority to educational reforms, considering that these would inevitably result in further political demands. For this reason he was also unsympathetic to Gladstone's efforts to abolish paper duties, which would have reduced the cost of books. When the Conservative-dominated Lords rejected the bill, Palmerston refused to stand by Gladstone's measure. Instead, he referred the matter to the Committee of Privileges, where the bill was discreetly buried.[46] He was also a major obstacle to further parliamentary reform, declaring in 1857: 'My Belief is that . . . the Country at large, including the Great Bulk of the Liberal Party, do not want or wish for any considerable changes in our Electoral System.'[47] He was especially scornful about proposals to introduce the secret ballot. 'A true Englishman', he said, 'hates doing a thing in secret or in the dark' and would not like to be seen 'sneaking to the ballot-box and poking in a piece of paper, looking round to see that no one could read it.'[48] Overall, it is hardly surprising that Disraeli should have considered Palmerston 'the Tory chief of a Radical Cabinet'.[49]

PALMERSTON'S CONTRIBUTION TO THE LIBERAL PARTY

Disraeli and other Conservatives hoped that Palmerston would go back to them. But Palmerston had already rejected this option: 'having acted for twenty-two years with the Whigs, and after having gained by, and while acting with them, any little political reputation I may have acquired it would not . . . be at all agreeable to me to go slap over the opposite camp'.[50] Far from retracing his political steps, as Winston Churchill was later to do, Palmerston in fact presided over the transformation of the party to which he belonged. This was something of a paradox: the most strongly individualistic of all the nineteenth-century prime ministers unwittingly put together the basis of the modern Liberal party.

This involved a threefold contribution. First, he had to maintain the Whigs as a strong base which, in turn, meant restricting the opportunities of the Conservatives. Palmerston ensured that during his lifetime the latter never recovered from the great split of 1846 to form a stable government. Palmerston established a personal ascendancy between 1855 and 1865 which no other political leader was able to threaten. The 1857 general election was in many ways a vote of personal confidence rather than the election of a political party. Nevertheless, because he was a Whig, his personal success rubbed off on the Whigs and prevented them from falling into the sort of decline they had experienced earlier in the century.

Second, he had to expand the base by joining other political groupings to the Whigs. Palmerston proved more adept than any of his contemporaries in putting together coalitions. One was assembled in 1855 specifically to win the Crimean War. The other, comprising Whigs, radicals and Peelites, followed the Willis's Rooms meeting in 1859. This was intended to provide a more permanent alliance; in the words of A.J.P. Taylor, it was 'not a coalition of groups which looked back to the past, but a coalition which anticipated the future.'[51] During his second ministry the new coalition began to organise itself as the Liberal party. This occurred despite Palmerston, who tended to delegate party organisation and finances to the Whips. It is doubtful, however, whether this progress could have been achieved without the stable leadership he provided.

Finally, Palmerston ensured that the coalition of different groups was permanent. He prevented the Whigs from being frightened off by the radicals and Peelites, thereby giving time for the union to set properly. As Southgate maintains, 'While Palmerston lived, Whiggery could feel safe'.[52] On the other hand the continued leadership of Palmerston impeded the further progress of Liberalism. This has therefore been called 'the Indian summer of Whiggery', a period indistinguishable from the 'age of Palmerston'. This ended abruptly with his death in 1865, which initiated the age of Gladstone and Disraeli.

11

PARLIAMENTARY REFORM
1867 and beyond

Lord John Russell, and others in his party, had confidently predicted that the Great Reform Act of 1832 would be a 'final settlement' of the parliamentary question. This, like all such prognostications, proved premature. During the Victorian era, two further Reform Acts followed in 1867 and 1884 to extend the franchise and redistribute seats, although the basis for full universal suffrage was not achieved until those of 1918 and 1928. This chapter will examine the period leading up to 1867; interpretations of the passing and effects of the 1867 Act; and the need for and results of the 1884 Act.

DEVELOPMENTS 1832–67

Despite the stir it had caused at the time, the 1832 Reform Act was limited in its impact; as Wright argues, 'Only the intolerably diseased sections of the old system were completely cut out'.[1] Among the remaining anomalies and inconsistencies was the uneven representation and distribution of seats; ten counties in southern England with a combined population of 3.3 million had 156 seats, while Middlesex, Lancashire, and West Yorkshire had 3.7 million people but only 58 seats. The boroughs (many of which were rural) had 62 per cent of the seats with only 43 per cent of the voters, at the expense of the counties, for which the figures were 38 per cent and 57 per cent respectively; among the boroughs were eight with fewer than 200 electors. Finally, less than 15 per cent of adult males had the vote after 1832: the electorate was 813,000 out of a total population of 24 million.

The 1830s and 1840s saw considerable pressure for further parliamentary reform. The Chartists, in particular, saw the 1832 Act as a sell-out to the aristocracy and upper middle class and demanded a comprehensive overhaul of the entire system (see Chapter 8). The collapse of the movement in 1848 for the moment weakened the demand for more radical solutions like universal suffrage. Instead, reform was picked up again by isolated politicians with strictly limited intentions. One of these, despite his earlier stand, was 'Finality Jack' Russell. By 1851 he considered it necessary to extend the franchise into at least the upper level of the working class, as a means of preventing the revival of political radicalism. Several measures were therefore considered. In 1851 Russell brought before the cabinet a bill which would have made the basis of the franchise qualification in the boroughs a £10 rateable value and would have given the vote in the counties to £20 tenants. This, however, failed to make it through cabinet discussion. He tried in 1852 to introduce the same bill into the Commons but had to withdraw it under a combined assault from both Whigs and Conservatives. In 1854 Russell tried again with a third bill which reduced the county franchise to £10 occupiers and the borough franchise to a £6 rateable value. Again it failed, as did a bill introduced by Disraeli in 1858. Russell's attempt in 1860 was opposed by the Conservatives and Whigs, who saw no need for it, as well as by the radicals, who regarded it as too cautious.

A number of factors contributed to the failure of any attempt to secure further reform during the 1850s. Perhaps the greatest of these was indifference. The collapse of Chartism was followed by a period of greatly reduced activism for parliamentary reform, while the Anti-Corn Law League never really moved into the realm of political activism once it had achieved its specific objective of repealing the Corn Laws. It could be argued that the growth of economic prosperity in mid-Victorian Britain reduced the immediate necessity for parliamentary reform, while foreign affairs held public attention in a quite unprecedented way. Such distractions from parliamentary reform included the Crimean War and events in Italy and Poland, to say nothing of the incidents, analysed in Chapter 10, which gave Palmerston the opportunity to 'play to the gallery'.

Even the sporadic efforts of Russell were frustrated. The House of Commons was largely hostile to reform because, at this stage, it saw no need for it. In any case, its social composition was a natural barrier to any degree of democratisation. In 1841, it has been calculated, 342 members were related to the peerage and 240 others were members of the landed gentry; this meant that fewer than 100 were without privileged connections. Most MPs ignored Russell and aligned themselves with Palmerston, whose views on the extension of the franchise were well known. Indeed, he and the Conservative leader, Derby, made a tactical agreement to ensure that the issue was not raised in parliament between 1859 and 1865, while he failed to refer to it at all during the 1865 election campaign. There was no shortage of MPs willing to articulate arguments against reform. The two best-known were Cranborne for the Conservatives, and the Liberal, Lowe. The latter said in 1865:

> I regard as one of the greatest dangers with which this country can be threatened a proposal to subvert the existing order of things, and to transfer power from the hands of property and intelligence to the hands of men whose daily life is necessarily employed in daily struggle for existence.[2]

Despite the resistance of the likes of Palmerston and Lowe, the profile of parliamentary reform was gradually raised during the 1860s. Partly responsible for this was Gladstone, who added a moral emphasis. He considered that a working-class aristocracy had developed which had come to accept middle-class values such as industry, sobriety and thrift. He also maintained that enfranchising the upper section of the working class would reduce its susceptibility to socialism by attaching it to the principles of capitalism. Pressure was also reviving from below. The National Reform Union, formed in 1864, demanded three-year parliaments, secret ballot, equal electoral districts and a ratepayer franchise. The Reform League, originating in the same year, also pressed for universal manhood suffrage. Meanwhile, external factors had also been encouraging the revival of popular enthusiasm for reform. The most important of these was the American Civil War. Whereas the majority of government ministers had been more sympathetic to the Confederacy, public opinion favoured the Union. The sort of enthusiasm this engendered could, when the time was appropriate, be transferred to the issue of domestic reform. Much the same applied to the visit of Garibaldi in 1864; in fact the committee which organised his reception eventually transformed itself into the Reform League.

By 1866, therefore, there was a raised level of consciousness throughout the country and a consensus in the House of Commons that the issue of parliamentary reform would have to be given another airing. With the death of Palmerston, the main obstacle to this had been removed. The key questions were: what form would any new bill take; who would introduce it; and what would be its fate?

THE SHAPING OF THE 1867 ACT

The process of parliamentary reform between 1866 and 1867 produced some unexpected twists.

Russell's Liberal government introduced a bill in 1866, extending the franchise in the boroughs to £7 householders and, in the counties, to £14 tenants. This measure, which would have expanded the electorate by some 400,000, caused immediate dissension within the Liberal party. It was savaged from the left by the radicals, who wanted household suffrage, and opposed on the right by the Whigs, who considered that the franchise was insufficiently selective. Derby and Disraeli saw in this a unique opportunity for the Conservatives to help the Liberals destroy themselves. This was accomplished by an alliance with the right-wing Liberal dissidents, the 'Adullamites', led by Elcho and Lowe. In June 1866 this combination introduced an amendment which modified the proposed changes. When this was passed, Russell resigned and Derby found himself in power at the head of a minority Conservative government.

Logic would have suggested the introduction of a more restricted bill to enfranchise a group somewhere between the £7 rental proposed by the Liberals and the existing £10. And yet Derby and Disraeli actually intended to drop the franchise level still further – until, that is, Cranborne threatened to split the Conservatives with a revolt from the right. To prevent this, Derby and Disraeli drew up a new bill which actually made very few alterations to the system established in 1832. It soon became obvious, however, that the Liberals would not support it. Hence Disraeli reverted to a measure which was even more radical than his original one. After a number of Liberal amendments the bill was enacted in August 1867; the House of Lords, mindful of its experience in 1832, offered only minimal resistance. The 1867 Reform Act extended the borough franchise to all householders and £10 lodgers, and the county franchise to £12 ratepayers and £5 copyholders and leaseholders. Some seats were also redistributed: forty-five were removed from boroughs with a population of under 10,000. Of these, fifteen went to boroughs without an MP; twenty-five to the counties; one each to Birmingham, Manchester, Liverpool and Leeds; and one to the University of London.

This strange turn of events, in which the Conservatives produced a reform which was infinitely more progressive than that proposed by the Liberals, has attracted a variety of explanations. One is a Liberal myth that the working man owed the vote less to Disraeli than to the constant pressure exerted by Gladstone throughout 1867 after the Conservatives had defeated Russell's measure in 1866. The new electorate subsequently acknowledged the real source of their extended franchise by voting the Liberals into power in the 1868 general election. This interpretation now has very few adherents since it does not really hold water; although in favour of a measure of reform, Gladstone had never wanted household suffrage and had consistently voted against the 1867 bill.

The second is a Conservative myth which was popularised by Moneypenny and Buckle,[3] the original biographers of Disraeli. This claims that Disraeli from the outset wanted to create a much larger electorate in the belief that it was likely to be fundamentally Conservative; indeed, he was really preparing his party and the country for his own vision of Conservative democracy. This still has a few influential advocates, including G. Himmelfarb,[4] who argues that Disraeli was firmly wedded to the concept of Tory democracy and that the Conservative party was far more attuned to the needs and aspirations of the working class than were the Liberals. On the other hand, such an approach has been extensively criticised, not least by the modern biographer of Disraeli, R. Blake: Disraeli 'was never a Tory democrat' and, in any case, he did his best to neutralise the effect of household suffrage 'by redrawing the county and borough boundaries'.[5] Whatever Disraeli's motives were, he cannot be seen as 'a far-sighted statesman, a Tory democrat or the educator of his party.'[6]

This brings us to a third possibility – that changes were introduced in 1867 for pragmatic reasons. In the words of Walton: 'The nature of the Act was determined by the exigencies of party strife in a complex and fragmented political system.'[7] This is also the position of Blake, who maintains that Disraeli and Derby 'had the wide franchise of 1867 forced on them as the price of staying in power.' Disraeli realised that he had to adapt to new circumstances – and he was better at doing this than most. 'It was like a moonlight steeplechase. In negotiating their fences few of them saw where they were going, nor much cared so long as they got there first.'[8] M. Cowling goes still further, stressing the importance of cynical party politics. Disraeli moved towards household suffrage not through principle or through careful calculation about the party's future, but rather because of the pressure of events. He adds: 'Disraeli's was a policy of consistent opportunism'.[9] The actual methods involved are aptly summarised by Feuchtwanger: 'In the session of 1867 Disraeli practised the tactics he had used so often since he became leader of his Party, the attempt to link up with any available group to secure a majority.'[10]

An overall interpretation might be advanced as follows. Having turned out Russell and Gladstone in 1866, the Conservatives had no option but to introduce their own measure of parliamentary reform. Disraeli was receptive to the lesson of 1832 – that the party taking the initiative could select the recipients of franchise extension, whereas the party opposing reform could expect only a period in political exile. But he could hardly expect the Liberals to support the reintroduction of Russell's bill of 1866. His own had to be substantially different, going either above or below the Liberal baseline. Since the Conservatives were in a minority of 290 to 360, Disraeli had to keep his own party together and, in addition, get some support from the Liberals. The former could be accomplished by a mild measure, pitched somewhere above Russell's. But when Disraeli tried this in order to appease Cranborne, he quickly realised that there would be no chance of any Liberal support. Such backing could come only from the radicals, and then only if the proposals were sufficiently progressive. Disraeli therefore opted for a bold stroke to take the old enemy completely by surprise. This was, above all, a tactical *coup*.

This is not to deny that Disraeli had some sense of the electoral implications of his stroke. Why were most of the Liberals so insistent on stopping the franchise at £6 or £7 householders? It was probably because they were confident of the support of the well-to-do working class, but considered the next layer down an unknown quantity. Disraeli saw no reason why this might not be captured by the Conservatives. There would, after all, be no secret ballot and the influence of industrial masters could therefore be brought to bear. Alternatively, the redistribution of seats would to some extent neutralise the franchise extensions, which would at least mean that the Liberals would not benefit unduly. At best, therefore, the Conservatives would gain, at worst they would not lose. All this was, of course, taking a calculated risk but, as Blake suggests, 'moonlight steeplechasing' was in Disraeli's political nature.[11]

There is a further controversy. How important was the pressure of public opinion in the passage of the 1867 Reform Act? The bald facts are that the replacement of Russell by Derby in 1866 was followed by an increase in public interest and pressure in the form of meetings and demonstrations. In July disturbances occurred at Hyde Park, during the course of which a 1,400-yard stretch of railings was pulled down and destroyed.

This was less violent than the events in Bristol and Nottingham in 1831. But, as with the First Reform Act, the *threat* of violence has been seen as a significant factor in forcing the pace; history, in other words, was repeating itself. This is certainly the line taken by the original biographer of Gladstone, John Morley. He argues that the House of Commons which passed the 1867 Act had actually been elected 'to support Palmerston' and that the reason for its reversal 'would seem to be that the tide of public opinion had suddenly swelled to flood'; particularly important were the Hyde Park riots and huge demonstrations and open air meetings held in Glasgow, London, Birmingham and elsewhere.[12] G.M. Trevelyan agrees, referring to the solidarity between the middle and working classes which characterised 'the agitation in the country over which Bright presided in the autumn of 1866.'[13] More recently, R. Harrison has claimed that historians have underestimated the fears of revolution among contemporaries. The Hyde Park demonstration appeared menacing and politicians were ready to concede limited measures at this stage to avoid having to grant universal suffrage in the future. The Conservatives were, therefore, pushed by the disturbances into picking up reform again.[14]

There are, however, anomalies in this approach. There was a time-lapse of six months between the disturbances and the introduction of the Conservative reform bill. Since such bills could be – and were – drawn up at very short notice, this scarcely indicates a knee-jerk reaction by the government. The alternative argument is therefore that public opinion was not as significant a factor as in 1832. As Cowling states, 'The passage of the Reform Act in 1867 was effected in a context of public agitation: it cannot be explained as a simple consequence.' He also maintains that 'There was no "capitulation" to popular pressure'.[15] 'The final verdict', says Feuchtwanger, 'must be that the public reform movement did not do much more than act the part of the chorus in this play'.[16]

Contemporaries were somewhat apprehensive about the likely impact of the 1867 Act. Derby, for example, referred to it as 'a leap in the dark', while the historian, Carlyle, likened it to 'shooting Niagara'. Did the effects justify these forebodings?

Some of the changes were extensive. The total electorate expanded from 1.4 million to 2.52 million and there were now working-class majorities among the voters of all the major cities. Yet these were accommodated to the political system with surprising ease. Both parties built up a more effective and centralised bureaucracy. J.E. Gorst transformed the organisation of the Conservative party by establishing in 1871 the central office as the focus for party propaganda. The Liberal equivalent was the National Liberal Federation. Both parties emphasised the importance of constituency organisation. The best example was the Birmingham Liberal Association which developed a highly successful method of ensuring that all three seats allocated to Birmingham were generally captured by the Liberals. Each constituency developed local clubs, with the intention of attracting working-class members and promoting permanent party allegiance. As a result, both parties were broadly based. Neither was based exclusively on a particular class, even though specific occupational and sectional groups might tend one way or the other. Because party loyalties divided vertically rather than horizontally, the wider franchise had a stabilising effect as both Conservatives and Liberals became more genuinely national parties. Furthermore, the two-party system returned as a regular feature for the first time since the repeal of the Corn Laws. Governments now alternated more frequently because it was not too difficult for a significant number of voters to switch their support from one election to another. The absorption of the new electorate was reassuring to all leading Liberals and Conservatives, making the prospect of changes in the future less traumatic.

FURTHER REFORMS, AFTER 1867

These soon became necessary. The 1867 Reform Act had a number of anomalies which needed urgent attention.

The most obvious was an imbalance in the franchise qualifications, which increased the electorate in the boroughs by 135 per cent but in the counties by only 45 per cent.[17] This was accompanied by a disproportionate distribution of parliamentary seats. For example, the South-West had forty-five constituencies for

76,612 electors and the South-East forty-one for 80,177; the North-East, by contrast, had only thirty-two for 232,431. More specifically, Wiltshire and Dorset, with a total population of 450,000, had twenty-five MPs, while London's 3 million were represented by twenty-four members.[18] In the absence of secret ballot, there was also plenty of scope for corruption and intimidation: according to *The Times* on 22 June 1868:

> Unceasing clamour prevails; proposers, seconders, and candidates speak in dumb show, or confide their sentiments to the reporters; heads are broken, blood flows from numerous noses, and the judgement of the electors is generally subjected to a severe training as a preliminary to the voting of the following day.[19]

The last of these problems was the first to be addressed. The Ballot Act of 1872, produced during Gladstone's first ministry, considerably reduced the scope for intimidation by ending open voting at the hustings. On the other hand, it had very little effect on corruption. This was dealt with separately, during Gladstone's second ministry, by the Corrupt and Illegal Practices Act (1883). This was considered especially urgent in the light of the evidence of electoral corruption revealed by the Royal Commission of 1880. The Liberals were willing to press ahead with such a measure partly because they were more heavily stretched than the Conservatives by the heavy expenses involved in unrestrained electioneering. The Conservatives gave way with grace. After all, what possible reason could they have given for opposing the bill?

Meanwhile, there had also been momentum for further extending the franchise, a process which was much more rapid than it had been after 1832. In 1877 the Liberals formally committed themselves to extend the suffrage to rural householders and thereby eliminate the difference between county and borough franchises. In 1884, therefore, Gladstone introduced a franchise bill. Although this passed through the Commons, the Conservative-dominated Lords threatened to reject it unless it were accompanied by a redistribution act. Lord Salisbury claimed that the Liberals would otherwise make a net gain of nearly fifty seats. It now looked as if there might be a constitutional crisis. Certainly, the radical wing of the Liberal party, under Joseph Chamberlain, did what it could to stir up public opinion, presenting the issue as 'the peers v. the people'. The Queen was sufficiently worried about the prospect of a major constitutional crisis to request a meeting between Gladstone and Salisbury. In the end, a settlement was reached by negotiation between Gladstone and Salisbury, together with their deputies. The subsequent legislation was pushed through the Commons and Lords with surprising ease, each of the two parties following the instructions of its leadership.

The attitudes of both Gladstone and Salisbury require some explanation here. The former was reconciled to a further extension of the franchise partly because he was projecting himself increasingly as a populist politician and, according to Gash, wanted to 'round off his term of office on a creditable reforming note'[20] and partly to compensate for the government's unpopularity over Egypt. It is also possible that the increase in the Irish representation which would inevitably follow would strengthen Gladstone's hand over Home Rule, a cause he had now adopted. Salisbury, meanwhile, was not especially in favour, but saw no advantage in resisting the increase in the electorate from a point of *principle*. The Conservatives might even pick up many of the new county votes; in any case, they were benefiting from the growing support of the middle class, probably in reaction to the extension of the franchise in the working class, and this process could be expected to continue. The key to Salisbury's attitude was that the Conservatives must be given a fighting chance by a redistribution of seats which would not automatically load the new franchise proposals in the Liberals' favour. This explains the introduction of two measures rather than one: the Franchise Act (1884) and the Redistribution Act (1885).

Public opinion has again been put forward as a significant influence behind the events of 1884. W.A. Hayes, for example, maintains that 'At bottom the course of events in mid-November reflected the importance of the battle out-of-doors, and more broadly, demonstrated the critical role played by popular opinion in the making of the Third Reform Act.'[21] It could certainly be argued that public opinion was taken into account more in 1884 than in 1867. On the other hand, it was hardly a threat of 1832 proportions and was exploited in a much more moderate manner. The danger of public upheaval was stressed by the party leaders to strengthen their own political positions: Gladstone needed the Conservatives to withdraw the stranglehold in the Lords, Salisbury wanted Gladstone to rethink his proposal. But the threat was never more than latent and both Gladstone and Salisbury responded rapidly to the Queen's request that they should negotiate an agreement. It might even be said that the Queen intervened less because of any possibility of revolution than the real prospect that she would succeed in ending a rather artificial dispute.

The new reform measures made a substantial difference. By the Franchise Act of 1884, all householders in the counties received the franchise, achieving uniformity with those in the boroughs. This effectively doubled the electorate from 2.5 million to just under 5 million. The Redistribution Act of 1885 removed both MPs from boroughs with fewer than 15,000 people and one MP from those with fewer than 50,000. The 142 seats now available were redistributed according to population. A major feature was the creation of the single-member constituency as the norm: this now applied to 647 out of a total of 670. The imbalance in seat distribution between the North and South was finally ended. Cornwall's seats, for example, were now reduced from forty-four to seven; Lancashire, by contrast, increased its representation from fourteen to fifty-eight. In the light of such changes, Read argues that 'These two Liberal measures, plus the Corrupt and Illegal Practices Prevention Act of 1883, and the 1885 Registration Act, amounted to the largest single instalment of parliamentary reform undertaken during the nineteenth century'.[22] There were also significant side-effects. Party activism was further stimulated at local level as the single-member constituency took hold. The composition and character of the Liberal party were particularly affected. The traditional pattern of securing the election of both a Whig and a Liberal was ended by the introduction of single-member constituencies, so that the Whigs now rapidly became extinct.

Yet major deficiencies still remained in the period before 1914. Several categories of adult males, for example domestic servants, were deprived of the vote and even those who were entitled had to satisfy a twelve-month residence qualification and go through a complex process of registration. It has been estimated that the electoral registers contained no more than 63 per cent of adult males. Of the 5 million or so who were not enfranchised, about 2.5 million had the necessary qualification but had failed to fulfil the requirements for registration.[23] Above all, the entire population of women were denied the vote for a series of specious reasons which were still used by the establishments of both the major political parties. The final achievement of democracy therefore had to wait until the Franchise Acts of 1918 and 1928, by which time Britain was lagging behind most of the countries of Europe.

12

DISRAELI AND THE
CONSERVATIVE PARTY

More than most of his contemporaries, Benjamin Disraeli's rise
to power was assisted by circumstances over which he had no
immediate control. For much of his early career in parliament,
which began in 1837, there was little to mark him out for high
office. His individuality, which bordered on eccentricity, alienated
all but a small group of personal followers. His first opportunity, however, came in 1846 with the resignation of Peel and
the split within the Conservative party over the repeal of the
Corn Laws. In Peel's absence Disraeli emerged, by 1849, as
a most capable leader of the Conservatives in the House of
Commons. But for nearly two decades he was unable to accomplish much in government, his only experience of which was a brief
term as Chancellor of the Exchequer under Derby in 1852. His
second chance came when, in 1865, the death of Palmerston
loosened the Whig grip on British politics, while the problems
experienced by Gladstone after 1872 gave him the opportunity in
1874 to lead the Conservatives to their first outright election
victory since 1841, thereby completing his own ascent of the
'greasy pole'.

Yet it would be a mistake to see Disraeli's career as a series of
fortuitous steps. More than any other British statesman in the
nineteenth century he had the ability to bend circumstances to his
use. In this he was aided by an unusual clarity of thought and by
the capacity to prevent his ideas from hardening into ideology. In
this respect he was more thoughtful than Palmerston but less
affected than Gladstone by underlying principle.

This chapter will first examine the development of Disraeli as a
party and national leader by 1874. It will then analyse the domestic
reforms of his second ministry and consider whether or not the

147

Plate 3 Benjamin Disraeli, Earl of Beaconsfield, 1804–1881. From photo by Jabez Hughes. By courtesy of the Mary Evans Picture Library, London.

term 'Disraelian Conservatism' has any meaning. The final section will deal with his defeat in the 1880 general election.

DISRAELI'S ACHIEVEMENT BY THE 1870s

Disraeli's major achievement was, by the 1870s, to restore the Conservative party to the political mainstream after the two decades it had spent in stagnant backwaters. This was not, however, accomplished in consistent stages, and historians are always ready to contrast his years of success with a long apprenticeship of failure. According to Blake, 'During those years Disraeli did very little. If he had died or retired in 1865 or 1866 his influence on his country and his party would have seemed to the historian to be as negative as that of Charles James Fox.'[1] Adelman makes a similar point: 'By 1865, after twenty years in the wilderness under the leadership of the Earl of Derby in the Lords and, more precariously, Disraeli in the Commons, little had been done to provide the Conservative Party with new supporters, new policies or any new enthusiasm.'[2]

There is certainly a contrast in Disraeli's career before and after 1866, but perhaps these views are a touch negative. Disraeli achieved a considerable amount during the earlier period, without which none of his later success would have been possible. Two of these achievements are particularly important: he formulated a series of ideas which were to be of practical use later; and he kept together what was left of the Conservative party after the rupture over the repeal of the Corn Laws. Although these were years of frustration, even of despair, Disraeli built the essentials of his policy, without which he could not have responded to more favourable circumstances after 1866 with a sudden and remarkable burst of activity.

Disraeli was one of the nineteenth century's most prolific writers. But there has been a tendency recently to downplay the significance of much of his political thought. Against this trend, P. Smith points to the underlying continuity of his ideas: 'Disraeli's concept of Toryism was almost fully formed by 1846, and in essentials it never changed.'[3] The most important sources dating from the early period were his *Vindication of the English Constitution in a Letter to a Noble and a Learned Lord* and *The Spirit of Whiggism* (1836), together with two novels, *Coningsby* and *Sybil* (1844–5). The overall view emerging from these was that Britain had come under the grip of a Whig oligarchy, of 'a small knot of great families who have no object but their own aggrandizement, and who seek to gratify it by all possible means'.[4] The Whigs had actually widened the gap between themselves and the working classes, thereby reducing Britain to 'two nations'. Toryism, he considered, was more progressive than Whiggism since 'It appeals with a keener sympathy to the passions of the millions; it studies their interests with a more comprehensive solicitude.'[5] With the right approach, the Conservatives could bridge the gap between the two nations. It would, of course, be necessary to entrust Britain's cohesion to its natural guarantors – the aristocracy, gentry, Church and monarchy. Disraeli hoped thereby to stimulate a more closely integrated hierarchial paternalism. This would eliminate the selfish aims of Whiggism and maintain the 'popular principles'. He believed that 'The Tory party in this country is the national party; it is the really democratic party of England'.[6] The way in which the support of the working classes would be guaranteed would be a steady stream of social reform; in *Sybil* he maintained that the essential purpose was 'to secure the social welfare of the people'.[7]

It is, of course, important to distinguish between ideas and ideology. The latter tends to dictate the course taken by a political party. Disraeli's intention, by contrast, was to use his ideas not so much to transform his party as to sharpen its presentation and broaden its appeal to the electorate.

This was desperately needed. Disraeli picked up the Conservative leadership in the Commons at a point of crisis in the party's political development. The traditional reactionary core had been softened by the more progressive policies of Canning, Huskisson and Robinson, while Peel had aimed more consciously at attracting the middle classes. On the other hand, Peel did very little to win over the working classes and he came increasingly under attack from Disraeli's Young England movement for being too narrow. Unfortunately, the crisis of 1846 – and the split in the party – for the time being prevented Disraeli from moving any further down the road. The most able Tories followed Peel into political exile, leaving behind them reactionary residue. Faced with this unpromising material, Disraeli's priority now had to be to save Conservatism, rather than to transform it. This meant having to ignore some personal preferences, making Blake's description of 'the years of frustration' particularly apposite.[8] This meant that he had virtually nothing to do with mid-Victorian social reform, almost all the milestones of which were set in place by the Whigs, the oligarchy so despised by Disraeli. The one change he did manage to persuade the party to adopt during this period was economic rather than social: the abandonment of the cause of protectionism. Disraeli argued convincingly that free trade was now irreversible and that the effects were by no means as dire for the landed interest as had been predicted.

Even so, the Conservative party remained in the state of deepest depression throughout the 1850s and early 1860s. According to Smith, 'It had failed to come to terms with urban and industrial Britain and its expanding social forces. It remained overwhelmingly the party of the landed and agricultural interest.'[9] As yet, therefore, Disraeli's more progressive ideas had had little impact.

Then, within half a decade, everything was transformed. The death of Palmerston in 1865 suddenly created a more fluid political situation. It removed the personal leadership which had made the Whigs the natural party of government. It also released forces within that party which created unexpected instability as radicals and Peelite Liberals threatened to clash with traditionalist Whigs. Disraeli now came into his own. All the years of frustration fell away and he had the chance to give free rein to his ideas. He displayed sudden genius, as Vincent maintains, in seeing that 'you can only fight one political culture with another.'[10] Equally important, however, was the *opportunist* way in which he did this.

Disraeli's involvement between 1866 and 1867 in extending the franchise was the first example of this synthesis of political theory and practical necessity. He had the opportunity to apply some of the basic principles he had already enunciated, and succeeded in outflanking the reform measures of the Liberals. As explained in Chapter 11, he undercut their franchise proposals by including all householders. He reasoned that the only way to prevent a cascade of lower middle-class votes for the Liberals was to win the support of the working class. He was acting here on the principle that 'Of all men . . . I think working men should be most conservative' and that the Liberals were 'the active opponents of this class of voters'.[11] This was entirely consistent with Disraeli's earlier belief that the Whigs had distorted the electoral system by pitching the Reform Act of 1832 to maximise their own support. In aiming to reverse this in 1867 he showed that he could manipulate ideas with equal partiality; as Vincent maintains, to Disraeli ' "trust the people" was code for "distrust the Whigs" '.[12]

And yet there was no immediate pay-off. The time was not yet ripe for Disraeli to establish himself as uncontested national leader. In 1868 the electorate voted against Disraeli's government, handing a convincing victory to Gladstone and the Liberals. For a while Disraeli's own position was in jeopardy. Anti-Disraeli factions were gathering at local constituency levels, while at the top there were discussions at Burghley House in January 1872 over an alternative leader. At this point, however, Disraeli asserted himself more forcefully than ever before, making full use of the ideas he had formed earlier in his career. He carried the party by storm in a series of public speeches delivered in 1872 at the Free Trade Hall in Manchester and at the Crystal Palace. He returned to his theme that the traditional bases of Conservative policy – the aristocracy, Church and the monarchy – should now be combined with social reform. Hence Conservative policies would maintain the institutions of the country, preserve the Empire and 'elevate the condition of the people'.[13]

The crucial test, of course, was whether Disraeli could persuade the electorate to give him a mandate for such policies. Again, his opportunism and timing proved impeccable. He took a major gamble in 1873 when he declined the premiership after Gladstone's defeat. This worked, and his leadership of the party was permanently secured: the following year he won the 1874 election and became Prime Minister with the first Conservative majority since the days of Peel.

His handling of the election campaign was masterly. He made the most of the deficiencies of the Liberals and sought to win over groups who had been antagonised by the reforms of Gladstone's first ministry. These included a significant part of the landed gentry, most of the Anglican clergy and many Nonconformists. Finally, much of the newly enfranchised working class, who had voted Liberal in 1868, had since been antagonised by Gladstone's legislation on trade unions. Disraeli took advantage of their disillusionment to build a temporary alliance. This enabled the Conservatives to win an overall majority for the first time since 1841. He also launched an effective personal attack on Gladstone, accusing him of 'blundering and plundering' and stressing that Gladstone had 'harassed every trade, worried every profession, and assailed or menaced every class, institution, and species of property in the country'.[14] He pointed to the apparent feebleness of Gladstone's foreign policy, including as it did the payment of compensation to the United States government over the *Alabama* incident and

Britain's incapacity in face of the events leading up to the Franco-Prussian War in 1870.

By 1874, therefore, Disraeli had finally come good, through a combination of brilliant opportunism on his part and wounds self-inflicted by the Liberals. But the strategy of victory could not have been developed without the long years of political survival and intellectual preparation.

DISRAELI'S DOMESTIC ACHIEVEMENTS 1874–80

What use did Disraeli make of this apparent regeneration? He has been given much credit for his domestic achievements as Prime Minister between 1874 and 1880. Ward, for example, argues that:

> his legislative successes were impressive. Prime ministers do not have to be personally involved in every Act of their ministers. But they set the tone of and take the ultimate responsibility for their governments. And the tone of Disraeli's ministry in 1874 and 1875 was such to make it the major social reforming government of the century.[15]

There was indeed much that was positive, especially with Conservative legislation concerning labour relations. The Conspiracy and Protection of Property Act of 1875 legalised picketing, thus removing an anomaly left by previous Liberal legislation. Blake goes so far as to say that this 'satisfactorily settled the position of labour for a generation',[16] while Smith maintains that 'The labour legislation of 1875 was a remarkable stroke, and easily the most important of the government's social reforms.'[17] This was followed by the Employers and Workmen Act (1875); both sides of industry were placed on an equal legal footing in that all breaches of contract were covered by civil law instead of the former inequity of the criminal law covering breaches by employees, civil law those by employers. Disraeli believed, with some justification, that 'We have settled the long and vexatious contest between capital and labour'.[18] He was also confident, although with less basis, that this legislation would 'gain and retain for the Conservatives the lasting affection of the working classes'.[19]

Also worthy of credit, although less successful than the labour legislation, were the laws affecting working conditions and public health. The former continued a long line of previous legislation, all of which had gradually reduced the hours and raised the minimum age. The 1874 Factory Act cut the working day from ten and a half to ten hours and increased the minium age from 8 to 10, while the 1878 Factory and Workshops Act remedied a structural deficiency of the 1867 Act by bringing workshops with fewer than fifty employees under the inspection of the government rather than of local authorities. The Artisans' Dwellings Act of 1875 was also a significant development, described by Disraeli as 'our chief measure'.[20] This gave local authorities the power to demolish slum properties after compulsory purchase. Unfortunately, it was permissive rather than compulsory in its scope, as were the regulations, under the 1875 Sale of Food and Drugs Act, to prevent the adulteration of food. Central government, in other words, was not yet willing to accept the responsibility of forcing local authorities to institute reform: there was still a strong residue of *laissez-faire* in Disraeli's measures.

Smith points to two Conservative acts of this period which did *not* reflect to Disraeli's credit. The Merchant Shipping Act (1876) was intended to reduce the unscrupulous practice of overloading unseaworthy vessels and claiming on insurance. The initiative, however, belonged very much to a back-bench Liberal MP, Samuel Plimsoll, and was resisted for as long as possible by Disraeli himself. In addition, the law concerning the painting of a loadline was nullified by the absence of any regulation specifying its precise location. Meanwhile, the Rivers Pollution Act of the previous year was designed to prevent the flow of poisonous liquids into rivers and streams. But this had totally inadequate definitions of pollution and, in any case, was applied with notorious inconsistency against offending factories.

Disraeli therefore produced a range of social legislation which, with the exceptions mentioned, equalled or even surpassed those of other governments of the period. But the key question is to what extent did all this involve a distinctively 'Conservative' approach? Was Disraeli now developing his earlier ideas – which, as we have seen were vitally important for Conservative recovery – into a blueprint for reform? Was 'Disraelian Conservatism' now a deliberate party policy, the first perhaps in modern British history?

Disraeli's own words would suggest so. He seemed to place social reform firmly on the party agenda, arguing that 'the first consideration of a Minister should be the people's health . . . Pure air, pure water, the inspection of unhealthy habitations, the adulteration of food, these and many kindred matters may be legitimately dealt with by the legislature.'[21] This approach was once very much supported in secondary sources, especially by historians in the 1920s. Wilkinson, for example, maintained that 'Throughout his career in Parliament he consistently supported all measures of social reform'[22] and that this added up to the distinctive brand of 'Disraelian Conservatism' which he used as the title of his book.

More recent opinion, however, is generally against the notion that Disraeli was giving Conservatism a blueprint of social reform. Smith, for one, argues that the social reforms cannot be viewed 'as the embodiment of any Conservative social "policy"'. Instead, 'It was empirical, piecemeal reform, dealing with problems as and when they were pushed into prominence by their inherent size and urgency.'[23] According to Walton, Disraeli's legislation was 'in no sense a paternalist initiative'; instead, 'Disraeli presided over the passing of the legislation without supplying a detailed agenda.'[24] Several reasons are given for such views.

In the first place, there was an underlying continuity of social legislation in the late 1860s and the 1870s which transcended party differences. There were, in fact, precedents in most previous governments for Disraeli's measures, which therefore prevented these from being distinctively Conservative. Working-class legislation had already been planned by Gladstone's first ministry, but had not been properly completed, while the Torrens Act of 1868 would have anticipated the Artisans' Dwellings Act if the House of Lords had not rejected the clauses concerning compulsory purchase. Other measures also followed up earlier initiatives. The Royal Commission set up by Gladstone's government in 1873 had anticipated the reforms on merchant shipping. The factory legislation has been seen as merely a consolidation of earlier measures, while even the 1875 Public Health Act consolidated some of the earlier work of Gladstone's ministry which in 1872 had set up sanitary districts.

Second, and arising out of this argument, it is possible to see so-called 'Conservatism' as heavily diluted by a bipartisan approach to social reform. There was a surprising degree of co-operation between Conservative and Liberals over key measures; indeed the latter often applied necessary pressure to get legislation through parliament. The Liberal front-bencher, Lowe, argued strongly for the clauses on peaceful picketing contained within the Conspiracy and Protection of Property Act. The Liberal MP Plimsoll combined with those Conservative members with seaport constituencies to press for the Merchant Shipping Act, and similarly members of both parties supported the measures relating to the working class, public health and factory reform.

Third, this co-operation between the two parties meant that there was no need for Disraeli to identify a specific programme and force it through the Commons against strong opposition. Indeed, there is some question as to whether Disraeli exerted overall leadership anyway. Lord Randolph Churchill later said that there was 'no master-mind pervading and controlling every branch of the administration.'[25] Much of the initiative therefore came from individual ministers, rather than from a planned response from the Prime Minister. The main responsibility for introducing and seeing reforms through rested with Cross at the Home Office, Sclater-Booth on the Local Government Board, Sandon in the Education Department and Adderley at the Board of Trade. Thus, according to Walton, 'Most of the actual legislation merely emerged: there was no need for an overall plan or set of priorities to identify problems and bring them into the parliamentary arena'.[26] Walton further cuts the Prime Minister down to size by arguing that 'The only *Disraelian* aspects were rhetorical.'[27]

Where does this leave us in assessing Disraeli's impact? We have established the importance of Disraeli's ideas in reviving the Conservative party by the late 1860s. And yet we seem to be close to the point of arguing that this was all a facade, a series of tactical changes designed to enhance the electoral prospects of the party, but without a genuine underlying commitment to reform.

Such a view would be as misleading, however, as one which accredited Disraeli with establishing a new party ideology. What he actually did was to make it acceptable for the Conservatives to introduce social reforms after a long period spent resisting them. To insist that the Conservatives had no detailed plan or that they merely continued the work of the Liberals may well be true, but it is also begging the question. Disraeli's intention was to use his earlier ideas and newly established powers of rhetoric to revive his party – not to introduce social transformation, but to move towards the middle ground of politics in order to contest with the Liberals the support of an enlarged electorate. In this respect, the strategy behind the social reform in Disraeli's second ministry was identical to his views on the extension of the franchise in 1867. The result of this was bound to be an air of half-heartedness; this was well expressed by Salt, a Conservative back-bencher, who believed that Disraeli's government passed 'suet-pudding legislation; it was flat,

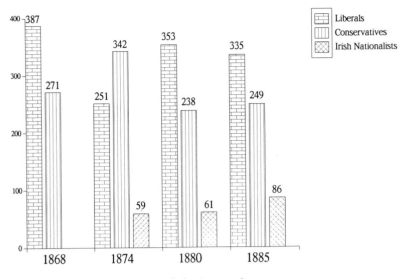

Figure 4 General election results 1868–85

insipid, dull, but it was very wise and very wholesome.'[28] It is also not really surprising that Disraeli tended to take the same attitude about his own role in social reform as about the form to be taken by specific acts. His was a 'permissive' rather than a 'compulsory' approach; he provided an environment in which reform could emerge, not a systematic programme for change.

CONSERVATIVE DEFEAT 1880

The 1880 general election produced results which were a mirror-image of those of 1874 as the Conservatives now slid to a 137-seat defeat:

	1880	*(1874)*
Conservatives	238	(342)
Liberals	353	(251)

Before the modern era, all general election results came as a surprise, since there were no public opinion polls to provide an advance prediction. But the outcome in 1880 was a particular shock to

157

Disraeli, who saw it as a poor reward from the working class for the efforts of his ministry on their behalf; after all, 'almost the whole domestic legislation of the past six years [had] concerned itself in improving their conditions and lightening their burdens'.[29] Like many disappointed party leaders before and after him, Disraeli therefore blamed 'the fickleness of the multitude'.[30] On reflection, however, he ascribed his defeat to objective factors, especially what he referred to as 'Hard Times', which was 'the alleged cause of our downfall'.[31]

To some extent, Disraeli was indeed the victim of circumstances. The Great Depression of the 1870s put his government very much on the spot. On the one hand, the tenant farmers and other members of the agricultural interest, traditionally Conservative supporters, clearly expected Disraeli to reintroduce protection to save their livelihood. On the other hand, to have done so would have led to an immediate rise in the price of food and increased the sufferings of the working class. In electoral terms, protection would probably have enabled the Conservatives to sweep the county seats in 1880; but the cost would have been the loss of almost all working-class votes in the boroughs. As it was, they managed to hold some of their borough seats, although the price for not causing the total defection of the working-class vote was the loss of twenty-seven seats in the counties, enough to swing the election to the Liberals.

But Disraeli was deluding himself in blaming objective factors entirely for his defeat. Another reason was that the Conservative government had run out of steam – in very much the same way as he had perceived the last part of the previous Liberal ministry as a 'range of exhausted volcanoes'.[32] As we have seen, the Conservatives contributed much to the general pattern of social reform in the 1870s. The flow, however, seemed to have stopped by 1876. By the time of the 1880 election, therefore, there was a lapse of nearly four years since the introduction of the measures which had most benefited the working class. At the same time the Conservatives were confronted by a revived Liberal party with a programme for further reform. In these circumstances it is hardly surprising that a substantial part of the working class should have voted Liberal, in anticipation, rather than Conservative, out of gratitude.

The Conservatives were also affected by two changes of direction towards the end of the ministry. One was Disraeli's elevation, as Lord Beaconsfield, to the House of Lords. The other was a conscious switch in the focus of his government from domestic to foreign policy. In themselves, these might have been interpreted as positive developments. After all, Disraeli received the accolade of statesmanship which was always denied to his rival, Gladstone. And Disraeli could claim considerable credit for the outcome of the Congress of Berlin (1878) which, for the time being at least, brought a respite to the crisis in the Balkans. On the other hand, there was much about Disraeli's foreign policy which was open to criticism (see Chapter 14) and Gladstone seized the opportunity to challenge the Conservatives for the high moral ground, especially over the apparent indifference of Disraeli over the sufferings of the Balkan Christians at the hands of the Turks. At the same time, convention dictated that Disraeli, now a peer, should not descend to the lower levels of public debate and answer Gladstone in kind. The latter was therefore left with all the hallmarks of personal victory.

Finally, there is even evidence of a downturn in the efficiency of the Conservative party machinery. The creation of the National Union (1867) and the Central Office (1870) did not have the expected impact on party organisation. Adelman argues that a struggle developed between the new organisers and the traditionalists within the party. The latter, in the form of the party whips, took over more and more of the responsibility from the man who had done most to transform the structure, J.A. Gorst.[33] However, the 1880 election made the party leadership rethink its priorities and bring Gorst back as party agent.

It had other effects as well. The Conservatives had been dealt such a psychological blow that many began to distrust the enlarged electorate, to harden their attitudes towards it and to show less inclination to promote or accept domestic change. Instead, they seemed to prefer a defensive stance, hoping no doubt to polarise the support of those parts of the population who feared that changes were occurring too quickly. The lead seemed to be provided by Disraeli himself. After resigning as Prime Minister in 1880, he dropped all reference to social reform and declared that the policy of the Conservative party was 'to maintain the Empire and preserve the Constitution'. Whether this was a temporary tactical retreat, or whether it was a more fundamental change of direction, will be discussed in Chapter 15.

13

GLADSTONE, LIBERALISM AND IRELAND

Few politicians have undergone such a profound change or have had such a turbulent career as W.E. Gladstone. Shortly after entering parliament in 1832, he was described by Macaulay as 'the rising hope of the stern unbending Tories'.[1] This seemed an apt description of a staunch upholder of all the privileges of the established Church, a defender of protection, and an opponent of almost all the domestic reforms of the Whigs. After 1841, however, Gladstone underwent a political transformation. Under the influence of Peel, whom he served as President of the Board of Trade between 1843 and 1845, he was converted to the cause of economic *laissez-faire*. One of the 'pivotal' events of this period was the debate over the Maynooth grant,[2] during which he abandoned his earlier belief that the Church should exert political power. In 1846 he supported the repeal of the Corn Laws and subsequently left the Conservative party as one of the Peelites (see Chapter 7).

For fifteen years Gladstone existed in a state of political limbo between the two parties. In 1852, however, he joined a Whig–Peelite coalition under Aberdeen and his budget of the next year continued the free trade policies already begun by Peel. In 1859 he decided to join the Whigs and radicals and increased his rapport with the masses, who, he considered, had an innate goodness. As a result, he clashed with the then Prime Minister, Palmerston, whom he thoroughly disliked.

Nevertheless, he served with distinction as Chancellor of the Exchequer between 1859 and 1866. Shortly after Palmerston's death in 1865, Gladstone assumed the leadership of a party in the process of transformation and brought together under his own brand of Liberalism the three main groups – Whigs, radicals and Peelites. He then led these to victory in the general election of 1868.

Plate 4 William Ewart Gladstone, 1809–1898. From photo by Mayall. By courtesy of the Mary Evans Picture Library, London.

Gladstone was Prime Minister four times: 1868–74, 1880–5, 1886 and 1892–4. His first ministry began with a series of reforms generally held to have been based on the precepts of 'Gladstonian Liberalism'. During the second ministry, however, the reforming impetus within Britain slowed. After 1885 Gladstone subordinated all else to the Irish issue and, in the process, divided the Liberal party just as surely as Peel had split the Conservatives over the repeal of the Corn Laws. This was responsible for the defeat of Gladstone's first Home Rule Bill in 1886. Another opportunity came during his fourth ministry, but the second Home Rule Bill was rejected by the House of Lords in 1893. Gladstone retired from active politics in 1894 without having accomplished his main aim.

This chapter will examine four main issues. What was the meaning of 'Gladstonian Liberalism'? To what extent was this applied to the reforms of his first ministry? What were the motives behind his Irish policy – and why did these not succeed? Finally, how effective was Gladstone as a party leader?

GLADSTONIAN LIBERALISM

Gladstone's version of Liberalism was built up over a long period and consisted of a variety of influences.

The underlying influence was religious rather than secular. Unlike many Liberals, who looked to Locke, Bentham and Mill for a secular ideology, Gladstone combined a profound belief in Christian morality with a sense of mission. He said in 1868 'The Almighty seems to sustain and spare me for some purpose of his own, deeply unworthy as I know myself to be'.[3] The result has been described as an 'equation of private morality with public action',[4] to an extent unequalled by any of his contemporaries. This was to operate, however, at an *individual* level. By the time he became Liberal leader, Gladstone had long since abandoned his original belief that religious influence should be exercised formally through the domination of the State by the Church. He became convinced, instead, that Christian morality in public life must be accompanied by full toleration for all other religious denominations and also for free-thinkers and atheists. Hence his support for the 1847 bill to admit Jews to the House of Commons and for the atheist MP, Bradlaugh, who refused to take the religious oath of allegiance in 1880.

Gladstonian Liberalism also contained a belief in the inherent 'goodness' of the masses, by comparison with the increasing selfishness of the governing classes. He was especially impressed by the moderation shown by the cotton operatives in Lancashire despite the hardships they suffered during the American Civil War. Surely, he argued, they could be entrusted with greater political responsibility? He said in 1864 that 'every man, who is not presumably incapacitated by some consideration of personal unfitness or of political danger, is morally entitled to come within the pale of the constitution'.[5] For this reason he was in favour of extending the franchise and was closely involved in the reform proposals of 1866 and 1884.

Political power, wielded from above, was seen as a trust which was to be carried out on behalf of, and for the benefit of, the masses. Gladstone disliked privilege and entrenched corruption, which he was prepared to sweep away wherever it manifested itself. This necessitated administrative efficiency and the elimination of waste through financial stringency. According to Magnus, Gladstone 'loathed waste because he regarded all money as a trust committed by God to man'.[6] He acknowledged his debt to Peel here, writing in 1889 that Peel had taught him 'purity in patronage, financial strictness, loyal adherence to the principle of public economy'.[7]

Finally, Gladstone had an unshakable commitment to economic *laissez-faire*, to which he gave a moral and semi-religious tone. Wealth was a 'trust' which should be conserved and increased so that it could 'fructify in the pockets of the people'.[8] This, he believed, meant a permanent commitment to the budgetary policies he had followed in 1853 and 1860 which were themselves a continuation of Peel's reforms of 1842 and 1845. Gladstone considered it essential to promote incentives which, in turn, coloured his attitude to income tax. This he consistently sought to eliminate, reducing it to 3d in the pound in 1868 and promising its abolition in the 1874 election campaign.

Gladstonian Liberalism was, however, limited and in some ways showed Gladstone's Tory origins. As Adelman points out, 'he never had very much sympathy with the more obvious causes of nineteenth-century Liberalism – democracy, equality, social improvement, republicanism'.[9] He retained, in particular, a belief in the importance of the landed aristocracy. He wrote to his son in 1875: 'Nowhere in the world is the position of the landed proprietor so high as in this country.'[10] He was also confident about the worth of the hereditary system. He suspected 'that a very large proportion of the people of England have a sneaking kindness for this hereditary principle'.[11] Gladstone considered that 'The natural condition of a healthy society is that governing functions should be discharged in the main by the leisured class'.[12]

Gladstone disapproved of some of the more progressive elements within the programmes of both the radicals and the Conservatives. In 1885 he wrote 'I deeply deplore the leaning of both parties to socialism, which I radically disapprove'.[13] He felt that this particular problem had actually been promoted by 'Tory democracy' and by the 'gradual disintegration of liberal aristocracy'.[14] Part of his objection was financial: when it came to public expenditure Gladstone was parsimonious and he tended to confuse welfare policies with wastefulness. But, more fundamentally, Gladstone had no sympathy with any notion of redistributing wealth; he had no intention of developing a graduated income tax for this purpose and strongly opposed an attempt to introduce death duties in 1894. He opposed any concept of the welfare state since he firmly believed in one of the cardinal Victorian virtues: 'self-help'. Nor had he any vision of the readjustment of the social order which might be accomplished by education. The extent to which he aimed to improve the condition of the working classes must, therefore, be highly questionable, and the limitations of his vision were open to increasing criticism from the radical wing of the party.

GLADSTONE'S FIRST MINISTRY 1868–74

Gladstone's first government was one of the most promising of the century, comprising a mixture of Whigs like Granville and Clarendon, moderates like Forster, and two radicals: Chamberlain and Bright. Like the cabinet itself, Gladstone maintained a balance between progressive reform on the one hand and conservatism and continuity on the other. Both of these influences can be seen within four specific examples of his legislation, as can the combination of strengths and shortcomings which was so characteristic of Gladstonian Liberalism.

The 1870 Education Act was perhaps the best example of this duality. On the one hand, it reflected Gladstonian Liberalism through the basic intention of spreading Christianity by extending literacy. On the other, it was essentially conservative. It aimed to promote widespread obedience and conformity to the existing system rather than break down class barriers. It also continued to emphasise the importance of self-help. Although the state became more heavily involved in education, it was never Gladstone's intention to use educational reform to establish a welfare state or anticipate radical side-effects. In any case, the actual measures were hardly radical, the purpose being to complement the voluntary system, not, in Forster's words, 'to destroy the existing system in introducing a new one'.[15] The Act was not, however, popular. Gladstone fell between two stools. His belief in religious toleration did not go far enough in the Act to satisfy the Nonconformists who were offended by the proposals to give grants to Church schools, while the Anglican establishment objected to the non-denominational teaching in Board schools.

One of Gladstone's priorities was to remove inefficiency and its partner, inequality of opportunity. This was especially the case with the home civil service, which was reformed in 1871. The overhaul included the establishment of clerical, executive and administrative grades and the opening of each to public examination. On the positive side, this reform succeeded in replacing aristocracy by meritocracy, establishing a new civil service tradition which was to last well into the twentieth century. In this respect it was creative and innovative. On the other hand, it might be argued that the impetus was as much Whig as it was Liberal. The measures had all been proposed in the Northcote-Trevelyan Report of 1854, even though no real attempt had been made by the Whig governments to implement it. The measure should really be seen, therefore, as one of consolidation.

A similar distinction might be made in connection with the University Tests Act of 1871, by which teaching posts at the universities of Oxford and Cambridge were no longer restricted to members of the Church of England. This was very much in line with Gladstone's policy of removing any inequality or discrimination practised on religious grounds. It was not, however, entirely without precedent, since a similar reform had already been carried out by the 1854 Whig government on behalf of undergraduates.

Gladstone's policy towards working-class organisations revealed an underlying intention to remove constraints on combination. Opposition to trade unions, he argued, was based on vested interests which were interfering with individual liberty. The Trade Union Act of 1871 therefore granted such bodies full legal status and additionally recognised the right to strike. But, in the same year, Gladstone negated the positive effects of this change by banning picketing in the Criminal Law Amendment Act. This apparent inconsistency shows that Gladstone did not develop a full programme on behalf of the working class. In this respect, Gladstonian Liberalism was no more progressive than Disraelian Conservatism: bearing in mind Disraeli's subsequent decision to legalise picketing, perhaps less so. On the other hand, restrictions on picketing had a certain Gladstonian logic, since they fitted in with his dislike of any form of coercion or pressure on the freedom of the individual from any group. This was possibly one of the many Peelite legacies in his policies.

Gladstonian Liberalism expressed itself in Cardwell's army reforms as a quest for financial saving and enhanced efficiency; in Cardwell's words, the measures were intended to 'combine in one harmonious whole all the branches of our military forces'.[16] In some respects the reforms were a success, opening the army to talent, ending the purchase of commissions, reorganising the regimental system along territorial lines, and redrawing the balance between service in the colours and the reserves. The humanitarian side was shown in the alternation of service at home and abroad and the abolition of flogging in peacetime. The unpopularity of the reforms with the privileged sections of society showed that their social impact were not insignificant. But were the reforms effective militarily? On the one hand, they brought a considerable improvement in the quality of recruits and officers, together with improved weapons in the form of the Martini-Henry rifle. The campaigns in Egypt, Afghanistan and South Africa owed much to the changes. On the other hand, it was not yet possible to predict whether they could meet the other need of the British army: the possible fulfilment of European commitments. The interim test provided by the Boer War (1899–1902) gave a depressing foretaste of developments to come.

One of Gladstone's particular aversions was the impact of excessive alcohol consumption on working-class life. Although surprisingly tolerant of occasional instances of drunkenness, Gladstone saw fully the destructive potential of regular abuse: the threat to financial security and therefore to the capacity for 'self-help', as well as the potential collapse of Christian-based morality. The answer was not to try to prohibit alcohol altogether, since this would constitute an attack on the individual's freedom of choice. He aimed, rather, to induce a more responsible social attitude. The 1872 Licensing Act therefore controlled the sale of alcohol through the public houses. Magistrates were empowered to grant licences to approved houses and to close down others where they considered that there were too many. Closing times were also imposed. The Act created a furore among the brewers, who subsequently supported the Conservatives to a man, without satisfying the Nonconformist desire for more stringent and effective controls on the sale and consumption of alcohol.

In a way such measures show that Gladstonian Liberalism had an unintentional capacity for antagonising a wide range of public opinion and interest groups. A mark of Gladstone's statesmanship as a reformer – and limitations as a politician – is that he seemed not to care.

GLADSTONE AND IRELAND

On being informed in 1868 that he was about to be invited to form a government, Gladstone is reported to have said 'My mission is to pacify Ireland'. The Irish problem spanned all four of Gladstone's ministries, taking up an increasingly large amount of his time, and diverting his attention from other issues. It consisted of four main components, which gradually narrowed down to two, eventually to one. What were these, and how did Gladstone deal with them?

The first was an historical relic which caused considerable resentment among the 88 per cent of the Irish population who were Catholic. This was the disproportionate power of the Anglican Church, which included the right to exact tithes of up to 10 per cent of the population's annual income. Although a devout Anglican himself, Gladstone had no wish to perpetuate religious subjugation of this kind. His Disestablishment of the Irish Church Act (1869) therefore aimed to reset the balance. Anglicanism was no longer the official religion of Ireland, while most of the Church's property was confiscated, some to be used to endow schools or hospitals, the rest to enable the Church to finance and govern itself without having to exploit the Catholic laity. Gladstone clearly deserves credit for having removed a long-standing anomaly and for calming some of the religious passion in the Irish situation.

On the other hand, the 1869 Act had a comparatively limited effect since the main focus of popular resentment was the nature of land tenure in Ireland, the second problem with which Gladstone had to grapple. A large proportion of the land was owned by Anglo-Irish landlords, many of them permanent absentees. Much of the land was let and then sub-let in tiny portions, driving the majority of the population into the intensive cultivation of potatoes, the only crop which could be sustained on less than an acre. Even then, there was considerable distress because of unpredictable evictions, while any improvements made almost invariably led to an increase in rents.

Gladstone addressed the land problem through two pieces of legislation. The First Irish Land Act of 1870 empowered the courts to prevent landlords from exacting 'exorbitant' rents and to enforce the payment of compensation for tenants who had been evicted, especially after improving their holdings. This was not, however, a success. The courts defined 'exorbitant' rents in favour of the landlords and compensation was paid usually only to evicted tenants who had made improvements. The Act did nothing to address the fundamental issue, which was the need for security of tenure – a vital basis for security in a country where the vast majority of the population were tied in some way to the land. As a result pressure was exerted by organisations such as the Irish Land League for the 'three Fs': fair rents, fixity of tenure and free sale. To his credit, Gladstone intensified his efforts for land reform. He introduced a bill in 1880 to secure compensation for evicted tenants, but this was thrown out by the House of Lords. He followed up in 1881 with the Second Irish Land Act, which introduced the principle of the three Fs, together with land courts to enforce fair rents. Unfortunately, these measures were too late to solve the Irish problem. History, in the meantime, had moved on through two more developments.

The third component of the Irish problem was the interplay between, on the one hand, protest and violence and, on the other, government coercion. This showed Gladstone at a loss. Trying to work out an acceptable land scheme, he had to divert his attention time and again to containing outbreaks of popular disapproval which he had not anticipated and which left him baffled. Disappointment with the First Irish Land Act of 1870 led to an increase in popular protest in Ireland, which was countered by a Coercion Act introduced by Gladstone in 1871. A similar sequence of events occurred after the passing of the Second Irish Land Act in 1881 as the Land League, now after more radical solutions, sought deliberately to sabotage the operation of that reform. Gladstone's response was to imprison Parnell and other Leaguers in Kilmainham Gaol, although this was ended by an agreement for mutual co-operation in 1882. Unfortunately, in 1882 an extremist faction committed an atrocity known as the Phoenix Park Murders, which left Gladstone with little alternative but to reimpose coercion measures. This constant interaction between threat and counter-threat made it more and more difficult for Gladstone to focus on land reform and forced him to come to terms with something more fundamental.

This was Home Rule, the fourth and most volatile component of the Irish situation. This solution had originated in Dublin with Isaac Butt's organisation of the Home Rule League. It entered Westminster as a result of the political activism of Biggar and Parnell. The latter united the Home Rule League and the Land League in a demand for the introduction of a Dublin parliament and for a switch from the social and economic policy so far pursued to a political solution. Although initially unimpressed by the argument for Home Rule, Gladstone decided some time between 1882 and 1885 to integrate it into Liberal policy. He introduced the first Home Rule Bill in April 1886, the purpose of which was to provide Ireland with a parliament in Dublin which would have jurisdiction over internal affairs; foreign affairs, defence and trade would, however, continue to be controlled by Westminster, at which Ireland would no longer be represented.

Gladstone's decision to accept the principle of Home Rule – and to commit his and the Liberal party's resources to its enactment – was the most important of his political career. It is hardly surprising, therefore, that his motive for doing so has become the subject of a major historical debate, with three substantially differing explanations now available.

The first, and most traditional, might be described as the theory of 'conversion through conviction'. Gladstone had already tried various measures, ranging from land reform to coercion. Gradually, however, he came to accept that a more fundamental solution had to be found to deal with all aspects of the Irish problem. This view is based on the belief that Gladstone had a positive regard for Ireland; according to Hammond, for example,

> what distinguished him . . . was that from first to last he thought of the Irish as a people, and he held that the ultimate test of a policy was whether or not it helped this people to satisfy its self-respect and to find its dignity and happiness in its self-governing life.[17]

Gladstone was convinced that the spirit of Irish nationalism had to be accommodated, a view which was entirely consistent with his earlier sympathies for Italian and Polish nationalism. If, he pointed out, Britain was to avoid the reputation for repression which had attached itself to Austria and Russia, then Ireland must be liberated. This would, in turn, safeguard the future of Britain's wider role in the world. 'Within this vast Empire there is but one spot where the people are discontented with their relation to the central power. That spot is Ireland.'[18] Gladstone arrived at this point of view, Hammond argues, because he was prepared to accept the need for conversion; he 'was the largest-minded man of his age' and his policy over Ireland was 'a superb example of magnanimity'.[19] Despite its record of failure, therefore, the Home Rule policy shows Gladstone at his very best.

There is a second, and very different, explanation. This could be categorised as conversion through 'convenience' rather than through 'conviction'. According to Vincent, 'Gladstone did not idealize the Irish'.[20] Far from adopting a positive and generous view of their needs, he subordinated them to his own political requirement. This was no less than a fundamental realignment of support behind him within the Liberal party. Vincent argues that 'What Gladstone was doing was not passing Home Rule, but carrying out the reorganization of party structure'.[21] Hamer seems to go along with this: 'Gladstone's reaction to the growing disorganization of Liberal politics was characteristic: he became increasingly interested in the possibility of discovering a new unifying policy, a policy which would "organize the action of the Liberal Party"'.[22] Gladstone therefore believed that what the party needed was 'concentration on a single subordinating issue'. In his analysis, 'it was Ireland that began to emerge as the great cause that might control and subordinate all other political questions and thus create order out of the prevailing chaos'.[23] Little did Gladstone know that his policy was to deepen the very crisis within the party that he was trying to overcome.

The third view is that there was no real change at all. Gladstone progressed quite logically from measures aimed to reform land tenure to a policy of Home Rule. According to Loughlin, 'the relationship between the land and Home Rule bills was not haphazard . . . Gladstone conceived both bills as vitally related parts of one comprehensive scheme aimed at solving the Irish problem'.[24] Furthermore: 'Gladstone had been convinced in 1882 that a comprehensive solution to the land question necessitated some kind of local government authority to actually put it into effect.'[25] The combined land and Home Rule schemes, therefore, were designed to achieve a new settlement, based on Irish autonomy and with the 'removal of the land issue as a source of social strife'.[26] This, in Gladstone's mind, would have the additional advantage of restoring the landlord to a fully responsible role within the Irish hierarchy, an indication of the more conservative influences upon his thinking.

Whichever explanation of Gladstone's motive is accepted, the actual course of his Home Rule policy was stormy. Gladstone lost the vote on the first Home Rule Bill in 1886 by 343 votes (including 93 dissident Liberals) to 313. When Gladstone appealed to the electorate the Liberals were heavily defeated by a combination of Conservatives and Liberal Unionists. His chance did not come again until 1893. The second Home Rule Bill was similar to the first except that Ireland was to be given representation at Westminster as well as in Dublin. Historians generally acknowledge Gladstone's supreme achievement in getting the bill through the Commons despite a powerful rearguard action by Chamberlain and the Liberal Unionists. Gladstone spoke for the bill with formidable presence in the Commons, but this counted for nothing as the House of Lords consigned the bill to a defeat which, in effect, ended Gladstone's career.

Three closely connected factors contributed to the eventual failure of Gladstone's Home Rule policy. The first was Gladstone's strategy over taking on the task of Home Rule. This was highly questionable. In particular, he has been criticised for mishandling the announcement of his policy at the outset. Instead of coming out into the open in 1885, he kept his own counsel and his real views were made known as a result of a press leak (usually known as the Hawarden Kite) by his son, Herbert. But why would Gladstone have risked wrong-footing a new policy by giving it an apparently devious inception? The basic point is that Gladstone was in a highly awkward position. He wanted to promote Home Rule as an issue which transcended party politics. Gladstone realised that the passage of Home Rule was more likely to succeed if there were common ground between the parties. Any announcement of his conversion to Home Rule during the highly charged atmosphere of a general election campaign would, he believed, have the reverse effect of giving the Conservatives an issue over which to express their immediate opposition. Similarly, he anticipated deep divisions within the Liberal party and therefore needed time to persuade the various factions to go along with him. This would, in his words, require 'a healthful, slow fermentation in many minds, working towards the final product'.[27] As events turned out, the 'Hawarden Kite' served to accelerate the very two problems which Gladstone had hoped, through his silence, to avoid.

Far from accepting a bipartisan approach, the Conservatives orchestrated an aggressive and highly organised campaign against Gladstone's policy. No holds were barred as Lord Randolph Churchill stirred up opposition to Home Rule among Irish Protestants. This was done quite deliberately as a party tactic; Churchill wrote in 1886: 'I decided some time ago that if the G.O.M. went for Home Rule, the Orange Card would be the one to play'.[28] In doing this he raised the temperature of debate in the House of Commons by pointing to the real prospect of civil war in Ireland if Home Rule went ahead. But the ultimate expression of Conservative opposition to Home Rule came in 1893 through the use of their entrenched majority in the House of Lords. Although it was passed by the House of Commons by forty-three votes, it was rejected by one of the largest majorities ever seen in the Lords: 419 to 41. The only way of challenging this was by launching a major offensive against the Upper House which, in turn, would have precipitated a constitutional crisis, thereby changing the ground of the contest from Ireland to Britain. This was not something that the Liberals were prepared to let Gladstone do. The Conservatives therefore successfully made use of an obstructive power for which the Liberals lacked a remedy.

The third major reason for the defeat of Home Rule was the extensive opposition to it within the Liberal party. Dissident Liberals, who subsequently became Liberal Unionists, were to be found on both wings of the party. On the right, a substantial number of Whigs, especially Lord Hartington, opposed Home Rule because they considered that it would be exploited by the Irish Nationalists to become a minimalist demand. It would also considerably enhance the power and status of the Catholic Church at the expense of Protestantism. The left wing can be subdivided into 'old' and 'new' radicals. The former included one of the most respected members of the entire party, John Bright, who argued: 'I will never surrender to a Parliamentary party from Ireland'.[29] The importance of this point of view was that it helped detach many of the more traditionalist radicals from their long-standing alliance with Gladstone and to deliver their support, instead, to the new radicals.

The leader of the latter group was Joseph Chamberlain, who completely rejected Gladstone's Home Rule policy, seeing the solution instead in the extension of powers of local government 'consistent with the integrity of the Empire and the supremacy of Parliament'.[30] He certainly opposed any separate Irish legislature, the end of Irish representation at Westminster and the apportionment of areas of responsibility: 'Where in all this is the integrity of the Empire?',[31] he asked. In part, Chamberlain may have been motivated by ambition. If the Liberal party were to be connected to a cause which would inevitably bring electoral defeat, then it made sense for Chamberlain to dissociate himself for the time being and rejoin the party when both the issue and its sponsor had gone from the scene. He might then even return from self-imposed exile as the next Liberal leader. In the meantime, he deprived the Liberals of a substantial part of the radical wing it had possessed throughout the nineteenth century. No party can suffer such a loss with equanimity.

GLADSTONE AS PARTY LEADER

In the early stages Gladstone proved remarkably successful as a party leader, repeating the earlier achievement of Peel. Just as Peel had moved the Tories away from the influence of Wellington, Gladstone adjusted the Liberals to a new world without Palmerston. He was able to pacify the Whigs, give fresh hope to the radicals and find a permanent political home for the Peelites. He was also able to mobilise the party as a force for progressive reform within the broad guidelines of Gladstonian Liberalism. Within months of assuming the leadership, Gladstone showed an ability to rally his party in a new offensive. He achieved a notable success in the Commons, defeating Disraeli in 1868 on a resolution for the separation of Church and State in Ireland. In the subsequent general election Gladstone played a major personal role in projecting a new Liberal image to an electorate enlarged by the 1867 Reform Act, thereby snatching the initiative from Disraeli who had confidently expected to be re-elected.

During the early part of his first ministry Gladstone displayed a sensitive understanding of the requirements of party leadership. He tried to balance the radical and conservative elements within his policies and actions: Gladstonian Liberalism, in this respect, was the crossing point between the radicals and Whigs. In these early years the party responded positively, the two wings seeing Gladstone as a counterbalance against each other. There was also a large middle ground within the party which gave him unquestioning support and which completely trusted his leadership and judgement. Gladstone's position was, in effect, above the Liberal party rather than within it.

But such harmony was fragile. Liberal unity under Gladstone's benevolent leadership needed a combination of purposeful reform and political success. The first of these was removed after 1872 as Gladstone's first ministry became, in Disraeli's phrase, 'a range of exhausted volcanoes'. The second was reversed in 1873 by the defeat of the Irish University Bill. This was followed by the heavy defeat of the Liberals in the 1874 general election. Suddenly Gladstone's relationship with the party appeared cut off from it rather than elevated above it. In 1875 he went so far as to resign the leadership on the grounds that 'I felt myself to be in some measure out of touch with some of the tendencies of the Liberal Party, especially in religious matters. I deeply desired an interval between parliament and the grave.'[32]

Although he returned in 1876, he gradually altered his relationship with the party, especially after winning the 1880 general election. He badly wanted to recapture from the Conservatives the reforming initiative but, at the same time, did not wish to respond to the more radical pressures now being exerted by Chamberlain. The result, between 1880 and 1885, was a government which, in Ramm's words, cast a 'backward look to 1874 but found it impossible to pick up the legislative or policy threads of the first administration'.[33] The internal state of the party did not, he felt, enable him to do this. What particularly disturbed him was the growth of factionalism, of which the Chamberlain radicals were the main example. He had already written in 1878 that 'the sects, which nestle within the party, cannot be treated . . . tenderly', and that the 'divisive courses of sectional opinion' would cause a 'loss of collective working power' and hence reduce the party's 'aggregate energy'.[34]

What was the answer? A number of historians, such as Ramm and Vincent, emphasise Gladstone's determination to move the Liberal party on – from a policy based on a programme of reform to one which embraced a major national issue. This would have the advantages of directing the energy of reform into a crusade while reuniting the factions of the party behind the common effort. His own leadership would transcend the party structure even more than it had in the past. He would remain detached from the details of party management[35] and assume the role of national statesmanship. This approach had already received a trial run while Gladstone had been in opposition. In 1880 he had concentrated Liberal energies on a great onslaught against 'Beaconsfieldism' in foreign policy and on the need to adopt a more moral and less pragmatic approach to developments in the Balkans. This had helped win the 1880 election. As we have already seen he was, by 1885, willing to accept the challenge of committing the Liberals to another 'great question'.[36]

Irish Home Rule, however, proved notoriously difficult to handle within the fragile constraints of the party. In his frustration, Gladstone revealed several serious weaknesses as a party leader, some of which could be seen as the excessive application of earlier strengths. In the first place, his detachment and ambivalent approach to policy-making meant that he refused to commit himself until he was ready. The 'Hawarden Kite' proved the worst possible way of preparing the party for its new role. Whether or not Gladstone had any hand in it, he gravely underestimated its capacity for exacerbating sectionalism. Second, Gladstone completely failed to develop a consensus within the party. In trying to thwart Chamberlain, he succeeded only in driving him out. With more patience and a larger measure of pragmatism and compromise he might have been able to use Chamberlain and to achieve a blend of radicalism and Gladstonian Liberalism: after all, this was eventually accomplished by Campbell-Bannerman despite – or because of – the absence of a 'national issue'. Third, and most important, Gladstone insisted on placing his own views in the forefront of party policy. Few would question the passion, and often the nobility, of his commitment to great causes. But this seriously undermined his effectiveness as a leader since he inflicted suffering on his party by connecting it irretrievably to the fulfilment of his personal crusades.[37]

Towards the end of his career Gladstone made some effort to moderate his style. In 1891 he partially succeeded in providing in the Newcastle Programme a synthesis between a variety of policies and a 'national issue': Irish Home Rule was placed within the context of a broader set of reform proposals. But this came too late to win back the defectors; to have stood any chance of success it should have been developed earlier to complement the Round Table Conference on Liberal reunion held in 1887.

THE IMPACT OF THE HOME RULE ISSUE ON THE LIBERAL PARTY

How serious was the effect of Gladstone's Home Rule policy on the Liberal party?

It certainly had a profound electoral impact. The Liberals lost the general election of 1886 as a direct result of the defection of the Liberal Unionists and were able to form a government in 1892 only with the unreliable support of the Irish Nationalists. Gladstone himself tried to quantify the damage. In his pamphlet *The Irish Question*, he stated that there was 'very great inequality among classes';[38] about four out of five normal middle-class Liberal voters had defected to the Liberal Unionists and Conservatives, compared with some 5 per cent of working-class Liberals. This could be taken as an indication that there was not much wrong with the Liberal appeal to the mass electorate. On the other hand, the Liberals were clearly failing to appeal to an electorate which had been greatly enlarged in 1884 in sufficient numbers. The 5 per cent deficit in the working class may therefore have been more significant than the 80 per cent in the middle class. The Liberals should have greatly enlarged their vote from the former source, as they were eventually to do in their landslide in 1906.

This, of course, raises the question of whether it was Ireland, or something else, which cut off the flow of working-class support for the Liberals. In the absence of public opinion poll findings, it is difficult to determine the motivation for party allegiance. It would be a reasonable deduction, however, that what counted most for the majority of the working-class electorate was not the Irish issue at all: rather, it was the drying up of social reform. At the same time, it needs to be asked whether the two are connected. Did Gladstone's preoccupation with Home Rule for Ireland actually prevent the Liberals from pursuing reform in Britain? Two answers are possible.

One is that 'Ireland had become the cuckoo in the nest, crowding out the measures with which Parliament should have been occupying itself at a time when restive social discontent was strongly marked'.[39] This meant that the impetus for social reform passed from the hands of Gladstone to those of Chamberlain. But Ireland

intervened again: because of the strength of his views over Home
Rule, Chamberlain eventually made common cause with the
Conservatives, even joining Salisbury's ministry in 1895 as Colonial
Secretary. The Liberal party therefore lost a major impetus to
reform and, until the Irish issue was dropped, it proved incapable of
making constructive use of what was left of its radical wing. Once
Ireland receded in importance, radicalism returned to Liberalism,
revitalised it and enabled it to defeat a Conservative party which, in
turn, had become divided over the issue of tariff reform. By this
argument, therefore, Gladstone diverted his own reforming energies
and lost the radicals – both because of his obsession with one issue
above all others.

The alternative argument is that the Irish issue made little difference – because Gladstone was in any case becoming increasingly
conservative by comparison with the radical wing of the party.
Gladstone has been seen by some historians as innately traditionalist in his views and instinctively opposed to the more radical
proposals of Chamberlain. His Home Rule solution was actually in
keeping with this conservatism since he expected the Irish landowning class to re-establish itself as the natural ruling elite and for
the rest of the Irish population to restore its deferential links with it.
Home Rule would force the landowners to re-examine their
attitudes and to justify their political influence, just as the various
reform acts had forced the British landowning classes to come to
terms with an enlarged electorate. But the same principle applied:
that enlightened land ownership was a sound basis for order,
stability and deference. By this argument, Gladstone's adoption of
the single-issue approach did not make a great deal of difference to
the Liberal party since he had already moved substantially away
from the radical wing on British issues.

The comments on Gladstone's leadership, made in the previous
section, would suggest a third view. The Liberal party was in the
process of changing. Gladstone was painfully aware of the growing
gap between himself and the radicals over the latter's preference for
programme policies. He was beginning to feel his age – and his
conservatism – by the time of his third ministry, which meant that
he was prepared to adopt a cause of which he had previously been
wary. The adoption of Home Rule was in this respect a symptom of
the Liberal crisis. But, of course, it also contributed to the intensifi-
cation of this crisis by strengthening the position of the
Conservatives through the defection of the Liberal Unionists. This

meant that the Liberal vote was severely depleted and any Liberal government was dependent on the uncertain support of the Irish Nationalists. Thus the symptom became a cause and the process of regeneration could not begin until the Irish issue was – albeit temporarily – removed.

14

THE FOREIGN POLICY OF DISRAELI AND GLADSTONE

Before becoming Prime Minister, neither Disraeli nor Gladstone had had much direct experience of foreign policy or relations with Europe. Neither had ever held the post of Foreign Secretary. Gladstone, it is true, had served Peel as Colonial Secretary (1845–6) but in this capacity had been responsible for *imperial* issues; the rest of his time he had been involved in domestic policy as President of the Board of Trade (1843–5) and Chancellor of the Exchequer (1852–5 and 1859–66). Disraeli's ministerial experience had also been gained as Chancellor of the Exchequer (1852, 1858–9 and 1866–8). The foreign policy of the period 1841–65 had been dominated instead by Aberdeen and Palmerston; the influence of Disraeli and Gladstone was expressed only occasionally and on occasion (as over the Don Pacifico affair in 1850) they found themselves on the same side in their criticism of government policy.

After 1868, however, their involvement in both foreign and imperial affairs was surprisingly direct for a prime minister, whose function normally was to preside over the work of the various government departments without undue interference in any of them. During their ministries, Disraeli (1868 and 1874–80) and Gladstone (1868–74, 1880–5, 1886 and 1892–4) intervened more directly in foreign policy than any other prime minister of the century, with the possible exceptions of Palmerston and Salisbury. This was partly because they had developed strong views about Britain's role in Europe and partly because the room for manoeuvre was now more restricted and involved greater potential dangers than before. Both were therefore convinced that this was an area of responsibility which could not be delegated properly. This inevitably meant clashes with their foreign secretaries. During his second ministry, Disraeli was served by the Earl of Derby, son of the former prime minister, who was not inclined to his leader's imperial and opportunist emphasis. Disraeli therefore gradually took the initiative and actually complained in May 1876 of 'the want of order and discipline in your office'.[1] Disraeli was particularly influential over the conduct of the Eastern Question between 1875 and 1878. He was Britain's principal plenipotentiary at the Congress of Berlin, his foreign secretary, Salisbury, playing a supporting role. Similarly, Gladstone pressed his own ideas vigorously on Granville and prevented the latter from developing an individual style as foreign secretary. In all Granville's despatches 'the ideas were Gladstone's'.[2] During the 1870s, therefore, prime ministers dictated foreign policy, while their foreign secretaries acted as influences for moderation and caution.

This chapter will compare and contrast the basic ideas and attitudes of Disraeli and Gladstone in connection with foreign policy before analysing their record in more detail. The focus will be Europe, especially the Eastern Question, since imperial policies are covered in Chapter 15.

DISRAELI AND GLADSTONE COMPARED

British foreign policy had previously been based on maintaining European equilibrium and upholding the Vienna Settlement, a course which had enabled Britain to avoid direct European entanglements. During the era of Palmerston, Britain's aloofness had been based to some extent on her own strength and the confidence that the continental powers were held in balance with each other. This situation had been transformed, however, by the Crimean War in the 1850s and the events in central Europe in the 1860s. The withdrawal of Russia into diplomatic isolation was counterbalanced by the rise of a united Germany. More than any other single factor this destroyed the previous balance which had worked so well in Britain's interests.

Both Disraeli and Gladstone were affected by the changed international scene which brought with it the comparative decline of Britain as a European power. Both had to grapple with the problems of German military supremacy and with the diplomatic skills of the German Chancellor, Bismarck. The obvious course for both Liberal and Conservative governments was to keep out of European entanglements without surrendering Britain's capacity to influence events. Here, however, the basic perceptions of Disraeli and

Gladstone diverged. The former still hoped to exert a Palmerstonian influence, with Britain as the focal point of diplomacy; he said in his Guildhall speech in 1879: 'So long as the power and advice of England are felt in the councils of Europe, peace, I believe, will be maintained, and for a long period'.[3] Furthermore, Disraeli would seize any opportunity which presented itself to pursue British interests in the traditional way. Gladstone's emphasis was altogether different. He saw Britain in a multilateral perspective, as part of a Concert of Europe which he hoped to revive. British interests should be subordinated to international law and the rights of all nations, which would be upheld by carefully planned collective action rather than by the opportunist intervention which Disraeli seemed to prefer.

Underlying this differing approach to diplomacy was a contrasting perception of Europe. Disraeli was more insular, viewing Europe with suspicion and making his calculations on the assumption that there were no underlying moral principles to observe or values to uphold. Gladstone, by contrast, had a deep attachment to Europe as a cultural ideal, as, in the words of Sandiford, 'an almost perfect synthesis of Christianity and Hellenism'.[4] He frequently visited Europe, spoke German, French, Italian and Greek, and corresponded regularly with personal friends and politicians. He considered that Britain had a spiritual and cultural role in Europe, together with an obligation to protect the interests of the weak rather than aggressively pursue Britain's own interests. Gladstone considered that Disraeli's foreign policy undermined 'all the most fundamental interests of Christian society'.[5] In the words of Knaplund, 'He advocated applying the principles of the Sermon on the Mount in dealing with foreign nations-law, justice, and the equal rights of all nations should prevail and be recognized.'[6] Unlike Palmerston and Disraeli, he was not, therefore, one of the 'Victorian chauvinists'.[7]

The contrast in aims and methods was sharpest over the Eastern Question. This was a complex web made up of a variety of strands, comprising the decline of Turkey as a major power; the attempts of the Balkan Christians to throw off an oppressive and increasingly inefficient administration exercised by the Turks; and the growing interest shown in the area by Austria, Germany and Russia. Gladstone was inclined instinctively to sympathise with the Balkan Christians in their struggle against Turkish rule, while Disraeli was much more concerned about the effects of the disintegration of

Turkey in diplomatic terms. This meant that for Gladstone the greatest threat in the region was the Ottoman Empire, whereas for Disraeli it was Russia. According to Seton-Watson: 'While, then, Disraeli clung to the very last to his illusions on Turkey and identified British interests with the artificial maintenance of a decadent state, Gladstone saw the future lay with the nations whom the Ottoman tyranny had so long submerged'.[8]

COMMENTS ON DISRAELI'S FOREIGN POLICY

In some respects Disraeli can be seen as the natural successor in foreign policy to Palmerston. He was essentially an opportunist and always placed Britain's immediate interests above any underlying principle or moral consideration. This was most apparent over the Eastern Question. To Disraeli the threat was the disintegration of the Ottoman Empire caused by internal disruption by the Balkan Christians fostered by Russia. This was an entirely pragmatic approach and a pursuit of the traditional fear of Russian expansion which had been shown by Canning and Palmerston. His handling of the Balkans problem showed a master of short-term strategy but some indecision about longer-term objectives. His policy between 1875 and 1877 was based very much on immediate reactions and expedients rather than any systematic planning. Not surprisingly, this met with very mixed success.

There were obvious errors of judgement. One was his acceptance of the advice of the British ambassador at Constantinople not to support the Berlin memorandum – an attempt made by Germany, Austria and Russia to put pressure on Turkey to reform and introduce an armistice with the Balkan Christians. Disraeli's decision only served to bolster Turkey's determination not to moderate her actions in her Christian provinces. This helped fan the flames of revolt in Serbia and Bulgaria, which in turn eventually involved Russia, who declared war on Turkey in 1877. Chamberlain heavily criticises Disraeli for splitting his cabinet over the crisis and for moving to 'an uncritically pro-Turkish position'.[9] Seaman goes even further: 'On balance, the crisis in the Near East from 1875 to 1878 may be said to have been to a great extent created by Disraeli's initial abandonment of concerted action when refusing to associate England with the Berlin Memorandum.'[10]

On the other hand, Disraeli did take several decisive steps in 1878. He hastened the end of the Russo-Turkish war by sending the

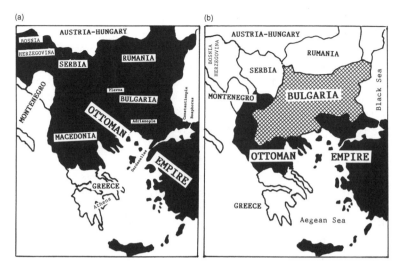

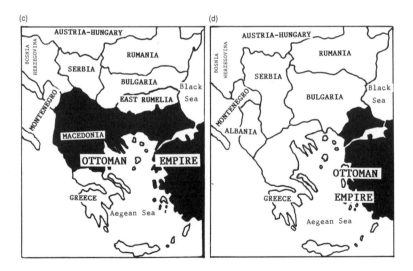

Figure 5 The Eastern Question 1870–1914. (a) The Balkans in 1870.
(b) After the Treaty of San Stefano 1878. (c) After the Treaty of Berlin 1878.
(d) After the Treaty of Bucharest 1913

British fleet to Constantinople in the wake of the Russian capture of Adrianople. He also reacted swiftly to the signing of the Treaty of San Stefano which he considered very much against Britain's interest in that it involved the retraction of Turkish rule in Europe and the establishment of a large new Bulgarian state which he feared would become a Russian satellite in the Balkans. Disraeli played a vital role at the 1878 Congress of Berlin, along with Andrassy, Gortchakov, Bismarck and Abdul Hamid. Most of the negotiation was carried out secretly behind the diplomatic scenes. The whole process, however, was dominated by an underlying agreement between Bismarck and Disraeli, between whom there was a considerable similarity. Both were ruthless, opportunist and determined to use the Congress to design a settlement in the Balkans which would be much more in the interests of their respective states. The result of their activities was the Treaty of Berlin.

How successful was Disraeli's policy in 1878? This is one of the major controversies of nineteenth-century foreign policy and involves a complex interweave of issues. The answer depends upon how these are unravelled and on whether they are placed within a short-term or long-term perspective.

On the one hand, Disraeli can be seen as having achieved a considerable success. He claimed on his return from Berlin that he had accomplished 'Peace with Honour'. *The Times* agreed: 'He has, at all events, averted a terrible war; he has, at the same time, maintained the dignity and authority of his country; and he has in all probability established affairs in the East upon a basis on which a really stable edifice may be erected.'[11] Queen Victoria enthused: 'High and low are delighted, excepting Mr Gladstone who is frantic'.[12] Disraeli dismissed the latter's criticisms in a series of devastating phrases. Gladstone, he said, was 'a sophisticated rhetorician inebriated with the exuberance of his own verbosity and gifted with an egotistical imagination that can at all times command an interminable and inconsistent series of arguments to malign an opponent and glorify himself'.[13]

Some modern historians also consider that Disraeli had pulled off something remarkable. The usual argument is that Disraeli made a positive contribution to the stability of the Balkans by helping dismantle the Treaty of San Stefano. In the process, he frustrated a blatant attempt to spread Russian influence through an enlarged satellite state which would have permanently distorted the balance of nationalities within the Balkans. A Russian-dominated Bulgaria would have been created at the expense of Serbs and Greeks, a recipe for future irredentism and further Balkan conflict. Bulgaria, in other words, would have replaced Turkey as the target of resentment. As it was, the Treaty of Berlin reduced Bulgaria to more realistic dimensions and, at the same time, confirmed the full independence of Serbia, Montenegro and Rumania from the Ottoman Empire. The territorial balance was therefore reset to a point halfway between the Treaty of San Stefano and the Ottoman boundaries before the Russo-Turkish War.

This settlement had major advantages for British diplomacy in a wider European context. Disraeli stated in a letter on 4 November 1880 that 'next to making a tolerable settlement for the Porte', his intention was 'to break up, and permanently prevent, the alliance of the three Empires'.[14] In this, arguably, he succeeded. The League of the Three Emperors, or *Dreikaiserbund*, was undermined by a settlement which set Austrian and Russian ambitions against each other in the future and destroyed any remaining vestiges of the Holy Alliance. Britain could therefore feel more secure in a Europe which lacked a traditional alliance of the three autocracies.

In addition, Disraeli and Bismarck between them accomplished a settlement which gave something to all the powers interested in the Balkans, ensuring that all aspirations were balanced against each other. The Ottoman Empire was shaved at the edges, but otherwise left intact through the restoration of Macedonia. This kept Turkey as a bulwark, thus meeting a traditional objective of British foreign policy. Russia was pacified for the trisection of 'Big Bulgaria' by being allowed to retain Bessarabia. Austria was satisfied by the option of occupying at a time of her own choosing the provinces of Bosnia and Herzegovina. The British territorial gain was the island of Cyprus which ensured a British naval presence in the eastern Mediterranean. Overall, it has been argued, the Treaty of Berlin was 'followed by almost as long a period of peace between the European great powers as the interval separating the Crimean War from the Congress of Vienna. As one of the two principal plenipotentiaries at Berlin Disraeli must share with Bismarck some part of the credit'.[15]

There is, of course, another side. Far from protecting Europe from conflict for the following thirty-six years, the situation in the Balkans contributed to the growing tensions and to the drawing of the battle-lines for the First World War. The Berlin settlement was followed by a steady accumulation of incidents, crises and armed conflicts which gives some credibility to Gladstone's accusation that Disraeli was short-sighted.

In the first place the break-up of Big Bulgaria frustrated Russia's aims to such an extent that the latter did everything possible to undermine Bulgaria in the future;[16] one instance of this was the Bulgarian crisis of 1885, which induced the Bulgarian government to look to Austria and Germany for protection against Russian encroachment. Henceforward Germany had a surrogate within the Balkans which enabled her to spread her influence as far as Turkey itself. It did not take very long, therefore, for a new line of influence to develop diagonally from central into south-eastern Europe. As Ensor maintains, 'Had the San Stefano settlement stood, Germany's ambition could scarcely have developed in this later direction'.[17] A further side-effect of this was that Turkey gradually moved away from a pro-British stance into the ranks of German-dominated satellites. This proved far more serious than any possible Russian threat and meant the reversal of a whole century of British foreign policy.

Second, Russian ambitions were intensified by the future developments in Bulgaria. Fearing the expansionism of Germany and Austria-Hungary, Russia now switched her support to those Balkan states which were suspicious of Bulgaria and the central European powers, namely Serbia, Rumania and Greece. Thus a potentially dangerous great-power rivalry was steadily built up in the very area which Disraeli had supposedly neutralised at Berlin.

Third, the Congress of Berlin created dangerous trouble-spots in the Balkans which reacted with the inter-power rivalries. For example, the return of Macedonia to Turkey provided the cause for the first Balkan War (1912) in which Bulgaria, Serbia and Greece liberated it from Turkey. The second Balkan War (1913), which was concerned with the division of the spoils, resulted in the defeat of Bulgaria by Greece and Serbia. As a result, the two states which lost the Balkan Wars, Turkey and Bulgaria, came ever closer under the influence of Germany and Austria, while Serbia tightened her ties with Russia. Hence the major powers were doubly aligned against each other. On a European scale, the Dual Alliance (Austria-Hungary and Germany) was confronted by the Franco-Russian Alliance, while, in the Balkans, Germany and Austria-Hungary were firmly aligned with Bulgaria and Turkey against Russia and Serbia. All that was missing for a general conflagration was a specific flashpoint.

This was provided by the fourth deficiency of the Berlin settlement, the allocation of Bosnia-Herzegovina to Austria-Hungary. When the annexation was eventually carried out in 1908, Serbia, which also claimed Bosnia, was permanently embittered – to the extent of supporting liberation movements within Bosnia itself. This convinced Austria that Serbia was a major threat. From 1912 onwards, therefore, Austria considered it essential to settle the Serbian question once and for all and was stiffened in her resolution to do so by Germany's promise of unconditional support. The result was a deliberate and calculated over-reaction to the assassination at Sarajevo in June 1914 which eventually plunged Europe into war. This could be seen as the explosion of a charge set in 1878; or to reverse the perspective and use the metaphor of A.J.P. Taylor, the decision on Bosnia-Herzegovina originally taken at Berlin 'contained the seeds of future disaster'.[18]

It is hardly surprising, therefore, that not all historians agree with Blake that Disraeli secured three decades of peace for Europe. An altogether different perspective is provided by L.S. Stavrianos: 'The direct and logical outcome of the Berlin settlement was the Serbian-Bulgarian War of 1885, the Bosnian crisis of 1908, the two Balkan Wars of 1912–1913, and the murder of Archduke Francis Ferdinand in 1914.'[19] In this context, Brasher makes another important point. 'When one considers the dismal history of the Balkans between 1878 and 1914 it is reasonable to think that Gladstone's advocacy of support for Balkan nationalism was not only morally justified but also politically wise.'[20] This is supportable. Although Gladstone had no diplomatic solution to the 1878 crisis and almost certainly would have failed to carry the day in Berlin as Disraeli did, he nevertheless perceived that the underlying danger in the area was not so much the collapse of Ottoman rule as the emergence of frustrated nationalism. Thus Disraeli succeeded brilliantly – but in solving the wrong problem.

COMMENTS ON GLADSTONE'S FOREIGN POLICY

As we have seen, the focus of Gladstone's foreign policy was multilateral diplomacy. He considered that Britain should play a role which transcended self-interest and set an example to the rest of Europe of how to base foreign policy on international law and moral principle. He was less concerned than Disraeli about his public image; indeed, for most of his first ministry he accepted unpopularity as an occupational hazard. In opposition after 1874 he made it one of his priorities to educate public opinion to reject Disraeli's opportunism.

Gladstone's first ministry was dominated by issues which provided little opportunity for him to project a positive image. His response was partly successful. This was especially true of his handling of the potential dangers to Britain posed by the Franco-Prussian War (1870–1). Gladstone had done all that was possible to prevent the outbreak of war in the first place. Britain had tried to reduce the tension by putting diplomatic pressure on Spain to withdraw the Hohenzollern candidature and by advising France not to press the demand for non-renewal in the future. This was unsuccessful, but mainly because of the provocative line pursued by Napoleon III and Bismarck's determination to take advantage of it in the Ems telegram. Gladstone was therefore caught between two leaders who clearly preferred war to any loss of face – and who probably wanted it anyway. When war did break out, Gladstone acted positively to prevent any possibility of British involvement while, at the same time, safeguarding Belgian neutrality – seen by all political parties as an essential British interest – by securing an undertaking from both Prussia and France that it would not be violated.

On the other hand, Gladstone failed completely in his proposal for multilateral action to influence the 1871 peace settlement. He felt particularly strongly about the violation of national self-determination which would occur if Bismarck went ahead with his proposal to transfer the French provinces of Alsace and Lorraine to the newly established state of Germany. But in his attempt to find allies to put pressure on Bismarck to desist, Gladstone found himself isolated. Neither Russia nor Italy expressed any interest, and Gladstone was even opposed by the rest of his cabinet. He was, of course, to be proved right in his view that 'this violent laceration and transfer is to lead us from bad to worse, and to be the beginning of a new series of European complications'.[21] But prescience in this case could not be converted by practical policy into diplomatic foresight.

Gladstone encountered another check in 1871 over Russia's unilateral repudiation of the Black Sea clauses of the Treaty of Paris (1856). He tried in the London conference of 1871 to submit the issue to international discussion and, in the process, to revive the Concert of Europe. But in reality he could do no more than recognise Russia's action. His face-saving device was that nations should not in future renounce unilaterally any clause previously agreed multilaterally without the consent of the other parties. But this was hardly convincing and it was never invoked in the future. There is, however, a positive side to all this. Britain's long-standing antagonism towards Russia was partly diluted. Diplomatic concessions sometimes have a longer-term reward and it could be argued that Disraeli was the one who reaped it. In 1878 Russia proved surprisingly willing to take part in the Congress of Berlin and in large part dismantle the advantages she had already secured in the war with Turkey. She might have been much more reluctant had Gladstone succeeded somehow in forcing the Russian government to change its mind over the Black Sea clauses in 1871.

The third embarrassment Gladstone had to face was the *Alabama* issue. The United States government had consistently claimed compensation for the destruction caused during the American Civil War by this and other ships built in Britain. Palmerston and Russell had ignored this, while Disraeli's government had undertaken to submit the issue to international arbitration. This was honoured by Gladstone, who agreed to abide by the decision made in Geneva that Britain should pay the United States £3.25 million in compensation. This outcome was, of course, criticised in the press and in parliament, and there was much reminiscing about the era of Palmerston.[22] On the other hand, the *Alabama* settlement was useful as a precedent for future diplomacy between Britain and the United States and allowed a number of remaining differences between the two countries to be settled peacefully. This was to be a significant help to Disraeli and Salisbury: in all their concerns about developments in Europe and how Britain should react to them, they could always be confident of the benevolent neutrality of the United States.

Was foreign policy a catalyst in the growing unpopularity of Gladstone's first ministry? It was – to the extent that his methods were consistently unglamorous and well outside the previous Palmerstonian tradition. Each achievement was a carefully manufactured compromise, involving no actual expression of British power or authority; if anything, it might well have given the impression of a concession made from a position of weakness. The fact that none of the problems Gladstone had to face were of his direct making is hardly the point: he did not bear comparison with the lingering memory of Palmerston, flawed and inappropriate though that might be. As long as Gladstone maintained the domestic impetus through active reform, he could more than hold his own over foreign policy; after all, domestic policy had always been seen as Gladstone's particular strength. But when this particular impetus slowed, Gladstone became doubly vulnerable and the perceived deficiencies of his foreign policy were much more likely to be held against him. Foreign policy did not lose the 1874 general election; this was due more to the coalition of interests built up as a result of domestic policies. Nevertheless, it did prevent the Liberals from launching a convincing response to the Conservative argument that the Liberals were bankrupt at home *and* abroad.

Gladstone gave up the leadership of the Liberal party for a while after losing power in 1874. This enabled him to articulate more forcefully his views on foreign policy but, at the same time, distanced him from the realities of power and responsibility. This was particularly apparent over the Eastern Question, which absorbed much of Gladstone's attention between 1875 and 1880.

The inter-party consensus about the Ottoman Empire which had existed during the 1850s and early 1860s now disappeared. While Disraeli allowed the traditional fear of Russian expansionism to steer him towards a policy of supporting Turkey irrespective of the latter's activities, Gladstone approached the problem from an entirely different perspective. He had two considerations. One was a thorough antipathy to the Ottoman Empire, the other a sympathy for the national aspirations of the Balkan peoples.

While the two were closely related, the first was expressed more forcefully. Gladstone's conception of Turkey was blatantly one-sided. He described her culture as 'inferior' and her government as 'a bottomless pit of iniquity and fraud'.[23] The full measure of his hatred became apparent in his pamphlet on *The Bulgarian Horrors and the Question of the East*. In this Gladstone argued that Turkey had defiled the diplomatic and military support previously given to her: 'The successes of the Crimean War, purchased . . . by a vast expenditure of French and English life and treasure, gave to Turkey for the first time perhaps in her blood-stained history, twenty years of a repose'.[24] The only solution to the Balkans crisis was the end of Ottoman misrule. 'Let the Turks now carry away their abuses in the only possible way, namely by carrying off themselves . . . One and all, bag and baggage, shall, I hope, clear out from the province they have desolated and profaned.'[25] He also launched an attack on Disraeli's apparent attachment to Turkey, criticising the Treaty of

Berlin in his 'Midlothian campaigns' and reiterating his commitment to non-intervention, international law and national self-determination.

Was Gladstone right in his approach to the Eastern Question? The traditional view, expressed by his first biographer, Morley, stresses the moral and principled elements of Gladstone's policies. Ensor considered that Gladstone had an extra component – that of sound diplomatic sense: that the creation of independent states in the Balkans would have exerted more effective constraint on an expansionist Russia than did a declining Turkey. The deficiencies of the Treaty of Berlin, already analysed, provided plenty of evidence for the inadequacies of Disraeli's pro-Turkish and anti-Russian approach; in satisfying these, the Berlin settlement stored up a host of problems for the future. These fully justified Gladstone's reservations.

There is, however, another possible argument. Disraeli was right to believe that an enlarged Bulgaria might become a Russian satellite. Abbott believes that the eventual creation of Russian satellites in the Balkans by 1946 'would seem to indicate that Disraeli was perhaps correct in his distrust of the ability of the Balkan states to thwart the ambitions of Russia on their own'.[26] The Gladstonian emphasis on satisfied nationalism as a solution to the Balkans problem may therefore have been overstated. There is even doubt as to whether, in any case, Gladstone fully believed in national self-determination. Sandiford argues that Gladstone's dislike of the Ottoman regime did not lead inevitably to his unqualified support for Balkan nationalism. His preference was for a substantial measure of reform which would render the dissolution of the Empire unnecessary. On the other hand, he frankly doubted whether the Turks were capable of delivering such reforms, in which case he was quite willing to see the introduction of nation-states within former Turkish territories. He was not, however, in favour of an enlarged Bulgaria and hence opposed the Treaty of San Stefano.

All this suggests that, while he was able to see the weaknesses of Disraeli's measures, he had no real solutions of his own. For this reason, Gladstone's overseas policies became increasingly pragmatic, even tortuous, after his return to power in 1880. This, however, was expressed primarily in imperial developments; Gladstone had virtually no further involvement in Europe.

BRITAIN'S POSITION IN 1885

Britain's position in 1885 was very different from that in 1860. Queen Victoria said to Gladstone 'Look at our relations abroad! No one trusts or relies on us'.[27] There was some truth in this. Russia was still a threat in the eastern Mediterranean, the Balkans, the Middle East and central Asia; France was antagonistic over North Africa and South-East Asia; and Germany had gained a firm foothold in Africa and, more seriously, ascendancy in south-eastern Europe and the Ottoman Empire. The theme of Chapter 19 will be how governments from 1885 onwards tried to deal with this problem and redress the balance.

15

BRITISH IMPERIALISM AND THE SCRAMBLE FOR AFRICA

During the eighteenth century Britain had been involved in a series of conflicts which had had both a European and a colonial dimension. The result had been the conquest of India and Canada. Other significant gains, such as the Cape of Good Hope, had been made during the Napoleonic War. Although there were further acquisitions over the next fifty years or so, these were much more limited in size; examples were Singapore, annexed in 1824, Aden (1839), New Zealand (1840), Hong Kong (1842), Natal (1843), Rangoon (1854), Oudh (1856) and Lagos (1861).

By the middle of the nineteenth century several factors had combined to limit the scope of colonial expansion. One was the growth of trade with all parts of the world, which had been far less closely connected with conquest than a hundred years earlier. There was no need to extend into the interior the coastal enclaves in Africa and Asia, threats to which could normally be dealt with by 'informal influence'. Anything more than this was seen by the British government as a major and unnecessary expense. Indeed, a parliamentary Select Committee advised in 1865 that no further colonies should be acquired by Britain in West Africa. For a while longer this became standard official policy and accorded with another trend. Ever since the Durham Report of 1839, the British government had encouraged internal self-government in the colonies, including New Zealand, New South Wales, South Australia, Tasmania and Queensland. The process was taken a stage further in 1867 by the establishment of the Dominion of Canada, while Gladstone aimed initially at conferring similar status on other colonies.

Yet, far from presiding over any contraction of the British Empire, all prime ministers from 1868 onwards contributed to a

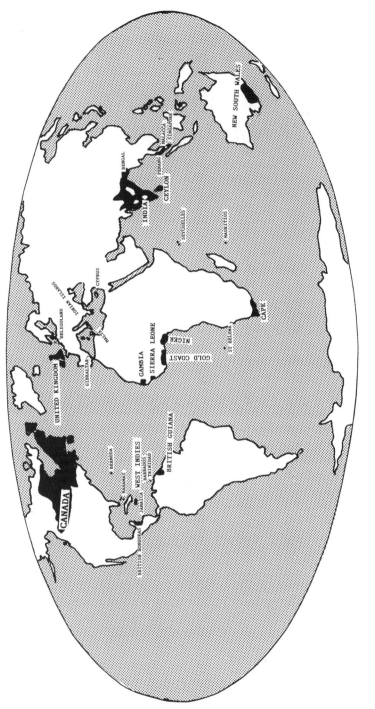

Figure 6 The British Empire in 1820

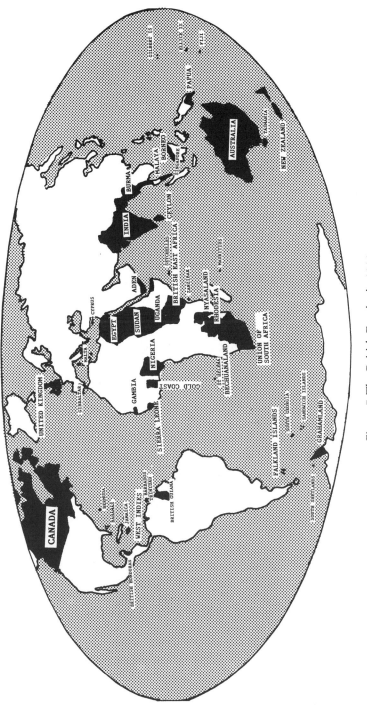

Figure 7 The British Empire in 1914

rapid acceleration in its further growth. Between 1875 and 1914 an extra 4 million square miles and 90 million people came under direct British sovereignty. In the Pacific, Britain annexed Fiji, part of New Guinea, North Borneo, Sarawak and the Cook Islands. In Asia, she took over Burma and sought actively to exclude Russian influence from Afghanistan and Persia. In Africa, colonisation by European powers was so rapid that it was described as a 'Scramble', Britain's share of the spoils being Egypt, Sudan, part of Somaliland, Bechuanaland, Zululand, Northern and Southern Rhodesia, Nyasaland, Uganda, Ashanti and Nigeria. In the process, Britain became involved in two major wars with the Boers, and military campaigns or expeditions in Zululand, East, West and Central Africa, Afghanistan and Tibet.

This chapter will examine the general reasons given for this remarkable change and then compare the specific policies and achievements of individual statesmen and their parties. Finally, it will suggest ways in which Britain's imperial policy affected her foreign policy in the period before 1914.

INTERPRETATIONS OF BRITISH IMPERIALISM

Britain's involvement in the Scramble for Africa has been the subject of a variety of interpretations. Their emphasis is – respectively – economic, diplomatic, strategic and susceptibility to pressure groups.

The best-known economic case was advanced by the Liberal writer J.A. Hobson whose *Imperialism: A Study* was published in 1902. He argued that industrialisation in Britain had generated enormous amounts of 'surplus capital' which could not 'find investments within the country', and therefore sought outlets overseas. Consequently, Britain and other industrial powers had to 'place larger and larger portions of their economic resources outside the area of their present political domain, and then stimulate a policy of political expansion so as to take in the new areas'.[1] This thesis does not, however, fit the facts: most British investment went to Canada, the United States and Latin America and not to pre-colonial Africa. Hence the accumulation of surplus capital cannot be regarded as the primary stimulus to imperial expansion.

On the other hand, it would be simplistic to argue that economic factors had no influence at all on British imperialism. The exploitation of raw materials was very much a factor, corresponding as it

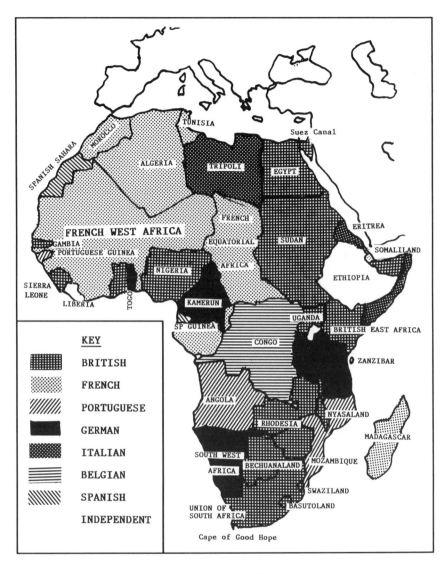

Figure 8 After the Scramble for Africa

did with a new phase in Britain's requirements. The more traditional materials like cotton, essential to the earlier stages of the
Industrial Revolution, had developed relatively stable sources of
supply. But the later Industrial Revolution created demands for new
resources: vegetable oils for industrial lubricants and for soap;
rubber for tyres and electrical insulation; and ivory for piano keys
and billiard balls. There was also a rapid increase in demand for
cocoa by confectionery giants such as Cadbury and Rowntree. All
of these items were found in abundance in West Africa, an area
which had a long-standing commercial connection with Merseyside.
Recognition of the value of such resources undoubtedly caused the
British government to take seriously the threats of expansion in
West Africa by France in the early 1880s and by Germany later
in the same decade. According, therefore, to J. Forbes Munro, 'The
protection and promotion of existing mercantile interests, and to a
lesser extent, the manufacturing interests, figured prominently in
the making of Britain's colonial empire in West Africa'.[2] M.E.
Chamberlain agrees, adding that West Africa was the region in
which the Scramble began, even if Britain's participation was
'largely defensive'.[3]

An entirely different explanation of imperial expansion is
provided by W.L. Langer[4] and A.J.P. Taylor,[5] who use diplomatic
rather than economic terms. This is an approach endorsed by
D.K. Fieldhouse, who believes that 'imperialism may be seen as the
extension into the periphery of the political struggle in Europe'.[6]
D. Thomson uses a similar analogy: 'The naked power politics of
the new colonialism were the projection, on to an overseas screen,
of the inter-state frictions and rivalries of Europe'.[7] According to
A.J.P. Taylor, the projectionist was the German Chancellor,
Bismarck, who was so concerned that France might try to build an
alliance against Germany that he sought to bring the Third Republic
under the influence of the Second Reich. This meant distancing both
from Britain. Hence 'Bismarck quarrelled with England in order to
draw closer to France.' The method of quarrel was 'the deliberately
provocative claim to ownerless lands, in which the German government had hitherto shown no interest'.[8] French and German expansion, in turn, provoked Britain into her own bout of colonisation in
West, East and Southern Africa.

This interpretation has been criticised for exaggerating the role of
a single individual; J.M. MacKenzie, for example, believes that it
'smacks too much of the influence of "great men" upon history, and

the forces at work in Africa were much too powerful and complex to be controlled or manipulated by single political figures'.[9] It could certainly be argued that the 'diplomatic view' promotes stereotypes: Germany as the schemer, France the accomplice and Britain the dupe. On the other hand, it is possible to see the Scramble as the result of less planned and more spontaneous reactions to diplomacy. Bismarck might well have reacted to events, even if he did not promote them, and British governments probably suspected Bismarck of pursuing a devious course. Imperialism could, therefore, have been a by-product of suspicion and miscalculation; in this sense it would have been partially caused by diplomacy, but not in the way explained by the 'diplomatic' historians.

A third explanation, which relates more explicitly – and convincingly – to Britain's role in northern and southern Africa, is the argument of 'strategic interest'. According to R. Robinson and J. Gallagher, Britain was drawn into Africa through 'the persistent crisis in Egypt' and the threat posed to British interests by the Boer Republics in South Africa. Britain's main concern, the argument goes, was to protect sea routes to India, the most valuable part of the British Empire, through the Suez Canal and round the Cape of Good Hope. Unfortunately, local problems made the northern and southern tips of Africa very unstable. The Egyptian Khedive was threatened, in 1881, by a major revolt led by Arabi Pasha, who aimed at freeing Egypt from all European influence. The British occupation of 1882 was not the end of the matter, for the great Islamic revolt in the Sudan against Anglo-Egyptian rule necessitated military action by Kitchener, culminating in the Battle of Omdurman in 1898. British rule was dragged further up the Nile and into East Africa by the need to outflank the Islamic threat and to counter the moves of France and Germany. 'From start to finish the partition of tropical Africa was driven by the persistent crisis in Egypt. When the British entered Egypt on their own, the Scramble began.'[10]

Meanwhile, the Boer Republics of the Transvaal and the Orange Free State were threatening the long-term British scheme for a loose federation of South African states which would also incorporate the Cape and Natal. The alternative could well be a United States of South Africa, dominated by a republican Transvaal and bitterly hostile to any British influence. Again, therefore, the British government was receptive to pressure to acquire territory as a means of outflanking or isolating the challenge, in this case promoting the colonisation of Bechuanaland on the western border of the Transvaal, and the Rhodesias to the north. The overall result of the two separate processes of expansion was a stretch of territory from the Cape to the Mediterranean broken only by German East Africa.

In some respects, imperialism was encouraged by popular pressure from within Britain. This was exerted by commercial lobbies and groups based in Lancashire and West Yorkshire. Intense interest was also expressed by missionaries, newspaper editors and journalists, learned societies and, above all, the Royal Colonial Institute. Prominent politicians like Joseph Chamberlain even articulated a philosophy of imperialism, while in 1907 Lord Curzon declared that 'Imperialism is animated by the supreme idea', which worked two ways. 'To the people of the mother state it must be a discipline, an inspiration and a faith', while to the people in the colonies it must give 'the sense of partnership in a great idea, the consecrating influence of a lofty purpose'.[11] Such extravagant phrases may not have been universally accepted but they did confirm that much of the residual resistance to territorial expansion had been swept away in a general acceptance of imperialism as a positive force, even as a moral obligation.

At the same time, British imperialism was also dragged into Africa by two forces on the spot. One was the local 'commercial factor' which, under the leadership of men like Rhodes, McKinnon and Goldie, assumed an increasingly political guise. Rhodes, who had made his fortunes from the diamond mines at Kimberley and the gold reef at Johannesburg, turned his attention to territorial expansion north of the Limpopo, his ultimate intention being to build a rail-route from Cape Town to Cairo. The British government, by granting a Royal Charter to Rhodes's British South Africa Company in 1889, directly sanctioned his activities in Matabeland and Mashonaland as a relatively inexpensive means of outflanking the Boers, although it was taken by surprise by the further extension of British interest beyond the Zambezi. Similarly, McKinnon's British East Africa Company, which was given a Charter in 1888 to safeguard British interests against German threats, eventually pulled the British Crown into unexpectedly large areas of Kenya and Uganda. In West Africa the substantial British enclave of Nigeria was the direct result of the energy and ambition of another empire builder, George Goldie, operating through the Royal Niger Company.

The second local force could be described as the 'indigenous factor', or the resistance of kingdoms or tribal groups and cultures to British influence. Islamic leaders in the Sudan, for example, sought through the *jihad*, or holy war, to purge themselves of the infidel; instead they laid themselves open to further invasion. Numerous Negro and Bantu states and confederacies also resisted the British, examples being the Ashanti in West Africa, Buganda in East Africa, and the Zulus and Matabele in southern Africa.

None of these influences would have counted for very much without advances in medicine and technology which made rapid and large-scale penetration into the African interior possible. The introduction of quinine, for example, greatly reduced the death rate of Europeans from malaria in West Africa, while improvements in engineering facilitated railway links in southern and East Africa and steamer services on the great lakes of the Rift Valley and the Niger, Congo, Shire and Zambezi rivers. There was also a revolution in weapon technology as the use of maxim and gatling guns made possible the conquest of complete tribes by a handful of British adventurers backed up by volunteer forces. This explains the apparent ease with which Rhodes's British South Africa Police was able in 1893 to overwhelm the Matabele at Shangani and Bembesi and thereby overthrow the military state of Lobengula. This was in contrast to the defeat at Isandhlwana of a much larger force of regular British troops armed with rifles – but not with machine guns – by the Zulus under Cetewayo. The eventual disparity in weapon technology between conquerors and conquered reduced the apparent risks of imperialism and made repetitions of Isandhlwana less and less likely. It also convinced successive British governments that corners could now be cut on costs – always a vital consideration.

DISRAELI'S IMPERIAL POLICIES

Turning now to more specific issues on British imperialism, what were the attitudes of the political parties and statesmen? And with what success were specific policies implemented?

During the 1870s and early 1880s a major change appears to have taken place in the attitude of most Conservatives to empire. In preceding decades they had often opposed Palmerston's assertive foreign policy and had at times been accused of being 'Little Englanders'. In 1852, furthermore, Disraeli had referred to Britain's 'wretched colonies' as 'a millstone round our necks'.[12] After becoming the Conservative leader, however, Disraeli made a series of more positive public statements. At the time of the Franco-Prussian War he maintained that 'England is no longer a mere European Power; she is the metropolis of a great maritime empire, extending to the boundaries of the farthest ocean',[13] while in 1872 he affirmed that Conservative policy was 'to maintain the institutions of the country, to uphold the Empire of England, and to elevate the condition of the people'.[14]

There is a division of opinion about whether these statements did actually show a transformation. Some historians maintain that there was no underlying inconsistency here. S.R. Stembridge argues that Disraeli was referring, in his 1852 speech, to specific colonies like Nova Scotia and New Brunswick and that he had always shown underlying support for imperialism.[15] There is therefore nothing fundamentally new about Disraeli's statements. The alternative view is that Disraeli did change his line and, in the process, reorientated the ideology of the Conservative party.[16] To a large extent Disraeli was motivated by opportunism. Blake points to imperialism as 'probably a bigger electoral asset in winning working-class support during the last quarter of the century than anything else', while Gann and Duignan emphasise its importance in consolidating party loyalty within Conservative associations, clubs and officers' messes.[17] Whether or not Disraeli was actually convinced by his own rhetoric on empire is also debatable. It could be argued that he was among the first to give imperialism a positive image as a civilising mission. On the other hand, Bentley is more doubtful, maintaining that Disraeli lacked a conscious and systematic policy on imperialism during the period 1874–80; instead, he 'bounced from one expedient to another in response to events'.[18]

If this was indeed his approach, it produced some remarkable successes. The most notable of these was his purchase of the Suez Canal shares from the bankrupt khedive in 1875, which has been described as 'a personal *coup* on Disraeli's part, conducted with skill and resolution'. The Prime Minister presented the result to the Queen with characteristic aplomb: 'It is just settled; you have it, Madam. The French Government has been out-generalled.'[19] The purchase was of considerable importance for the future. It was not so much that Britain secured a majority of the shares as that France was denied outright control after a decade of close involvement which had started with the actual construction of the project by a French consortium. The purchase greatly increased Britain's use of the Canal and eventually cut by 75 per cent the cost of shipping goods to and from Australia and New Zealand. Disraeli also benefited from his decision in 1876 to secure for the Queen the additional title 'Empress of India'. This was not an original scheme, since it had been on the cards ever since the Indian Mutiny of 1857–8. But it showed that Disraeli had an understanding of the way in which imperialism might be used to boost Britain's image abroad. He was elevating the British monarchy to the level of the three European emperors and, in the process, emphasising that Britain was a world and not a continental power.

Disraeli's ministries were marred, however, by two disasters, for which he must accept at least part of the blame. He failed, for example, to control Frere's deliberate policy of expansionism in southern Africa and was too diverted by playing the role of statesman over the Balkans to see the crisis building up in Zululand. The result was Isandhlwana, the worst humiliation ever suffered by a British army in Africa. It is true that this was reversed at Ulundi. But even this was mishandled. Anxious to restore British prestige, Disraeli insisted on the elimination of Zulu military power, the effect of which was to make the Boers in the Transvaal less dependent on British protection and therefore more assertive in their demands for independence. In destroying a lesser threat, therefore, Disraeli released a greater one, which resulted in the first Boer War of 1880–1. He also made miscalculations over Afghanistan: his handling of the 1878 crisis has been described as 'inept and ill-judged in the extreme'.[20] He failed to control the excesses of Lord Lytton (his own appointment as Viceroy) and allowed himself to be talked into a major and unsuccessful military intervention. Disraeli's record here, and elsewhere, was strongly attacked by Gladstone, who referred to 'false phantoms of glory' and to 'mischievous and ruinous misdeeds'.[21]

GLADSTONE'S IMPERIAL POLICIES

Whereas Disraeli gradually and willingly accepted a more openly imperial role for Britain, Gladstone's attitude seems more paradoxical.

There was certainly no personal conversion to imperialism. Gladstone had a long record of hostility to expansion. In 1872 he considered that Britain's Empire was 'satiated',[22] adding in an article entitled *England's Mission* (1878) that the government's prime obligation was to take 'care of her own children within her own shores'.[23] In 1881 he said of recent additions in South Africa that 'Nothing will induce me to submit to these colonial annexations',[24] while, according to his biographer, Magnus, he 'coupled imperialism with militarism and called the compound "jingoism"'.[25]

And yet Gladstone was actually responsible – at an earlier stage than Disraeli – for the further expansion of the British Empire into West Africa (where a military expedition was despatched under Wolseley in 1873), Malaysia and Fiji. Even greater changes took place during his second ministry, with the acquisition of Egypt in 1882. Gladstone, it seems, had been forced to come to terms with a process which he instinctively distrusted. This was partly because he realised the widespread appeal imperialism now had. 'The sentiment of empire may be called innate in every Briton', so much so that it was 'part of our patrimony' and 'interwoven with all our habits of mental action upon public affairs'.[26] He therefore had to accept that his own perception was not that of the broad public. Even so, Gladstone found all further additions distasteful. Although these might sometimes be necessary, 'it ought to be understood that they are, as a rule, new burdens added to the old, and that in augmenting space they diminish power'.[27] It followed that Gladstone entirely lacked Disraeli's new-found enthusiasm for imperialism, emphasising instead the necessity of the moment: he described the situation leading to the occupation of Egypt as 'not one which we made, but one that we found', which meant that 'we never had any option'.[28] Whereas Disraeli may be seen as the willing convert, Gladstone remained a reluctant imperialist.

It is not surprising, therefore, that Gladstone's reputation as a statesman owes very little to any contributions made to the British Empire. L.C.B. Seaman's view is especially critical: 'There is little to be said in favour of Gladstone's handling of foreign and colonial affairs from 1880 to 1885', since he displayed 'almost continuous incompetence, administrative inefficiency and at times almost wilful self-deception.'[29] Historians are particularly quick to point out Gladstone's underlying inconsistencies. He said one thing in opposition, often virulently attacking Disraeli, only to find himself doing something entirely different when he came to power. It could be considered perverse 'to sympathise with nationalism in Ireland and the Transvaal, but to regard it as pernicious in Egypt',[30] or to withdraw from South Africa by the Convention of Pretoria while remaining in full occupation of Egypt.[31] Gladstone can also be charged with sending the wrong message and inviting future trouble. In opposition he had discredited the government's policy by appearing to side with the Boers, while after taking office he had granted independence too willingly and rapidly. This made the Boers feel that they had a legitimate grievance and was undoubtedly an encouragement for them to press further claims in the future.[32] At times, Gladstone also displayed serious indecision. By delaying in sending relief to help Gordon hold Khartoum against the forces of the Mahdi, Gladstone was suddenly confronted by the spectre of a sacked city and a dead hero. No prime minister ever attracted more personal blame for an external disaster.

It is possible, however, to overstate the case against Gladstone. He should also be given credit for the moral courage shown in defending the rights of occupied peoples; certainly the Aborigines Protection Society and the missionary lobbies had more time for Gladstone than for any other statesman of the late nineteenth century. He also had the ability to take swift and decisive action when necessary. His occupation of Egypt can in many ways be considered a bold and successful stroke. It removed the threat of a military *coup* against the Egyptian government, safeguarded Britain's vital interest in the Suez Canal, and restored some of the credibility of his government at a bad time. Conversely, Gladstone knew when to leave well alone. He avoided the sort of involvement in Afghanistan which had been handled so badly by Disraeli, and effectively quietened the situation there over the next two decades. He also had the common sense to see as a gross exaggeration the whole notion of a Russian threat to the Indian sub-continent via some of the most inhospitable terrain on earth.

SALISBURY, ROSEBERY AND CHAMBERLAIN

Disraeli and Gladstone dominated British politics for more than two decades, their attacks on each other preserving the appearance of a partisan approach to imperialism. Under their successors, however, the Conservative and Liberal parties approached a broad consensus.

Lord Salisbury backed away from Disraeli's exuberant justification of imperialism, showing little interest in expansion in Africa for its own sake. According to R.Taylor, 'His aim was not to splash Africa with the red of the British Empire';[33] indeed, there is some evidence that he hoped for a return to the pre-Disraelian emphasis

1906 general election. Chamberlain's legacy was therefore domestic and negative rather than positive and imperial.

THE IMPACT OF IMPERIALISM ON FOREIGN POLICY

Imperialism has been seen as the projection overseas of European power-politics. It can be argued, however, that the reverse also applied – that imperial commitments and rivalries affected relations between the European states and helped shape their *foreign* policies between 1870 and 1914. In the case of Britain, this process involved both a shaping and a reshaping.

British statesmen had always had the problem of upholding interests both in Europe and overseas. One solution, pursued by Canning, Palmerston and Disraeli, had been to promote a balance of power on the Continent with Britain, as a peripheral state, ready to become involved if necessary. The other had been to promote co-operation through the idea of the Concert of Europe, as upheld by Castlereagh and Gladstone. But both of these expedients were rendered impossible by the deep rift with two European states. Gladstone's occupation of Egypt in 1882 alienated the French for two decades and the two countries came close to war over the Fashoda crisis in 1898. Russia, meanwhile, was seen as a constant threat to the Indian sub-continent, adding an imperial dimension to the more traditional fears Britain had of her activities in the Balkans and eastern Mediterranean. Deteriorating relations forced Britain for a while into an uncharacteristic policy of isolation, although her leaders graced this with the description of 'Splendid'.

Shortly after the turn of the century Britain's approach went into reverse. The Anglo-French Entente (1904) and the Anglo-Russian Convention (1907) brought agreement over remaining colonial con-flicts – with France in North and West Africa, and with Russia in Tibet, Afghanistan and Persia. It is often argued that this showed a reordering of priorities by British statesmen, who now saw commit-ments and crises in Europe as of greater importance than those overseas. Imperialism, in other words, had exhausted its influence, restoring to British foreign policy its more traditional concern with Europe. This view is simplistic. An equally valid alternative is that British imperial interests were exerting as much influence as ever on foreign policy; they were now under more intensive pressure than ever before – but not from France or Russia. This time the threat came from Germany which was combining imperial rivalry with an unprecedented challenge to British naval supremacy. This deliberate strategy, known as *Weltpolitik*, was formulated by the German Chancellor, Bulow, and by Admiral Tirpitz, the latter informing the Kaiser that Britain would have to 'concede to Your Majesty such a measure of maritime influence which will make it possible for Your Majesty to conduct a great overseas policy'.[39]

After Britain had decided as a matter of some urgency to settle her disputes with France and Russia, Germany sought to revive them through a calculated, but unsuccessful, use of colonial pressure points. Bulow's attempt at Algeçiras in 1905 to exploit the Moroccan crisis served only to tighten and perpetuate the Anglo-French Entente. The Agadir incident and the second Moroccan crisis (1911) provoked an official warning to Germany in Lloyd George's Mansion House speech, and created an atmosphere in which Anglo-French and Anglo-Russian fleet manoeuvres were considered necessary. Imperial factors continued to interact with British and European diplomacy, inevitably contributing to the international tensions which affected Europe in the build-up to the First World War.

16

CONSERVATIVE
ASCENDANCY 1885–1905

In the three decades before 1830 the Tories had appeared the natural governing party of Britain. Then, after 1830, the balance had shifted in favour of the Whigs, or Liberals, who held power for forty-two years out of the total of fifty-five between 1830 and 1885. During this period the Conservatives had won only two of the thirteen general elections, those of 1841 and 1874.

Between 1885 and 1905, however, the Conservatives re-emerged as the dominant force in British politics. They were in power for seventeen of the twenty years, under Lord Salisbury, who was Prime Minister three times (1885, 1886–92 and 1895–1902) and Balfour, Prime Minister between 1902 and 1905. They also achieved impressive victories in the general elections of 1886, 1895 and 1900, while in 1892 they fell only four seats short of the Liberal total:

	1886	1892	1895	1900
Conservatives	317	268	340	334
Liberal Unionists	77	46	71	68
Liberals	191	272	177	184
Irish Nationalists	85	80	82	82

And yet, in 1906, they suffered their greatest ever electoral defeat to a newly revived and reinvigorated Liberal party, and they had to wait another sixteen years until the formation of the next Conservative government.

This chapter will analyse the political balance between 1885 and 1905 by examining the vulnerabilty of the Liberals during the 1880s and 1890s, together with the advantages of the Conservatives. It will

	1906
Conservatives	133
Liberal Unionists	24
Liberals	400
Irish Nationalists	83
Labour	30

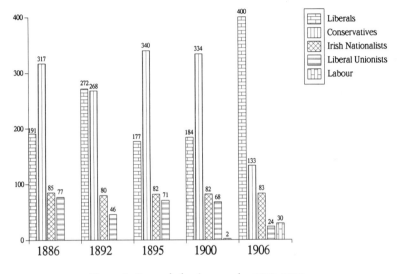

Figure 9 General election results 1886–1906

then reverse the process by explaining the post-1900 decline of the Conservatives and the growing strength of the Liberals.

LIBERAL DECLINE

Conservative political strength was, of course, built partly on Liberal weakness.

This weakness was so apparent that, during the 1890s, there were gloomy – if premature – predictions of Liberalism's early demise. James Stansfeld, for example, believed that the Liberals would soon be 'succeeded by a Party of the Centre'.[1] Rosebery, who succeeded Gladstone as Liberal leader and Prime Minister in 1894, expressed a different fear after the 1895 election, namely the eventual elimination of the moderate left and centre: 'It is always possible that that may happen here which has happened in Belgium – the elimination of Liberalism, leaving the two forces of Socialism and Reaction face to face.'[2]

There were two broad reasons for the upheaval within the Liberal party. One was the serious split over the Home Rule issue, which saw the defection of Joseph Chamberlain and a significant number of Liberal Unionists. The other was a prolonged crisis among the remaining parliamentary Liberals which exacerbated the impact of this division and delayed the party's recovery from it.

Chamberlain's hostility to Home Rule had been fundamental; he had been 'absolutely opposed to such a policy',[3] and felt that it had drawn the party's attention away from urgently needed social reform. In the circumstances he preferred to cut himself off from a party which, he felt, had become obsessed with a single issue and even the concerted efforts applied at the 1887 Round Table Conference failed to win back the defectors. Chamberlain had already come to the conclusion that he might get more out of the other side of the House, and maintained that 'this country could not be better governed than by a Conservative Ministry in an insignificant minority' and 'under the eyes of a watchful Liberal majority'.[4] The damage inflicted on the Liberals came in two instalments. The first was the loss of between sixty and eighty MPs, who set themselves up as a separate political group – the Liberal Unionists – with their own organisation and whips. The second was the decision taken by some of these during the 1890s to join the Conservative ranks, Chamberlain himself serving as Colonial Secretary between 1895 and 1903. It is true that a substantial proportion of Liberal Unionists refrained from going this far, and retained a separate identity from the Conservatives. But those who went the whole way set a trend followed by upper middle-class business men who transferred their contributions from one party to the other.

The remainder of the Liberal party suffered a crisis of identity during the 1890s. At the top was the problem of finding a suitable successor to Gladstone as leader. After a fierce debate within the Liberal party, Rosebery came through as a compromise, although with extensive internal opposition from the left wing who disliked having to look to the Whigs for leadership. After its heavy defeat in the 1895 general election, the Liberal party continued to dissipate its energies in the leadership debate. Harcourt succeeded Rosebery in 1896 but was discredited almost immediately when, through a negative and lacklustre performance, he failed to pin the Conservative government down over the crisis caused by the Jameson Raid. As a result, Rosebery made a brief but undistinguished return. It was not until the emergence of Campbell-Bannerman in 1898 that effective party leadership was restored.

With problems as fundamental as these, it is not surprising that the Liberals were unable to hold on to power in the second half of the 1890s. There is some evidence that they did not even wish to do so. Rosebery felt a sense of relief at Liberal defeat in 1895 since it provided 'a necessary prelude to the resurrection and reconstitution of the party'.[5] This raised a question, however, which proved very difficult to answer. What was to be the future role of the party? There was as much controversy over this as over the leadership. Most agreed with the party mouthpiece, the *Speaker*, that the Liberals should oppose whatever the Conservatives did in order to re-establish in the public mind a clear difference between 'the party of progress and the party of reaction'.[6] Others, like Haldane, preferred a period of consolidation and regrouping, until 'the ground is cleared of the rubbish which covers it'.[7] Rosebery, however, came to the conclusion that the Liberals needed to focus on a single great issue rather than on a programme. The party needed to be 'purged' from within of all remaining Gladstonian influences, including Home Rule and the Newcastle Programme. The problem was that there was no single issue to hand which could reconcile and unite. Rosebery's own preference was for reforming the House of Lords, but there were those in the party who considered that the priority at the turn of the century was the expansion and consolidation of the British Empire. These 'Liberal Imperialists' were opposed, however, by the 'pro-Boers' during the South African conflict and, in any case, the Conservatives were still the true party of empire.

Inept leadership and indecisive policies were complemented by a weakening of the party structure. With the flight of support and capital to the Conservatives, the Liberals faced a crisis of funding. This showed itself most seriously in the number of seats the Liberals allowed the Conservatives to retain unopposed: 114 in 1895 and 138 in 1900. This was not the way to win elections. The party had already lost its previous hold on the middle class. If it was to make a comeback against the Conservatives, it needed to regain this and, at the same time, to achieve substantial support from the enlarged working-class electorate. But much of this was withheld, giving rise to the formation of the Labour party in 1900: this, in the words of Adelman, was 'a fitting comment on the failures of the Liberal party in the age of Rosebery and Harcourt'.[8]

CONSERVATIVE CONSOLIDATION

It was indeed fortunate for the Conservatives that they should have encountered the opposition in such a sorry state. But there were other benefits for which they could claim no direct responsibility.

One of these was the electoral system, which distorted the majorities of winning parties. During the 1880s and 1890s this worked in favour of the Conservatives and against the Liberals. In 1900, for example, the Conservatives and Liberal Unionists between them secured 51 per cent of the popular vote for their combined 402 seats, while the Liberals gained just under 47 per cent for their 184. The reform measures of the 1880s also worked in favour of the Conservatives. It has been estimated, for example, that some 1 million men at any one time were unenfranchised because their changes of jobs or of residence meant that they could not meet the twelve-month residence qualification. It would be safe to assume that most of these would not have voted Conservative. Conversely, those higher up the social scale benefited from the dual vote which meant that they could claim representation through the constituencies in which they lived and worked. Comprising at least 7 per cent of the electorate, these were among the main defectors from the Liberals. In addition, the Conservatives gained considerably from the 1885 Redistribution Act which created single-member constituencies and enabled them to make deep inroads into Liberal-held boroughs. According to J. Belchem, 'Redistribution was a triumph for Salisbury. His hard bargaining not only confirmed his undisputed leadership of the party, but also produced a settlement geared to the suburban geo-politics of middle-class conservatism.'[9]

The Conservative party also underwent a change in the basis of its support – at exactly the right time to maximise its attraction to Liberal defectors. This was due less to any conscious party policy than to a development entirely beyond its control. The agricultural depression of the 1870s and 1880s considerably reduced the traditional Conservative core, opening the party more to influence from the middle classes. The following table[10] shows the resulting changes in the percentages of the three main social and occupational categories of Conservative MPs:

214

	1868	1885	1900
Landed interest	46	23	20
Commerce and industry	31	50	52
Professions	9	16	18

This transformation greatly reassured a significant minority of Liberal voters, party members and MPs that they could safely transfer their allegiance without perpetuating what they had once perceived to be a landed oligarchy.

This analysis should, of course, include the contributions made by the Conservative party itself to its ascendancy between 1885 and 1905. One of the party's greatest assets was Lord Salisbury, described by Blake as the most successful of Conservative leaders,[11] even though it is more difficult to attach to him the sort of memorable image which goes with Peel, Disraeli, Baldwin or Churchill. He was, nevertheless, realistic, pragmatic and fully aware of the importance of sustaining the support of the Liberal Unionists through conceding a measure of reform. He also succeeded in keeping together the various components which made the Conservative party almost as much of a coalition as the Liberals. He was even prepared to reshape the party image, through use of the new label 'Unionist' to ease the conscience of new converts.

The same might be achieved by means of a programme of steady reform. Although not instinctively progressive, Salisbury did see an opportunity to outbid the Liberals and thereby make them unelectable in the future. At first this approach looked as if it might involve a substantial degree of social reform, especially in view of the policy of 'Tory Democracy' announced by Lord Randolph Churchill in his 1886 Dartford Speech. But Churchill was soon forced out of Salisbury's government after a split over his proposed budget, and the reforms actually introduced by the Salisbury government were much less extensive than Churchill had hoped. In any case, Salisbury was not in favour of direct government involvement in social issues, preferring the principle of 'self-help'. Even so, the Conservative governments of the 1880s and 1890s passed more reforming legislation than could be managed by Gladstone's second, third and fourth ministries, or by Gladstone's successor, Rosebery. These measures included the Labourers' Allotment Act (1887), the Mines Regulation Act (1887), the Tithe Act (1890), the

Factory Act (1891), and the Workmen's Compensation Act (1897). The most important of Salisbury's reforms was the Local Government Act of 1888, which did for the counties what the 1835 Municipal Corporations Act had accomplished for the boroughs, establishing sixty-two elected county councils and over sixty county boroughs – overall a major landmark in local government reform.

The Conservatives did not, however, pin all their hopes on one strategy. In addition to a policy of cautious reform designed to consolidate middle-class support, they were able to generate more popular enthusiasm through a more intensive focus on imperialism. This, as we have seen, had the additional advantage of dividing the Liberals. Lord Salisbury confirmed that 'the Conservative Party is the Imperial Party. I must work with it – who indeed am just such an one myself'.[12] As in Germany and France during the same period, imperial issues were a useful means of diverting potential discontent among the working classes into periodic surges of patriotism. These were accomplished especially by the Jubilees of 1887 and 1897, while the popular press reported in detail on Kitchener's campaign in the Sudan (including the Battle of Omdurman in 1898) and whipped up francophobia over the Fashoda Incident in the same year. At the turn of the century the public were caught up in the details of the Boer War and the campaign against the Boxers in China, reacting with wild jubilation to the relief of Mafeking and the march on Peking.

Underpinning the leadership and appeal of the Conservatives was a highly competent party machine, which had a steady source of funding and efficient managers in Middleton and Akers-Douglas. The Conservatives were able to compete aggressively in the Liberal heartlands – the great cities – a crucial development at a time when the electorate was expanding. A typical example was the Conservative campaign in London; here the Conservatives had a total of thirty party agents, the Liberals only three.[13] With such organisational advantages, optimists expected Conservative domination to extend well into the new century.

REVERSAL: THE 1906 'LANDSLIDE'

What actually happened was a spectacular change in the fortunes of both parties. In the 1906 election the Conservatives lost 201 seats to the Liberals, leaving themselves a paltry 133, while the Liberals gained 216 to add to their previous total of 184. A necessary precondition for this metamorphosis was for the Conservatives to have become infected with what they had come to see as the Liberal disease: a loss of popular confidence in their ability to govern, sustained hostility to their measures and obsession with a single issue over which the party divided.

At several stages in the nineteenth and early twentieth century, Britain's domestic politics have been transformed as involvement in a foreign conflict has upset apparent equilibrium. In this case the Boer War (1899–1902) proved the principal catalyst for change. Initial military failures inevitably brought public condemnation of the government of the day, as in the cases of Aberdeen in 1855 and Neville Chamberlain in 1940. But the successful resistance shown by untrained farmers came as a profound psychological shock to a public which had come to believe in the power of the British Empire. It called into question the effectiveness of Britain's military preparedness, administrative support and political leadership. This was not the last time that a major power was humiliated by guerrilla tactics, or that a government with a large majority and successful domestic record was discredited as a result: much the same happened in the United States to the Johnson administration in the 1960s.

The Boer War did have a positive result: it stimulated an unprecedented degree of co-operation between Britain and the dominions of the Empire. But this rebounded against the Conservatives. Joseph Chamberlain, inspired by the prospect of closer imperial integration, launched a campaign for tariff reform. This was based on the principle of imposing duties on foreign imports, while promoting the import of colonial raw materials in exchange for the export of British manufactured goods. This split the Conservative party as fundamentally as Home Rule had split the Liberals. Balfour tried to hold the party together but a number of Conservatives, including Winston Churchill, crossed the floor to join the Liberals. The irony of Chamberlain splitting his adopted party was not lost on the one he had originally abandoned.

By 1902 the Conservatives had begun to develop a more negative image in other ways. Their new leader, Balfour, was much less effective than Salisbury had been. Although endowed with a formidable intellect, he never really rose to the challenge of the combative politics at a time when the Conservatives were under attack, and he lacked Salisbury's sense of opportunism and capacity for survival. The Liberals, it seemed, gained far more from the transition from Rosebery to Campbell-Bannerman than the Conservatives from Salisbury to Balfour.

The Conservatives were also vulnerable to accusations that they had become indifferent to the social needs of the people. Although they had been in power for twenty years, they had not managed to introduce a single major item of social reform, in singular contrast to the achievements of Disraeli's second government between 1874 and 1880. This was more and more alluded to after 1900 as part of a campaign of criticism which included the government's handling of the Taff Vale case in 1901 and the 'Chinese slavery' affair in South Africa. Balfour's response to the latter was complacent and he completely underestimated public concern over the treatment of over 50,000 foreign labourers imported into the Transvaal with his express permission. Even where Balfour made a positive attempt to address a major national issue in his Education Act (1902), he succeeded inadvertently in stirring up the hornets' nest of Nonconformist opinion, which committed itself wholeheartedly to the Liberals for the first time since the late 1860s.

The decline of the Conservatives was paralleled by the revival of the Liberals. Again, the catalyst was the Boer War, which removed the Irish shadow from the party and diverted attention from internal wrangles. By 1902 the Liberal party had become more accommodating and less obsessive about the issues it espoused. The policy of Campbell-Bannerman was to promote the party as a 'Broad Church', in which no policy or faction should be allowed to predominate. According to Hamer, 'the major achievement of Campbell-Bannerman as Liberal leader before 1905 was to bring Liberals to accept that strength and organic unity, rather than disintegration, could result from the co-existence in their party of many different sections and tendencies of opinion'.[14] The Liberals therefore improved their chances of electoral revival by becoming less dogmatic. Lacking a single-issue approach they were able to put together a coalition which in many ways was a revival of the party which had developed immediately after the death of Palmerston. The party also rediscovered its dynamic, launching concerted attacks on Conservative initiatives like the 1902 Education Act and Chamberlain's proposals for tariff reform. The latter helped re-create the more traditional free trade ideology of the party and to focus on a

218

fundamental bread and butter issue which was bound to attract more working-class votes.

Meanwhile, the organisation of the Liberal party was being overhauled by Herbert Gladstone, whose self-imposed task as Chief Whip after 1899 was to achieve greater integration and to promote an image of Liberalism as 'an alternative government' at a time when this was becoming more and more necessary. A major influence on the 'Broad Church' strategy, he helped patch up the old Liberal party and toned down specific commitments; he particularly favoured ambiguity over Home Rule and ensured that this could not be thrown at the Liberals by the Conservatives in any future election campaign. Thus, although Ireland remained on the Liberal agenda, it ceased to obstruct the party's other policies. Gladstone also forestalled the possibility of a strong Labour challenge for the working-class vote by forming a secret agreement with Ramsay MacDonald in 1903. This avoided direct competition by giving Labour a free run in selected constituencies in return for their not placing a candidate against the Liberal in most of the others.

By 1906 the Liberal organisation was in a much higher state of readiness than at any time since 1880 and, in the words of Russell, proceeded to lay 'the charges for the landslide'.[15] It maintained a high level of morale, produced effective campaign songs and organised an unprecented number of party meetings. The best Liberal speakers, like Lloyd George and Churchill, toured other constituencies, a practice which was not carried out in the Conservative party. The Liberals also made more effective use of the motor car for canvassing and polling. And this time the Liberals allowed only five Conservative candidates to remain unopposed, compared with 153 in 1900.

Why did the Liberal recovery turn into a 'landslide'? Again, the British electoral system can claim some of the credit for a massive distortion. The 400 seats won by the Liberals were based on 2.76 million votes (only 49 per cent of the total), while the Conservatives and Liberal Unionists between them won only 157 seats with 2.45 million votes (just under 44 per cent). The distortion was further accentuated because every Liberal vote counted. Whereas it took an average of 15,606 votes to win a Conservative or Liberal Unionist seat, each Liberal win was accomplished with only 6,900. This occurred because of a series of uniquely favourable swings to the Liberals which were highest in Conservative strongholds and lowest in Liberal areas where, of course, they were not needed. The translation of votes into seats therefore accelerated ascendancy or decline and has much to do with the strange reversal of party fortunes between 1885 and 1905.

17

LIBERAL DOMESTIC
POLICIES 1905–14

After a decade in political exile, the Liberals found themselves back
in power in 1905. Following the landslide election victory of 1906,
the governments of Campbell-Bannerman (to 1908) and Asquith
(1908–15) set about a major programme of social reform. This
chapter will consider five questions. What was the nature of
Liberalism during this period, and how did it differ from
Gladstonian Liberalism? What changes did its social reforms
involve for the role of the State? How did the Liberals deal with
political obstacles from the House of Lords? How effectively did
Asquith's government cope with the three threats to stability
between 1911 and 1914: the Suffragettes, Ireland and industrial
unrest? And was there any indication by 1914 that this Liberal
government was to be the last?

EDWARDIAN LIBERALISM

The reforms rested on an ideological base generally known as 'New'
or 'Edwardian' Liberalism. This was a significant departure from
the more traditional 'Gladstonian' Liberalism in that it changed the
emphasis from the individual's 'self-help' to a more explicit recognition of the state's involvement in social issues. Why had this
change occurred?

Gladstonian Liberalism had promoted progressive reform but
with certain limitations. One was the insistence that the individual
was ultimately responsible for his own well-being. Another was
Gladstone's determination to control state expenditure and, if possible, to abolish income tax. These were powerful arguments against
any move to introduce any form of welfare state. Increasingly,
however, the Gladstonian Liberal party had been penetrated

by 'new radicalism', largely under the influence of Joseph Chamberlain. This argued strongly for more direct action by the State to control poverty and soften the impact of unemployment. Although some of the radicals, including Chamberlain himself, left the party over Irish Home Rule, many remained. Their views were merged with more traditional liberalism in the 1891 Newcastle Programme, which proposed the further extension of the franchise and a reform of the House of Lords; a greater degree of local autonomy, including Irish Home Rule; the ending of certain vested interests, especially on the land; and more extensive social reform to improve living conditions. These could all be taken as basic objectives of 'Edwardian Liberalism', which therefore had its roots in the 1890s.

The need for social reform was given a sharper focus, however, by revelations of the extent of poverty in late Victorian Britain. Charles Booth's *Life and Labour of the People of London* (completed in 1902) revealed dreadful conditions and demonstrated that poverty afflicted no less than 30 per cent of the population of London. Seebohm Rowntree added further details in his investigation, *Poverty: A Study of Town Life* (1901), based on a study of York. This included an analysis of the recurring cycle of poverty which affected a labourer in childhood, 'when his constitution is being built up', in early middle age, 'when he should be in his prime', and in old age.[1] Between them these works helped undermine the traditional view that poverty and unemployment were self-inflicted problems and, furthermore, identified the specific points at which individuals and families needed assistance. Thus was born the notion of *continuing* help – from childhood to old age, from cradle to grave.

To some this smacked of socialism, a framework which had been abhorred by Gladstone. But this was an oversimplification. Rather, it was an expression of 'social radicalism', since Edwardian Liberalism managed to combine the traditional emphasis on individualism with a new awareness of the organic society. This was shown, for example, in the writing of the Liberal intellectual, J.A. Hobson, according to whom new Liberalism

> aims primarily not to abolish the competitive system, to socialise all instruments of production, distribution, and exchange, and to convert all workers into public employees – but rather to supply all workers at cost price with all the

economic conditions requisite to the education and employment of their personal powers for their personal advantage and enjoyment.[2]

Lloyd George took this further in 1910. He argued that Liberalism 'has not abandoned the traditional ambition of the Liberal Party to establish freedom . . . but side by side with this effort it promotes measures for ameliorating the conditions of life for the multitude'.[3]

The role of the State had, therefore, to be modified. Liberalism now added a new dimension to liberty. Whereas Gladstone had focused on 'freedom to' and 'freedom of', the Edwardian Liberals added 'freedom from', which required more active government intervention in two areas. One was the economy. The traditional *laissez-faire* economic principles espoused by Gladstone now had to be changed. According to the Liberal theorist, Hobhouse,

> It is for the State to take care that the economic conditions are such that the normal man who is not defective in mind or body or will can by useful labour feed, house, and clothe himself and his family. The 'right to work' and the right to a 'living wage' are just as valid as the rights of person or property.[4]

Lloyd George considered that the State also had a fundamental duty to intervene directly, through a legislative programme and a redistribution of wealth by progressive taxation, to improve social conditions. This he saw as the *raison d'être* for any government, and he confidently predicted that 'there will soon be no civilized land in the world where proper provision for the aged, the broken, and the unfortunate amongst those who toil will not be regarded as the first charge upon the wealth of the land'.[5]

All this appears thoroughly idealistic. To an extent it was. The Liberal party had always been an alliance of principles and causes, ranging from Christian morality to temperance, from individual liberty to national self-determination. It should be no surprise, therefore, that the party should also have come to accept a social role for the State. At the same time, there was also a pragmatic reason for the evolution from 'Gladstonian' into 'Edwardian' Liberalism. The party clearly needed a revived image if it was to recover from its nadir of the 1890s and compete more aggressively with the Conservatives in the future. This meant appealing more directly to the enlarged working-class vote which had somehow eluded the Liberals since the 1884 Reform Act. Liberalism also had to try to prevent Labour from overtaking it on its left. Practical considerations therefore suggested a realignment of policies.

In addition, the party leadership had to find a national issue which would unite most of the sectional interests *within* the party. This could not be an external principle since the last of these to be tried had done devastating damage; Irish Home Rule was therefore downgraded as a priority. Instead, the idea of progressive and all-encompassing reform would have universal appeal and would offer something to all groups, thereby keeping them together and preventing further migration to the Conservative party. The one danger here was the possible alienation of the remaining Whigs, but these were now too few in number to be especially significant. In the meantime, greater internal cohesion would be accompanied by renewed offensive against the bastions of privilege to which Conservatism could retreat whenever it needed to regroup. One of the Liberal campaigns was therefore against the landed gentry, the traditional opponent of the Liberal party; another was to reform the licensing laws and thereby undermine a primary base of Conservative support – the brewing interest. Above all, there was an air of anticipation of a possible confrontation with Conservatism at the point where it was most entrenched: in the House of Lords.

It has been argued that the pragmatic motive for Liberal policy included an attempt to re-establish the party's middle-class base. This may seem surprising, given that much of the middle-class vote had already defected to the Conservatives from the time of the 1874 general election and the Liberals had tried to offset this by enlarging the working-class electorate. Yet the Liberal landslide of 1906 had eaten deeply into Conservative-dominated areas, and many middle-class voters had been reassured by Liberal opposition to any form of tariffs on foreign imports. Having won the confidence of the middle class, it is suggested, the Liberals aimed to retain it by introducing measures which hit the wealthy and the privileged, not the middle layers of society. Thus the party would prevent large-scale working-class defections to Labour through carefully calculated reforms while, at the same time, re-establishing its own middle-class base by ensuring that these reforms did not affect the productive or service sectors.

This is overprescriptive, however, and leans too heavily on a Marxist framework. An alternative viewpoint, which reduces the importance of 'class' as a factor in Edwardian Liberalism, is suggested by Bernstein: 'the Edwardian Liberal Party did not and could not direct its appeal along such class lines. The Liberals had always argued against class-based politics, having long accused the Conservatives of indulging in this. Instead, they focused on the "larger community interest".[6] The Liberals were suspicious of 'class' causes and preferred to mobilise on the basis of traditional and proven Liberal causes such as temperance, education and the House of Lords. All their strategies were *against* class-based appeal because their measures might have been interpreted by one class as being primarily in the interests of another. Instead, they aimed to *transcend* class interest. Hence they were able to hold off the Labour challenge before 1914 largely because they projected an image of reform which was not based on the middle class alone but embraced the interest of the working man. At the same time, the more progressive elements of the middle class were reassured by Asquith's determination not to have anything to do with socialism and by the restrictions placed on the electoral pact with Labour (see Chapter 18). As Sutton argues, what the Liberals actually set out to do was to 'mobilize "middle opinion" as a countervailing force to the "extremes" represented by class politics'.[7]

THE LEVELS OF STATE ACTION

To what extent was the theory of extended State intervention put into practice? The Liberals implemented different solutions for different problems, with the result that their changes lack the impression of an overall blueprint or master-plan. The State was called into action at five levels, each with an emphasis which differed from the others.

The *first* level involved the traditional device of State-imposed regulations, with the government setting or revising rules of conduct. There was nothing new in this method, which had been used throughout the nineteenth century, and the focus was very much on the continuation, or consolidation, of earlier legislation. Several measures, for example, were designed to benefit the workforce without introducing revolutionary new State powers. The 1906 Trades Disputes Act, for instance, stipulated that no cases could be brought against unions for damage done by strikes, thus reversing the Taff Vale judgement of 1901 and restoring the former powers of trade unions. The 1906 Workmen's Compensation Act was essentially an extension of a measure passed in 1897, obliging employers to pay compensation to employees injured at work. The 1909 Trade

Boards Act set up boards of government officials to supervise pay and conditions in sweated industries, while the 1911 Shops Act made it compulsory for employers to provide a half-day holiday each week; both of these were within the long tradition of factory legislation. Similarly, although there was a more general acceptance by the community of its responsibility for the welfare of children, the 1908 Children's Act was, nevertheless, primarily regulatory and involved no new government initiatives. It was confined to preventing the sale of alcohol and tobacco to children, to ending imprisonment for child offenders and to the introduction of juvenile courts.

The *second* level was the involvement of the State in providing services for the population. Underlying this were principles which were both traditional and new. The traditional approach, widely used by Gladstone and Disraeli, was the government empowering local authorities to introduce measures at their own expense. This was the basis of the 1906 School Meals Act, which allowed local education authorities to provide a free school meals service for children of the poor. This was initially a very cautious measure, involving the local levy of a special half-penny rate, although in 1914 the government undertook half the cost. There are two examples, however, of the government's provision of services after 1906 involving a new departure. One was the 1907 schools medical inspection service, which was centrally organised from a new medical department within the Board of Education and involved the regular visit to schools by doctors and nurses. The other was the 1909 Labour Exchanges Act, which was a nationally based and regionally operated scheme for providing information about vacancies to the unemployed. Thus, for the first time the State was accepting a new responsibility as an advisory service.

The *third* level was more complex. It introduced the principle of State intervention to improve the quality of people's lives while, at the same time, insisting that the people themselves were ultimately responsible. This was, therefore, a combination of State-assistance and self-help. The practical means of maintaining such a balance was 'social insurance', or a contributory benefit scheme of the type which already existed in Germany. The Liberals introduced 'social insurance' in the 1911 National Insurance Act, perhaps the most important, and certainly the most complex, of all their measures, involving an enormous amount of effort and planning by politicians, civil servants and advisers. The Act was eventually divided into two parts. The first, largely inspired by Lloyd George, introduced National Health Insurance; the second, organised by Churchill, added Unemployment Insurance.

Health cover was secured by payment of 4d per week into an Insurance Fund; to this the employer added 3d and the State 2d. In return, the worker was entitled to medical treatment, paid out of the Fund and, if absent through illness, to 10 shillings per week for up to fifty weeks; this would be followed by a disability pension of 5 shillings per week. These measures removed the shadow of impoverishment from many working families and ensured access to medical facilities for the first time. There was, of course, opposition. The Conservative party succeeded in whipping up discontent against the principle of compulsory contribution, while defects in Lloyd George's consultation before pushing the measure through parliament led to a 'doctors' revolt'. More seriously, the clauses concerning health were very much a scheme to deal with sickness once it had occurred rather than to try to prevent it. This, of course, was influenced by the whole principle of insurance: it only works financially when the majority of contributors make no claim on it. Hence modifications were necessary in the future, and the introduction of the National Health Service in 1946 saw a reduction in the emphasis on insurance.

Unemployment insurance worked on the same principle as health insurance. An Unemployment Fund was built up from the contributions of workers and employers, both of whom paid 2½d per week, the State adding 2d. In the event of unemployment, the benefit was 7 shillings per week for a total of fifteen weeks. Churchill justified the terms in ringing phrases: 'By sacrifices which are inconceivably small families can be secured against catastrophes which otherwise would smash them up for ever'.[8] There was, indeed, much that was positive. The taint of 'begging for charity' was removed altogether, to be replaced by an entitlement which had been earned. This had an important influence on future policy, the Blanesborough Committee stating in 1927 that 'an unemployment insurance scheme must now be regarded as a permanent feature of our code of social legislation'.[9] On the other hand, there were serious defects. Unemployment insurance did not cover all industries, and excluded wives and families from its scope. The benefits were also very low, on the assumption that they offered only a safety net. Future changes were therefore needed, including its extension to all industrial workers in 1920 and to domestic and agricultural workers in 1937.

The *fourth* level was the involvement of the State to introduce services which were not based on contributory schemes and which therefore dispensed altogether with the notion of 'self-help'. This was really the most radical of all the Liberal approaches and had no connection whatever with past procedures. It was restricted, however, to one area only – old age pensions – and was not repeated in the 1911 measures covering health and unemployment. Joseph Chamberlain had for some time argued for the introduction of a contributory pension scheme but the Liberal government preferred the even older advice of Charles Booth that pensions should be financed from general taxation. The reason for this decision was that contributory schemes would obviously take time to work, whereas the government was in a hurry to carry a reform for which there was a great demand. Lloyd George, for one, was willing to take this short cut because 'it is time we did something that appealed straight to the people'.[10] Hence the 1909 Old Age Pensions Act gave people over 70 an entitlement to 5 shillings per week provided that they had less than £21 per annum available from other sources. No contributions were sought for this.

The benefits were considerable, and the Conservative opposition were wrong in describing the Act as 'thinly disguised outdoor relief'. In fact the measures it introduced were designed to end the stigma attached to seeking relief and, above all, to remove the shadow of the workhouse from the elderly. Individual pride, always a very powerful emotion, was also salvaged now that pensions were presented as an entitlement, not as a form of charity. It is not surprising, therefore, that the Act was immensely popular. Richard Roberts describes the reactions of his mother, a shopkeeper in Salford: 'Old folk, my mother said, spending their allowance at the shop, "would bless the name of Lloyd George as if he were a saint from heaven".'[11]

As in the case of all the Liberal measures, there were shortcomings to the pension scheme. The terms were not generous but then, according to Churchill, 'We have not pretended to carry the toiler on to dry land; what we have done is to strap a lifebelt around him'.[12] There was a mean element in the withdrawal of proposals for a pension of 7s 6d for married couples, and Labour MPs like Philip Snowden had a point when they argued that the pensionable age was so high that few would actually reach it. Extensive changes were needed in the future, starting with the overhaul in 1925, before the modern combination of State and contributory pensions was reached.

The *fifth* level affected all the others and went well beyond what any previous government – Liberal or Conservative – would have considered acceptable. The Edwardian Liberals redefined the scope of the State's use of the Budget, giving this traditional financial tool a more explicitly social edge. The main reason for this was to pay for reforms which, like old age pensions, had already been introduced, and those, like national insurance, which were projected for the future. Lloyd George was confronted by the need to find £16 million to finance government reforms and, at the same time, to maintain the programme of Dreadnought construction. At the end of his 1909 Budget speech in the House of Commons, he declared: 'This is a War Budget. It is for raising money to wage implacable warfare against poverty and squalidness.'[13] At the same time, the Chancellor raised the necessary sums by the introduction of a second principle: the redistribution of wealth through graduated taxation. Hence income tax was increased to 1s 2d in the pound on incomes over £3,000; supertax was levied at 6d in the pound on incomes over £5,000; and unearned increments on land values were taxed at 20 per cent on resale. The increases in direct taxation were comparatively mild by later standards, but represented a permanent departure from the attempts made by Gladstonian Liberals to abolish direct taxation altogether. Graduated income tax was soon to be accepted by all parties, although fine-tuned according to party policy.

THE CONFLICT WITH THE HOUSE OF LORDS

Given their scope, it is hardly surprising that the Liberal government's social changes should have faced a major constitutional obstacle. The government had to remove this if its programme was to go ahead. The result may be considered a major achievement in its own right.

A conflict had always been on the cards. The Lords were dominated by a Conservative interest which would tolerate a Liberal government only so long as its policies were not substantially out of line with those the Conservatives might have introduced. But anything which looked like a fundamental change was instantly opposed with all the resources at the Lords' disposal. One example of this had been Gladstone's policy of Home Rule for Ireland. The next was the social legislation of Edwardian Liberalism, especially where specific policies looked like attacking entrenched financial privileges. As in the 1880s and 1890s the justification was that the Lords were acting in their legitimate role as 'watchdog of the constitution', although Lloyd George preferred to see the Lords as 'Mr Balfour's poodle'. The upper chamber obstructed the reforms of the Liberal government from 1906 onwards. It halted the Education Bill (1906), the Plural Voting Bill (1906), two further bills in 1907 and the Licensing Bill of 1908 and, of course, Lloyd George's 1909 Budget.

How did the Liberals react to all this? For some time they had accused the House of Lords of being partisan and the 1891 Newcastle Programme had included a call for its revision or end. But the leadership did not consider it appropriate to escalate early confrontations over, for example, the Education Bill into a full-scale constitutional crisis which would involve a further general election and a complete halt to all other government business. The rejection of the 1909 Budget, however, was another matter. The House of Lords had deliberately ignored a convention by overturning a finance bill for the first time for some 200 years. Such provocation could not possibly be ignored.

It is sometimes argued that the Budget was deliberately framed to *incite* the Lords. This seems unlikely, for two reasons. The first is that both Asquith and Lloyd George gave priority to their reform programme and wanted to maintain its impetus. A constitutional crisis would guarantee its complete halt. In any case, it is probable that Asquith had tried to sidestep confrontation in the first place by including in the Budget several measures such as land taxes, hoping that the Lords would abide by convention and not reject anything in a money bill. Second, Lloyd George was well aware of the need to revive the support of the rank and file who were somewhat disillusioned by the limited measures so far produced. He also had the next election in mind and had to find a quick way of conveying a policy which would get reform moving and appeal to most of the Liberal constituency. Thus the aim of the government was probably to speed up its social legislation by finding a way out of political entanglement.

Once the challenge was made, however, the Liberal government was determined to see the crisis through to the end. It realised that it had a good case for so doing. In the first place, the Lords were undermining the long-established right of the Commons to control

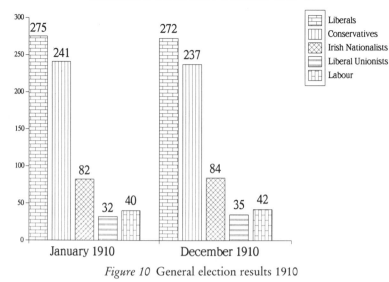

Figure 10 General election results 1910

taxation. Second, they were aiming to unmake a government which had a strong electoral mandate simply because the opposition in the House of Commons was too weak to do so. And third, they were upholding Conservative political and financial interests in the most blatant way. Lloyd George emphasised in a speech in October 1908 that the Lords were the aggressors. 'They', he warned 'are forcing revolution'.[14] The government was therefore able to project itself as taking *defensive* action. The first step was to fight a general election, in January 1910, on the issue of the Budget itself. The result was that the Liberals were returned with a reduced majority and a dependence on the Irish Nationalists – but now able to force the Lords to swallow the Budget. Asquith then proceeded to prepare a Parliament Bill to restrict the power of the Lords in the future. To ensure its success he requested the creation of 250 Liberal peers if the Lords held out against it. The King insisted on a second general election before he agreed to do this. The results of the December election being virtually identical with the first, Asquith remained in office and proceeded to reintroduce the Parliament Bill. Faced with the alarming prospect of being swamped by 250 new Liberal creations, the House of Lords had no alternative but to pass the measure.

All this seems to suggest that the Liberals had a carefully formulated strategy. This was not the case. To some extent the government muddled its way through the crisis, reacting to developments rather than anticipating them. For one thing, the cabinet was divided over precisely how the House of Lords should be reformed. Some ministers favoured the solution suggested by a cabinet committee in 1907 that there should be a joint sitting of the Commons and 100 representatives from the Lords whenever there was deadlock over legislation. Others preferred Campbell-Bannerman's device of converting the Lords' power of veto to one of delay. In the end, Asquith had to impose his own view on the cabinet, and the Campbell-Bannerman approach prevailed. The government was also thrown by the sudden death, at the height of the crisis, of Edward VII. It would have been insensitive and politically unwise for the government to have exerted pressure too quickly on his successor, George V. This explains why Lloyd George apparently reduced the pressure exerted by the Liberals and proposed a joint party conference; he even went so far as to offer the prospect of a coalition government to settle the issue. Asquith was not in favour of the latter but did not interfere, knowing that it would strengthen the hand he would play with the new King when the negotiations inevitably failed.

How successful were the Liberals in overcoming the obstacle represented by the House of Lords? On the one hand, they must be credited with a major achievement. They had taken on the most entrenched institution in the land and, for the first time since the seventeenth century, had forced it to agree to the reduction of its own authority. In this respect, the success of the Liberals in 1911 was even greater than that of the Whigs in 1832, since they had gone well beyond the scope of the 1832 conflict. The terms of the 1911 Parliament Act also reduced the inherent advantage possessed by the Conservatives by stipulating that all money bills had to be passed by the Lords and by reducing the veto on other bills to a delaying power of three sessions only. This enabled the Liberals to press ahead with their remaining legislative programme, the flagship of which was the National Insurance Act of 1911.

There is, however, another perspective. The 1911 Parliament Act stopped well short of what the Liberals had really wanted. The preamble of the Act referred to more sweeping reform in the future: 'it is intended to substitute for the House of Lords as it at present exists a Second Chamber constituted on a popular instead of heredi-tary basis.' But this was never taken up, partly because of disagree-ment within the cabinet as to how to proceed and partly because of the pressure of other business. Hence the Lords remained unreformed in their composition until the eventual introduction of life peers half a century later. The Liberals therefore lost a unique opportunity in following up while the issue was still warm; the longer the House of Lords continued to exist unreformed, the more difficult it would be to know what to do with it.

The House of Lords also had the final say. Between 1911 and 1914 it used the delaying power against a new range of Liberal measures, including the Irish Home Rule Bill, the Welsh Disestablishment Bill and the Plural Voting Bill. Reasoning that the government had legitimised its power by redefining it, the Lords saw no reason why they should not use it. They thus dampened what could well have been another reforming phase and a revival of Liberal zest. The outbreak of war in 1914 transformed the delaying power on these bills into what amounted to an absolute veto and preserved in aspic the impression of a government which had run out of ideas.

THREE THREATS TO STABILITY 1906–14

The Liberals faced a full range of problems between 1906 and 1914, the climax of which was the period around 1911–13. In addition to the conflict with the House of Lords, which has already been examined, they were confronted by a committed and active pressure group in the form of the suffragettes, by a large-scale eruption of industrial unrest and, to cap everything, by the renewed urgency of the Irish question.

There were good reasons why the Liberal government should have supported the demand for women's franchise. Liberalism had been at the forefront of all previous franchise extensions, even that of 1867, and Liberal MPs had been prominent in the late Victorian era in supporting the social emancipation of women. The Liberals recognised that further additions would have to be made to the male vote and it was not unreasonable to expect them to give careful consideration to the arguments of female suffragists, many of whom were, after all, Liberal supporters. And yet the Liberal party was strangely unreceptive. A surprising number of the rank and file accepted the traditional arguments that most women did not want the vote and that their proper role was in the home, not in political involvement. Constituency organisers also believed that the limited enfranchisement which would be most likely would result in women of property predominating and voting Conservative.

In such a situation the government had an obligation to lead and convert the rest of the party. Instead, it followed a disastrous policy of drifting and was forced in consequence to take a tough position in which it did not really believe.

The Liberal cabinet were not opposed on principle to the enfranchisement of women; indeed, Campbell-Bannerman, Lloyd George and Grey were known to be very much in favour. But the issue was given very low priority, partly because Asquith was not convinced about the need for women's suffrage and favoured the 'wait and see' expedient he adopted on several other issues. The initial approach was therefore dilatory and half-hearted. The government missed the opportunity of supporting one of the private member's bills of 1907, 1908 and 1909; any of these would have given them only indirect involvement while, at the same time, enabling them to control the change. From this stage onwards, the government found itself under increasing pressure from the National Union of Women's Suffrage Societies (NUWSS) and the more militant Women's Social and Political Union (WSPU). There was still a chance of political solution when the government introduced the Conciliation Bills of 1910 and 1911 which were designed to give women the franchise on the same grounds as men. Both, however, failed to get through because the government would allow them no more time in the Commons. When the suffragettes stepped up their campaign as a result, the government found it more difficult to justify another separate measure, in case it should be accused of yielding to external pressure. It did, however, try a low-key measure. In 1912 Asquith made late additions to the Plural Voting Bill to enfranchise a minority of women, but the Speaker ruled against accepting these on the grounds that they changed the nature of the original bill. Asquith's reaction is revealing: 'The Speaker's *coup d'état* has bowled over the Women for this session – a great relief'.[15]

The failure of these measures served only to infuriate the suffragettes, who stepped up their campaign. As this became more and more violent, the government found itself increasingly on the defensive and, as such, having to take measures to secure its reputation for being in control. Its response to the hunger-strike campaign in prison was the 'Cat and Mouse Act' of 1913, an ingenious but thoroughly insensitive solution which served only to intensify the vicious circle. There was still no end in sight to the confrontation by 1914 and it was the outbreak of war which changed the situation and resulted in the suffragette campaign being suspended.

Asquith must accept much of the responsibility for the crisis. He failed to go along with the prevailing view of his cabinet and lost several key opportunities to deal with the issue. His own argument, at least from 1910, was that it would not be possible to get a suffrage bill through the Commons because of likely opposition from the Irish Nationalists. This, however, smacks of an excuse for doing nothing. Asquith was, after all, in the driving seat over Home Rule and could have made a *quid pro quo* with the Irish Nationalists over women's suffrage had he been so inclined. Asquith's unwillingness to see through any of the measures which the Liberals initiated meant that his government became increasingly boxed in and had, eventually, to resort to a very uncharacteristic policy of coercion.

This was altogether a strange and sorry episode which blotted the record of a progressive and constructive government. Some historians would go further than this. Clarke, for example, maintains that in the act of bringing about social democracy through a burst of legislation, the Liberals completely failed to introduce *political* democracy.[16] It could certainly be said that the Liberals expended a great deal of effort in reducing the base of the House of Lords while begrudging the comparatively minor measures needed to complete democracy in the Commons. The most radical argument, however, is advanced by Morgan, who sees the Liberal failure over women's suffrage as a catalyst for subsequent political decline. 'Asquith's prejudice against Woman Suffrage almost certainly aggravated his myopia on electoral reform; and that, in turn, contributed to the failure of the "New Liberalism" and the rise of the Labour party.'[17] This particular interpretation, however, needs to be considered against the more general perspective provided at the end of the chapter.

The Liberal government was the first in modern times to face a concerted wave of militant strike action. This started with a threatened rail strike in 1907, and extended to stoppages in shipbuilding in the North-East in 1908, and to the coal mines of South Wales, Yorkshire, Durham and Northumberland. The worst period, however, was 1911-12. The Southampton docks came to a standstill in 1911 and the London docks in 1912. The entire Miners' Confederation went on strike for a minimum wage, calling out 2 million men. The rest of the period, 1913-14, saw a series of miners' strikes in the Midlands and the spread of industrial unrest to Dublin. In some instances there was violence and the government resorted on several occasions to the use of troops to restore order.

Potentially most serious of all, the National Union of Railwaymen, the Transport Workers' Federation and the Miners' Federation of Great Britain formed the Triple Alliance in a move towards a collective strike. This was forestalled, however, by the outbreak of war.

To what extent was the government responsible for this unrest? The underlying reasons for the crisis can hardly be placed at its door since they related to more general economic problems. Britain had entered a period of slump which had affected trade and driven unemployment upwards. During the period 1909–13, furthermore, prices rose more rapidly than wages, threatening a substantial part of the working class with impoverishment. The situation was at its worst in the staple industries, especially coal and shipbuilding, which experienced a decline in orders. The employers reacted swiftly, imposing wage-cuts and, when these precipitated strikes, lock-outs. In addition they sought to undermine trade union influence and employ non-unionised and 'blackleg' labour to nullify the effects of industrial action. This further embittered industrial relations. Britain was given a foretaste of the sort of underlying economic problem which was to become endemic during the inter-war period.

The situation was not of the government's making for another reason. Underlying some of the industrial action of this period was an imported influence: Syndicalism. This was based heavily on ideas and practices from France, as introduced into Britain by Thomas Mann. The main intention was to influence trade unions into taking joint and collective action to achieve political objectives. It was therefore considered by its opponents to have revolutionary connotations. Some historians, including Halévy, have argued that this was indeed the main influence behind the wave of unrest. This is probably an overstatement. Although Syndicalism probably helped fan the flames, it is more likely that the majority of trade union activity was conducted on traditional lines. This was partly because of the divisions within the trade union movement itself and the enormous diversity of its leadership and organisation. This meant that common action was not instinctive or inherent and therefore even less likely to be influenced entirely by foreign ideas.

Did the government do everything within its power to try to resolve the crisis? It was certainly conscious of the need to act as mediator between employers and employees. In fact, Lloyd George's handling of the strikes showed him in his best light. He used the services of the Board of Trade in 1907 to prevent a potentially damaging rail strike, while the following year Churchill did much to secure the return to work of the Amalgamated Engineers. In addition, the workers gained a great deal from the establishment of conciliation boards to negotiate on key issues such as conditions, hours and wages, while the National Insurance Act of 1911 attempted to alleviate the impact of unemployment. On the other hand, it could be argued that it had no overall strategy for tackling underlying grievances. It reacted to emergencies and was prepared to intervene only when absolutely necessary. Hence there is some justification in Read's view that 'the Liberal Government had pursued an unemployment policy, but it had not attempted to follow an overall labour policy'.[18]

To some extent the Irish issue had died down during the period of Conservative rule before 1905. But it was inevitable that it should reassert itself once the Liberals were returned to power.

The Liberals started by trying to find a way 'to reconcile Irish desires for self-government with English suspicions of Home Rule'.[19] They wanted above all to avoid the obsessive approach of Gladstone. The result was the Irish Council Bill, which would have provided devolution for eight government departments. But this was not acceptable to the Irish Nationalists, who considered it a solution more in line with Conservative policies. The Liberals were therefore forced back on to Gladstonian lines when, after the general election of January 1910, Asquith had to undertake to introduce Home Rule in the future in order to gain the support of the eighty-two Irish Nationalists in his constitutional struggle with the House of Lords. The 1912 bill was really a revival of Gladstone's second Home Rule Bill. It proposed an Irish executive and a two-chamber legislature in Dublin, while forty-two Irish MPs would continue to sit at Westminster. London would retain control over certain areas, especially foreign policy and defence.

By this time, however, the situation had become complicated as a result partly of objective factors and partly of deficiencies in Liberal strategy.

The most significant of the former was the emergence of extreme groups, such as Sinn Fein, which were more radical than the Irish Nationalists and less likely to compromise. At the other pole, the Protestant population of Ulster, who had been encouraged by Lord Randolph Churchill in 1886 to fight against Gladstone's first Home Rule Bill, had become even more determined that no further moves should be made in that direction, especially since Ulster had in the meantime developed a more advanced industrial economy based upon shipbuilding in Belfast. The Unionist case was strongly put by Carson, who warned of the possibility of armed resistance.

The Liberal government was also impeded in its search for a settlement by the continued opposition of the Conservatives. Home Rule was very much a party issue rather than a cross-party commitment. As such, the Conservatives did their best to resist it, partly because of their close connection with the Ulster position. Bonar Law, for example, closely identified with Ulster. In 1912 he said in a public speech at Blenheim: 'I say now, with a full sense of the responsibility which attaches to my position, that if any attempt be made under present conditions [to force Home Rule through Parliament], I can imagine no length of resistance to which Ulster will go in which I shall not be ready to support them.'[20] In other words, the Conservatives were officially lining up with the Ulster Unionists against Home Rule. Pressure was even attempted on the King to veto the Bill if it was passed, and even, perhaps, to dismiss ministers. The House of Lords, meanwhile, used the powers left to it after the 1911 Parliament Act to delay the third Home Rule Bill, which therefore had to be abandoned on the outbreak of war in 1914.

There can be little doubt, therefore, that the Conservative party used the Irish issue to destabilise and undermine the Liberals. Even so, the latter did not handle the Irish situation very effectively. Their key error was not to recognise the Ulster factor for what it was and thereby build into the settlement the principle of partition. This would have relieved much of the opposition's case. As it was, Asquith adopted a policy which became characteristic of him: 'wait and see'. He failed to include a plan for partition in the third Home Rule Bill, overruling Churchill and Haldane, who had argued strongly in the cabinet that Ulster should be allowed to opt out. Asquith's judgement was that the Ulster Unionists were using the issue to destroy Home Rule altogether, to try to force a general election and to bring back the Conservatives. He was probably right, but such an analysis did not allow for any last-minute concessions to defuse the situation.

The government's vulnerability was additionally exposed by the Curragh Incident and by the lack of firm measures to prevent the build-up of arms in Ireland; in 1914, for example, the Ulster Volunteers got away with importing a large consignment of rifles into Larne. To make matters worse, the Secretary for War openly stated that the British Army would not be instrumental in enforcing Home Rule; this greatly reduced the options open to the government and also encouraged Ulster to resist. Liberal policy, therefore, fell between two stools. It did not provide Ulster with what it wanted. Nor did it give the impression that it would deal firmly with any unrest from Ulster. The result was an increase in tension and the accumulation of weapons and the proliferation of paramilitary groups brought the country to the edge of civil war.

An alternative view is provided by Bernstein, who considers that the Liberals failed not because of any inconsistency but rather because they were too reasonable:

> the failure of liberalism in Ireland was not a failure of policy. It was the same as its failure in dealing with militant women and striking workers . . . An ideology rooted in the supremacy of rational discourse could not succeed when others had rejected reason, moderation and common sense as a means of resolving problems.[21]

But should not the Liberals have anticipated the results of not meeting genuine fears and aspirations half-way? The government, after all, was negotiating from a position of strength; rational discourse means, in part, taking account of deeply held conviction which is bound to be partisan and biased. The Liberals signally failed between 1911 and 1914 to be flexible but firm; instead they seemed inflexible but yielding, sending a clear signal to the pressure groups concerned to intensify their activity.

LIBERAL DECLINE

The year 1914 was the last one of Liberal rule in peacetime. In May 1915 the pressure of war forced Asquith to invite Conservatives to join a coalition government which then passed under the leadership of Lloyd George in December 1916. This proved to be the beginning of the end for the Liberals as a major force in British politics. They won 161 seats in 1918 and 116 in 1922, recovering slightly to 159 in 1923. Thereafter the party suffered electoral catastrophe. It plummeted to 40 seats in 1924, 59 in 1929 and 72 in 1931. These figures include all the factions into which the party was divided during this period, otherwise the picture would appear even bleaker.

The decline of the Liberals and the simultaneous rise of Labour is the major political change of the twentieth century. One issue concerns us here: did the process begin before 1914?

One view is that the seeds of Liberal decline had already been sown before the First World War, and that the Labour party had a direct connection with this. In 1936 Dangerfield argued that the signs of Liberal decline could be read as far back as 1906, even though this was the year of the Liberal landslide. The party was 'doomed' since it was like 'an army protected at all points except for one vital position on its flank':[22] this was exposed to infiltration by Labour members who steadily undermined it. The situation deteriorated further with the rising tide of violence and industrial unrest during the turbulent period 1910–14 which discredited the Liberal government and recruited support for Labour. To this could be added the crisis involving the suffragettes, which Morgan argues was directly responsible for the subsequent Liberal collapse.[23]

Other historians, such as Wilson, have minimised the importance of the decline of the Liberals before 1914.[24] A common argument is that the Liberal party was more than holding its own. For one thing, the Liberals had introduced a wider range of positive social legislation than any government before it, and had still not run out of steam. The Conservatives, by contrast, were unable to offer a credible alternative and had had to depend on their entrenched position in the House of Lords to combat Liberal policies. Their recovery since 1906 had therefore been only partial and there was certainly no guarantee that they would have won an election called in 1915. Labour, meanwhile, had not reached the point of breakthrough against the Liberal government and could not expect any direct benefits from the latter's discomfiture over industrial conflict and Syndicalism. In any case, Labour's performance in the 1910 elections had not been impressive and they, too, cannot have been sanguine about their prospects in 1915. Thus the Liberals were still reasonably secure in 1914, despite the various crises that confronted them. The decline came later, the result of self-inflicted wounds during the First World War, especially in the bitter rift between Asquith and Lloyd George. The decline was therefore accidental, and had no roots in the period before 1914. Wilson uses the analogy of a pedestrian struck by an automobile. 'A rampant omnibus (the First World War) . . . mounted the pavement and ran him over. After lingering painfully, he expired.'[25]

In the final analysis, what made the real difference was the impact of the First World War. The political scene in 1914 was one of equilibrium: the Liberals were just about holding their own, the Conservatives had not quite recovered, and Labour had not reached the point of electoral breakthrough. The Liberal decline was not caused primarily by the division between Asquith and Lloyd George; parties have recovered from far worse splits. A far more fundamental dynamic was needed. Between 1914 and 1918 two things happened. One was a social transformation, brought about by the levelling effect of four years of war. The other was the arrival of universal manhood suffrage in the Representation of the People Act (1918). The former raised the popularity of the Labour party, the latter eventually delivered it sufficient votes to accomplish an electoral breakthrough. Ironically, the main beneficiary of all this was the Conservative party, the recovery of which was out of all proportion to its own efforts.

18

THE RISE OF THE LABOUR PARTY BEFORE 1914

The name 'Labour party' was first used in 1906. It was a shortened form of 'Labour Representation Committee', which had been set up in 1900 to unite the various working-class and socialist groups within Britain. These included the handful of Labour MPs then within the Liberal party, the Scottish Parliamentary Labour Party, the Independent Labour Party (ILP), the Social Democratic Federation and the Fabian Society. The breakthrough for the Labour party came with the election of thirty MPs in 1906; these increased to forty and then forty-two during the two general elections of 1910. Although it was not until 1924 that Labour was able to form a government, this increase in electoral support was unparalleled in British political history.

There were, of course, precedents for smaller political parties during the nineteenth century. One type was the splinter group, like the Canningites, Peelites or Liberal Unionists, which all separated as mature sections of an existing party, eventually to join another. A second variety was a distinctive party with a strictly regional base; an example was the Irish Nationalists, who never established themselves outside their own area. But the growth of the Labour party was entirely different from both of these. It was essentially a new development – not a splinter group – which achieved a national – not a regional – base.

Accounts of the rise of Labour have often obscured the overall process under a welter of detail. The focus of this chapter will be on three distinct stages which can be identified before 1914, and an examination of each. The first was the growth of a new organisation in close association with one of the established parties, the Liberals – not changing that party's general outlook, but maintaining a separate identity as a section on its fringe. Second, this section gradually expanded and overlapped groups which had been developing entirely independently of the Liberals. These applied pressure for the emergence of a separate overall identity. Third, this separation did occur gradually during the 1890s and was formalised with the establishment of the Labour Representation Committee in 1900. A connection was maintained, however, with the Liberals between 1903 and 1914, this time as an electoral pact between two independent parties.

INITIAL ASSOCIATION WITH THE LIBERALS

It might be thought that the enlargement of the electorate in 1867 and 1884 would have created an automatic demand for a new party. And yet, in the early stages, the more obvious effect was to modify *existing* parties. The Liberals and Conservatives, having achieved a broad consensus about the extension of the franchise, tried to accommodate the extra voters within their own party ranks, and to aim their policies more directly at what they perceived to be the needs of the working class, whether through 'Gladstonian Liberalism' or the 'Tory Democracy' of Disraeli and Lord Randolph Churchill.

These reforms, however, showed the strong influence of *laissez-faire* and self-help, two principles which were felt to be inappropriate to working-class needs. There was, therefore, some disillusionment with the traditional parties. This showed itself partly in the swing from one party to the other, winning the 1868 and 1880 elections for the Liberals and the 1874 election for the Conservatives, and partly in the substantial number of non-voters, or abstainers, in elections after 1884. In other words, there was now a large part of the electorate which did not have a natural home within either of the two existing parties. If this untapped voting power were to polarise around a new party, the result could be devastating since, between 1885 and 1914, working-class constituents were in a majority in over 100 seats in Britain. There were distinct advantages in such a course. For example, a political dimension might be added to the organisations which had already been set up for the economic well-being of the working classes, particularly trade unions. This would make it possible to shift the focus of legislation away from *laissez-faire* and to develop State intervention – perhaps even socialism – as an alternative to the traditional influences of conservatism and liberalism.

Of course, such a step had enormous difficulties. A working-class organisation had virtually no chance of sustaining an independent existence at the outset. It would need, instead, to grow and develop within an existing political party.

Why was this? In the first place, the existing parties had already established contacts with the working classes and had geared their party organisations for this purpose, the Conservatives promoting entertainment via the brewing interest, the Liberals focusing more on the influence of the Nonconformist chapels. No newly formed group could hope to break connections like this immediately. It would be additionally hamstrung by the electoral system which favoured the major parties and made it extremely difficult for any third party to break their monopoly. Similarly, any minority party would be in serious financial difficulties as soon as it tried to take on more powerful opposition. It would have no means of supporting large numbers of candidates in elections, or of meeting the costs involved in campaigning which were, of course, unlimited until the Corrupt Practices Act of 1883. Even the election of an MP would cause difficulties since there was as yet no salary or subsistence independent of individual or party provision. A new party could not sustain itself properly until both of these difficulties had been met.

There were even conservative forces within the trade union movement which were opposed to the pursuit of a new policy within a new party, preferring instead to meet specific targets within an existing one. Hence early political spokesmen for trade unions tended to take for granted a Liberal connection at local constituency association level. This applied especially to the miners, who felt that more could be done on their behalf by an established party than by an inexperienced one struggling for survival. What was needed was a pressure group to remind that party from time to time of its reform agenda and to make sure that the interests of specific portions of the working class received due attention. There was at first even some antipathy to the notion of a separate party. Being in a tiny minority it would automatically be ridiculed and distrusted, and could have an adverse reflection on the working-class components of the Liberal party.

The answer, therefore, was an arrangement whereby a handful of working-class MPs were elected on a Labour ticket but within the broad church of the Liberal party. Known as 'Lib-Labs', these took part in all general elections between 1868 and 1895, although their handful of seats were subsumed within the overall Liberal totals. One of their main spokesmen was Henry Broadhurst, who defined the purpose of the Lib-Lab arrangement as 'a system by which you cordially co-operate with your friends, while reserving to yourself, should the need arise, your own independence of action'.[1] The implication here was that the Lib-Lab concept stopped short of integration with the Liberals. The Labour representatives retained an identifiable image on the fringe of the Liberal party and did not dismiss the possibility of eventually seceding from it. This would depend, of course, on future circumstances, ideas and influences.

INDEPENDENCE FROM THE LIBERALS

Meanwhile, several other groups claiming to represent working-class interests were developing *outside* the scope of Lib-Lab collaboration.

One was the Social Democratic Federation, established in 1884 by H.M. Hyndman, a theoretical determinist and follower of scientific socialism. The movement was split, however, by the inevitable Marxist division over whether the focus should be revolution or propaganda. The result was a second group, the more moderate Socialist League under William Morris. A third was the Fabian Society, also set up in 1884. Composed mainly of intellectuals, the core of whom were known as the 'Hampstead Marx Circle', these focused on the conversion of politicians to a gradualist socialism. Its strategy, which gave the Society its name, was described vividly by Frank Podmore, one of its leading members: 'For the right moment you must wait, as Fabius did most patiently, when warring against Hannibal, though many censured his delays; but when the time comes you must strike hard, as Fabius did, or your waiting will be in vain, and fruitless'.[2] The most important of the new groups, however, was the Independent Labour party, formed in 1893 under the leadership of Keir Hardie. Its aim was to entice trade unionists away from the Lib-Lab strategy they had been following and to promote a more explicit socialist programme based on the principle of 'the collective and communal ownership of all the means of production, distribution and exchange'.[3]

How important were these organisations in encouraging the Labour movement to emerge from its close association with the Liberal party? On the one hand, they did reveal an alternative political strategy and they succeeded in influencing a number of trade unionists with socialist ideas. As this occurred the politicians representing trade unionists had to accept the need to distance themselves at least partially from the Liberals in order to prevent a split from opening up within trade unionist ranks. This inevitably meant some movement towards the new groups, especially the socialist ideology of the Independent Labour party and the gradualist strategy of the Fabians.

On the other hand, the influence of the external working-class groups was less than total. For one thing, they set a bad example by competing, often viciously, with each other. Keir Hardie's Independent Labour Party was strongly opposed to revolution and hence denounced Hyndman's Social Democratic Federation (SDF); so did William Morris of the Socialist League, who argued that 'As Hyndman considers the SDF his property, let him take it and make what he can of it, and try if he can really make up a bogy of it to frighten the Government . . . we will begin again quite cleanhanded to try the more humdrum method of quiet propaganda'.[4] Beatrice Webb of the Fabians thought very little of the Independent Labour Party. She wrote in her diary on 12 March 1894 that 'The Independent Labour Party, with its lack of money, brains, and, to some extent, moral characteristics, is as yet more of a thorn in the side of the Liberals than an effective force on our side'.[5]

The external groups therefore lacked the power or credibility to control political changes in the 1890s even though they did influence them. The overall initiative lay with the trade union movement, which had been renovated by a process usually decribed as a transition from 'old' trade unionism to 'new'. Partly responsible for this was a greater degree of industrial militancy, expressed, for example, in the Great Dock Strike of 1889. Indeed, Ben Tillett, a union leader, believed that 'The regeneration of the Trade Union Movement dates from this great social event'.[6] It is true that there was a sudden downturn in union membership and activity between 1893 and 1894, due largely to the impact of industrial depression. Nevertheless, 'new' unionism picked up again after 1894, sustaining its growth until by 1900 there were almost 2 million trade union members. The Independent Labour Party, by contrast, had 10,000 members in 1895, falling to just over 5,000 by 1901,[7] while the membership of the Social Democratic Federation was a fraction of even that.

The decision to increase the distance with the Liberal party, therefore, had to be primarily a trade union one. There were two good reasons why this decision needed to be taken. One was that there was a class conflict developing at local constituency level as the Liberals were unwilling to adopt working-class candidates; one such victim was Ramsay MacDonald, who had failed to be adopted as a Liberal candidate because of his humble origins. Ramsay MacDonald later said: 'We did not leave the Liberals. They kicked us out and slammed the door in our faces'.[8] There was therefore no chance of Lib-Lab co-operation leading to a broader Lib-Lab party and the trade unionists decided not to attempt to move in this direction. In any case, a second strong reason presented itself for separation rather than integration. This was the comparative weakness of the Liberals in opposition from 1895 to 1905. This meant that the Liberal party would be able to pass no legislation on behalf of the working class and it was preferable for labour interests to try to build up their own strength and independence. Many even considered that independence would strengthen their electoral bargaining position with the Liberals, forcing the latter to concede more constituencies than before in order to have a clear run in their own strongholds: this was the only way in which they could hope to defeat the Conservatives.

This reasoning underlay the formation of the Labour Representation Committee. This comprised seven trade unionists, one Fabian, and two members from each of the Independent Labour Party and the Social Democratic Federation. Its purpose was to fashion 'a distinct Labour group in Parliament, who shall have their own whips'.[9] Of course, the Labour Representation Committee faced initial difficulties, such as the secession of the Social Democratic Federation in 1901. But it also grew in confidence. The Taff Vale judgement of 1901 was a further – if unintended – help. Ramsay MacDonald proved correct in his view that 'The recent decision of the House of Lords . . . should convince the unions that a labour party in Parliament is an immediate necessity';[10] it has been estimated that, as a direct result of the Taff Vale case, 127 new unions threw in their lot with the Labour Representation Committee, including the first of the miners' unions.

True to its original purpose, the Labour Representation Committee restrained its members from helping other parties. The 1903 Newcastle Conference adopted a resolution 'to abstain strictly from identifying themselves with or promoting the interests of any section of the Liberal or Conservative parties'.[11] This seemed to pay off as between 1902 and 1903 Labour managed to win three by-elections quite independently of Liberal support. The days of Lib-Labism seemed to be over.

A REDEFINED RELATIONSHIP

Or did they? Although Labour had emerged *out* of the Liberal party, it was not yet time to grow *away* from it. Instead, the relationship between the two was now to be redefined.

As an alternative to negotiating within the Liberal party, Labour now conducted diplomacy as a separate, if still unequal, partner. In 1903 Ramsay MacDonald formed with Herbert Gladstone an electoral agreement which redefined the relationship between the two parties. Gladstone would 'ascertain from qualified and responsible Labour leaders how far Labour candidates [could] be given an open field against a common enemy'; Liberal associations would then be persuaded to 'abstain from nominating a Liberal candidate and to unite in support of any recognized and competent Labour candidate who [supported] the general objects of the Liberal Party'.[12] Both the Liberals and Labour aimed to exploit the quirks of the electoral system which distorted a small majority of the overall vote into a large majority of seats. The Liberals hoped to reverse two successive defeats by the Conservatives (in 1895 and 1900) by letting loose Labour candidates in selected Conservative constituencies while, at the same time, preventing any Labour threat in their own or in those Conservative seats which they had targeted themselves. Labour, in turn, were using these Liberal calculations to achieve their own breakthrough. The pay-off was impressive. Out of the party's fifty candidates contesting the 1906 general election, Labour won thirty seats while, in the twenty-four constituencies where there was a direct contest with the Conservative, Labour won 60 per cent of the vote.

It now remained to be seen what practical use Labour would be able to make of these gains. How far would a still small party be able to influence a new Liberal government in possession of a huge majority? Would it be able to play the role of junior partner and contribute to the development of legislation? Or would it be entirely dependent on a few crumbs big brother condescended to give it? There are two ways of looking at this.

On the one hand, it has been argued that the Labour party exerted an influence which was quite disproportionate to its actual size. According to K. Hutchison:

> The very existence of such an independent political force was a considerable factor in the outpouring of social legislation that makes the period 1906 to 1911 in Britain comparable to the New Deal era in the United States . . . While all the credit cannot be given to the Labour Party, its advent surely created a climate favourable for such building operations.[13]

Labour MPs, furthermore, periodically prodded the Liberal government into action. This was especially important since there was still a residue within the Liberal party which wanted to apply the brakes because, argues Hutchison, they 'clung firmly to the economic philosophy of the nineteenth-century Whigs'.[14]

An alternative view is that Labour had comparatively little control over the Liberals and were able to exert only occasional influence – and then in specific ways, as tolerated by the Liberals themselves. Although, as Feuchtwanger concedes, this meant that Labour 'scored some success',[15] the scope for intervention was strictly limited. The greatest success was the involvement of Labour MPs and trade union officials in determining the eventual form and details of the 1906 Trades Disputes Act. This gave trade unions the right to strike and to picket without running the risk of legal action being taken against them by employers. But, as Belchem says, 'this was the last concession to sectionalism as the Liberals seized the initiative with a series of progressive measures which Labour could neither oppose nor amend'.[16] The Liberals were very much in control of the more ambitious programme of social reform and were not anxious to allow much Labour intervention. This was intensely frustrating to some Labour members, who would have preferred a different framework to the incipient welfare state. R.H. Tawney expressed the difference as follows:

> The middle and upper class view in social reform is that it should regulate the worker's *life* in order that he may *work* better. The working class view of economic reform is that it should regulate his *work*, in order that he may have a chance of living. Hence to working people licensing reform, insurance act, etc. seems beginning at the wrong end.[17]

There were also reservations about Liberal reforms concerning employment, especially the introduction of 'labour exchanges' which were seen initially as a device for providing work for strike-breakers or 'blacklegs'. The Labour party got nowhere in its attempts to persuade the Liberals to introduce a 'right-to-work' bill.

Even so, the Labour party preferred the Liberal reforms to no reforms at all, or to the prospects of a Conservative government. Between 1909 and 1914 the Liberal reforms hit a series of obstacles (see Chapter 17) and, for a while, Labour had no alternative but to suspend its criticism and support the beleaguered Liberals against a common enemy. In the process, it secured two pieces of legislation which were of considerable benefit. The first was the payment of MPs which Lloyd George introduced in 1911; this enabled the Labour party to consider putting up a larger number of candidates for future elections. Second, in 1913, trade unions were permitted to set up a political fund, which solved the problem of financing these future additions and, in the process, effectively reversed the Osborne Judgement of 1909. Labour was not, therefore, without compensation for frustrations it experienced during the Liberal ascendancy.

LABOUR IN 1914

How far had the Labour party progressed by 1914? To what extent was it vulnerable to setbacks and decline? According to Belchem, it is possible to see an adverse trend beginning to develop. 'Boosted by the pact, Labour reached its peak in 1906–7, after which support fell away.'[18]

In some respects this trend can be borne out, although the dates are open to question. After achieving its electoral breakthrough of thirty seats in 1906, Labour's impetus slowed in the next four years. It won forty in January 1910, which it increased to forty-two the following December. Labour's share of the total actually dropped between the two elections in 1910 from 7.6 to 7.1 per cent. Furthermore, Labour candidates won none of the thirty-five three-cornered contests and came third with twenty-nine. Worse still, between 1910 and 1914 Labour lost five seats in by-elections, some in Midlands coalfields, to reduce its total parliamentary representation to thirty-seven. Part of the problem was that the electoral system prevented Labour from becoming fully established unless one of the two major parties spiralled into insignificance. It was totally unrealistic to think in terms of displacing the Conservatives, since there was little overlap in their electoral appeal. Labour could only hope, therefore, to replace the Liberals as the party representing the majority of the working class and at least part of the middle. But what hope was there of this, given the strength of the Liberals since 1906?

The Labour party was still hampered by its somewhat restricted image. It depended for its support on a particular social stratum – the trade unionists or better-off members of the working class. It had still not established its credentials with the groups below these or, at the other end, with sufficient members of the middle class. In addition, the two major parties were both confident of retaining the share of the vote to which each had become accustomed. There were still working-class Conservatives, attracted by better recreational facilities or by the memories of Disraeli and 'Tory Democracy'. The Liberals still projected themselves as the major party for the working class and, since they had a far better chance of being elected, they were the more realistic choice for the working-class electorate. Labour even lacked a comprehensive overall programme. Before 1914 it represented a variety of views and lacked united or effective leadership. According to Beatrice Webb, 'The Labour MPs seem to me to be drifting into futility'. She complained that 'J.R. MacDonald has ceased to be a Socialist, . . . Snowden is embittered and Lansbury is wild. At present there is no co-operation among the Labour Members themselves nor between them and the trade union leaders.'[19]

On the other hand, there was some evidence that the Labour party was expanding steadily right up to the outbreak of the First World War. There had been substantial improvements, for example, in the party's structure. The number of constituency organisations had increased from 73 in 1906 to 179 by 1914.[20] With an influx of trade unionists, it has been estimated that membership of the Labour party had reached 2.1 million by 1915. Labour also benefited from improvements in its financial basis as the legalisation of affiliation fees paid by trade union members effectively reversed the Osborne Judgement. The Liberals, who introduced this legislation, failed to curb the flow of trade union funds to Labour, since the requirement for secret ballots among union members produced majorities of 71 per cent in 1913 and 1914 in favour of financing Labour candidates. This, in turn, attracted still more union members and enabled the party to contest more constituencies. According to Belchem, 'Labour marched forward in the pre-war years as trade-unionism expanded. No longer the preserve of the labour aristocracy, national trade unions eradicated regional and traditional loyalties, promoting a wider working-class identity.'[21]

Labour also made rapid inroads among existing voters in the Celtic fringe, and was building links which would bring it many women's votes in the future. To some extent the increase in Welsh union support for Labour was due to fundamental changes taking place in the occupational structure. Many of the miners decided to cut their links with the Liberals, especially those in South Wales. A significant proportion of their employers were Nonconformists, who were being deserted increasingly by the younger generation of miners. Thus political and social transformations overlapped as secular socialism began to replace Liberal nonconformity as the basis of Welsh radicalism. Meanwhile, the National Union of Women's Suffrage Societies assisted with the promotion of Labour at national and local level, through canvassing, in exchange for a Labour commitment to support women's suffrage. This was seen by some Labour supporters as a mixed blessing. On the one hand, it placed Labour on the side of what was widely regarded as the 'lunatic fringe' and may therefore have alienated some potential male voters. On the other hand, it established a strong future connection between the Labour party and middle-class women, who were prepared to support Labour for non-social reasons. This was important, because to gain credibility Labour needed to escape from its limited image of a party entirely for the working class.

Finally, the Labour party achieved spectacular successes in local politics. By 1914 it was fighting up to 18 per cent of municipal seats and increased its seats from 91 in 1906 to 171 in 1913 – a much faster rate of growth than in parliamentary politics. Labour had certain advantages locally. Candidates were able to focus clearly on munici-pal issues and to project the need for social reform, whereas to an extent the local Liberals were tied to the national programme of the Liberal government and were made to look conservative and unex-citing by comparison. They also seemed more backward in their funding schemes and attitudes to financial constraints.

By 1914, therefore, the Labour party had made extensive pro-gress. Yet it was still in a difficult position. It could not stand still but had not yet the means of going forward. It had outgrown the Liberal connection but was not yet strong enough to fight the Liberals openly. The question which was going to have to be addressed was whether or not the electoral agreement of 1906 and 1910 should be repeated in the election to be held at the latest in

1915. Labour would have wanted to put up more than 150 candidates, which could not possibly have been covered by a stand-aside policy by the Liberals. There would therefore have been more three-cornered contests, which could have cut deeply into the Liberal vote and given the election to the Conservatives. For this reason, the Liberals might have tried to undercut the baseline that they had already allowed Labour to build up: was Labour yet strong enough to withstand an all-out Liberal assault? It was fortunate for Labour's political future that the whole question was rendered hypothetical by the outbreak of war.

19

FROM SPLENDID ISOLATION TO WAR
British foreign policy 1895–1914

The term 'splendid isolation' refers to a period in British diplomacy when the British government preferred a policy of isolation to an alliance or close diplomatic ties with other powers. This is usually considered to have lasted from 1895 until 1902. Contemporary politicians certainly used the term; it appeared in the speeches of Salisbury, Rosebery, Harcourt, Goschen and Joseph Chamberlain, to name only a few. Historians, however, have been more wary. The first to use the description consistently was W.H. Dawson, who argued that Lord Salisbury deliberately opted for a policy of 'splendid isolation'.[1] This has been questioned by others, who maintain that if indeed Britain *was* in isolation, it was involuntary and far from 'splendid'. L. Penson, for example, considered that 'her isolation was a fact rather than a policy',[2] while Z. Steiner considers that 'splendid isolation' is 'a cliché which must be abandoned'.[3]

'Splendid' or not, there were good reasons at the end of the century for emerging from it. This was a gradual process involving the Anglo-Japanese Alliance of 1902, the Anglo-French Entente (1904) and the Anglo-Russian Convention (1907). The intention of these was not to increase Britain's involvement in Europe, or to seek a European-based security. They were primarily concerned with settling imperial and maritime problems.

But one thing led to another and Britain found herself increasingly involved by these new connections in European affairs. There were several issues which ensured that this occurred. One was the growing rivalry with Germany. Another was the delayed effect of the Treaty of Berlin which now threw up crises to threaten the equilibrium of the powers, which included Britain within its scope. This ensured that the last vestiges of isolation disappeared and

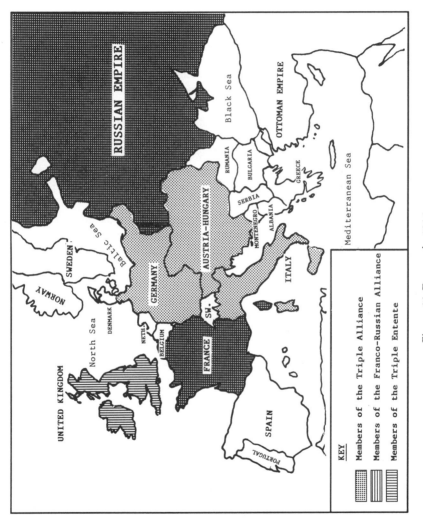

Figure 11 Europe in 1914

Britain even began to develop military co-operation with France and Russia. But even in 1914 Britain was not committed by the Ententes to going to war with Germany and her reason for so doing needs separate analysis.

'SPLENDID ISOLATION'?

Europe was dominated in 1895 by two alliance systems which included all the major powers on the Continent. The first of these started in 1879 as the Dual Alliance between Germany and Austria-Hungary, which guaranteed mutual assistance if either were attacked by Russia. Italy joined in 1882, to form the Triple Alliance; by this, Germany and Italy similarly undertook to assist each other against France. For a while, Russia was connected with Germany and Austria-Hungary by the *Dreikaiserbund* of 1873. Renewed in 1881, this was a much looser agreement which stopped well short of any military commitments. It was replaced, on its expiry in 1887, by the Reinsurance Treaty between Germany and Russia only. This complex diplomacy was the work of Bismarck, who intended to give Germany diplomatic security and to isolate her main rival, France, by preventing the latter's gravitation towards Russia. His successors maintained the Triple Alliance but allowed the crucial link with Russia to lapse. As a result a new system developed with the conclusion, between 1892 and 1894, of the Franco-Russian Alliance. Russia's obligation was now to support France in the event of an attack by Germany or by Germany and Italy; in return, France would assist Russia against an invasion by Germany or by Germany in conjunction with Austria-Hungary.

Britain was outside both alliance networks. It is true that in 1887 Salisbury drew up a Mediterranean agreement with Italy. But neither Gladstone nor Rosebery recognised nor acted in accordance with it and Salisbury did not revive it during his third ministry (1895-1902). There were no further attempts to establish such commitments and there is a case for seeing this as a deliberate choice made from a position of strength. In 1896 the First Lord of the Admiralty, Goschen, declared:

> There may be the isolation of those who are weak and who therefore are not courted because they can contribute nothing, and there is, on the other hand, the isolation of those who do not wish to be entangled in any complications and will hold

themselves free in every respect . . . Our isolation is not an isolation of weakness; it is deliberately chosen, the freedom to act as we choose in any circumstances that may arise.[4]

In the same year, Harcourt believed that Britain was avoiding 'permanent or entangling alliances'.[5] The Liberal opposition, especially Campbell-Bannerman, also emphasised the importance of maintaining Britain's 'freedom of individual action'.[6]

These attitudes were based on the belief that an equilibrium had been reached on the Continent and that it could be dangerous for Britain to interfere with it. In any case, there was no need. During the 1890s the purpose of the alliance systems was still avowedly defensive and the main areas of activity were overseas. In Britain's case, therefore, it made sense to focus on her imperial and maritime interests, neither of which appeared at this stage to need a continental alliance. Hence, at the turn of the century, foreign policy relating to Europe was subordinated to imperial policy concerned with interests in Africa and Asia. Salisbury added a further argument. Britain, he said, was less free to involve herself in the complexity of European diplomacy because any decisions had to be ratified by parliament. 'In a country like ours, no absolutely valid engagement could be entered into as to the course to be adopted at a future period . . . Questions of war or peace must be decided by the Parliament of the day.'[7] It must be said that this was used as an excuse for inaction since it did not prevent the government from entering undertakings when it later decided to do so.

The argument against there having been a period which can be designated 'splendid' isolation is based partly on historical perspective. Britain had aimed ever since 1815 to remain detached from alliances with the major continental powers, with the obvious exception of her collaboration with France and Turkey against Russia during the Crimean War (1854–6). The period 1895–1902 is merely a continuation of this process and deserves no special recognition. In any case, it could be argued that Britain was not, and could never be, entirely free from commitments in Europe. Although British governments had avoided giving any recent pledges of assistance to other states, there were several from the more distant past which still counted. One example was the Treaty of London of 1839, Article 7 of which guaranteed the independence and neutrality of Belgium. Another was the Treaty of Paris (1856) in which Britain had contributed to guaranteeing the future integrity of the Ottoman

Empire, Serbia, Moldavia and Wallachia. Thus Britain had commitments in both western and eastern Europe which might at any time involve her intervention against a potential aggressor.

It has also been said that Britain's isolation in the 1890s was the result of actual events, not of a deliberate policy. For over a decade successive British governments were confronted by a series of crises, involving almost every major power and indicating Britain's universal unpopularity. In 1894, for example, France and Germany forced Britain to abandon a treaty for the lease of territories in the Congo and there were disputes with Germany over Walfish Bay and Samoa. There were crises with Turkey over Armenia in 1896 and 1897, continuing threats of Russian expansion in Afghanistan, Tibet and Persia, and poor relations with the United States between 1895 and 1896 over Venezuela. Africa produced the most dangerous confrontations. Relations between Britain and Germany deteriorated over the Kaiser's telegram in 1896 congratulating President Kruger on having crushed the Jameson Raid. The Fashoda incident in the Sudan brought Britain as close as she had been at any time since 1815 to war with France, while a year later the sympathy of the whole of Europe was behind the Boers in their struggle against the forces of the British Empire. In all this time, it could be argued, virtually the only case of isolation through *choice* was Britain's decision in 1895 not to respond to an invitation from France and Russia to force Japan to disgorge some of her territorial gains made at the expense of China in the Treaty of Shimonoseki. In all other instances Britain was under pressure from activity of the European powers overseas which was all the more hectic because of the constraints imposed by the alliance system on the European scene. Isolation was a symptom of, rather than a deliberate response to, this pressure. The label 'splendid' was applied by the politicians of the time to preserve the illusion that Britain's governments and armed forces were fully in control of a deteriorating situation.

THE EMERGENCE FROM ISOLATION

Until the turn of the century most British politicians argued for maintaining isolation. There was even an official party consensus about this. Lord Salisbury, for example, continued to believe that 'Our treaty obligations will follow our national inclinations and will not precede them'.[8] But already alternative ideas were being put across by the Liberal Unionists, some of whom had crossed over to the Conservative party. By and large, they argued for closer ties with other powers; Chamberlain, for example, wanted an alliance with Germany, while Lansdowne eventually secured one with Japan.

Two basic developments undermined the logic of isolationism, whatever its emphasis. One was the end of Britain's claim to be the world's leading industrial power, the other the threat posed by Germany and Russia to Britain's imperial and maritime interests.

If isolation was 'splendid', it had to rest on an unquestionable position of strength. There was plenty of evidence, however, to show that Britain's industrial base was slipping back by comparison with other states. The best way of showing this is by comparing steel production, since this has the most direct bearing on military and naval armaments. Back in 1870 Britain had led the world with 0.7 million tons produced in that year, with Germany some way behind on 0.3 million. By 1900 both Germany and the United States had overtaken Britain, at 6.7 and 10 million tons respectively compared with Britain's 5 million. The gap widened rapidly: by 1910 the figures for Germany and the United States were 13.8 and 26 million, while for Britain only 5.9 million. Austria, France and Russia were all increasing their steel production at a faster pace than Britain at the turn of the century, if from a lower base. Although this type of development took some time to affect contemporary perceptions of power, politicians could not but be aware of the disconcerting statistics which undermined the claim, maintained since the days of Palmerston, that Britain was the greatest nation on earth.

If isolation was by default and drift, then something had to be done urgently to deal with the growing threat from other powers to Britain's naval and imperial role; it was on this, after all, that the whole notion of doing nothing in Europe was based. Germany was the most serious danger, especially since the German government was pursuing a policy of deliberate confrontation with Britain, systematically constructed by key advisers. Holstein, for example, believed that colonial pressure would force the British government to make concessions and thereby acknowledge the legitimacy of Germany's new world role. Tirpitz argued that Germany should also increase her battleship strength and thereby force Britain into protecting home waters at the expense of far-flung imperial commitments. This, Tirpitz told Kaiser Wilhelm II, would 'concede to Your Majesty such a measure of maritime influence which will make it possible for Your Majesty to conduct a great overseas policy'.[9] This pressure came at the worst possible time; France was building up her naval strength in the western Mediterranean and, more seriously, Russia was threatening to control the access to many of the north China ports as a result of her construction of a major naval base at Port Arthur. Faced with the escalation of threats overseas, it could be argued, Britain had, sooner or later, to seek accommodation with another power. Otherwise, isolation could only become more and more burdensome.

The emergence from isolation was therefore conditioned by a feeling of vulnerability and a consciousness of being deeply unpopular with the rest of the world. The first major power approached was Germany. This started as a bilateral attempt to resolve colonial disputes and led to the Anglo-German agreement on Portugal's colonies (1898) and the Anglo-German China agreement of 1900. Joseph Chamberlain, Salisbury's Colonial Secretary, wanted to go further. He favoured the end of isolation in principle, adding: 'We must not reject the idea of an alliance with those Powers whose interests most nearly approximate to our own'.[10] To Chamberlain this meant Germany, which would be a dangerous enemy but a powerful ally. Hence 'The natural alliance is between ourselves and the great German empire'.[11] For all Chamberlain's enthusiasm, however, the Anglo-German negotiations of 1898, 1899 and 1901 came to nothing. The basic problem was that Britain wanted German assistance against Russia in the Far East, but was not willing to meet the German condition: British membership of the Triple Alliance and a full role in Europe. To Britain this was unacceptable since any security provided by German help in the East would be more than offset by a dangerous increase in pressures on Britain from France and Russia in the West.

Even so, the Far East continued to present the British government with a serious problem. For all her commercial and financial interests in China, Britain's security was suspect. The fleet allocated to the China Seas and the north Pacific was outnumbered by the combined navies of Russia and France and yet any attempt to supplement existing forces in the area would mean drawing off from the Mediterranean, leaving the British presence there weaker than the French, or from the North Sea, increasing Britain's vulnerability to Germany. The solution advanced by Selborne and Lansdowne was an agreement with Japan. This retained the focus on the East while minimising the risk of military commitment in the West.

Salisbury himself was not convinced, but this hardly mattered since he retired in 1902, giving way to Balfour who was.

The preamble of the Anglo-Japanese Alliance of 1902 emphasised the mutual desire of the two signatory powers to 'maintain the *status quo* and general peace in the Extreme East'. By Article 2 both Britain and Japan undertook to observe 'strict neutrality' should either 'become involved in war with another Power'. Article 3, however, carried Britain's first new diplomatic commitment for some years. 'If . . . any other Power or Powers should join in hostilities against that ally, the other High Contracting party will come to its assitance, and will conduct the war in common, and make peace in mutual agreement with it.'[12] This meant, in effect, that Japan would be left to deal with Russia alone, but that if France joined Russia, Britain would come to Japan's assistance. In the meantime, Britain achieved the security she needed in the Far East, since the Anglo-Japanese forces outnumbered the Franco-Russian.

Two arguments have been advanced as to whether or not this alliance signalled the end of British isolation. On the one hand, it has been taken as a complete change of direction. The media at the time certainly felt this, although there were very mixed views as to how desirable Britain's new partner was. There was now a strong possibility of further diplomatic developments. As Rosebery said in a speech in Liverpool in 1902: 'The treaty with Japan may be our first treaty of the kind for many years, but, having made it, it cannot be the last'.[13] The case for there having been a major change has also been argued by some historians. Temperley and Penson, in particular, maintain that 'The Treaty was revolutionary, a departure not only from the principles of Salisbury but even from those of Canning, which deprecated increase of obligations by guarantees or alliances'.[14] But this view is by no means universally accepted. Albrecht Carrié, for example, maintains that 'isolation was thought of in Britain as primarily a European policy; the alliance with Japan could therefore be said to confirm, in a sense, the tradition of isolation.'[15] A.J.P. Taylor makes the identical point: 'The Alliance did not mark the end of British isolation; rather it confirmed it. Isolation meant aloofness from the European Balance of Power; and this was now more possible than before.'[16]

There is, of course, some truth in both arguments. Although Britain did not intend to abandon isolation in Europe, the effects of the Treaty were to create new threats and thereby limit her options so that European agreements had to be entered into. This was certainly the case in 1904. As Britain's new ally found herself on a collision course with Russia, culminating in the outbreak of the Russo-Japanese war, Britain suddenly became aware of her changing relationship with France. The basic problem was that Britain did not want to have to honour a commitment given to Japan to fight two powers, which would certainly apply if France were to join Russia. The answer was to ensure France's neutrality. Britain was also strongly motivated by the prospect of reducing colonial tensions in Africa and bringing to an end nasty incidents like the 1898 Fashoda crisis. There was also the possibility that France might be able to put pressure on Russia to come to an accommodation with Britain over similar conflicts in Asia. Thus the conflict between Russia and Japan was the main catalyst for the Anglo-French Entente.

Signed in 1904, this was primarily an agreement to eliminate colonial disputes, especially in north Africa. By Article 1 'His Britannic Majesty's Government declare that they have no intention of altering the political status of Egypt. The Government of the French Republic, for their part, declare that they will not obstruct the action of Great Britain in that country [Egypt]'.[17] The *quid pro quo* concerned Morocco. Article 2 stated that 'The Government of the French Republic declare that they have no intention of altering the political status of Morocco. His Britannic Majesty's Government, for their part, . . . declare that they will not obstruct the action taken by France.'[18] Did this indicate that Britain had finally emerged from isolation? It is tempting, in the light of what eventually happened in 1914, to see the Entente as the commitment of Britain to a counter-alliance system. But this was the intention neither of Balfour's government, which signed it, nor of Campbell-Bannerman's ministry, which endorsed it the following year. Their focus was still the British Empire rather than Europe and the Entente carried no commitments concerning the latter. On the other hand, now that a connection had been made with a European power, European involvements were bound to follow; an example was Britain's support for France at the 1906 Algeçiras Conference, dealt with in the next section.

The last stage in Britain's emergence from isolation was the signing in 1907 of the Convention with Russia and the Triple Entente with Russia and France. Again the focus was on eliminating imperial rivalries. Although defeat in the Far East had weakened Russia's threat to China, it had also served to divert her attention elsewhere, especially in Tibet, Afghanistan (the traditional pressure point against British India) and Persia. There was a strong argument, therefore, for reaching accommodation over these areas and making Russia more susceptible to French influence on Britain's behalf. Hence the Preamble of the Anglo-Russian Convention stated that Britain and Russia were 'animated by the sincere desire to settle by mutual agreement different questions concerning the interests of their States on the Continent of Asia'.[19] The subsequent Articles allowed for spheres of influence in Persia but ruled out annexations or internal interference in Afghanistan and Tibet.

As in the case of the Anglo-French Entente, this arrangement has been seen as clear evidence of Britain's acceptance of a European role. G.W. Monger, for example, considers that Britain's priority was 'to change the balance of forces in Europe and in particular to create a counterpoise to Germany'.[20] On the other hand, some historians see the Convention entirely within the context of Britain's traditional overseas policy; according to K. Wilson, 'like the Agreement with France, that with Russia was made not for the sake of the balance of power in Europe but for the sake of Britain's own Imperial interests.'[21] An alternative perspective is that Britain was seeking through diplomacy to solve traditional imperial problems but, in the process, unintentionally set up new European links and commitments which meant that isolation entirely disappeared as an option. The Entente with France and the Convention with Russia therefore helped reorientate Britain's imperial policy into the very European commitments which had for the past decade been carefully avoided.

GROWING COMMITMENTS

This transition was not a deliberate one. Sir Edward Grey, the Liberal Foreign Secretary, said in 1906 that 'alliances, especially continental alliances, are not in accordance with our traditions'.[22] Far from accepting European obligations, the Liberal government once again invoked the principle of the Concert of Europe and sought to revive the idealism which had been missing since the era of Gladstone. This meant emphasising the common interest of nations and the primacy of international law. It did *not* mean specific commitments to reset the balance of European power in Britain's favour. Nevertheless, Britain was thrust more and more into the turbulent diplomacy of Europe by a series of developments which made isolation a practical impossibility. These worked concurrently and overlapped each other.

The first became apparent very quickly: diplomatic undertakings on imperial issues carried obligations which had *European* implications. The Morocco crises of 1906 and 1911 clearly illustrate this. In a deliberate attempt to test Britain's new friendship with France, Germany declared her intention to uphold the full independence of Morocco and, at the 1906 Algeçiras Conference, challenged France's special interest in the area. This might have been a case for polite neutrality on the part of Britain – except that Article 9 of the Anglo-French Entente had stipulated that 'The two Governments agree to afford to one another their diplomatic support, in order to obtain the execution of the clauses of the present Declaration regarding Egypt and Morocco'.[23] It was therefore quite impossible for Britain to avoid becoming involved in the confrontation with Germany. Hence Grey fulfilled Britain's obligation at Algeçiras by orchestrating support for France from Russia, Spain and Italy. Even tighter links were forged in 1911 over the second Moroccan crisis, when Germany sent a gunboat to Agadir. Two statements of policy, made by members of the British government, seemed to indicate that the Entente was tightening into something resembling an alliance. One was Lloyd George's Mansion House speech, which warned that Britain could not be expected to stand by 'where her interests were vitally affected'. The other, and more important, was Grey's declaration to parliament:

> The ideal of splendid isolation contemplated a balance of power in Europe to which we were not to be a party, and from which we were to be able to stand aside in the happy position of having no obligations and being able to take advantage of any difficulties which arose in Europe from friction between opposing Powers. That policy is not a possible one now.[24]

The second development transforming Britain's imperial agreements into European commitments was the explosion of the delayed time charges set in 1878 when the statesmen at the Congress of Berlin had resolved one set of problems by storing up others for the future (see Chapter 14). One of these had been the allocation of Bosnia-Herzegovina to Austria-Hungary. The Austrian government eventually made good its claim and annexed Bosnia in 1908 – to the disappointment of Serbia, which immediately appealed to Russia. At the subsequent conference, however, France and Britain decided on a cautious approach since Austria was clearly intent on pursuing her claim to the point of war – and with a guarantee of German support. Britain's reaction can be seen in two ways. On the one hand, it might be interpreted as Britain showing the limits of her new commitments. On the other, bearing in mind that France acted similarly – to the disappointment of her ally Russia – it could be argued that this was merely a crisis which the Entente powers ducked. But they were the more determined to avoid doing so again. In particular, this tightened Britain's resolve to meet the German naval building challenge and to intensify her own programme.

The third factor drawing Britain further into Europe was the German threat itself. This was not immediately recognised by the Liberal government. Grey wanted at the outset to re-establish good relations with Germany, which many Liberals preferred to closer diplomatic connections with Russia, a regime which they regarded as an abhorrent autocracy. Hence there were several attempts at coming to terms with Germany, including proposals for arms reductions in 1907 and the Haldane mission in 1912; there was actually a decrease in the number of new Dreadnoughts built – from three in 1906 to two in 1907. But the unencouraging German response, especially in 1907, was a severe blow to the pacifists within the Liberal party and a clear warning to the leadership that Germany would need to be handled with extreme caution – even suspicion. This became even more apparent with the Bosnia crisis of 1908, which did much to accelerate the levels of Dreadnought construction to six in 1909 and ten between 1910 and 1911. Much of the initiative for this was taken by the First Sea Lord, Fisher, who added his voice to warnings about the growing German peril. Major changes also occurred in the army, under the auspices of the Secretary for War, Haldane. A general staff was established in 1907 and an Expeditionary Force of 160,000 troops was organised for immediate action if necessary. These were backed up by 300,000 Territorials and an updated network of supplies and equipment. The underlying assumption was that they might actually have to be used – confirmation, therefore, that the Entente was beginning to evolve into alliance. These reforms were not designed for imperial campaigns, therefore, but as a precaution in case of continental involvement.

All of these factors led Britain to prepare for war as an option and to seek closer naval and military collaboration with France. The

Committee for Imperial Defence (CID) actually discussed the scenario of British involvement in a general European war, with the military and naval command giving their own somewhat different suggestions as to how this should be organised. According to the secretary for the CID, Hankey: 'from that time onward there was never any doubt what would be the Grand Strategy in the event of our being drawn into a continental war in support of France. Unquestionably the Expeditionary Force, or the greater part of it, would have been sent to France as it was in 1914'.[25] According to Kennedy all the quarrels between the War Office and the Admiralty were about '*how* to support the French, not *whether* to support them'.[26] Although there was still no detailed and specific military *commitment*, the decision to synchronise naval responsibilites within the China Sea, the Mediterranean and the North Sea carried an ever-increasing moral obligation to France which went far beyond anything originally envisaged in the 1904 Entente.

1914: THE DECISION FOR WAR

By 1914, Britain had therefore shed all vestiges of 'splendid isolation', having experienced aggressive competition from Germany and undertaken a number of obligations towards France. As yet, however, Britain still had no military commitments enshrined within a treaty and, in theory at least, still had a major degree of choice in her future actions.

Sir Edward Grey acted initially on the assumption that war with Germany was completely unnecessary – and for a while he appeared to be right. Anglo-German relations actually improved. The potentially dangerous Balkan Wars (1912–13) were localised largely as a result of diplomatic co-operation between Britain and Germany. The situation could easily have slid into direct confrontation between Austria-Hungary and Russia, but the former was restrained by Germany and the latter by Britain and France. The British government also saw Germany as a decreasing threat because of the widening gap between their respective naval building programmes. Indeed, several efforts, including the Haldane mission, were made to try to bring about more explicit co-operation. There was also agreement on all remaining colonial issues, especially in Africa.

The assassination at Sarajevo on 28 June 1914 came as a major blow, leading eventually to the Austrian ultimatum to Serbia and the prospects of direct confrontation between all the continental powers. Even so, Grey assumed that the crisis could be contained by the type of negotiation which had already succeeded in limiting the scope of the Balkan Wars. Why should the situation in Bosnia-Herzegovina be any different? On 25 July, therefore, Grey suggested mediation between Serbia, Austria-Hungary and Russia, by Britain, France, Germany and Italy. When Germany refused, Grey followed up with a proposal for a European conference. When this met a negative response, Grey requested from Germany a suggestion as to 'any method by which the influence of the four Powers could be used together to prevent a war between Austria and Russia'.[27] Again, nothing happened.

By this stage, Grey had switched his attention to trying to persuade his cabinet to stand by France if the latter were attacked by Germany. He emphasised the importance of being willing to give such an undertaking for the sake of Britain's future reputation – which now rested on much more than the fulfilment of the narrow obligations imposed by the 1904 Entente. He was supported by Churchill, Haldane and Asquith but the outcome of several meetings at the end of July was inconclusive because of the opposition of the majority of the ministers, including Burns, Beauchamp, Simon and Morley. The Conservative opposition sought to influence the deliberations; Lansdowne and Bonar Law wrote that 'it would be fatal to the honour and security of the United Kingdom to hesitate in supporting France and Russia at this juncture; and we offer our unconditional support to the Government in any measures they may consider necessary to this object'.[28] Even on 1 August the British government could give the French no guarantee. Things were, however, beginning to move: the cabinet did decide to treat any violation of Belgian neutrality as a *casus belli* and also proved receptive to Grey's argument that the British navy had some obligation to defend the Channel, given that the French had agreed to confine their naval role to the Mediterranean.

But Britain was finally impelled to act not when the Germans declared war on France on 3 August, but when they invaded Belgium the following day. Does this mean that Belgium was the main factor in Britain's declaration of war on Germany? The usual argument is that emphasising Belgian integrity was the only way in which Grey could get his cabinet behind him for the vital task of helping France. The defence of a small and helpless state against a military regime with a recent record of aggression had an irresistible appeal and countered the pacifist principles of all but two members of the cabinet. In assisting Belgium, of course, Britain would be sending the Expeditionary Force to France, thus carrying out every conceivable obligation she might have incurred.

There is an alternative view, which ascribes a secondary role to the Belgian issue. Wilson, indeed, argues that the importance of the invasion of Belgium in pushing Britain into war has been exaggerated. Instead, there was a strong element of *internal* politics. In insisting on the need to help France, Grey threatened on 1 August to resign if the cabinet continued to adopt an 'uncompromising policy of non-intervention at all costs'.[29] He was assisted by the letter of Lansdowne and Bonar Law, which seemed to indicate that the Conservatives were making a bid for power. If, as appeared likely, Asquith resigned along with Grey, the result would have to be either a coalition cabinet or a new Conservative government; neither would prevent the slide to war and the latter might even accelerate it. All but two Liberal cabinet ministers came to the conclusion that unity had to prevail if the Liberals were to remain in power, and the Belgian issue made their conversion more palatable.

Whichever way the events of July and August 1914 are viewed, the personal influence of Sir Edward Grey was considerable. Were his actions in any way at fault? It has been said that Grey's policy towards Germany was inconclusive and that he sent the wrong messages, inadvertently encouraging the German government to increase the pressure. Then Grey suddenly cried halt and Germany let loose the dogs of war. His policies were, from the start, over-ambitious. According to Ekstein and Steiner, 'He believed Britain could act as a mediator while supporting France and Russia against Germany'.[30]

On the other hand, it might be argued that nothing that Grey did – or did not do – made any difference to the German invasion of Belgium. Recent historical interpretation has tended very much to stress Germany's desire to go to war in 1914 as the way out of a major dilemma. It was considered in Berlin that German security was being endangered by a rapid increase in the military power of the Franco-Russian Alliance; both countries were catching up quickly and the Russian programme of rearmament would be complete (ironically) by 1917. At a meeting between the Kaiser and his generals, held on 8 December 1912, von Moltke, the Chief of General Staff, said that war was inevitable and, he added, 'the sooner the better'.[31] Germany, after all, had the means of inflicting a swift and crushing defeat on France by means of the Schlieffen Plan, which involved the invasion of northern France via Belgium. In the aftermath of the Sarajevo crisis, therefore, Bethmann Hollweg was content to ignore the peace offers made by Grey, in the knowledge that 'If war must break out, better now than in one or two years' time, when the Entente will be stronger'.[32]

Thus Grey was trying to constrain a government which had already capitulated to the advice of its military leadership and which saw war as a way out of, and not into, a hole. For Britain, therefore, all ways pointed to military conflict – or a return to isolation which, far from being 'splendid', would now be utterly humiliating.

20

GOVERNMENT POLICY AND THE ECONOMY 1815–1914

Several of the earlier chapters included sections on the economic measures of specific governments. It is now time to provide a more general perspective on economic policy as a whole between 1815 and 1914, placing it within the broad canvas of political history referred to in Chapter 1.

Historians have attempted to break the period down into economic phases. W.W. Rostow, for example, maintains that the period 1815–47 was one of adjustment and reconstruction.[1] This was followed, between 1847 and 1873, by the so-called 'mid-Victorian boom' which, in turn, gave way to the Great Depression (1873–1900) and Edwardian recovery (1900–14). R. Tames uses a similar breakdown, although with slightly differing dates.[2] The years 1815–42 saw the 'crisis of capitalism', 1842–73 the 'great Victorian boom', 1873–96 'the Great Depression' and 1896–1914 the 'Indian summer' of the British economy. The two interpretations have a common dynamic; the implication is that periods one and three correspond as the search for renewal and revival, while two and four indicate expansion and fulfilment.

This chapter will condense the process into two main periods: 1815–73 and 1873–1914. Within this framework the focus will be the role of the government in Britain's economic growth. It will be argued that between 1815 and 1873 the government gradually dismantled the traditional apparatus of a controlled economy and in its place introduced *laissez-faire* which was effectively complete by the late 1860s. During the second period, 1873–1914, the economy experienced substantial changes which indicated that *laissez-faire* was no longer entirely appropriate. Governments of the period did not, however, see fit to adjust the approach which had been introduced; they preferred, instead, to stay with *laissez-faire*, with the effects that will be examined.

MOVING TO ECONOMIC *LAISSEZ-FAIRE* 1815–70

At the beginning of the eighteenth century the British economy had been circumscribed by a series of laws which were collectively known as the mercantilist system. In the first half of the nineteenth century, however, these were gradually removed. The Statute of Apprentices, which prescribed a minimum period of training, was repealed in 1814. Legislation defining in minute detail the quality of cloth was reversed by the governments of the 1820s and 1830s. In 1824, for example, Liverpool's government repealed the Acts prescribing the manufacture of boots, while legislation concerning the quality of bread was ended in 1822 and 1836.

Governments also targeted the Usury Laws which limited interest charges to 5 per cent. The Bank Charter Act of 1833 empowered the Bank of England to operate outside the scope of the Laws, which, in turn, were formally repealed by Gladstone in 1854. Meanwhile, restrictions imposed by the Bubble Act of 1720 were lifted from joint-stock companies. Most significant of all was the lifting of restrictions on imports. Some of these had been intended as a major source of government revenue. Others had come within the scope of the Navigation Acts, which had prevented the import of goods from foreign countries unless they were carried in British ships. The purpose had originally been to protect the English mercantile marine against its major competitors, the Dutch, who, during the seventeenth century, had dominated up to two-thirds of Europe's carrying trade. Import duties were steadily reduced throughout the first half of the nineteenth century. Huskisson, for example, reduced duties on a wide range of raw materials and other goods. This process was continued by Peel's Budgets of 1842 and 1845, which removed altogether the duties on 600 articles and greatly reduced those on 500 others. Huskisson relaxed the full operation of the Navigation Acts and they were eventually repealed in 1849. The most persistent form of protection, and the last to be introduced, was the Corn Law of 1815. This was gradually discredited during the 1830s and 1840s by the mercantile and industrial interests who argued that the special concessions given to agriculture were distorting the pattern of Britain's economic growth. The climax came, in 1846, with the repeal of the Corn Laws of 1815 and 1828.

By 1850, therefore, the full panoply of mercantilist restrictions had been swept away, to be replaced by a policy of minimal State intervention in the economy. There is some dispute, however, as to whether this change was a pragmatic response to prevailing conditions, or whether it was influenced directly by economic theorists. Perhaps it makes most sense to see it as a combination of the two. The process began as the mercantilist system gradually became obsolete, but it was accelerated by new ideas.

Recent historians have, nevertheless, rightly emphasised that there was no sudden movement into an 'age of *laissez-faire*'. Instead, there was considerable continuity between the early nineteenth century and the late eighteenth. P. Deane argues that 'The beginnings of a purposeful government economic policy can be traced back to Pitt the Younger'.[3] Certainly Pitt made more systematic use of the Budget as an instrument of financial policy, reduced a number of duties and experimented with new taxes. But even he was not deliberately innovative. All prime ministers and chancellors of the period 1750–1850 were faced with the undeniable truth that mercantilism and the policies of restriction were not working. Almost all the regulations were difficult to enforce and were being widely evaded. Joint companies were set up by private Acts of Parliament which ignored the Bubble Act, the Usury Laws were bypassed by private agreements between money-lenders and entrepreneurs, and the import duties were reduced to a mockery by the widespread smuggling conducted along all parts of the English and Scottish coastline. Detailed regulations had become ineffectual and it made increasing sense for governments to rationalise them in a way which would reduce the administrative costs of their enforcement.

It would be a serious distortion, however, to claim that *laissez-faire* economic policies derived from pragmatic considerations alone. The period saw an outpouring of literature on the economy which was quite unprecedented in its intensity. The first and arguably the most influential of the 'Classical economists' was Adam Smith, who favoured 'a strong presumption against government activity beyond its fundamental duties of protection against its foreign foes and maintenance of justice'.[4] His views were reinforced by Ricardo who, in his *Principles of Political Economy and Taxation*, argued for the fair and free competition of the market in determining wage levels. This is why Gregg calls him 'the high priest of the manufacturers'.[5] The successors of Smith and Ricardo were Senior and McCulloch. According to Senior in 1830: 'the duty of the Government is to keep the peace, to protect all its subjects from the violence and fraud and malice of one another, and, having done so, to leave them to pursue what they believe to be their own interests in the way which they deem advisable'.[6] John Stuart Mill argued in 1848 in his *Principles of Political Economy* that *laissez-faire* should operate as the general principle and that 'the burthen of making out a strong case [rests] not on those who resist, but on those who recommend government interference'.[7]

The writings of the Classical economists exercised a widespread influence, direct and indirect, at a variety of levels. They had a considerable readership: *The Wealth of Nations*, for example, went through five editions during Adam Smith's lifetime. Popularised versions were also provided – for example, by Harriet Martineau's monthly *Illustrations of Political Economy*. On a loftier level, the *Economist*, founded by James Wilson, regularly propagated the principles of *laissez-faire* on behalf of the Anti-Corn Law League, while other press organs included the *Leeds Mercury*. The ideas of *laissez-faire* also penetrated both political parties. Although some Tories and Conservatives were influenced, more notable was the wholesale, rather than partial, conversion of the Whigs and Liberals. Within parliament individual MPs made it their business to translate economic principles into political policy. One such was Ricardo; another, later in the century, was John Stuart Mill.

Finally, the ideas of *laissez-faire* penetrated governments directly. Peel, for example, was converted in the early 1840s; by 1846 he was regularly articulating the views of the Classical economists. In the railway debate of 1846 he argued for 'the great principle of permitting this commercial country the free application of individual enterprise and capital'.[8] Below the cabinet level, but still within the executive, a number of civil servants acted as a major influence on government policy. Particularly important were MacGregor, Porter and Hume at the Board of Trade between 1828 and 1841. According to A.J. Taylor: 'All were convinced free traders in the full tradition of Adam Smith and through their work, particularly in the collection and deployment of statistical evidence, they exercised a powerful influence on the deliberations of the Select Committee on Import Duties in 1840 and on the commercial legislation of the succeeding decade'.[9] L. Brown goes so far as to say that 'In the eighteen-twenties the Board of Trade had led the movement for commercial liberalism'.[10]

P. Deane expresses this influence as the creation of an awareness of the need for more systematic planning and thought, whether this applied to Huskisson, Canning or Peel:

> They tried to evolve consistent policies in the light of the teachings of the leading economists . . . They did not always take the undiluted advice of the economists but they did realize more than any of their eighteenth-century predecessors that the execution of the appropriate economic policy required serious thought and positive action.[11]

How important was government policy in promoting the economic progress of Britain during the first half of the nineteenth century? It might be argued that it is impossible to quantify the economic effect of political withdrawal: after all, how can one measure the success of the *absence* of a policy? In one respect, however, the government's policy on *laissez-faire* was positive. It set up a framework for future economic expansion and undoubtedly stimulated exports by reducing the costs of imports. At times limited intervention was necessary, although on a far smaller scale than in the eighteenth century. In order to promote *laissez-faire* it had to create the appropriate environment; this meant the imposition of certain constraints to ensure that competition was purposeful and sound. Hence the importance of Peel's Bank Charter Act and Companies Act, together with the legislation controlling the spread of the railways. It is arguable that the reduction of import duties stimulated growth, while the currency and corporate regulations prevented it from dissipating.

All this is not to say that government policy was the only factor in Britain's economic growth. It would have counted for nothing without other factors. These included entrepreneurial skills, the backwardness of Britain's competitors, and the various booms. R. Tames argues that the most important of these were the railway booms since 'The lag between railway promotion and railway construction, however, gave a much-needed boost at this difficult time and as a consequence Britain was saved from the revolutionary wave which engulfed Europe in 1848'.[12] The economy was also assisted by a rapid increase in business optimism after gold was discovered in 1848 in Western Australia and in 1849 in California. A government practising *laissez-faire* principles could not hope to initiate these circumstances, merely to enable entrepreneurs to take advantage of them by providing favourable conditions.

STAYING WITH ECONOMIC *LAISSEZ-FAIRE*
1870–1914

Throughout the first half of the nineteenth century Britain was unquestionably the world's leading industrial and commercial power. After about 1870, however, the gap narrowed and then disappeared as Germany and the United States in particular increased their own industrial output. Figure 12 shows the changing share each of the three countries had of the world's steel production between 1875 and 1913, while Figure 13 indicates how far behind Britain had fallen in the manufacture of chemicals. It is quite evident from these that Britain's leading rivals were catching up and taking the lead during this period. The United States was experiencing a boom after a prolonged recession caused by the Civil War, while Germany was riding the crest of an economic and industrial wave after political unification in 1871. At the same time, Britain was, in comparative terms, slowing down; Figure 14, for example, compares British, German and American growth rates in industrial output, industrial productivity and exports. Figure 15 reveals that even her population growth fell far behind that of her rivals.

A remarkable economic transformation was therefore taking place – to Britain's underlying disadvantage. But this was not accompanied by a change in the government's policy on *laissez-faire*. Indeed, the degree of government abstention during this crucial period was remarkable. According to Hobsbawm 'Britain was the only country which systematically refused any fiscal protection to its industries, and the only country in which the government neither built, nor helped to finance (directly or indirectly), nor even planned any part of the railway system'.[13] It needs to be asked why this was and to what extent Britain's relative economic decline was due to political factors – or government policies – and to what extent it was the inevitable result of factors beyond the government's control.

What are the facts of government non-intervention in the economy? Hobsbawm is right to stress the contrast between Britain and Germany over capital projects and industrial infrastructure. British governments quite deliberately refused to follow the example of almost every other industrial state which was subsidising the building of railways or canals. Another example of 'negative intervention' was the failure to provide protection for British goods against foreign competition. The government could

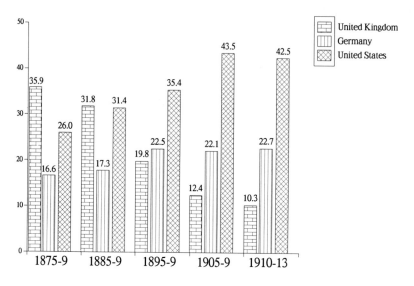

Figure 12 Production of steel 1875–1913 (% of world production)

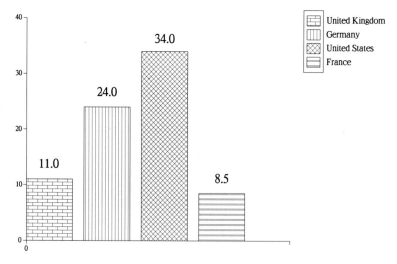

Figure 13 Production of chemicals in 1913 (% of world production)

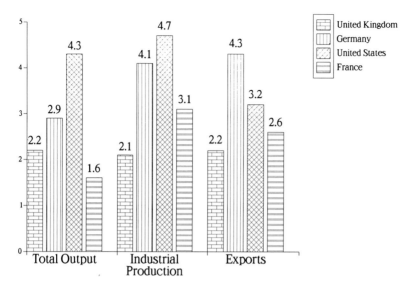

Figure 14 Economic growth rates 1870–1914 (% per annum)

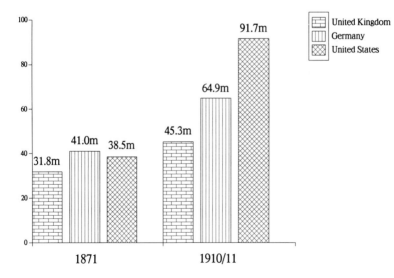

Figure 15 Total populations 1871–1911

scarcely plead ignorance here, since there was no shortage of pressure groups to point out the growing threat of Germany and the United States. The British government, however, refused consistently to follow the example of Germany which, in 1879, imposed tariff barriers. It ignored the pleas in the 1880s of MPs representing Bradford and Sheffield for protection for woollens and steel utensils. There was remarkable political consensus here. The Liberals remained ideologically committed to *laissez-faire* and the Conservatives, who were more divided on the issue, decided to lie low on tariffs in order to attract to their ranks the Liberal Unionists who were abandoning Gladstone over the issue of Irish Home Rule. In this respect, Conservative economic policy played a secondary role to political considerations. Admittedly there was a strong campaign at the turn of the century for tariff reform. But this emerged as a fringe movement within the Conservative party. It was led by Joseph Chamberlain, whose political credentials had already been called into question for the damage he had inflicted on the Liberal party over Ireland. In the minds of many politicians his economic case was seriously undermined by the political dangers with which he now threatened the Conservative party.

A third example of the British government's refusal to interfere with the economy was its determination to maintain the British currency in connection with the gold standard, even though, as Pollard points out, the Bank of England cannot be considered a governmental bank. According to Pollard, 'The Government had no direct access to the decision making of the Bank of England whatever . . . Instead of setting the tone, the Government asked for and frequently took the advice of the Bank and the City on questions of monetary policy and related issues'.[14] In Germany, the *Reichsbank* provided a more stable economic environment for investment in German industry, whereas the Bank of England held such low gold reserves that it was more liable than the French and German banks to cause fluctuations in the interest rates.

What were the reasons for this political abstention from the economic sphere? One was that the politicians who administered the State after 1873 all had connections with an earlier period in which economic *laissez-faire* and free trade had established complete ascendancy. It was asking a great deal of someone like Gladstone to turn his back on his Peelite past; had he made this economic transition he would have called into question many of his earlier political changes between 1846 and 1868.

Another major reason was that the sectors of the economy which would have benefited most from a change of policy had no real political influence. Pollard points to a basic paradox – that 'the middle classes, and especially the industrial middle classes, failed to capture power on the basis of the growing economic superiority of the commercial and industrial sectors as against the agrarian'.[15] This was mainly because much of the productive middle class was absorbed into the upper classes, which meant that the measure of their economic success was translated into social terms and that they therefore became part of the traditional political elite. Those who remained distinctively middle class either devoted their energies to their businesses or entered politics at the local level, where there were fewer traditional hierarchies to break into. Meanwhile, political institutions remained very much under the control of those whose interests were best served by maintaining the economic *status quo*; especially important were the landed classes and the financial and commercial groups. Industrial groups were very much in a minority. Even in the most radical of all the parliaments elected before 1914 – that produced by the 1906 Liberal landslide – over 20 per cent of MPs were connected with the land and nearly 50 per cent with finance and insurance.

In both political parties, therefore, there was a predominance of those interests which were closely related to the aristocratic principle, to the public school and to the non-industrial part of the economy. This meant that industry always lost out to the landed interests and to services like finance and insurance when it came to the interpretation by the government of the day of the most important priorities of economic policy. On the issue of Chamberlain's tariff reform, there was a particularly close alliance between city and agricultural interests. Large landowners were now against protection because Chamberlain's tariff reform envisaged a special relationship with the Empire which would clearly downgrade British agriculture: the use of imperial markets for British exports in return for imperial supplies of raw materials and food. The City was opposed to Chamberlain's policy because it already benefited from the existing pattern where Britain's most important contribution to the world economy was shifting from industry to the service sector, finance, investment and insurance.

Did this policy – or absence of a policy – have much effect? Can it really be held accountable for the comparative decline of Britain's economic performance between 1870 and 1914? On the one hand, it could be argued that the British government impeded industrial growth in Britain precisely because it did not follow the example of continental governments in promoting theirs. Belgian, German and French governments, for example, made it possible for industry to release funds for other forms of essential infrastructure, while they themselves concentrated on extending transport links. In addition, the lack of a firm policy by the British government in connection with the Bank of England meant that there were more fluctuations in interest rates in Britain than among her competitors, thus further affecting the availability of investment. Where the British government did occasionally intervene in specifically economic issues, the results were generally negative. One example was the Electric Lighting Act of 1882 which enabled local authorities to take over private companies, thereby reducing the attraction of the electricity industry to private investors. Another Act required car speeds to be limited to 4 miles per hour and vehicles to be preceded by a man on foot carrying a red flag. Notorious though these instances were, they were very much exceptions to the general rule of abstention from economic regulation.

There are, however, several prominent reasons for the slowing down or retardation of British industrial output which go well beyond any government neglect. One is the early start experienced by British industry. It would be unreasonable to have expected Britain to have maintained her economic lead indefinitely and there was bound to be a degree of catching up by other countries sooner or later. A second possibility is that British entrepreneurial skills were no longer as distinctive as they had once been. One problem for industry was that a lower proportion of profits was ploughed back into infrastructural improvements; instead, an increasing number of second- and third-generation industrialists used part of their wealth to gain access to the higher social levels. This helps explain the political predominance of the traditional elites as well as the curiously negative attitudes within Britain to the manufacturing classes, a contrast to the high esteem in which they were held in Germany and the United States.

Third, Britain was hampered by a slowing down of technological innovations: she actually fell behind in engineering and chemicals. One reason for this was that Britain was better supplied with labour than, for example, the United States, which therefore had more incentive to develop new technology. In addition, Britain possessed a larger proportion of machinery which, although obsolete, was still operational. Perhaps this was because British industry was accustomed to building to specification, which meant in effect building to last. Technological growth has to be based partly on an acceptance of obsolescence: in the United States, this promoted mass-production which was foreign to British methods until the 1920s and 1930s.

A fourth argument is that the British economy depended too heavily on a few select, or staple, industries, such as iron, steel, shipbuilding and textiles. These were at the expense of newer industries, such as man-made fibres and motor vehicles, which expanded more rapidly in Germany. Instead, more and more investment was ploughed into industries which had already reached saturation point and which, after the First World War, were to be undercut by rivals which could produce more cheaply. And finally, Britain had a smaller internal market at a time when Germany and the United States were exerting their major challenge. This is quite clear from the comparative changes in population growth. This, of course, was well beyond the control of the British government. Recent history suggests that the most successful industrial states, like Germany, the United States and Japan, are those which have substantial internal markets to act as a base for developing industries to the position where they can produce cost-effective goods to undercut the opposition in the export markets.

THE CONTRAST WITH SOCIAL POLICIES

Throughout the nineteenth century there was a fundamental contrast between the policies of various governments to issues which were economic and those which were more obviously social. As we have seen, economic policy moved towards, and then remained with, the broad principles of *laissez-faire*, even if from time to time there were exceptions to *laissez-faire* within this trend. Social policies followed a very different dynamic, to which we now turn.

281

21

GOVERNMENT POLICY TOWARDS SOCIAL PROBLEMS 1815–1914

The government's social policies originated from the effects of economic change, but they were not part of a policy which included the economy. Hence historians have tended to see the economy as being primarily geared to *laissez-faire* (although this was never in the purest sense), while social policies reflect a more obvious move towards State intervention, even collectivism.

At the turn of the century A.V. Dicey argued that 1865 formed a dividing line in the attitude of the government to social issues. Before that date policy had been dominated by individualism and Benthamite principles, whereas afterwards Britain came increasingly under collectivist influences.[1] This analysis served a useful purpose in that it showed the nineteenth-century origins of the collectivist State. But the consensus of modern historians is that Dicey did not go far enough back and that the break he assumed occurred in 1865 was too sharp. Instead, it is possible to see movement towards State intervention in social issues during the *first* half of the century. G. Kitson Clark, for example, divides the nineteenth century into three main phases. The first was the traditional order before 1832, the second a transitional period between 1832 and 1867, and the third, lasting from 1867 to 1885, was when 'modern society, modern democracy and the modern State were beginning to take shape'.[2] The fact that these are the dates of the Reform Acts is no coincidence, since parliamentary reform both reflected current necessity and provided an impetus for further social changes.

This chapter will use the broad periods suggested by Dicey while, at the same time, emphasising the continuity between them which more recent research has highlighted.

THE BEGINNING OF GOVERNMENT
INTERVENTION 1815–70

Throughout the first half of the nineteenth century, there appears to be a contradiction. On the one hand, governments increasingly removed constraints on trade and industry while, on the other, they intervened in the social sphere to deal with some of the worst results of the Industrial Revolution. But this was a meaningful dichotomy. Both forms of action involved government intervention – one to emancipate the economy from outmoded constraints, the other to alleviate the side-effects of this emancipation. In both instances government action was needed and a limited degree of collectivism in the social sector was quite compatible with *laissez-faire* in the economic. The period 1815–40 saw the origins of intervention by governments in social issues, while, between 1840 and 1865, a series of political decisions led to the emergence of an institutional framework for intervention, albeit somewhat limited at this stage.

A number of reasons can be advanced for the growth of this intervention. One is that the impact of the Industrial Revolution had been so appalling it could not simply be ignored. Evidence was provided by the reports of select committees; that of 1840 argued that the dangers to public health were so serious that 'There do not appear to be any practicable means of removing them without legislative interference.'[3] In the meantime, awareness had been raised by a wide variety of individuals including Methodists; Evangelicals such as William Wilberforce, Anthony Ashley and John Wood; trade unionists like John Doherty; and factory owners like Robert Owen and John Fielden. There was also no shortage of pressure groups and theorists, especially the Benthamites, whose influence was apparent in the Poor Law Amendment Act of 1834 and the institutions which that created. Particularly influential was Edwin Chadwick, who argued that although the greatest happiness of the population related directly to the national wealth, the loss of any individual's labour had a detrimental effect on the whole economy. To some extent, he said, existing processes should be changed to allow labour to find its natural level; this meant amending the Poor Law. But in other instances more direct State action was needed to prevent losses through avoidable ill-health. The answer in both cases was a more obvious role for State supervision: a central body with overall control of inspection and of local committees.

Ideas and pressures were accentuated by fear. At least part of the establishment felt that unchecked poverty and squalor might increase political unrest and even threaten revolution. There were also 'panics', or reactions to specific crises like the cholera epidemics of 1832, 1837 and 1847, and the typhus outbreaks in 1837 and 1839. These made governments much more receptive to reports on the details of insanitary conditions.

For anything to happen, however, governments needed to be willing to take the initiative. From 1830 onwards they were. The 1832 Reform Act had acted as a catalyst for further reform and the Whigs were receptive to arguments for social reform for reasons given in Chapter 6. They were also able to distinguish between economic and social motives for legislation. Macaulay gave a typical statement of the official position in 1846. Speaking in the House of Commons he upheld the principle of free trade, but with a reservation about the application of *laissez-faire* to the non-economic sector:

> I am not aware of any exceptions to that principle; but you would fall into error if you apply it to the transactions which are not purely commercial . . . the principle of non-interference is one that cannot be applied without great restriction where the public health or the public morality is concerned.[4]

There were also administrative influences behind the changes to the political approach to social reform. In particular, a new pattern had developed, within the Civil Service, of political neutrality and professional competence. According to P. Deane, 'This was another departure from the eighteenth-century pattern where government officials had characteristically been the lackeys of the landed aristocracy. It was the beginning of a new kind of bureaucracy, an officialdom from which today's Civil Service can trace direct descent.'[5] This meant that reform was a process which might be initiated at official as well as at ministerial level, thus doubling the scope for political action.

A significant number of changes was actually introduced during the period 1815–70. A consistent pattern gradually emerged; this lacked any counterpart in economic policy – which tended to be based more on *ad hoc* measures. At the outset pressure was applied by groups convinced that reform was necessary. This was followed by an official enquiry or investigation such as the Poor Law Commission (1832–4), the Royal Commission on the Employment of Women and Children (1842) and the Health of the Towns Commission (1844–5). Investigations, in turn, produced reports – such as the *Report of the Health of Towns Committee* (1840) and the *Report on an Inquiry into the Sanitary Condition of the Labouring Population of Great Britain* (1842). The outcome was often specific legislation. This affected three main areas – poverty, working conditions and public health – and included the Poor Law Amendment Act of 1834; the Factory Acts of 1831, 1833, 1844, 1847, 1850 and 1867; the Mines Act of 1842; the Coal Mines Inspection Act (1850); the Mines Regulation and Inspection Act (1860); the Public Health Act of 1848; and the Sanitation Act (1866).

These laws led to what Deane has called 'revolution in social administration'.[6] The Poor Law Amendment Act (1834), for example, set up a new unit in the form of the parish union and, at the same time, standardised on a national level the methods by which the poor were to be treated. Above the whole system was a group of commissioners. A further development occurred in 1847 when the Poor Law Commission was replaced by the Poor Law Board subject to ministerial and hence parliamentary control. Administrative changes were also made for public health. These started with the provisions within the New Poor Law for unions to appoint medical officers. Chadwick, who had been a prominent member of the Poor Law Commission, took up the further fight for State intervention to prevent the spread of disease. The Public Health Act of 1848 set up the General Board of Health, which had powers to inspect and recommend. Local government initiatives were also apparent. The Municipal Corporations Act of 1835 and the subsequent reform of the counties acted as a catalyst for local reforming initiatives. For example, Manchester banned back-to-back housing in 1844, while Liverpool appointed a medical officer of health in 1847, in advance of the nationally imposed requirement. London also took some initiatives in the form of the City of London Sewers Act (1851), which included prohibitions on cellar-dwellings and enabled the clearance of slum areas.

Perspectives differ on the effectiveness of these changes. On the one hand, P. Deane argues that

> In the 1830s and 1840s, therefore, and still more in the 1850s the State was steadily taking responsibility for wider and wider control of private enterprise in the interest of society as

a whole . . . So far from being triumphant by the 1850s, the *laissez-faire* movement had been finally routed by new techniques of government control of the economy which had their own built-in tendency to develop, grow and multiply.[7]

On the other hand, it would be premature to speak in terms of a collectivist system in full operation by the middle of the nineteenth century since there were still several major obstacles to its further spread.

One was the widespread opposition shown to State interference, usually and misguidedly expressed in terms of individual liberty. *Laissez-faire* was therefore invoked in the name of social as well as economic freedom. Opposition, for example, forced the abolition of the General Board of Health in 1858 and the transfer of its responsibilities to the Privy Council. In part this was influenced by a campaign against the Board in *The Times* which preferred 'to take its chance of cholera' than 'be bullied into health'. It also presented an alarming picture of John Bull being 'scrubbed, and rubbed, and small-tooth combed until the tears came into his eyes'.[8] Although Dr Simon proved a committed and efficient adviser, and several health inspectors were appointed, there was nevertheless a break in the development of a comprehensive system which could ensure a more effective check on sanitary conditions. The threads had to be taken up again by the governments of Gladstone and Disraeli after 1868.

Another obstacle was that there were, as yet, no influential theorists for extensive government intervention. It was more a case of justifying the government being unable to follow the same pattern as in the economy. At this stage in the nineteenth century State action was negative and preventive rather than positive and supportive. It was designed to set limits on intervention quite as much as to extend that intervention. This distinguishes the early collectivist measures from the more advanced policies of the Welfare State. The former associated poverty with idleness, the latter with other, more objective, criteria.

By the 1860s, therefore, there was still a major shortfall in state intervention in those areas of society most in need of reform. The Royal Commission of 1869 made a comment which could perhaps be applied to all areas tackled: 'the English public health system of the sixties was thus chiefly characterised by not being a system at all'.[9] Part of the reason for this was that the approach was mainly negative. 'Its object was to release man from the thrall of disease in order that he might produce efficiently. In attempting thus to prevent nuisance, it failed lamentably to attack the roots of ill-health positively.' [10]

THE GROWTH OF COLLECTIVISM 1870–1914

Between 1870 and 1906 the scope of social reform expanded steadily as a mass of legislation emerged during the era of Gladstone and Disraeli, and that of Salisbury and Balfour. Factory conditions and hours were further regulated in the Acts of 1867, 1874, 1878 and 1891. The Public Health Act of 1872 subdivided England and Wales into more logically defined health authorities, while the appointment of a public health officer by each authority now became compulsory. A further stride was made in 1875 by the Public Health Act, which consolidated earlier legislation and introduced regulations on details. Further reorganisation in 1888 and 1894 meant that, according to Midwinter, 'It was in the field of public health that central authority bit quickly and deeply in the last quarter of the nineteenth century.' [11] There was also a perceptible softening of attitudes towards poverty; time brought a more flexible use of the Poor Law, which meant the partial return of outdoor relief and the use of workhouses as refuges rather than places of punishment. Finally, advances were made in the State funding of education by means of Forster's Act (1870), Sandon's Act (1876) and Balfour's Act (1902). How can this obvious acceleration of State intervention be explained?

The first reason was the political transformation which took place in the 1860s. The death of Palmerston in 1865 enabled the rapid evolution of the Whig–Radical–Peelite coalition into the Gladstonian Liberal party. At the same time, the rise of Disraeli gave a more progressive emphasis to the Conservatives. Both parties, newly reactivated, contested with each other the support of an electorate enlarged by the 1867 Reform Act. The solution of both party leaders was to sponsor a series of reforms. Gladstonian Liberalism focused more on the great institutions, while Disraelian Conservatism looked more directly at the social needs of the working class. Together they pushed back the boundaries of State intervention. Party policy was backed by the contributions made to progressive reform in central and local administration. The Civil Service at Whitehall was particularly influential. Senior officials shaped the legislation,[12] acting as a progressive influence, in contrast with some European states where the civil service was actually obstructive. Local government also became more and more collectivist. This was made possible by the administrative overhaul which set up municipal boroughs in 1882 and the county councils and county boroughs in 1888.

At the service of politicians and officials was a wide range of technical expertise. Major developments had taken place in civil engineering, which made possible the massive projects of laying sewers and drains for which late Victorian England is rightly renowned. Much the same applied to architectural progress and the use of improved materials in house construction. Scientific progress was also made, especially in identifying the specific causes of cholera and typhus; State intervention against filth was therefore given an additional impetus based on medical knowledge. The promotion of antiseptics and anaesthetics also provided an incentive to improve hospital conditions.

The growth of social collectivism was also related to the reduced threat of revolution and political radicalism. Those who wielded power were now more willing to share it with the levels below them, which meant the extension of the franchise to the working classes in 1867 and 1884 (see Chapter 11). In part this was due to the evolution of British labour into moderate and non-Marxist channels; 'new model unionism', for example, acted increasingly by negotiation rather than through political pressure. Both political parties were therefore convinced that political reform could be carried through without the risk of opening the floodgates. The corollary, however, was that this new electorate would expect further attention to its social needs – and that this expectation would now influence the outcome of general elections. Governments therefore saw collectivism as a party-political issue. As such, they had to give more attention to health, housing and trade union rights. There was also much greater pressure than before to increase educational provision as a means of guaranteeing political moderation within the working-class electorate in the future. This is what the Liberal MP Lowe had in mind when he said that 'we must now educate our masters'.[13]

Finally, governments continued to be bombarded with ideas, petitions and campaigns from all quarters. For instance, middle-class temperance movements persuaded Liberal ministries to bring licensing within the scope of State intervention. Influence was also exerted by Christian academics; J.R. Seeley argued that the scope of religion was 'much more national and political, much less personal than is commonly supposed'.[14] The Liberals also paid heed to the Christian socialism of F.D. Maurice, Charles Kingsley and Thomas Hughes and were, of course, permeated by the Nonconformist conscience.

Social reform had therefore taken a permanent place within the political arena. Before 1906, however, there were still major constraints on government action which postponed any introduction of a Welfare State. One was the reluctance of any of the prime ministers of the period – Gladstone, Disraeli, Salisbury, Rosebery and Balfour – to consider raising income tax; indeed, Gladstone always hoped to be able to abolish it. There was no possibility that collectivism could be transformed into a Welfare State until governments accepted responsibility for the individual's social well-being.

For the moment they remained heavily committed to the principle of 'self-help', which was given massive publicity by the works of Samuel Smiles. These included *Self-Help* (1859), *Character* (1871), *Thrift* (1875) and *Duty* (1887). The first became one of the greatest best-sellers of the whole of the nineteenth century, far outstripping any novel in popularity.[15] The best-known phrase was: 'God helps those who help themselves. Go thou and do likewise'. Although not totally convinced by *laissez-faire*, Smiles nevertheless had very definite views about the limitations of State intervention in social issues: 'Some call for Caesars, others for Nationality, and others for Acts of Parliament . . . Whatever is done *for* men and classes to a certain extent takes away the stimulus and necessity of doing for themselves.'[16] His rationale behind this was that 'All life is a struggle. Amongst workmen, competition is a struggle to advance towards high wages. Amongst masters, to make the highest profits . . . Stop competition, and you stop individualism.'[17]

Clearly, then, collectivism had not yet reached its most advanced form. This was to come at the turn of the century with its evolution into an incipient form of the Welfare State. The details of this are covered in Chapter 17, which refers to the various types of collectivism introduced by Liberal governments of the period 1905–14. These were partly a logical extension of state involvement through tried and tested channels, partly a breaking of new ground. They included traditional State-imposed regulations like the 1906 Trades Disputes Act, the 1906 Workmen's Compensation Act, the 1908

Children's Act and the 1911 Shops Act. The State also provided new services under the School Meals Act (1906) and the Labour Exchanges Act (1909). In the 1911 National Insurance Act the Liberals developed the principle of 'social insurance' which balanced State assistance and self-help. A more progressive form of collectivism was the Old Age Pensions Act of 1909, since it did not require a contribution from those to be covered immediately. The funding of these measures was also a departure from previous Liberal and Conservative policies; the 1909 Budget dispensed once and for all with the idea of aiming to abolish direct taxation and, instead, aimed to use death duties and supertax as a means of redistributing wealth.

In contrast to the broad consensus between the parties during the era of Gladstone and Disraeli, a wide gap opened up between the social policies of the Edwardian Liberal and Conservative parties. The Liberals of Asquith and Lloyd George were acting partly for altruistic reasons, partly from political necessity. At the turn of the century pressure intensified on behalf of those who were still among the poor and exploited – and who were obviously not benefiting from the growth of collectivism. The Liberals took direct note of the investigations of Rowntree, of the Rev. Andrew Mearn's *Bitter Cry of Outcast London* (1883), William Booth's *In Darkest England* (1890), Jack London's *On the Edge of the Abyss* (1901), Charles Booth's *Life and Labour of the People of London* (1902), and Rowntree's investigation of 1901. Together, these formed the most extensive and detailed study of poverty and squalor produced throughout the whole of the nineteenth century. It was fortunate that they came at a time when the Liberal party was seeking a new identity and a new role which would enable it to compete more effectively against the Conservatives, win more of the working-class vote and escape the long shadow that Ireland had placed over Gladstone's governments. It could be argued, therefore, that social collectivism crossed the threshold into the Welfare State because it was politically expedient for it to do so.

How extensive were the Liberal measures in practice? They certainly constituted a major change in the way in which poverty and unemployment were regarded. The traditional *laissez-faire* approach was replaced by increased government intervention, which inevitably meant centralisation and the growth of bureaucracy. Also, the future development of welfare services was based on the mixture of contributory and non-contributory benefits as established before 1914. The 1945–51 Labour government changed the proportions of these, reducing the importance of insurance for health care, retaining it for unemployment and introducing it for pensions. It also provided a considerable increase in the benefits and a safety net for those unable to make contributions. But it was the scope that changed, not the basic principle.

On the other hand, the Welfare State was still in incipient form and would be unable to develop any further until the government assumed more direct responsibility for the causes of poverty and other areas of concern. This, in turn, meant a willingness to take a greater degree of control over economic policy. The eventual emergence of the full Welfare State in the period after the Second World War owed much to the foundations of the Liberal governments before the First World War. But another essential prerequisite was the abandonment of the remnants of *laissez-faire* in the economy between the World Wars. The State in the twentieth century gave more attention to seeking to reduce social problems not just through social policy but also by seeking partially to reshape the economy. This brought a convergence in the political treatment of social and economic issues which was entirely lacking in the period 1815–1914.

22

BRITAIN AND IRELAND
1800–1921

Ireland was linked to Britain in 1800 by the Act of Union. This ended in 1921 as the three southern provinces became the Irish Free State and two-thirds of the northern province, Ulster, remained within the United Kingdom. Within the last seven years of the period a major conflict had developed between the republicans on the one hand and the Ulster unionists on the other. The former saw Britain as a colonial power exploiting the Irish population, while the latter believed equally passionately in continued integration.

The polarised loyalties of the early twentieth century should not, however, lead us to suppose that 'it was always thus'. At no time before 1914 could the independence and partition of Ireland have been considered inevitable. Other solutions, such as 'Home Rule' were more strongly favoured, while the Ulster 'unionists' and the Irish 'republicans' had always been heavily outnumbered by the more moderate 'radicals' and 'nationalists'. This chapter will trace and interpret the main political developments of the period and consider the impact on them of social and economic problems. Its purpose will be to show that the outcome of 1921 does not appear to match up with the long-term trends since 1800 – and to account for this paradox.

THE PERIOD OF 'RADICALISM' 1800–46

By the Act of Union of 1800 the Irish parliament was replaced by direct representation in Westminster in the form of one hundred MPs in the House of Commons and twenty-eight Irish temporal peers and four Bishops in the House of Lords. The administration in Dublin remained unchanged; based in Dublin, it continued to be appointed directly by the British government. These provisions were highly significant for the future.

In the first place there was a major redistribution of seats. In the former Irish parliament there had been a huge disparity in favour of the borough seats over the counties; this was reversed in Westminster, where the counties were given sixty-four seats to the boroughs' thirty-five. This was important because the boroughs were in the grip of Protestants, whereas the county seats contained a majority of Catholic voters who had been enfranchised in 1797. Some historians have argued that this developed a political consciousness which had been lacking before.[1] It is perhaps too early to talk of the emergence of Irish nationalism. But the Act of Union did create, albeit unintentionally, a substantial political group which could be influenced by radical ideas. Radicalism, an essential prerequisite for nationalism, needed in turn a grievance upon which to grow.

The Act of Union provided two. One was the monopoly on executive powers by Protestant appointees of the British government; this applied especially to the office of Chief Secretary for Ireland. It is possible to exaggerate the damage done to Ireland by this system and to use too glibly terms like 'exploitation'. The administration was genuinely paternalistic and more than matched the social improvements and collectivist policies which were gaining ground in Britain. But even mild rule is unacceptable when it is considered alien rule. Daniel O'Connell, for example, stated in 1842 that 'the Union produced the most disastrous results to Ireland'.[2] In the first three decades of the nineteenth century the sense of being dominated by a foreign power was greatly accentuated by the second grievance left by the Act of Union: religious inequality. Those, especially the Younger Pitt, who had framed the Act had always intended that it should be accompanied by Catholic emancipation, which would allow Catholic members to be elected to Westminster. Unfortunately, this had been vetoed by George III on the grounds that this would infringe his coronation oath. He wrote to Pitt on 31 January 1799: 'though a strong friend of the union of the two kingdoms, I should become an enemy to the measure if I thought a change in the situation of the Roman Catholics would attend the measure'.[3]

The exclusion of Catholics from Westminster provided the ammunition for the greatest Irish radical of the entire period – the landowner and barrister, Daniel O'Connell. The first of his spectacular incursions into politics was to ensure that Catholics 'be allowed to partake of the advantages of the Constitution'.[4] He also hoped to redistribute the wealth of the Established (Protestant) Church for public works and to end the anomalous system of tithes paid by Catholics for its upkeep. His Catholic Association, formed in 1823, raised the political temperature in Ireland so much that when he won the County Clare by-election in 1828 he sent a message to Westminster which could not possibly be ignored. If he were denied the right to take up his seat there would be a risk of extensive disturbances. O'Connell told his supporters that when he reached England he would ask 'What is to be done with Ireland? What is to be done with the Catholics? They must either crush us or conciliate us. There is no going on as we are.'[5] Wellington and Peel acted swiftly to prevent revolution. Most of the Tories and all of the Whigs voted through the Catholic Emancipation Act in 1829, finally remedying one of the worst deficiencies of the Act of Union.

Catholic emancipation was also an important catalyst for further political change. In Britain it cleared the way for further reforms of the establishment; as shown in Chapter 3, the Whigs were now able to argue that parliamentary reform was not only necessary but inevitable. The Tories were hamstrung by serious internal divisions as their right wing were prepared, in expressing their opposition to emancipation, to bring Wellington's government down in 1830. This resulted in ten years of Whig rule. In Ireland, meanwhile, Catholic emancipation put a new construction on to politics. According to Norman, it 'gave the Catholic Church a national existence for the first time'.[6] O'Connell's campaign had therefore radicalised the Catholic vote and provided the Church with a role which transcended class barriers. The question now arising was to what further use force would be put.

Certainly O'Connell had no intention of bringing about any social upheaval. He did not campaign on behalf of the peasantry, of whom he remained suspicious. He wrote in 1833: 'I desire no social revolution, no social change'.[7] His focus was very much on political reform, although his precise motives were not always clear. He was not a nationalist as such and did not base his particular appeal on any Irish cultural or historical tradition. As a middle-class radical he was no democrat and the early 1830s were spent looking for a precise political role. In fact, he found himself in a position of unusual influence at Westminster. During the 1820s there had usually been about seventy Tories and thirty Whigs representing

Ireland. In 1832 the Tories were down to twenty-nine and the Whigs up to thirty-six, the remaining thirty-nine comprising O'Connellites. These allied with the Whigs in the expectation that they were more likely to deliver what O'Connell sought. What was this?

At first O'Connell's priority was to secure a number of much needed changes for Ireland. One of these was the reform of the Board of Works in 1831, which was now able to loan up to £500,000 for projects for land drainage, fisheries and other forms of enterprise. Then, in 1831 a national system was set up for primary schools and a new board took over responsibility for the grant of £30,000 per annum. Both of these were considerably ahead of developments in Britain. The 1832 Reform Act, of course, amended the Irish electoral system, while the Irish Church Temporalities Act (1833) ensured that the revenues were administered by an ecclesiastical commission. From 1837 progress was also made in the Irish administration – at the time under Drummond: Catholics were admitted to a variety of offices, including magistracies. In general, Anglo-Irish relations seemed to have entered a happier and more positive phase.

Despite this, O'Connell's name came increasingly to be linked with demands for the repeal of the Act of Union altogether. He was not at first fully convinced that this should be done, arguing in 1833 that: 'As long as I could see the utility of the British Parliament – and an immense utility may exist – I should prefer seeing the House doing injustice to my countrymen rather than that should be done by a local legislature.'[8] It is possible, therefore, that O'Connell used the issue of repeal as a tactical threat to keep the Whigs under his influence and in a reformist mode. Gradually, however, he came into the open. In 1840 he put forward a scheme for an Irish House of Commons which would contain 173 members for the counties and 127 for the boroughs. He followed this in 1843 with a programme which included 'The capability and capacity of the Irish nation for an independent legislature'.[9] He was by now convinced of the need for repeal, adding in a speech in 1843: 'What numberless advantages would not the Irish enjoy if they possessed their own country?'[10] Unfortunately, Peel's ministry (1841-6) had no special relationship with O'Connell and resorted to tough measures like the Arms Act in 1843. In the same year Peel warned that: 'There is no influence, no power, no authority, which the prerogatives of the Crown and the existing law gave to the Government, which will not be exercised for the purpose of maintaining the Union.'[11] O'Connell was convicted of conspiracy in 1844 and given a year in detention, which severely affected his leadership and health. Peel, now aware of the potential dangers in Ireland, sought to pursue a more restrained policy of reform, the most useful of which was the Maynooth grant and the Irish University Bill of 1845. But by this time it was clear that the honeymoon in Anglo-Irish relations was over. By the time of his death in 1851, O'Connell was no longer in control of the repeal movement; it was evident that he had mobilised forces which were far more radical than he had originally intended. Why was this?

THE GREAT FAMINE AND MID-CENTURY CONFUSION 1845–68

Ireland in the middle of the nineteenth century was preoccupied with the potato famine of 1845–6, the worst disaster ever to have befallen the country. The famine had several major consequences for the future development of Ireland.

The first and most important was the widespread emigration which, far more than the deaths caused by the famine, reduced Ireland's population from 8.2 million in 1841 to 5.4 million by 1871. This had both internal and external side-effects. Within Ireland the number of small-holders declined by half. Much of their land was bought up by speculators, who were more inclined to evict their tenants. This created a serious land problem, which became increasingly caught up in political developments after 1850. Outside Ireland, and especially in the United States, there was an ever-growing population of disillusioned exiles. This exerted increasing pressure on Irish politics and gave ready support to the more extreme organisations. In the words of G. Morton, this 'made it impossible for either British statesmen or Irish politicians to attempt to solve Ireland's problems as if they were simply a matter of domestic concern'.[12]

This, in any case, proved increasingly difficult, for the second effect of the great famine had been to increase the distrust of British policy in Ireland. To some extent this was undeserved. Peel's government had attempted to alleviate the crisis by appointing 473 medical officers and by importing corn from North America to the value of £100,000 for sale at low prices through food depots. Russell's ministry, which succeeded Peel in 1846, encouraged the development of roads through the Board of Works in order to bring more effective relief of famine. The Poor Law was amended in 1847, which appointed permanent officials and organised outdoor relief, while Russell's Land Improvement Act made available £1.5 million for agricultural improvements. In total the governments of Peel and Russell provided £9.5 million. Even so, British policies were heavily criticised. The main grounds for complaint were that *laissez-faire* economic policies undermined the effectiveness of social assistance and that food continued to be exported from Ireland for profit throughout the crisis. There was much anger that both Peel and Russell had rejected the suggestion from Irish MPs that such exports should be suspended. One of the radicals, Mitchel, went so far as to argue that the famine was a method deliberately devised by the British government 'for the entire subjugation of the island – the slaughter of a portion of its people, and the pauperization of the rest'.[13]

For a while, however, there was no consistent political force within Ireland to attempt to redefine relations with Britain. To the British government this was an advantage in that there was a temporary lull in the sort of pressure which had been applied to it by O'Connell. The Irish population experienced the negative side of this – a period of political confusion. This was not actually caused by the famine: a split had already begun to develop between O'Connell and his more nationalistic supporters. But there can be no doubt that the appalling suffering of the 1840s added weight to the likes of Lalor, Dillon, Duffy, O'Brien, Reilly, Magee, Martin and Mitchel, who departed from the moderation of O'Connell and established the Young Ireland movement. Plans were laid for nationalist revolution in 1848. There was little popular support, however, and most of the leaders were transported until 1854.

By 1849, therefore, O'Connell's Repeal Association and its natio- nalist wing, Young Ireland, were both defunct. For a while the vacuum was filled by two lesser and more moderate organisations. One was the Tenant League. Formed in 1850, this comprised Catholics and Protestants and attempted to bridge the gap between urban and rural interests and grievances. It also used parliamentary tactics to bring the question of land into the political arena. It was, however, short-lived; it collapsed in 1858 from internal splits and through lack of support from the North. The other organisation was the so-called 'Independent opposition', which also shifted the focus to land issues. It worked on the principle of not supporting any government unless it introduced appropriate measures for Ireland. Twenty MPs were returned in the 1852 general election, but they gradually moved back to the Liberals and ceased to exist as a separate force after the 1859 election.

In the meantime, the confused situation following the famine had given birth to the most extreme movement of the nineteenth century. The Fenians, set up in 1858 by James Stephens, added the ingredient of republicanism to the political caldron. The members were expected to 'swear allegiance to the Irish Republic, now virtually established',[14] and to prepare for armed revolution. They were opposed to any constitutional negotiation, had no interest in reform, and failed entirely to take up the question of land tenure. Their quarrel with Britain was entirely political and ideological. Known as the Irish Republican Brotherhood (IRB) from 1865, its support was sporadic and confined to small pockets in Munster and Leinster; in Connaught and Ulster it made very little impression.

How important was Fenianism as a factor in Irish politics? In the short term, it did not achieve any of its objectives. The rebellion it organised in 1867 was a complete failure and the organisers were imprisoned. Some of these later escaped to the United States. In the longer term, of course, the IRB provided the foundations for Sinn Fein and the Irish Republican Army (IRA), which were to grow rapidly between 1916 and 1921. In the meantime, however, its effects were actually counterproductive and helped revive a more moderate Irish bloc.

This was based not on republicanism but on nationalism. The violence of the Fenians had convinced the remnants of the O'Connellites, Young Ireland, the Tenants League and the Independents that the way forward had to be through political pressure on the British government, not through armed insurrection against it. The Catholic Church was also in favour of the more moderate course and strongly opposed the openly secular policies of republicanism. By the end of the 1860s, therefore, Irish opinion was once again beginning to polarise. In the 1830s and 1840s Irish voters had been attracted by O'Connell's campaign for 'Repeal'. After the intervening period of confusion the body of support built up by O'Connell found a new cause: 'Home Rule'. In many ways, this was to be a natural successor to 'Repeal', as was Parnell's nationalism to O'Connell's radicalism.

IRISH NATIONALISTS, HOME RULE AND BRITISH GOVERNMENT POLICIES 1868–1914

It appeared, in 1868, that there was a real chance of resolving some of the major problems which still affected Ireland. The Liberal party had come to power under the leadership of Gladstone, who regarded it as his personal mission 'to pacify Ireland'. More than any other politician of the nineteenth century, he raised the importance of Ireland; in 1869 he said, a touch verbosely, of the Fenian outrages:

> then it was when these phenomena came home to the popular mind and produced that attitude of attention and preparedness on the part of the whole population of this country which qualified them to embrace, in a manner foreign to their habits of other times, the vast importance of the Irish controversy.[15]

With the support of Irish Liberals, Gladstone set about introducing a series of reforms to tackle what he considered to be the major issues of the day. These are analysed in Chapter 13. He focused intially on the ecclesiastical question through the Irish Church Act of 1869, while his solutions to the problems of land tenure were contained in the First and Second Irish Land Acts of 1870 and 1881. But Gladstone's measures were invariably too late to satisfy the ever-increasing demands from pressure groups like the Irish Land League and Nationalists like Butt and Parnell. Gradually he found himself resorting to measures of coercion, which included the imprisonment of Parnell and other Leaguers in Kilmainham Gaol between 1881 and 1882. Some time between 1882 and 1885 Gladstone decided that the only feasible solution to the Irish problem was 'Home Rule', a concession now being demanded by the Nationalists.

There is no doubt that Gladstone had been under considerable pressure. Between 1874 and 1885 Irish politics were dominated by the quest for Home Rule. As explained by Butt, this would mean a common imperial parliament and separate domestic parliaments for England, Scotland and Ireland, but one common government. In 1873 the Home Rule League was founded and Home Rule achieved its first major success in the 1874 general election. From this stage onwards the movement was captured by more militant politicians like Parnell, who was elected president of the reorganised Home Rule Confederation in place of Butt in 1877. For a while, Parnell flirted with the Fenians. He was connected with Fenian agrarian radicalism and Fenians made up a substantial part of the membership of his Land League. After his release from Kilmainham Gaol in 1882, however, Parnell appeared to move towards a moderate policy. He condemned the murders of Chief Secretary Cavendish and Under-Secretary Burke in Phoenix Park (1882) and, with the formation of the National League in the same year, Parnell became the unquestioned leader of the Irish Nationalists at Westminster. His machinations in parliament were immensely frustrating for all British parties, but were highly successful in increasing the pressure for Home Rule. He expressed his displeasure at Gladstone's delay in converting to Home Rule by supporting the Conservatives after the 1885 election. Once Gladstone's commitment to Home Rule had become clear, Parnell switched his strategy, voted with the Liberals on a motion on agrarian reform in England and unseated the Conservative government in 1885. From this stage onwards, the policies of Parnell and Gladstone converged.

But the objective of these policies was not met. Gladstone's first Home Rule Bill was defeated in the Commons in 1886, the second in the Lords in 1893. The Liberal party entered a period of division and decline which was accentuated by the whole question of Home Rule. Some historians maintain that the Irish issue brought about a revolution within British politics between 1885 and 1905, resulting in a period of Conservative ascendancy and temporarily depressing the ability of the Liberals to compete effectively (see Chapter 16). Home Rule, in other words, did to the Liberals what the repeal of the Corn Laws had done to the Conservatives after 1846. An alternative viewpoint is that it merely confirmed an existing process. According to E. Norman 'All the inherent weaknesses of the Liberal party . . . were moving it to destruction by the mid eighties, before Home Rule arrived to administer the dispatching blow.'[16]

Whether or not the Liberal crisis was mainly due to Irish issues, it can certainly be said that Conservative ascendancy had a direct impact on Irish aspirations. The name by which the party was known throughout this period – the Unionists – was an indication that the new priority was to find an alternative to Home Rule. The ministries of Salisbury and Balfour followed a dual policy of land reform and devolution. The former was embodied, for example, in the Wyndham Act of 1903, which enabled tenants to buy their land from landlords with money advanced by the government and repayable over $68\frac{1}{2}$ years. Devolution was less successful; the proposals made by Wyndham for the establishment of an additional body – an Irish council – were so strongly opposed that Wyndham was forced to resign.

It might be thought that the defeat of the Home Rule Bills and the substitution of Conservative for Liberal measures would have a depressing effect on the Irish Nationalists and possibly lead to the revival of Fenianism. It is true that the Nationalists turned in on themselves, dividing into pro- and anti-Parnellite factions. It was not until 1905 that unity was restored under the leadership of John Redmond. Nevertheless, the fortunes of the Irish Nationalists picked up with the revival of the Liberals (see Chapter 17), who came to power again in 1905 and won a landslide election victory the following year.

It would also be a mistake to see Ireland reverting to a repressed condition. In many ways the opening decade of the twentieth century was one of remarkable stability, moderation and progress. The Irish Nationalists revived their tactical alliance with the Liberals and were infinitely more important than any rumblings on the republican fringe of Irish politics. Ireland herself was experiencing a great cultural resurgence which was expressed in the form partly of a Gaelic revival and partly of the impressive literary output of poets and writers like Yeats, Synge, Joyce, Shaw and O'Casey. There was also a generally constructive connection with Britain. Government policy aimed at rectifying financial injustices so that by 1912 expenditure on Ireland exceeded taxation by some £2 million and £108 million had been advanced to enable land purchase. A long-standing grievance was settled by the establishment of a national university in 1909 and, of course, the social reforms of Asquith's government (such as the 1911 National Insurance Act) applied as much to Ireland as to Britain.

Although these were unquestionably happier times, the Irish Nationalists continued to think in terms of Home Rule. Asquith considered it just and expedient to grant it. He announced in the Albert Hall at the end of 1909: 'The solution of the problem can be found only in one way – by a policy which, while explicitly safeguarding the supreme and indefeasible authority of the Imperial Parliament, will set up in Ireland a system of full self-government in regard to purely Irish affairs.'[17] He therefore introduced the Third Home Rule Bill in 1912, which Redmond's Irish Nationalists supported with enthusiasm: 'We on these benches stand precisely where Parnell stood. We want peace with this country. We deny that we are separatists, and we say we are willing, as Parnell was willing, to accept a subordinate Parliament created by statute of this Imperial Legislature as a final settlement of Ireland's claims.'[18]

Almost all the factors which had prevented the passing of Gladstone's measures now appeared to have been cancelled out. First, the Liberals had largely overcome the split which had ensured the defeat of the first Home Rule Bill in the House of Commons in 1885. Almost all were reconciled to a measure which they regarded as inevitable and the number of Liberal Unionists prepared to support the Conservatives had been reduced by 1912 from seventy-seven to thirty-five. Second, the Conservatives could not summon sufficient support to defeat the Bill; the state of the parties after the second general election of 1910 was as follows:

In favour of home rule		Against home rule	
272	Liberals	237	Conservatives (Unionists)
84	Irish Nationalists	35	Liberal Unionists
42	Labour		
396		272	

Finally, the House of Lords had also been neutralised. Although it voted against accepting the third Home Rule Bill in 1912, its power of veto had been reduced by the 1911 Parliament Act to one of delay. This meant that Home Rule could come into existence, without further constitutional obstacles, in 1914. What could now prevent it?

THE END OF HOME RULE AND THE ORIGINS OF INDEPENDENCE AND PARTITION

Home Rule would have been the logical outcome of the growth of political forces in the nineteenth century. History, however, is littered with examples of an unexpected twist which nullifies an apparently inexorable trend. Ireland is one of these. The Irish Nationalists seemed to have channelled most of the earlier movements into a coherent policy which was on the point of being conceded by a large majority at Westminster. The election of 1910 shows their absolute command of seats at Westminster.

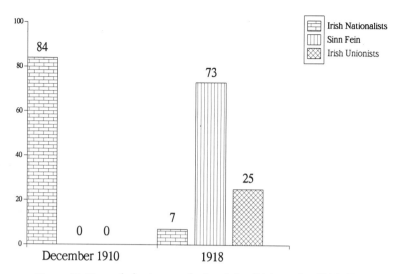

Figure 16 General election results involving Irish parties 1910–18

Irish Nationalists	84
Irish Unionists	0
Sinn Fein	0

By the time of the next election this position of strength had been totally destroyed. The figures for 1918 were as follows:

Irish Nationalists	7
Irish Unionists	25
Sinn Fein	73

What had happened between 1914 and 1918, therefore, was a considerable increase in support for two more extreme parties at the expense of the moderate grouping. The Irish Unionists, concentrated especially in the province of Ulster, had already emerged as an obstacle to a negotiated settlement before 1914. Sinn Fein developed partly as a backlash against the Ulster Unionists and partly as a protest against the additional burdens placed on Ireland by the British government as a direct consequence of the First World War. In this respect war acted as a catalyst for revolution.

The resistance within Ireland came from people of Anglo-Irish and Scots-Irish descent. The desire to retain the union with Britain was in part a fear of the Catholic majority; increasingly, 'Home Rule' was projected as 'Rome Rule'. In part it was economic, since Ulster was more heavily industrialised and had much closer economic connections with the British mainland, relying heavily upon it for raw materials and markets. The problem was that an independent Ireland might seek to protect itself with tariff walls. It might also fall prey to the agricultural interest of the peasantry, which would undermine the industrial growth which had taken place in the late nineteenth century. Ulster had also been less badly affected by the famine and the land wars of the nineteenth century, and its population had actually increased while the rest of Ireland's had declined.

The campaign in Ulster against Home Rule began in 1886 with the formation of the Ulster Loyalist Anti-Repeal Union, which was replaced in 1904 by the Ulster Unionist Council. These established close links with the Conservative party at Westminster in a desperate bid to outmanoeuvre the Liberals and Irish Nationalists. For a while they succeeded, the Conservative opposition managing to defeat Gladstone's first Home Rule Bill in the Commons and the second in the Lords. During this period the activities of the Ulster Unionists were relatively restrained. There was, after all, a guarantee that the permanent Conservative majority in the House of Lords would be able to veto Home Rule; the Ulster Unionists were content, therefore, to act as the Irish conscience of the British Conservatives.

By 1914, however, the situation was very different. The Lords had lost their permanent veto and the Conservatives were helpless; the Ulster Unionists therefore took matters increasingly into their own hands. They put pressure on the House of Lords to delay the third Home Rule Bill as long as possible while they mobilised for direct action. The delay between 1912, when the Bill passed the Commons, and 1914, when the suspensory delay finally lapsed, was crucial. The Ulster Unionists had time to organise a Volunteer force of 100,000 men, smuggle in consignments of rifles (as, for example, into Larne) and to make it absolutely clear that Home Rule would be resisted by force. Edward Carson, a barrister and former Irish Solicitor-General, set up a provisional government in Ulster, acting on a warning he had already given in 1911 that

> We must be prepared, in the event of a Home Rule Bill passing, with such measures as will carry on for ourselves the government of those districts of which we have control. We must be prepared – and time is precious in these things – the

morning Home Rule passes, ourselves to become responsible for the government of the Protestant Province of Ulster.[19]

To make matters worse, the outbreak of the First World War prevented the British government pushing ahead with the policy it had come increasingly to favour: Home Rule with special guarantees for the North. The whole question was frozen until Britain had dealt with the German threat. By the time this option was picked up again by Lloyd George in 1916 there had been further changes. The rapid increase in the influence of Ulster Unionism in the North had a serious backlash: the dramatic rise of Irish republicanism in the South. To the IRB was added Sinn Fein, formed in 1905 by Arthur Griffith. Its name 'Ourselves Alone' indicated an early rejection of the Home Rule solution and a demand for a constitution based on entirely separate governments. The economy would be protected and English influences would be eradicated. In response to the mobilisation in Ulster, Sinn Fein and the IRB established a force of 200,000 Volunteers in the South. At first the Irish Nationalists tried to maintain a degree of control over this, but were gradually superseded by the republicans, who planned and launched the Easter Uprising against British rule in 1916. This resulted in the deaths of 450 rebels and 103 soldiers and the executions of 14 leaders, including the organiser, Pearse. The executions, although understandable within the context of the war, damaged Britain's reputation in Ireland and created martyrs for the republican cause. There was a sudden increase in popular support for Sinn Fein and for the paramilitary organisation it formed called the Irish Republican Army. Lloyd George, who at this point led a coalition government in Britain, tried to win back the initiative by introducing Home Rule immediately rather than waiting for the end of the War; this, however, foundered on the question of Ulster and on the determination of Sinn Fein and the IRA to win complete independence. Sinn Fein's performance in the 1918 general election confirmed the increased support for the republicans. To publicise their proposal to break altogether with Britain, Sinn Fein refused to take up their seventy-three seats at Westminster, instead setting up the *Dail Eireann* in Dublin and electing Eamon de Valera the new Irish leader. To all intents and purposes, Home Rule was now dead.

The First World War had been a decisive factor in these developments. All over Europe it was a catalyst for revolution: two regimes were overthrown in Russia during the course of 1917, Austria-

Hungary broke asunder in 1918, and in Germany the monarchy was replaced by a republic. It is often stated that Britain escaped revolution in any political sense and that the most drastic political change was the sudden decline of the Liberal party. This, of course, ignores the Irish situation and confines the impact of war to Great Britain rather than considering its effect on the United Kingdom as a whole. The events in Ireland between 1916 and 1922 were unquestionably part of a revolution – in the sense that they produced within a short period an outcome which was at variance with all longer-term trends. It is true that the first blows to Home Rule were delivered *before* the War by the Ulster Unionists. But the backlash, which saw the defeat of the moderate nationalists by the more extreme republicans, occurred *during* the War, and is explicable only within the context of the War.

Perhaps the most important factor was the attempt made by the British government in April 1918 to extend to Ireland the 1916 conscription law. This was widely opposed, to the great benefit of the republicans. It has been argued that even by 1918 Sinn Fein had not been fully established in Ireland, and that the Easter Rising had somewhat undermined its credibility. What the conscription law did was to provide Sinn Fein with a new focus which could be used to good effect in the 1918 election. E. Norman goes further: 'The anti-conscription movement had revived the fortunes of Sinn Fein at a time when they would otherwise have wilted into extinction.'[20] This is, of course, impossible to prove. It does indicate, nevertheless, that the rise of Sinn Fein was by no means inevitable; even within the generally destabilising context of war it took further unexpected twists, such as the conscription issue, to bring it to the verge of power. There is a further point: the impact of a wartime measure interacted with the peculiarities of the British electoral system to convert a less than total shift in popular support into an electoral landslide. In the 1918 election Sinn Fein won 70 per cent of the Irish seats at Westminster with 47 per cent of the Irish vote. As a proportion of the total United Kingdom vote, Sinn Fein achieved 4.5 per cent, compared with 2.7 per cent for the Ulster Unionists and 2.2 per cent for the Irish Nationalists, or a combined opposition to Sinn Fein of 4.9 per cent. Ironically, the destabilising impact of the War was converted into a political revolution by the continuity of the British electoral system. The South had an overwhelming case for independence as a republic and the North for partition and continued union with Britain.

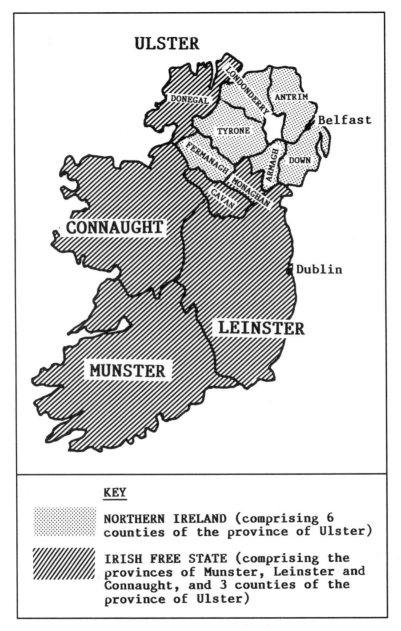

ULSTER

DONEGAL

LONDONDERRY

ANTRIM

Belfast

TYRONE

FERMANAGH

ARMAGH

DOWN

MONAGHAN

CAVAN

CONNAUGHT

Dublin

LEINSTER

MUNSTER

KEY

NORTHERN IRELAND (comprising 6 counties of the province of Ulster)

IRISH FREE STATE (comprising the provinces of Munster, Leinster and Connaught, and 3 counties of the province of Ulster)

Figure 17 Ireland by 1922

Events between 1919 and 1921 confirmed this trend. The IRA carried out a series of attacks on the British authorities to lend credibility to Sinn Fein's claim to control the South. The British government responded by using ex-service volunteers, who were nicknamed the 'Black and Tans', and the auxiliary division of the Irish Constabulary, or Auxis. In the ensuing chaos, in which atrocities were committed by both sides, Lloyd George decided that the only feasible solution was now independence and partition. Hence the 1920 Government of Ireland Act divided Ulster into two parts. Six counties of Ulster were to remain within the United Kingdom, while the remaining three were to join the provinces of Connaught, Leinster and Munster in a separate Irish state. In both cases, Britain would retain overall control: the proposed constitution was therefore not dissimilar to that intended in 1914. The Ulster Unionists accepted the Act and established a government under Sir James Craig. In the South, however, Sinn Fein rejected the scheme and, in 1921, the British government was forced to acknowledge the new Irish Free State. In 1949, this was converted into the Republic of Eire, which broke the last remaining link with Britain by leaving the Commonwealth.

23

PRIMARY SOURCES FOR BRITISH POLITICAL HISTORY 1815–1914

Primary sources are those produced during the period being studied – in this case, the Georgian, Victorian and Edwardian eras. They have been described as the raw material from which history is made and they play a vital role in interpretations to be found in secondary sources. Interest in primary sources was initiated by the nineteenth-century German historical school but, during the second half of the twentieth, has been given a new focus within the British educational system. The scope of primary sources has also been greatly expanded and now goes far beyond the original concentration on diplomatic and official documents. Every student of history is now familiar with the shades and variety of primary sources, and also with the questions which need to be asked of them. Are they reliable and are they useful?

The response generally given to this question is that reliability and usefulness depend entirely upon what the historian envisages as their function. This will be considered in greater depth in relation to diaries, memoirs and autobiographies; diplomatic documents; correspondence; speeches; newspapers; statistics; novels; and cartoons.

DIARIES, MEMOIRS AND AUTOBIOGRAPHIES

The most personal of all primary sources is the diary. One motive for keeping a regular account is to prepare a reliable *aide-mémoire*. This would be useful as a systematic record either for the eventual preparation of personal memoirs or for subsequent reference for speeches, diplomatic negotiations, or even cabinet meetings. Another motive might be to provide an outlet for personal views, impressions and frustrations. Either reason would involve the interaction between the author and the events of the day, the author helping shape the events and, at the same time, commenting on them.

As such, diaries provide the historian with first-hand and vivid descriptions, which can be used retrospectively to supplement more formal records such as cabinet minutes. The personal views they contain illustrate and enliven the more formal approach of official documents. When kept over a long period of time, they provide perhaps the greatest form of continuity, illuminating changing attitudes as well as constant principles. A detailed and frank diary might confirm – or modify – the conventional evaluation of a particular individual personality, revealing especially personal charisma or eccentricities. At times, a diary might convey information or details not otherwise available and it is especially informative to compare two or more diaries covering the same period.

On the other hand, all diaries are open to question as to the motivation behind their entries; this must inevitably affect their reliabilty as a source. The historian needs to consider the position of the diarist, since here there is an unusual opportunity to exaggerate (or, alternatively, to minimise) the author's role in particular events. There is also considerable scope for bias. This may be expressed directly, in the form of commitment or antipathy, or indirectly through the selection of material. The latter raises the additional questions of the motives for inclusion and exclusion and the historian has to undertake the difficult task of assessing the extent of the diarist's concern for personal posterity and reputation. Finally, the habits of the diarist will undoubtedly affect the overall character of the work. A daily record is likely to provide a more precise recall of detail but will also contain a great deal that is redundant. A weekly diary, on the other hand, is more likely to have a sense of underlying perspective but, since this is based on selection, may be more prone to distorting the events covered.

Many prominent politicians of the nineteenth century kept more or less regular diaries: Peel, Palmerston, Gladstone, Disraeli and Salisbury were the main examples. But personal records kept by persons on the periphery of power can be just as informative. For instance, a penetrating view of the differences between the various components making up the Labour Representation Committee was provided by Beatrice Webb's Diary. She revealed the disagreements between the Independent Labour Party and the Fabians, and the disillusionment of Ramsay MacDonald ('I think he would welcome a really conclusive reason for joining the Liberal Party'). She described Keir Hardie as 'used up', with 'no real faith left in the Labour movement as a revolutionary force' and the rank and file as 'puzzled and disheartened'. Overall, Labour members were failing to 'impress the House of Commons' and 'There is little leadership but a great deal of anti-leadership.'[1] This was a frank and detailed analysis of the labour movement made possible within the privacy of a personal diary; obviously a document for publication would have contained a much more guarded approach. On the other hand, the entry shows a particular standpoint within the labour movement, a Fabian point of view in opposition particularly to the socialism of the Independent Labour Party. It would therefore be interesting to compare Webb's observations with those of other members of the Labour movement.

Memoirs and autobiographies have certain similarities with diaries. They, too, are personal recollections based on the interaction between an individual and the society in which he or she lived and worked. On the other hand, memoirs and autobiographies are based on a more ordered and systematic selection of material; they have a more obvious development of themes and argument; and they put more emphasis on the 'times' as well as the 'life' of the subject. They may also contain more obvious self-justification, a greater emphasis on motivation over a longer period of time, and the use of non-personal, often privileged material. Autobiographies and memoirs may well use diaries as their raw material, which in itself poses problems of distortion. What would be the motive for omitting certain diary entries? Could this amount to a new form of bias? Alternatively, if memoirs are not based on diaries, how accurate is the memory of the writer? How much of the material is third-hand and not personal at all?

A good example from the first half of the nineteenth century was the Greville Memoirs, which combine a personal recollection of key events and a series of observations of events and personalities. One of these was a detailed description of Peel's parliamentary skills: 'No matter how unruly the House, how impatient or fatigued, the moment he rises all is silence, and he is sure of being heard with profound attention and respect.'[2]

Autobiographies are confined largely to the late nineteenth and early twentieth centuries. One of the most commonly quoted is that of Philip Snowden, which provided a clear insight into the early activism of Labour at local level, conveying the enthusiasm and spontaneity: 'The Party quickly developed a large number of local speakers. Many young men who were Nonconformist local preachers were attracted to the movement by the ethical appeal of Socialism. Their experience in speaking was a great help to the Party propaganda'.[3]

Similarly, Emmeline Pankhurst provided valuable information about the methods used by the suffragettes to disrupt the meetings held by Liberal candidates during general election campaigns. The impression gained is of an uncanny ability to cause maximum inconvenience with comparatively few resources. For example, 'We attended every meeting addressed by Mr Churchill. We heckled him unmercifully; we spoiled his best points by flinging back such obvious retorts that the crowds roared with laughter'.[4] These extracts are less frank, however, and therefore less revealing than the thoughts of Beatrice Webb. In the last analysis, diaries allow for greater spontaneity because the author has no immediate motive to censor his or her views. By contrast, memoirs and autobiographies are more likely to be expurgated since they are a step closer to being publicised or even published.

DIPLOMATIC DOCUMENTS

Diplomatic documents are perhaps the most used of all the sources covering the nineteenth century. This is a generic term for a variety of materials produced by and for the British government, usually in conjuction with other governments.

The type most commonly quoted is the treaty, which normally has two elements, although in varying proportions. One is the 'reflective' purpose, which is to provide a comprehensive settlement and so neutralise the causes of past tension and conflict. The other element is 'projective', the focus of which is on future territorial settlement or arrangements for military security. Examples include the Treaties of Vienna (1815) and Paris (1856), which were evenly reflective and projective, and the Treaty of Berlin (1878) which combined the resolution of the Balkan conflict with the definition of future boundaries in the region in accordance with longer-term aims of statesmen like Bismarck and Disraeli. Treaties which were more completely projective were those drawn up between Britain and other powers for security needs considered necessary for the future. The loosest form was 'détente', progressing through 'rapprochement', 'convention' and 'entente' to the tightest in form,

312

which is the 'alliance'. Examples from this range include the Anglo-Russian Convention (1907), the Anglo-French Entente (1904) and the Anglo-Japanese Alliance (1902).

All treaties of the nineteenth century had a common format. This comprised a preamble, which was a useful summary of the official ideology behind the treaty; a series of clauses or articles which contained the details of the agreement; and additional protocols which might, although not usually in British diplomacy, be secret. There are several benefits in such documents to the historian of British history. For one thing, they are the easiest to authenticate and are therefore the least likely to to be forged. For another, their preambles contain an excellent summary of the multiplicity of viewpoints, which might even be seen as an agreed balance of biases.

On the other hand, there must be reservations about the use of diplomatic documents. Treaties are by their nature legalistic and, as such, offer a very restricted understanding of the background of a particular situation. This is because a 'balance of biases' is achievable only through a 'balance of omissions'. Treaties rarely exist in isolation and have to be seen within the context of voluminous correspondence, official and secret, and the records and minutes of related meetings and conferences. These reveal the details of the process leading up to the formation of a treaty and the difficulties which have to be overcome. Quite often the changing shape of diplomacy is explicable only within the context of such material. Even these have their limitations. Late nineteenth-century documents were contained within bound volumes, usually referred to as 'Blue Books' and officially compiled by the Foreign and Colonial Offices. But the limitations of typing and printing facilities inevitably limited output: how much more must this have applied to the records maintained in the standardised civil service handwriting at the time of Palmerston? The practical difficulties of making and keeping multiple records must therefore have restricted severely the details of discussion. It is therefore essential for the historian to supplement official diplomatic documents with private papers and correspondence, with memoirs and autobiographies, and with press reports.

CORRESPONDENCE

There is possibly a greater range within correspondence than within any other primary source. The letter can be adapted to highly personal needs on the one hand or to official State policy on the other. It can also be secret or open, and can express a seemingly infinite variety of intentions. The fact that a letter exists at all implies an impulse behind it. In the case of politically motivated letters, the historian can gain a valuable insight into a specific character or incident.

In the first place, a letter can convey in the clearest terms justification for a particular course of action. Peel, for example, wrote to Canning on 17 April 1827 explaining why he felt it 'necessary to record the grounds on which I felt myself compelled to decline being a member of the Administration over which you are to preside as Prime Minister'.[5] Encapsulated within two paragraphs is Peel's own analysis of Canningite Toryism and a foretaste of his subsequent rivalry with Palmerston. Another opponent of Palmerston was Gladstone, who explained confidentially to Sir John Acton in June 1864 why he had agreed to overcome his aversion to some of Palmerston's policies to join his cabinet. This provides a rare insight into Gladstone's uncharacteristic preference for pragmatism to moral instinct and helps avoid developing too stereotyped a view of his political motives.[6]

Second, correspondence may illuminate the development of policy. A single letter may foreshadow a change in political strategy by suggesting, perhaps tentatively, the outlines of proposed action. This is what Peel did in a letter to Goulburn on 3 January 1833, which explained his views on restoring support for the Tory party by a policy of moderation which anticipated the celebrated Tamworth Manifesto.[7] Or it may be a means of clarifying a policy in the face of criticism. Hence Lord Salisbury replied on 7 November 1886 to Lord Randolph Churchill with what might have been the watchword of his government, 'Our Bills must be tentative and cautious, not sweeping and dramatic'.[8] Here the historian has a useful insight into Salisbury's attitude to domestic policy which would not be possible from an official document. A letter may also show up the influence of junior officials and demonstrate that policy at times may feed upwards. In 1903 the Liberal Chief Whip, Herbert Gladstone, formed an electoral pact with Ramsay MacDonald. What is not generally known is that he was persuaded to do so as the result of a carefully presented argument drawn up by his secretary, Jesse Herbert, on 6 March 1903.[9]

Third, there is considerable scope in letters for sounding off and expressing forthright views. These are especially useful to the historian since they indicate problems which public documents would aim to conceal: stress, divisions and disillusionment. Peel described in a letter to Arbuthnot (14 August 1845) the difficulties of premiership: 'It is impossible for me not to feel that the duties are incompatible, and above all human strength – at least above mine'.[10] Gladstone gave to a fellow cabinet minister (on 8 January 1874) a frank and realistic appraisal of a government in decline. He ended with the desperate question: 'can we by any measures materially mend the position of the party for an impending election?'[11] At times, the party leadership had to be alerted by officials to organisational difficulties. The Liberal Chief Whip wrote to Gladstone on 12 September 1867 itemising the expenses under the new electoral conditions following the passage of the 1867 Reform Act and concluding – hopefully – 'I don't think it possible to manage properly without say £10,000 to £15,000'.[12] This would counterbalance the natural tendency of the historian to assume that the Liberals expected to benefit from parliamentary reform: they could well have been ambivalent and perhaps surprised by the ease with which they eventually won the 1868 election. Correspondence fulfils the important purpose of reminding the historian that nothing can be taken for granted.

Finally, much can be inferred, or read between the lines. On 23 September 1819, for example, Lord Liverpool wrote a frank letter to Canning in which he argued that the government must be seen to support action taken by the magistrates to uphold public order, particularly through the introduction of parliamentary measures. On the other hand, there is an uncomfortable feeling that the magistrates had not been fully justified in taking the action they did at Peterloo.[13] This type of reservation could well enhance an argument that the ideological base of so-called Tory 'repression' after 1815 has been exaggerated. It also shows more generally that the historian, in analysing correspondence, needs to be as alert to what is implied as to what is explicitly stated.

SPEECHES

With the advent of radio and television came a revolution in the methods of public speaking. During the nineteenth century, however, this form of communication was confined to two main variants – the parliamentary speech and the public address, either at a meeting or at a rally. The former was the vehicle to announce, or denounce, government policy and the form taken was controlled and logical exposition. Public meetings, by contrast, elicited emotive generalisations within the context of mass oratory. Arguably the greatest speaker of the nineteenth century was W.E. Gladstone, who was equally at home with the cut and thrust of parliamentary debate and the more energetic projection of his principles from the hustings.

The main advantage of the speech as an historical source is that it provides an insight into the speaker's character through his use of vocabulary and tone. Was his approach emotive or reasoned? The basic emphasis of the speech could be seen through the target of his oratory: was he conciliatory or hostile? Speeches were also the main means of announcing policies to the public – either direct, or through newspapers, or within parliament. There are, of course, certain disadvantages of speeches as a source for the historian. The selection of material by the speaker inevitably shows a restricted view of policy: how much has been revealed – and what has been concealed? There are additional disadvantages in the processes of recording. The most complete records were, of course, *Hansard*, but there were many possibilities for distortion through selective reporting in the press; points might be taken out of context in order to provide the essence of a speech within the space available. In any case, the written record of any speech excludes visual evidence of the projection of the speaker's personality, the devices and tricks used in his oratory, and the impact on his audience.

Four examples of nineteenth-century parliamentary oratory are especially worth pursuing. The first two concern the issue of parliamentary reform. On 2 March 1831 the Whig MP Macaulay delivered a carefully reasoned but impassioned plea for the enfranchisement of the middle classes which has gone down as a classic justification for introducing measured change as a prophylactic against uncontrollable radicalism: 'we exclude from all share in the government vast masses of property and intelligence – vast numbers of those who are most interested in preserving tranquillity, and who know best how to preserve it. We do more. We drive over to the side of revolution those whom we shut out of power.'[14] The Conservative case was put by Peel on 6 July 1831. Although less frequently quoted than Macaulay's, it is a no less impressive example of how reform proposals can be projected as potentially harmful not so much because they are revolutionary as because they are not really needed. This was already a line which had been taken

– and bungled – by the Duke of Wellington, but Peel gave it renewed respectability:

> do not force this Reform Bill upon the country, upon the assumption that the unanimous voice of the people demands it. I doubt the existence of any such ground; and if you do find hereafter that you have been mistaken – if you find that the people have only been acting under an excitement produced by temporary causes – if they are already sobering down from their enthusiasm for the days of July, let the House remember, that when the steady good sense and reason of the people of England shall return, they will be the first to reproach us with the baseness of having sacrificed the constitution in the vain hope of conciliating the favour of a temporary burst of popular feeling; they will be the first to blame us for deferring this question to popular opinion, instead of acting upon our own judgement.[15]

Foreign policy proved an even more fruitful area for parliamentary debate and specific issues such as the Opium War invoked arguments both for preserving British interests and for observing moral principles. Over the Don Pacifico incident, Palmerston tried to synthesise the two. He insisted, on 25 June 1850, that: 'as the Roman, in days of old, held himself free from indignity, when he could say *Civis Romanus sum*; so also a British subject, in whatever land he may be, shall feel confident that the watchful eye and strong arm of England will protect him against injustice and wrong'.[16] Gladstone clearly gave this careful thought overnight for, on 27 June, he took the offensive against Palmerston:

> What then, Sir, was a Roman citizen? He was a member of a privileged caste: he belonged to a conquering race, to a nation that held all others bound down by the strong arm of power. For him there was to be an exceptional system of law; for him were principles to be asserted, and by him rights were to be enjoyed, that were denied to the rest of the world. Is such, then, the view of the noble Lord, as to the relation that is to subsist between England and other countries?[17]

This is one of the high points of nineteenth-century oratory, reflecting a different conception of freedom and moral judgement. It might also be considered to have captured the fundamental contrast between Palmerstonian Whiggery and Gladstonian Liberalism. On the other hand, such a conclusion would be simplistic, since the whole purpose of speeches is to persuade by marshalling details which might, in other circumstances, be presented very differently.

NEWSPAPERS AND PERIODICALS

The most transitory of all written sources are newspapers. They lack the degree of self-consciousness of some other forms of material because, in the words of G. Wilkinson, they 'are time-specific and do not have an eye for posterity'.[18] This has a distinct advantage. There is no source which provides such a detailed account of and reflection on events – at regular, often daily, intervals. Newspapers can therefore provide the spine for research on contemporary sources, partly because of the sheer volume available, and partly because they are bound by their transitory nature to reflect the major issues literally of the day.

The historian has to establish the precise nature of the relationship between the newspaper and the society it serves. To what extent does it reflect contemporary views and to what extent does it manufacture them? All newspapers claim to articulate the view of the common man, when the role they are generally fulfilling is to convey the view of the interest of the paper's owner. This may seem to reduce the usefulness of the newspaper as a source. On the other hand, the historian can find such manipulation a useful commentary on the formulation of public opinion and on the channels used. In any case, the extent of bias can generally be cross-checked by comparing different newspapers within the same period. Substantial parts of any paper will be relatively free of editorial bias, providing a considerable amount of detail in the form of minor articles and advertisements which reflect the social life at the time, especially taste, leisure, fashions.

Eight newspapers and periodicals can be cited to illustrate the range and variety in the nineteenth century. The most influential at the national level was *The Times*, which was the main medium for reporting political developments and providing key extracts from the speeches of politicians. Obviously parliamentary speeches would be covered in more detail in *Hansard*, but what of the addresses made outside the context of parliament? But for *The Times* there would have been no public record of Palmerston's speeches to his constituents in Tiverton during the 1859 general election campaign.

The majority of the papers of the nineteenth century reflected sectional interests and therefore provide a valuable insight into different levels of society. The *Farmers' Magazine* promoted the interest of agriculturalists and put up a leading case for the retention of the Corn laws. In this respect it was an important organ for the articulation of the arguments of an influential pressure group. The *Leeds Mercury* was a paper for middle-class radicals, which reflected the enthusiasm of that section of the population for the 1832 Reform Act: 'By that Act, a mighty and ancient system of corruption and abuse will receive its death-blow. The reform Act will be an epoch as well known in our particular history as the Reformation is in the annals of religion'.[19]

The *Poor Man's Guardian*, by contrast, represented the views of working-class radicals, and therefore provided a very different perspective on 1832: 'The Bill was never intended to do you one particle of good. The object of its promoters was not to change that "glorious constitution", which has entailed upon you so much misery, but to make it immortal'.[20] The *Nonconformist* was critical of the Anglican and Tory establishment and, as can be seen in an article published on 1 January 1880, had strong political leanings: 'Taken broadly, the Liberal Party has striven to follow the fiery pillar of conscience into this promised land . . . speaking generally it has striven to be "the party of Christ" . . . the party of moral principles as against that of selfish and corrupt interests'.[21]

Two papers attempted to be more analytical and to represent a wider cross-section of opinion. The *Fortnightly Review*, edited by John Morley, was a journal intended for the more intellectual radical market. It comprised articles written by political commentators, often in a position of power. In 1874 it predicted an electoral transformation based on its premise that 'the middle-class, or its effective strength, has swung round to Conservatism'.[22] In 1882 it contained an equally surprising article, written by the Conservative party organiser, J.A. Gorst: 'If the Tory party is to continue to exist as a power in the State, it must become a popular party.'[23] The *Fortnightly Review* therefore offered the opportunity for a more academic analysis of British institutions and political trends without having to grind an ideological axe. The *Annual Register* was also a stage removed from any specific sectional interest; its function was to provide a major review of events, once a year, together with a commentary. In 1824, for example, it revealed the growing acceptance of free trade in commerce: 'All the relics of the commercial code, constructed with such perverse ingenuity by our barbarous ancestors . . . are fast being demolished under the new enlightened policy of their present successors.'[24] This extract shows, however, that no paper can realistically aspire to regular impartiality. Even though not permanently representing any specific group, it may well advance a sectional interest at a particular time. This means that the historian needs to examine a variety of the paper's issues in order to detect whether there is a balance of editorial viewpoints over a longer period.

STATISTICS

Statistics are the product of the modern technological society. They cover population growth and distribution, the breakdown of layers of the workforce, the distribution of industries and agriculture, the volume of imports and exports, the variation of wages, the cost of living, and the incidence of crime, disease and poverty. Such material is often considered inherently one of the most reliable forms of primary source because it is likely to be the most neutral. It has, for example, a specific index, normally numerical, which is not directly attached to a political or ideological framework.

On the other hand, it may well have been manipulated. This could have been done by contemporaries seeking to support a particular thesis. The historian would therefore need to be aware of the possibilities of selection, omission, even distortion – all amounting to the expression of party bias. Even where such politicisation has not occurred, there is still the possibility of figures being falsified through accidental error at some stage in their compilation. The historian therefore carries a major responsibility. In the first place, he has to interpret a mass of data which has an underlying logic but no inherent meaning. He also needs to make *appropriate* use of data and to avoid distortion through inaccurate comparisons between different types of figures. Finally, he has to beware of simplistic generalisations based on superficial reading of the figures; for example, statistics showing a rapid increase in industrialisation need to be related to the original industrial baseline since the rate of growth from a low baseline is likely to be significantly higher than from a more highly developed one.

All of these points apply to the nineteenth century since there were less regular and systematic and sophisticated forms of collection and collation. There were also fewer checks carried out against the possibility of deliberate manipulation and distortion. Above all, fewer statistics are available from this period for cross-checking. B.R. Mitchell, for example, points out the 'notorious paucity of information on retail prices before the end of the nineteenth century'.[25] Indeed, until the 1880s, recorded data were few and far-between. This is partly because of the limitations in the technology of communications: printing was confined to key documents and before the era of the typewriter, written material meant precisely that. This has not, however, prevented economic historians from making inferences about, for example, the fortunes of Chartism. Rostow formulated an argument, based on an 'index of prosperity', that Chartism prospered in times of slump but declined when the economy recovered. This is an ingenious use of very limited material showing fluctuations in the price of grain, but would be more convincing if it could be confirmed by statistics showing the increase in trade union membership in the 'high' periods. Unfortunately, no such figures exist.

The historian has other opportunities for generalising, on the basis of the Russeaux price index covering the period 1800–1913, the Schumpeter-Gilboy price index (1714–1823) and the Sauerbeck-Statist price index (1900–65). But before 1914 there are comparatively few constraints on interpretation. Compared with his twentieth-century counterpart, the historian of the nineteenth century is more secure against having his thesis refuted but is less likely to have it confirmed.

NOVELS

There is a certain common ground between History and the novel, in that both cover connecting links between events and therefore deal with causation. The underlying approach is different in that the historian aims to explain what has actually occurred and the motivation of individuals who really lived. The novelist, on the other hand, explores the human psyche through imaginative constructions. Where history and literature overlap is in the attitudes of a particular period. The literary analyst will wish to explore the novel's potential for, in Shakespeare's phrase, holding the mirror up to nature, while the historian will adjust the mirror so that it reflects contemporary society and social attitudes. There is, however, an obvious deficiency here. The reflection of society will be one-sided and hence incomplete; the novelist can hardly be expected to aim at the level of impartiality aspired to by the historian, since this could well devalue the effectiveness of the plot or characterisation. Where possible, the historian will therefore need to cross-check social descriptions in novels with details from other sources and, ideally, to compare two fundamentally contrasting approaches to the same issue within two different novels. The range of novels available for the Victorian and early Edwardian eras is extensive. For convenience, they can be subdivided into three broad categories: quality, popular and political.

The quality novel experienced something of a renaissance in the nineteenth century. Georgian England is given a focus which might be called microscopic, in that it included a fine analysis of the mores of the upper middle class in specific areas of Hampshire; the pre-occupations of the nation as a whole seem not to intrude at all. This says something about the self-contained units into which England was divided before the days of the mass society. The growing interaction between social and economic groups is shown more clearly in George Eliot's *Middlemarch* and Gaskell's *Mary Barton*. A more detailed picture of economic and political dislocation is provided in Kingsley's *Alton Locke*, while Dickens provides a series of detailed views of Victorian society. These include the workhouse in *Oliver Twist*, the education system in *David Copperfield*, the prevalent economic attitudes in *Little Dorrit*, and the legal system and the Civil Service in *Bleak House*.

In terms of popular literature, two writers were particularly widely read during the last four decades of the period covered by this book: Rudyard Kipling and Henry Rider Haggard. Both had strongly imperial themes; while Kipling wrote mainly of India, Rider Haggard's novels had an African focus. Although the latter wrote 'outrageous adventures' for 'healthy amusement', his numerous works – with deceptively romantic names – provide an exceptionally clear reflection of patriotism and popular prejudices at the turn of the century. Generations of late Victorians and early Edwardians, brought up on a regular diet of Rider Haggard and Kipling, could hardly fail to develop an emotional commitment to the whole concept of Empire and to accept the underlying validity of Britain's overseas role.

Rider Haggard's novels took for granted the natural superiority of the British – more specifically the English – to other European peoples; the dedication in *Allan Quartermain*, for example, exhorts Rider Haggard's son to aspire to that highest status a human being can reach: 'the state and dignity of English gentlemen'. There is also a recurring theme of the English hero conquering an opponent of another race in a 'fair fight'. Occasionally, the author seems to be carried away in an orgy of patriotism referring to the combatants by their race rather than their name: hence 'our great Englishman' (*King Solomon's Mines*) or, more dismissively, 'the Arab' (*Allan and the Holy Flower*) or the 'Portugee' (*The People of the Mist*). Rider Haggard also reflected the late Victorian preference for pure racial groups and the dislike of miscegenation. The black man was accepted and even idealised in his 'natural' or tribal role. This led to a particular respect for the Zulus, probably heightened by the latter's temporary triumph at Isandhlwana in 1879. Thus sub-heroic roles were often played by black warriors, like Umbopa and Umslopogaas, while *Nada the Lily*, reputedly the most bloodthirsty book ever written, was the author's attempt to create an idyllic picture of the spartan virtues of Zululand. Conversely, the villains in his books were often half-caste Arabs (as in *The People of the Mist*) or mixed-race Portuguese (as in *Marie*).

The third category of literature – political novels – are of particular value to the historian. They reflect the inner mind of the politicians of the day, providing a valuable extra resource to supplement official State papers and personal diaries. In *Coningsby*, for example, Disraeli revealed the extent of his criticism of Peel's brand of Conservatism. This is shown in an extract from a conversation between two Conservative agents (and implied Peelites), Tadpole and Taper. Although fictional, this is a clear indication of Disraeli's stereotyped view of revived Conservatism, and shows that the vehemence with which he attacked Peel's leadership in 1846 was not due merely to the proposed repeal of the Corn Laws.

> 'True, terribly true', said Mr Taper. 'That we should ever live to see a Tory Government again! We have reason to be very grateful.'
> 'Hush!' said Mr Tadpole. 'That time has gone by for Tory Governments; what the country requires is a sound Conservative Government.'
> 'A sound Conservative Government', said Taper musingly. 'I understand: Tory men and Whig measures.'[26]

Disraeli's other major novel, *Sybil*, had a broader perspective, as its subtitle *The Two Nations* implies. Part of its aim was to show the growth of social divergence within Victorian Britain and it offered, albeit implicitly, a vision of the way in which Toryism could achieve reconciliation by broadening the base of its support well beyond the more restricted Peelite vision. Any understanding of Disraelian, as opposed to Peelite, Conservatism must be based at least in part on an appreciation of the importance of *Sybil* as a receptacle for Disraeli's broader political aspirations. The lasting significance of this particular novel is that its title came to be associated with a new political trend: 'single-nation toryism'.

CARTOONS

One particular type of source may, at first sight, be seen as inappropriate for use by the historian. The cartoon is, by its very nature, one-sided. All humour depends on the display of bias: after all, whoever heard of the carefully balanced joke? To some extent, therefore, the historian must suspend his usual striving for impartiality in order to appreciate the point being made. On the other hand, the joke can reveal a great deal about the society in which it was produced and the people at which it was aimed.

The style employed underwent a considerable change during the course of the nineteenth century. The cartoons of the early decades were far more complex than those which eventually replaced them. Although they focused on an easily identifiable theme, the extent of detail was such that they required careful study before the point became fully apparent (see Figure 18). Gradually, however, the focus sharpened, and the cartoonist's intention was to convey the point immediately and succinctly (see Figures 19–25).

There were many different types of cartoon, with varying degrees of subtlety. In most instances, the cartoonist occupied a detached position as an observer of political developments, adding a wry comment of his own to circumstances he had no intention of trying to influence. At times, the cartoonist would focus on individual politicians. 'The rising generation in parliament' (Figure 19) encapsulates two views of Conservatism – Peel as the embodiment of common sense, Disraeli as the iconoclast. 'There's always something' (Figure 20) depicts Palmerston as Russell's ungovernable partner, although Palmerston is more dignified than Disraeli and his form of eccentricity is somehow more acceptable. Both cartoons have a common defect. They provide a totally one-sided view of the conflict they portray. But this is inevitable, since all cartoons depend on distilling a character into one characteristic: in this instance, Palmerston's arrogance and Disraeli's rebelliousness.

The focus of some cartoons was an issue rather than a personality. A famous example was the cartoon (Figure 21) showing Disraeli winning the race for the passage of the 1867 Reform Act. The horse race is a much used scenario, but this particular version shows an additional insight in its prophetic allusion to the next general election. This comment within a comment shows an unusual degree of subtlety, which is altogether missing in the next example. The 1886 cartoon on the 'live shell' (Figure 22) grossly oversimplifies the responses of the two party leaders to the Irish issue, wrongly implying that their responses were identical. On the other hand, this might be seen as an accurate reflection of the weariness of public opinion with a long-standing problem.

An increasingly popular device used by cartoonists was the political metaphor. The favourite was the British lion, seen in Figure 23 as under pressure from imperial problems. This cartoon conveys the sense of restrained power. Britain is shown as assailed by a series of irritants, to which her response would be reluctant but forceful. There is an underlying certainty that the problems are not sufficiently serious to inflict any real damage. Thus the message is in part frustration and in part confidence in the strength of the British Empire. There is no anticipation of the twentieth-century's use of the metaphor in a more destructive sense: the 'war of the flea' came to signify the effectiveness of guerrilla warfare against major powers like the United States and the Soviet Union.

On occasion, the cartoonist abandoned his position as observer and, instead, became a campaigner. Figure 18 is a powerful indictment of the corruption of the pre-1832 parliamentary system, with the strong implication that reform was vitally needed. During the 1840s and 1850s public health was taken up by *Punch* as an issue needing a political solution. A series of cholera epidemics turned the attention of the cartoonists to the effects of Britain's inadequate sewers; hence the government was exhorted to greater expenditure in order to overcome the side-effects of pollution (Figure 24). Not all campaigns were constructive. Occasionally there were examples of the deliberate selection of a stereotyped target. Over women's suffrage, *Punch* took a heavy-handed swipe at a pressure group (Figure 25) claiming, at the same time, to be adopting a reasonable attitude. Thus cartoons could sometimes seek to mould opinion as well as to reflect it, and in a way which could be reactionary as well as progressive.

Figure 18 The reformers' attack on the old rotten tree (Source: Cruickshank 1832)

THE RISING GENERATION—IN PARLIAMENT.

Peel. "WELL, MY LITTLE MAN, WHAT ARE YOU GOING TO DO THIS SESSION, EH?"

D——li (the Juvenile). "WHY—AW—AW—I 'VE MADE ARRANGEMENTS—AW—TO SMASH—AW—EVERYBODY."

Figure 19 The rising generation – in Parliament (Source: *Punch* 1847; by courtesy of the Mary Evans Picture Library, London)

THERE'S ALWAYS SOMETHING.

" I 'M VERY SORRY, PALMERSTON, THAT YOU CANNOT AGREE WITH YOUR FELLOW SERVANTS ; BUT AS I DON'T FEEL
INCLINED TO PART WITH JOHN, YOU MUST GO, OF COURSE."

JANUARY 10, 1852.

Figure 20 There's always something (Source: *Punch* 1851; by courtesy of
the Mary Evans Picture Library, London)

THE DERBY, 1867. DIZZY WINS WITH "REFORM BILL."

Mr. Punch. "DON'T BE TOO SURE; WAIT TILL HE'S *WEIGHED.*"

Figure 21 The Derby, 1867 (Source: *Punch* 1867; by courtesy of the Mary Evans Picture Library, London)

THE LIVE SHELL.

(WHICH OF 'EM WILL THROW IT OVERBOARD?)

Figure 22 The live shell (Source: *Punch* 1886; by courtesy of the Mary Evans Picture Library, London)

Figure 23 If they will irritate him, they must take the consequences (Source: *Judy* 1879; by courtesy of the Mary Evans Picture Library, London)

Figure 24 A court for King Cholera (Source: *Punch* 1852; by courtesy of the Mary Evans Picture Library, London)

THE SHRIEKING SISTER.

The Sensible Woman. "*YOU* HELP OUR CAUSE? WHY, YOU'RE ITS WORST ENEMY!"

Figure 25 The shrieking sister (Source: *Punch* 1906; by courtesy of the
Mary Evans Picture Library, London)

CONCLUSION

The late twentieth century has seen a remarkable increase in the number of secondary works published. The reason for this is an interaction between different levels of historical activity, but the catalyst is the increased significance attached to the primary source and a never-ending quest to see it in a new light.

The impetus comes from the enormous quantity of detailed research, usually connected with, or the follow-up to, a doctoral thesis. This may unearth new sources, but is more likely to reinterpret existing ones or to focus on documents which have previously been ignored or marginalised. The result is the development of an increasingly elaborate patchwork of detailed studies which have two important functions. One is to bring obscure primary sources within the range of any serious student of history. The other is to regenerate historical debate on a wide variety of issues – partly through the sources themselves, partly through the interpretation attached to them within the thesis or monograph. Other secondary works follow, representing a wide range of viewpoints. These, in turn, attract the 'synthesisers', who aim to provide a more composite interpretation covering a wider period. This, of course, has been the main intention of Chapters 2–22 in this book.

NOTES

1 AN INTRODUCTION TO BRITISH POLITICAL HISTORY 1815–1914

1 In J. Gardiner (ed.) *What is History Today?* (Atlantic Highlands, NJ 1988), pp. 19–20.
2 ibid., p. 21.
3 ibid., p. 22.
4 See E. Halévy *A History of the English People in the Nineteenth Century* (trans. London 1926), vol. 2; and Sir L. Woodward *The Age of Reform* (Oxford 1938).
5 G. Macaulay *A History of England* (1848), ch. 1.
6 Sir L. Namier, quoted in A. Marwick *The Nature of History* (London 1970), p. 92.
7 K. Marx and F. Engels *Manifesto of the Communist Party* (1848), ch. 1.
8 See Macdonagh 'The Nineteenth-century Revolution in Government: A Reappraisal', *Historical Journal* 1, 1958; J. Hart 'Nineteenth-century Social Reform: a Tory Interpretation of History' in M.W. Flinn and T.C. Smout (eds) *Essays in Social History* (Oxford 1974); and D. Roberts: 'Jeremy Bentham and the Victorian Administrative State', *Victorian Studies* 2, 1959.

2 BRITAIN AND THE THREAT OF REVOLUTION 1789–1832

1 E. Halévy *A History of the English People in the Nineteenth Century* (trans. London 1926), vol. 1, part 3, ch. 1.
2 E. Hobsbawm *Industry and Empire* (London 1968), p. 55.
3 J.L. and B. Hammond *The Town Labourer* (1917 and 1978), p. 71.
4 P. Gregg *A Social and Economic History of Britain 1760–1870* (London 1950).
5 H.T. Dickinson *British Radicalism and the French Revolution* (Oxford 1985), ch. 1.
6 See T. Paine *Rights of Man 1791–92* (repr. New York 1969).

7 Halévy, op. cit., p. 426.
8 Dickinson, op. cit., ch. 1.
9 ibid., p. 3.
10 Halévy, op. cit., ch. 1.
11 ibid., ch. 1.
12 E.P. Thompson *The Making of the English Working Class* (London 1963), ch. 11.
13 Gregg, op. cit.
14 Gregg, op. cit., p. 86.
15 H. Arendt *On Revolution* (London 1963), p. 112.
16 Burke, quoted in J. Bowle *Western Political Thought* (London 1947), ch. 9.
17 M.I. Thomis and P. Holt *Threats of Revolution in Britain, 1789-1848* (London 1977), ch. 2.
18 See E.J. Evans *The Forging of the Modern State* (London 1983).
19 M.I. Thomis *The Town Labourer and the Industrial Revolution* (London 1974).
20 F.O. Darvall *Popular Disturbances and Public Order in Regency England* (London 1934), ch. 15.
21 N. Gash *Aristocracy and People: Britain 1815-1865* (London 1979), ch. 3.
22 Evans, op. cit., ch. 19.
23 J. Marlow *The Peterloo Massacre* (London 1969), conclusion.
24 ibid.
25 Thomis and Holt, op. cit, ch. 6.
26 A. Briggs *The Age of Improvement* (London 1959), p. 233.
27 J.T. Ward (ed.) *Popular Movements 1830-1850* (London 1970), introduction.
28 Thomis and Holt, op. cit., ch. 6.
29 Ward, op. cit., introduction.
30 For an analysis of Eldon's views see J.C.D. Clark *English Society 1688-1832* (Cambridge 1985), ch. 6.
31 Dickinson, op. cit., ch. 1.
32 ibid.
33 Thomis and Holt, op. cit., ch. 6.

3 TORY RULE 1812-30

1 E. Halévy *A History of the English People in the Nineteenth Century* (trans. London 1926), vol. 2, part 1, ch. 1.
2 ibid., vol. 2, part 2, ch. 1.
3 Sir L. Woodward *The Age of Reform* (Oxford 1938), book 1, ch. 1.
4 W.R. Brock *Lord Liverpool and Liberal Toryism 1820 to 1827* (Cambridge 1941), ch. 6.
5 See D. Beales *From Castlereagh to Gladstone 1815-1885* (London 1969).
6 A. Wood *Nineteenth Century Britain 1815-1914* (London 1960), ch. 6.
7 Quoted in R. Brown and C. Daniels *Documents and Debates: Nineteenth Century Britain* (London 1975), ch. 2.
8 J.E. Cookson *Lord Liverpool's Administration 1815-1822* (Edinburgh

and London 1975), conclusion.
9 N. Gash *Aristocracy and People: Britain 1815–1865* (London 1979), ch. 4.
10 ibid., ch. 3.
11 ibid., ch. 3.
12 E.J. Evans *The Forging of the Modern State* (London 1983), ch. 20.
13 Gash.
14 ibid.
15 Evans, op. cit., ch. 22.
16 B.W. Hill *British Parliamentary Parties 1742–1832* (London 1985), ch. 13.
17 M. Bentley *Politics without Democracy* (London 1984), ch. 1.
18 Gash, op. cit., ch. 5.
19 A. Briggs *The Age of Improvement* (London 1959), p. 234.
20 R. Stewart *Party and Politics* (London 1989), ch 2.
21 J.C.D. Clark *English Society 1688–1832* (London 1985).
22 A. Mitchell *The Whigs in Opposition 1815–1830* (Oxford 1967).
23 E.A. Wasson *Whig Renaissance* (New York 1987), ch. 5.

4 THE FOREIGN POLICY OF CASTLEREAGH AND CANNING

1 J.W. Derry *Castlereagh* (London 1976), ch. 4.
2 ibid., ch. 4.
3 ibid., ch. 4.
4 W. Hinde *Castlereagh* (London 1981), ch. 14.
5 C. von Clausewitz *On War* (1832, English trans. London 1908), book 1, ch. 1.
6 Hinde, op. cit., ch. 14.
7 Derry, op. cit., ch. 1.
8 ibid., ch. 4.
9 ibid., ch. 4.
10 D.R. Ward *Foreign Affairs 1815–1865* (London 1972), ch. 3.
11 Derry, op. cit., ch. 4.
12 J. Clarke *British Diplomacy and Foreign Policy 1782–1865* (London 1989), ch. 4.
13 ibid., ch. 4.
14 H. Martineau, quoted in Derry, op. cit., ch. 1.
15 See D. Southgate *The Most English Minister* (London 1966).
16 Ward, op. cit., ch. 4.
17 Derry, op. cit., ch. 4.
18 P. Dixon *Canning* (London 1976), ch. 9.
19 P.J.V. Rolo *George Canning. Three Biographical Studies* (London 1965), p. 209.
20 Clarke, op. cit., ch. 6.
21 Dixon, op. cit., ch. 9.
22 ibid., ch. 9.
23 Rolo, op. cit., p. 220.
24 Dixon, op. cit., ch. 9.

25 ibid., ch. 9.
26 Rolo, op. cit., p. 130.
27 Dixon, op. cit., ch. 9.
28 E.J. Evans *The Forging of the Modern State* (London 1983), p. 200.
29 Rolo, op. cit., p. 260.

5 THE 1832 REFORM ACT

1 I.R. Christie *Wilkes, Wyvill and Reform* (London 1962), quoted in D.G. Wright *Democracy and Reform 1815–1885* (London 1970), ch. 2.
2 E.J. Evans *The Great Reform Act of 1832* (London 1983), p. 11.
3 ibid.
4 D.G. Wright *Democracy and Reform 1815–1885* (London 1970), ch. 4.
5 E.J. Evans *The Forging of the Modern State* (London 1983), ch. 23.
6 Wright, op. cit., ch. 4.
7 Wright, op. cit., document 7.
8 ibid., p. 32.
9 A. Llewellyn *The Decade of Reform: The 1830s* (London 1972), ch. 2.
10 ibid., ch. 2.
11 ibid., ch. 2.
12 Wright, op. cit., document 8a.
13 J.W. Hunt *Reaction and Reform 1815–1841* (London 1972), p. 106.
14 C. Flick 'The Fall of Wellington's Government', *Journal of Modern History*, 1965.
15 R.W. Davies 'The Tories, the Whigs, and Catholic Emancipation, 1827–1829', *English Historical Review*, 1982.
16 N. Gash *Aristocracy and People: Britain 1815–1865* (London 1979), ch. 5.
17 ibid., ch. 5.
18 ibid., ch. 5.
19 G.B. Finlayson *England in the Eighteen Thirties. Decade of Reform* (London 1969), ch. 1.
20 Gash, op. cit., ch. 5.
21 Finlayson, op. cit., ch. 1.
22 Llewellyn, op. cit., ch. 2.
23 D. Close 'The Formation of a Two-party Alignment in the House of Commons between 1832 and 1841', *English Historical Review*, 1969.

6 WHIG REFORMS IN THE 1830s

1 A.D. Kriegel 'A Convergence of Ethics: Saints and Whigs in British Antislavery', *Journal of British Studies* 26, 1987.
2 ibid., p. 446.
3 ibid., p. 448.
4 ibid., p. 449.
5 G.B. Finlayson 'The Politics of Municipal Reform, 1835', *English Historical Review*, 1966.
6 ibid.

7 From *A Fragment on Government* (1776), quoted in M. Bruce *The Coming of the Welfare State* (London 1961), p. 93.

8 J.W. Hunt *Reaction and Reform 1815–1841* (London 1972), p. 116.

9 Finlayson, op. cit.

10 M. Bruce *The Coming of the Welfare State* (London 1961), p. 93.

11 Kriegel, op. cit., p. 425.

12 R.H. Tawney *Religion and the Rise of Capitalism* (London 1926 and 1938), p. 242.

13 M. Blaug 'The Myth of the Old Poor Law and the Making of the New', *The Journal of Economic History*, 1963; 'The Poor Law Report Reexamined', *Journal of Economic History,* 1963.

14 U. Henriques *Before the Welfare State* (London 1979), p. 44.

15 P. Gregg *A Social and Economic History of Britain 1760–1870* (London 1950), p. 190.

16 E.J. Evans *The Forging of the Modern State* (London 1983), p. 225.

17 Bruce, op. cit., p. 105.

18 N. Brasher *Arguments in History* (London 1968), ch. 2.

19 E. Halévy *A History of the English People in the Nineteenth Century* (trans. London 1926), vol. 3, part 1, ch. 2.

20 A.D. Kriegel 'The Irish Policy of Lord Grey's Government', *English Historical Review*, Jan. 1971, p. 23.

21 Brasher, op. cit., ch. 2.

22 Hunt, op. cit., p. 136

23 I.D.C. Newbould 'William IV and the Dismissal of the Whigs', *Canadian Journal of History*, 1976.

24 A. Llewellyn *The Decade of Reform: The 1830s* (London 1972), ch. 3.

25 ibid., ch. 3.

26 ibid., ch. 3.

27 ibid., ch. 3.

7 SIR ROBERT PEEL AS PARTY LEADER AND NATIONAL STATESMAN

1 N. Gash *Sir Robert Peel* (London 1972), pp. 234–7.

2 E.J. Evans *The Forging of the Modern State* (London 1983), ch. 27.

3 R. Stewart *The Foundation of the Conservative Party 1830–1867* (London 1978), ch. 5.

4 P. Adelman *Peel and the Conservative Party 1830–1850* (London 1989), ch. 2.

5 L. Strachey and R. Fulford (eds) *The Greville Memoirs 1814–1860* (London 1938), vol. 3, pp. 18–19.

6 Adelman, op. cit., ch. 2.

7 N. Gash *The Age of Peel* (London 1968), part IV, document 4.

8 N. Gash 'The Historical Significance of the Tamworth Manifesto' in *Pillars of Government and Other Essays on State and Society c. 1770–c. 1880* (London 1986).

9 N. Gash 'Peel and the Party System 1830–1850', *Transactions of the Royal Historical Society*, 1951.

10 Evans, op. cit., ch. 27.

11 N. Gash *Aristocracy and People* (London 1979), p. 234.
12 Adelman, op. cit., ch. 4.
13 A.J.B. Hilton 'Peel: A Reappraisal', *The Historical Journal* 22, 1979.
14 Adelman, op. cit., ch. 4.
15 ibid., ch. 4.
16 ibid., ch. 4.
17 *Hansard* 15 May 1846.
18 I.D.C. Newbould 'Sir Robert Peel and the Conservative Party, 1832–1841: A study in failure?', *English Historical Review*, 1983.
19 Adelman, op. cit., ch. 4.
20 Evans, op. cit., ch. 27.
21 Adelman, op. cit., ch. 3.
22 N. Gash, 'Wellington and Peel' in D. Southgate (ed.) *The Conservative Leadership 1832–1932* (London 1974).
23 R. Blake *The Conservative Party from Peel to Churchill* (London 1970), ch. 2.
24 Adelman, op. cit., ch. 5.
25 ibid., ch. 5.
26 Evans, op. cit., ch. 27.

8 CHARTISM

1 N. Gash *Aristocracy and People* (London 1979), p. 187.
2 William Lovett *Life and Struggles*, ed. R.H. Tawney (London 1920), pp. 94–5.
3 A. Briggs *Chartist Studies* (London 1958), p. 2.
4 E. Hopkins *A Social History of the English Working Classes* (London 1979), p. 44.
5 P. Gregg *A Social and Economic History of Britain 1700–1870* (London 1950), p. 205.
6 R.C. Gammage *The History of the Chartist Movement from its Commencement Down to the Present Time* (London 1854).
7 H. Cunningham 'The Nature of Chartism', *Modern History Review*, 1990.
8 G. Stedman Jones 'The Language of Chartism', in J. Epstein and D. Thompson (eds) *The Chartist Experience: Studies in Working-Class Radicalism and Culture, 1830–60* (London 1982).
9 Briggs, op. cit., pp. 9 and 34.
10 Stedman Jones, op. cit.
11 ibid.
12 See G.D.H. Cole *Chartist Portraits* (London 1941).
13 W.W. Rostow *The British Economy of the Nineteenth Century* (London 1948).
14 Stedman Jones, op. cit.
15 Briggs, op. cit., p. 5.
16 Gregg, op. cit., p. 207.
17 Hopkins, op. cit., p. 49.
18 Gregg, op. cit., ch. 10.
19 Hopkins, op. cit., p. 47.

20 ibid., p. 47.
21 Briggs, op. cit., p. 290.
22 E.H. Haraszti *Chartism* (Budapest 1978).
23 D. Thompson *The Chartists* (London 1984), ch. 5.
24 ibid., ch. 5.
25 ibid., ch. 5.
26 Briggs, op. cit., p. 296.
27 R.C. Gammage *History of the Chartist Movement 1837–1854* (2nd edn London 1894), pp. 2–3.
28 F.C. Mather (ed.) *Chartism and Society* (London 1980), pp. 199–202.
29 Haraszti, op. cit., p. 181.
30 ibid., p. 182.
31 Gash, op. cit., ch. 7.
32 ibid., ch. 7.
33 Thompson, op. cit., ch. 5.
34 ibid., ch. 5.
35 E.J. Evans *The Forging of the Modern State* (London 1983), ch. 28.
36 Thompson, op. cit., ch. 5.
37 ibid., ch. 5.
38 J. West *A History of the Chartist Movement* (London 1920), pp. 294–6.

9 THE CORN LAWS AND THEIR REPEAL

1 J.D. Chambers and G.E. Mingay *The Agricultural Revolution 1750–1880* (London 1966), ch. 5.
2 D.G. Barnes *A History of the English Corn Laws* (London 1930).
3 C.R. Fay *The Corn Laws and Social England* (Cambridge 1932).
4 Chambers and Mingay, op. cit., p. 125.
5 J. Walker *British Economic and Social History 1700–1977* (London 1968), ch. 12.
6 P. Deane *The First Industrial Revolution* (Cambridge 1965), ch. 12.
7 K. Randell *Politics and the People* (London 1972), ch. 2.
8 Chambers and Mingay, op. cit., p. 153.
9 N. McCord *The Anti-Corn Law League 1838–1846* (London 1948), p. 26.
10 ibid., p. 61.
11 ibid., p. 32.
12 ibid., p. 137.
13 M. Lawson-Tancred 'The Anti-League and the Corn Law Crisis of 1846', *Historical Journal* 3 (2), 1960.
14 ibid.
15 ibid.
16 Deane, op. cit., p. 97.
17 Chambers and Mingay, op. cit., p. 159.
18 ibid., pp. 158–9.
19 D.C. Moore 'The Corn Laws and High Farming', *Economic History Review*, 1964.
20 Chambers and Mingay, op. cit., p. 168.
21 *Hansard*, 3rd series, 87, col. 1054.

22 R. Stewart *The Politics of Protection: Lord Derby and the Protectionist Party 1841–1852* (Cambridge 1971), ch. 9.
23 R. Blake *The Conservative Party from Peel to Churchill* (London 1970), ch. 3.
24 ibid., ch. 3.
25 Chambers and Mingay, op. cit., p. 166.
26 Stewart, op. cit., ch. 9.

10 PALMERSTON'S FOREIGN AND DOMESTIC POLICIES

1 A.J.P. Taylor 'Lord Palmerston', *History Today*, July 1951.
2 Quoted in N. Brasher *Arguments in History* (London 1968), ch. 4.
3 D. Judd *Palmerston* (London 1975), ch. 4.
4 M.E. Chamberlain *Lord Palmerston* (Cardiff 1987), document 42.
5 ibid., document 45.
6 ibid., document 46.
7 Judd, op. cit., ch. 3.
8 ibid., ch. 3.
9 Chamberlain, op. cit., document 33.
10 ibid., ch. 3.
11 M.E. Chamberlain *British Foreign Policy in the Age of Palmerston* (London 1980), ch. 3.
12 Chamberlain, *Palmerston*, op. cit., document 27.
13 ibid., document 58.
14 H.C.F. Bell *Lord Palmerston* (London 1936), quoted in D.R. Ward *Foreign Affairs 1815–1865* (London 1972), ch. 5.
15 P. Guedalla 'Lord Palmerston', in F.J.C. Hearnshaw (ed.) *The Political Principles of some Notable Prime Ministers of the Nineteenth Century* (New York 1926).
16 Sir C.K. Webster *The Foreign Policy of Palmerston 1830–1841*, quoted in D.R. Ward *Foreign Affairs 1815–1865* (London 1972), ch. 5.
17 J. Clark *British Diplomacy and Foreign Policy 1782–1865* (London 1989), ch. 6.
18 ibid., ch. 7.
19 Chamberlain, *Palmerston*, op. cit., ch. 3.
20 ibid., ch. 3.
21 ibid., ch. 3.
22 See D.R. Ward *Foreign Affairs 1815–1865* (London 1972), ch. 5.
23 Judd, op. cit., ch. 4.
24 ibid., ch. 4.
25 ibid., ch. 4.
26 ibid., ch. 4.
27 ibid., ch. 5.
28 ibid., ch. 5.
29 Brasher, op. cit., ch. 4.
30 D. Southgate *The Most English Minister* (New York 1966), p. 284.
31 Judd, op. cit., ch. 5.
32 Taylor, op. cit.
33 L.C.B. Seaman *Victorian England. Aspects of English and Imperial*

History 1837–1901, ch. 7.
34 Brasher, op. cit., ch. 4.
35 Seaman, op. cit., ch. 7.
36 Chamberlain, *Palmerston*, op. cit., p. 85.
37 Taylor, op. cit.
38 Judd, op. cit., ch. 4.
39 Guedalla, op. cit.
40 Judd, op. cit., ch. 2.
41 ibid., ch. 6.
42 Guedalla, op. cit.
43 Judd, op. cit., ch. 6.
44 ibid., ch. 6.
45 Chamberlain, *Palmerston*, op. cit., ch. 7.
46 Judd, op. cit., ch. 8.
47 ibid., ch. 8.
48 ibid., ch. 8.
49 ibid., ch. 8.
50 ibid., ch. 8.
51 Taylor, op. cit.
52 D. Southgate *The Passing of the Whigs 1832–1886* (London 1962), ch. 11.

11   PARLIAMENTARY REFORM: 1867 AND BEYOND

1 D.G. Wright *Democracy and Reform 1815–1885* (London 1970), p. 49.
2 ibid., ch. 6.
3 W.F. Moneypenny and G.E. Buckle *The Life of Benjamin Disraeli* (London 1910–20).
4 G. Himmelfarb 'The politics of democracy: the English Reform Act of 1867', *Journal of British Studies* 6 (1), 1966.
5 R. Blake *Disraeli* (London 1966), ch. 21.
6 ibid., ch. 21.
7 J.K. Walton *The Second Reform Act* (London 1987), ch. 3.
8 Blake, op. cit., ch. 21.
9 M. Cowling *1867: Disraeli, Gladstone and Revolution* (Cambridge 1967), ch. 1.
10 E.J. Feuchtwanger *Democracy and Empire: Britain 1865–1914* (London 1985), pp. 45–6.
11 Blake, op. cit., ch. 21.
12 J. Morley *The Life of William Ewart Gladstone* (London 1908), vol. 1, pp. 643–50.
13 See G.M. Trevelyan *British History in the Nineteenth Century and After, 1782–1919* (London 1937), pp. 335–8.
14 R. Harrison *Before the Socialists* (London 1965), ch. 3.
15 Cowling, op. cit., ch. 1.
16 Feuchtwanger, op. cit., ch. 1.
17 Wright, op. cit., ch. 7.
18 D. Read *England 1868–1914* (London 1979), ch. 7.
19 ibid., ch. 7.

20 N. Gash 'Parliament and Democracy in Britain: The Three Nineteenth-Century Reform Acts', in *Pillars of Government and other Essays on State and Society c. 1770–c. 1880* (London 1986).
21 W.A. Hayes *The Background and Passage of the Third Reform Act* (New York and London 1982), ch. 11.
22 Read, op. cit., ch. 17.
23 Wright, op. cit., ch. 9.

12 DISRAELI AND THE CONSERVATIVE PARTY

1 R. Blake *Disraeli* (London 1966), epilogue.
2 P. Adelman *Gladstone, Disraeli and Later Victorian Politics* (London 1970) ch. 2.
3 P. Smith *Disraelian Conservatism and Social Reform* (London 1967), introduction.
4 J.R. Vincent (ed.) *Disraeli, Derby and the Conservative Party* (Hassocks 1978), ch. 2.
5 B. Disraeli *Whigs and Whiggism* (London 1913), p. 340.
6 B. Disraeli *Vindication of the English Constitution in a Letter to a Noble and a Learned Lord*, pp. 182–3.
7 B. Disraeli *Sybil* (London 1845).
8 R. Blake *The Conservative Party from Peel to Churchill* (London 1970), ch. 3.
9 Smith, op. cit., introduction.
10 Vincent, op. cit., ch. 2.
11 *Parliamentary Debates*, 3rd series, vol. 112 (1850), 1176.
12 Vincent, op. cit., ch. 2.
13 T.E. Kebbel (ed.) *Selected Speeches of Benjamin Disraeli, Earl of Beaconsfield* (London 1882), vol. 2, p. 511.
14 Blake, *Disraeli*, op. cit., p. 533.
15 J.T. Ward 'Derby and Disraeli', in D. Southgate (ed.) *The Conservative Leadership 1832–1932* (London 1974).
16 Blake, *Disraeli*, op. cit., p. 555.
17 Smith, op. cit., ch. 5.
18 J.K. Walton *Disraeli* (London 1990), ch. 5.
19 N. Lowe *Mastering Modern British History* (London 1984), p. 249.
20 Walton, op. cit., ch. 5.
21 Kebbel, op. cit., vol. 2, p. 511.
22 W.J. Wilkinson *Tory Democracy* (New York 1925), p. 35.
23 Smith, op. cit., ch. 5.
24 Walton, op. cit., ch.5.
25 Smith, op. cit., ch. 5.
26 Walton, op. cit., ch. 5.
27 ibid., ch. 5.
28 Smith, op. cit., ch. 5.
29 ibid., ch. 6.
30 ibid., ch. 6.
31 Adelman, op. cit., ch. 2.

32 Blake, *Disraeli*, op. cit., ch. 23.
33 Adelman, op. cit., ch.3.

13 GLADSTONE, LIBERALISM AND IRELAND

1 Quoted in P. Magnus *Gladstone* (London 1954), ch. 3.
2 P. Butler *Gladstone: Church, State and Tractarianism* (Oxford 1982), conclusion.
3 N. Brasher *Arguments in History* (London 1968), ch. 5.
4 P. Stansky *Gladstone: A Progress in Politics* (Boston and Toronto 1979), epilogue.
5 Brasher, op. cit., ch. 5.
6 Stansky, op. cit., epilogue.
7 ibid., epilogue.
8 P. Adelman 'Gladstone and Liberalism: Changes in Political Outlook', *Modern History Review*, Feb. 1991, p. 25.
9 P. Adelman *Gladstone, Disraeli and Later Victorian Politics* (London 1970), ch. 1.
10 E.D. Steele 'Gladstone and Ireland', *Irish Historical Review* 17, 1970–1.
11 ibid.
12 ibid.
13 ibid.
14 ibid.
15 B.H. Abbott *Gladstone and Disraeli* (London 1972), ch. 3.
16 ibid., ch. 3.
17 J.L. Hammond *Gladstone and the Irish Nation* (London 1964), ch. 35.
18 ibid., ch. 35.
19 ibid., ch. 35.
20 J. Vincent 'Gladstone and Ireland', *Proceedings of the British Academy* 63, 1977.
21 ibid.
22 D.A. Hamer *Liberal Politics in the Age of Gladstone and Rosebery* (Oxford 1972), ch. 5.
23 ibid., ch. 5.
24 J. Loughlin *Gladstone, Home Rule and the Ulster Question 1882–93* (Dublin 1986), conclusion.
25 ibid., conclusion.
26 ibid., conclusion.
27 A. Ramm *William Ewart Gladstone* (Cardiff 1989), ch. 4.
28 Abbott, op. cit., ch. 5.
29 ibid., ch. 5.
30 G. Morton *Home Rule and the Irish Question* (London 1980), ch. 6.
31 ibid., ch. 6.
32 P. Adelman 'Gladstone and Liberalism: Changes in Political Outlook', *Modern History Review*, Feb. 1991.
33 Ramm, op. cit., ch. 4.
34 Hamer, op. cit., ch. 3.
35 ibid., ch. 3.
36 ibid., ch. 3.

37 This is argued, for example, by A.F. Thompson 'Gladstone', *History Today*, Nov. 1952.
38 E.D. Steele 'Gladstone and Ireland', *Irish Historical Review* 17, 1971.
39 Brasher, op. cit., ch. 5.

14   THE FOREIGN POLICY OF DISRAELI AND GLADSTONE

1 P.J.V. Rolo 'Derby', in K.M. Wilson (ed.) *British Foreign Secretaries and Foreign Policy From Crimean War to First World War* (London 1987).
2 A. Ramm 'Granville', in K.M. Wilson (ed.) *British Foreign Secretaries and Foreign Policy From Crimean War to First World War* (London 1987).
3 B.H. Abbott *Gladstone and Disraeli* (London 1972), ch. 4.
4 K.A.P. Sandiford 'Gladstone and Europe', in B.L. Kinzler (ed.) *The Gladstonian Turn of Mind: Essays Presented to J.B. Conacher* (Toronto 1985).
5 N. Brasher *Arguments in History* (London 1968) ch. 5.
6 P. Knaplund *Gladstone's Foreign Policy* (London 1970), ch. 1.
7 ibid., ch. 1.
8 R.W. Seton-Watson *Disraeli, Gladstone and the Eastern Question* (London 1962), epilogue.
9 M.E. Chamberlain *Pax Britannica? British Foreign Policy 1789–1914* (London and New York 1988), ch. 8.
10 L.C.B. Seaman *Victorian England* (London 1973), ch. 11.
11 *The Times* 16 July 1878.
12 R. Blake *Disraeli* (London 1966), ch. 27.
13 ibid., ch. 27.
14 R. Ensor *England 1870–1914* (Oxford 1936), ch. 2.
15 Blake, op. cit., ch. 27.
16 M.C. Morgan *Foreign Affairs 1886–1914* (London 1973), pp. 13–21.
17 Ensor, op. cit., ch. 2.
18 Quoted in N. Lowe *Mastering Modern British History* (London 1984), p. 259.
19 L.S. Stavrianos *The Balkans Since 1453* (New York 1958), p. 412.
20 Brasher, op. cit., ch. 6.
21 Abbott, op. cit., ch. 4.
22 P. Magnus *Gladstone* (London 1954), p. 207.
23 Sandiford, op. cit.
24 W.E. Gladstone *The Bulgarian Horrors and the Question of the East* (London 1876).
25 ibid.
26 Abbott, op. cit., ch. 4.
27 P. Hayes 'British Foreign Policy, 1867–1900: Continuity and Conflict', in T.R. Gourvish and A. O'Day (eds) *Later Victorian Britain, 1867–1900* (London 1988).

NOTES

15 BRITISH IMPERIALISM AND THE SCRAMBLE
FOR AFRICA

1 See J.A. Hobson *Imperialism: A Study* (London 1902).
2 J. Forbes Munro *Britain in Tropical Africa, 1880–1960. Economic Relationships and Impact* (London 1984), ch. 2.
3 M.E. Chamberlain *The Scramble for Africa* (London 1974), ch. 4.
4 W.L. Langer *The European Alliances and Alignments 1871–1890* (New York 1931); *The Diplomacy of Imperialism* (New York and London 1935).
5 A.J.P. Taylor *The Struggle for Mastery in Europe 1848–1918* (Oxford 1954).
6 D.K. Fieldhouse 'Imperialism; an Historiographical Revision', *Economic History Review* 14, 1961, pp. 187–209.
7 D. Thomson *Europe Since Napoleon* (London 1957), ch. 20.
8 Taylor., op. cit., ch. 17.
9 J.M. Mackenzie *The Partition of Africa 1880–1900 and European Imperialism in the Nineteenth Century* (London 1983), p. 33.
10 R. Robinson and J. Gallagher *Africa and the Victorians* (London 1961), p. 465.
11 R. Brown and C. Daniels (eds) *Documents and Debates: Nineteenth Century Britain* (London 1980), ch. 8.
12 J.K. Walton *Disraeli* (London 1990), ch. 4.
13 M.E. Chamberlain *Pax Britannica? British Foreign Policy 1789–1914* (London 1988), ch. 8.
14 N. Brasher *Arguments in History* (London 1968), ch. 6.
15 See also M.E. Chamberlain *Pax Britannica?*, p. 132.
16 See R. Blake *The Conservative Party from Peel to Churchill* (London 1970), ch. 4.
17 L.H. Gann and P. Duignan *The Rulers of British Africa* (London 1978), ch. 1.
18 M. Bentley *Politics without Democracy* (London 1984), p. 224.
19 W.F. Moneypenny and G.E. Buckle *The Life of Benjamin Disraeli* (London 1910–1920), vol. 5, p. 148.
20 Brasher, op. cit., ch. 6.
21 L.C.B. Seaman *Victorian England* (London 1973), ch. 11.
22 P. Knaplund *Gladstone and Britain's Imperial Policy* (London 1966), ch. 4.
23 ibid., ch. 5.
24 P. Magnus *Gladstone* (London 1954), ch. 12.
25 ibid., ch. 12.
26 Chamberlain, *Pax Britannica?*, op. cit., ch. 8.
27 Knaplund, op. cit., ch. 5.
28 Brasher, op. cit., ch. 5.
29 Seaman, op. cit., ch. 11.
30 Brasher, op. cit., ch. 5.
31 Chamberlain, *Pax Britannica?*, op. cit., ch. 8.
32 Seaman, op. cit., ch. 11.

347

33 Quoted in N. Lowe *Mastering Modern British History* (London 1984), p. 303.
34 D. Gillard 'Salisbury', in K.M. Wilson (ed.) *British Foreign Secretaries and Foreign Policy From Crimean War to First World War* (London 1987), p. 132.
35 ibid., p. 132.
36 Chamberlain, *Pax Britannica?*, op. cit., ch. 8.
37 P. Hayes 'British Foreign Policy 1867–1900: Continuity and Conflict', in T.R. Gourvish and A. O'Day (eds) *Later Victorian Britain, 1867–1900* (London 1988).
38 See M. Balfour *Britain and Joseph Chamberlain* (London 1985).
39 V.R. Berghahn *Germany and the Approach of War in 1914* (London 1973), ch. 2.

16 CONSERVATIVE ASCENDANCY 1885–1905

1 D.A. Hamer *Liberal Politics in the Age of Gladstone and Rosebery* (Oxford 1972), ch. 9.
2 ibid., ch. 9.
3 H. Browne *Joseph Chamberlain, Radical and Imperialist* (London 1974), document 12.
4 Hamer, op. cit., ch. 9.
5 ibid., ch. 9.
6 ibid., ch. 9.
7 ibid., ch. 9.
8 P. Adelman *Gladstone, Disraeli and Later Victorian Politics* (London 1970), ch. 4.
9 J. Belchem *Class, Party and the Political System in Britain 1867–1914* (Oxford 1990), ch. 2.
10 Adelman, op. cit., ch. 4.
11 R. Blake *The Conservative Party from Peel to Churchill* (London 1970).
12 J.P.D. Dunbabin 'The Politics of the Establishment of County Councils', *Historical Journal* 6, 1963.
13 See P. Thompson *Socialists, Liberals and Labour. The Struggle for London 1885–1914* (London 1967).
14 Hamer, op. cit., ch. 12.
15 A.K. Russell 'Laying the Charges for the Landslide: the Revival of Liberal Party Organisation, 1902–1905', in A.J.A. Morris (ed.) *Edwardian Radicalism 1900–1914* (London 1974).

17 LIBERAL DOMESTIC POLICIES 1905–14

1 S. Rowntree *Poverty: A Study of Town Life* (London 1901), pp. 136–7.
2 D. Sutton 'Liberalism, State Collectivism and the Social Relations of Citizenship', in M. Langan and B. Scwarz (eds) *Crises in the British State 1880–1930* (London 1985).
3 D. Lloyd George *Better Times* (London 1910), pp. 50–5.
4 K.W.W. Aikin *The Last Years of Liberal England 1900–1914* (London 1972), ch. 1.

5 Lloyd George, op. cit., pp. 50–5.
6 G.L. Bernstein *Liberalism and Liberal Politics in Edwardian England* (London 1986), introduction.
7 Sutton, op. cit.
8 M. Bruce *The Coming of the Welfare State* (London 1961), ch. 5.
9 ibid., ch. 5.
10 ibid.
11 R. Roberts *The Classic Slum* (London 1973), p. 84.
12 Bruce, op. cit., ch. 5.
13 *Hansard* 29 April 1909.
14 *The Times* 11 October 1909.
15 Aikin, op. cit., ch. 6.
16 P.F. Clarke *Lancashire and the New Liberalism* (Cambridge 1971), p. 339.
17 D. Morgan *Suffragists and Liberals: The Politics of Woman Suffrage in Britain* (London 1975), ch. 11.
18 D. Read *England 1868–1914* (London 1979), ch. 31.
19 Bernstein, op. cit., ch. 5.
20 ibid., ch. 7.
21 ibid., ch. 7.
22 G. Dangerfield *Strange Death of Liberal England* (London 1936), ch. 1.
23 Morgan, op. cit., ch. 11.
24 See T. Wilson *Downfall of the Liberal Party* (London 1966), pp. 16–18.
25 ibid., pp. 16–18.

18   THE RISE OF THE LABOUR PARTY BEFORE 1914

1 G. Phillips *The Rise of the Labour Party 1893–1931* (London 1992), ch. 2.
2 P. Adelman *The Rise of the Labour Party 1880–1945* (London 1972).
3 K. Hutchison *The Decline and Fall of British Capitalism* (Hamden, CT 1966), ch. 4.
4 Adelman, op. cit., ch. 1.
5 Hutchison, op. cit., ch. 4.
6 Adelman, op. cit., ch. 1.
7 Phillips, op. cit., ch. 2.
8 J Belchem *Class, Party and the Political System in Britain 1867–1914* (Oxford 1990), ch. 5.
9 Adelman, op. cit., ch. 2.
10 ibid., ch. 2.
11 A.F. Havighurst *Britain in Transition. The Twentieth Century* (Chicago and London 1962), p. 74.
12 ibid., p. 75.
13 Hutchison, op. cit., ch. 3.
14 ibid., ch. 3.
15 E.J. Feuchtwanger *Democracy and Empire. Britain 1865–1914* (London 1985), ch. 8.
16 Belchem, op. cit., ch. 5.

17 ibid., ch. 5.
18 ibid., ch. 5.
19 N. and J. Mackenzie (eds) *The Diary of Beatrice Webb* (London 1984), p. 180.
20 Phillips, op. cit., ch. 5.
21 Belchem, op. cit., ch. 5.

19 FROM SPLENDID ISOLATION TO WAR: BRITISH FOREIGN POLICY 1895–1914

1 W.H. Dawson, in *Cambridge History of Foreign Policy* (Cambridge 1923), vol. 3, p. 261.
2 L. Penson 'Obligations by Treaty: Their Place in British Foreign Policy 1898–1914', in A.O. Sarkission (ed.) *Studies in Diplomatic History and Historiography in Honour of G.P. Gooch* (London 1961), p. 76.
3 *Historical Journal* 7, 1964, p. 342.
4 C. Howard *Splendid Isolation* (London 1967), p. 22.
5 ibid., p. 23.
6 ibid., p. 25.
7 ibid., ch. 9.
8 ibid., ch. 7.
9 V.R. Berghahn *Germany and the Approach of War in 1914* (London 1973), ch. 2.
10 Howard, op. cit., ch. 4.
11 R. Langhorne *The Collapse of the Concert of Europe; International Politics 1890–1914* (London 1981), ch. 5.
12 M. Hurst (ed.) *Key Treaties for the Great Powers 1814–1914* (London 1972), document 157.
13 Howard, op. cit., ch. 10.
14 See H. Temperley and L. Penson *The Foundations of British Foreign Policy* (London 1938).
15 R. Albrecht Carrié *A Diplomatic History of Europe since the Congress of Vienna* (London 1958), ch. 7.
16 See A.J.P. Taylor *The Struggle for Mastery in Europe 1848–1918* (Oxford 1954).
17 Hurst, op. cit., document 165.
18 ibid.
19 Hurst, op. cit., 'Convention between Great Britain and Russia relating to Persia, Afghanistan, and Thibet', August 31, 1907.
20 See G.W. Monger *The End of Isolation* (London 1963).
21 K. Wilson 'British Power in the European Balance, 1906–14', in D. Dilks (ed.) *Retreat from Power. Studies in Britain's Foreign Policy of the Twentieth Century* (London 1981).
22 Howard, op. cit., epilogue.
23 Hurst, op. cit., document 165.
24 Wilson, op. cit.
25 P.M. Kennedy *The Rise of the Anglo-German Antagonism 1860–1914* (London 1980), ch. 22.
26 ibid., ch. 22.

27 *Report Presented to the Preliminary Peace Conference* (1919).
28 M.G. Ekstein and Z. Steiner 'The Sarajevo Crisis', in F.H. Hinsley (ed.)
   British Foreign Policy under Sir Edward Grey (Cambridge 1977).
29 K.M. Wilson *The Policy of the Entente. Essays on the Determinants of
   British Foreign Policy 1904–1914* (Cambridge 1985), ch. 8.
30 Ekstein and Steiner, op. cit.
31 Berghahn, op. cit., ch. 19.
32 W. Carr *A History of Germany 1815–1945* (London 1969), ch. 8.

20 GOVERNMENT POLICY AND THE ECONOMY 1815–1914

1 See W.W. Rostow *British Economy of the Nineteenth Century* (Oxford 1948), ch. 1.
2 See R. Tames *Economy and Society in Nineteenth Century Britain* (London 1972), ch. 1.
3 P. Deane *The First Industrial Revolution* (Cambridge 1965), ch. 13.
4 A. Smith *The Wealth of Nations* (1904 edn), vol. 1, p. 484.
5 P. Gregg *A Social and Economic History of Britain* (London 1950), p. 277.
6 A.J. Taylor *Laissez-faire and State Intervention in Nineteenth-Century Britain* (London 1972), ch. 3.
7 Quoted in ibid., p. 24.
8 *Hansard* 23 April 1846.
9 Taylor, op. cit., ch. 4.
10 L. Brown *Board of Trade and the Free Trade Movement 1830–42* (London 1958), p. 21.
11 Deane, op. cit., ch. 13.
12 Tames op. cit., ch. 1.
13 E.J. Hobsbawm *Industry and Empire* (London 1968), ch. 12.
14 S. Pollard *Britain's Prime and Britain's Decline. The British Economy 1870–1914* (London 1989), ch. 4.
15 ibid., ch. 4.

21 GOVERNMENT POLICY TOWARDS SOCIAL PROBLEMS 1815–1914

1 A.V. Dicey *Law and Public Opinion in England during the Nineteenth Century* (London 1914).
2 G. Kitson Clark *Churchmen and the Condition of England 1832–1885* (London 1973), introduction.
3 *Report of the Select Committee on the Health of Towns* (1840), 11, vii.
4 A.J. Taylor *Laissez-faire and State Intervention in Nineteenth-century Britain* (London 1972), ch. 6.
5 P. Deane *The First Industrial Revolution* (Cambridge 1965), ch. 13.
6 ibid., ch. 13.
7 ibid., ch. 13.
8 *The Times* 1 August 1854.

9 E.C. Midwinter *Victorian Social Reform* (London 1968), ch. 5.
10 ibid., ch. 5.
11 ibid., ch. 5.
12 J.R. Hay *The Development of the British Welfare State 1880–1975* (London 1978), introduction.
13 M. Bruce *The Coming of the Welfare State* (London 1961), ch. 4.
14 Kitson Clark, op. cit., ch. 8.
15 A. Briggs *Victorian People* (London 1954), ch. 5.
16 ibid., ch. 5.
17 ibid., ch. 5.

22 BRITAIN AND IRELAND 1800–1921

1 E. Norman *A History of Modern Ireland* (London 1971), ch. 2.
2 Quoted in R. Dunlop *Daniel O'Connell* (London 1900), p. 338.
3 G.C. Bolton *The Passing of the Irish Act of Union* (Oxford 1966), p. 207.
4 Norman, op. cit., ch. 3.
5 D. Gwynn *Daniel O'Connell; The Irish Liberator* (London), p. 200.
6 Norman, op. cit., ch. 3.
7 W.J. Fitzpatrick (ed.) *Correspondence of Daniel O'Connell the Liberator*, (London 1888), vol. 1, p. 326.
8 Norman, op. cit., ch. 4.
9 Dunlop, op. cit., p. 337
10 *Nation*, 20 May 1843.
11 Norman, op. cit., ch. 4.
12 G. Morton *Home Rule and the Irish Question* (London 1980), ch. 3.
13 Norman, op. cit., ch. 5.
14 J. O'Leary *Recollections of Fenians and Fenianism* (1896), vol. 1, p. 121.
15 *Parliamentary Debates*, 1869, 3rd series, 196, col. 1062.
16 Norman, op. cit., ch. 8.
17 *The Times* 11 December 1909.
18 *Parliamentary Debates*, 5th series, vol. 36, col. 1445.
19 I. Colvin *The Life of Lord Carson* (London 1934), vol. 2, p. 79.
20 Norman, op. cit., ch. 10.

23 PRIMARY SOURCES FOR BRITISH POLITICAL HISTORY 1815–1914

1 P. Adelman *The Rise of the Labour Party 1880–1945* (London 1972), document 17(b).
2 P. Adelman *Peel and the Conservative Party 1830–1850* (London 1989), document 10.
3 P. Snowden *An Autobiograhy* (London 1934), vol. 1, p. 74.
4 E. Pankhurst *My Own Story* (London 1914), pp. 51–2.
5 Adelman *Peel and the Conservative Party*, op. cit., document 10.
6 ibid., document 31.
7 ibid., document 8.
8 P. Adelman *Gladstone, Disraeli and Later Victorian Politics* (London

1970), document 34.

9 Adelman *The Rise of the Labour Party*, op. cit., document 15.
10 Adelman *Peel and the Conservative Party*, op. cit., document 13.
11 Adelman *Gladstone, Disraeli and Later Victorian Politics*, op. cit., document 5.
12 ibid., document 13.
13 Adelman *Peel and the Conservative Party*, op. cit., document 1.
14 *Hansard*, 1831, 3rd series, vol. 2, cols. 1108–9.
15 Adelman *Peel and the Conservative Party*, op. cit., document 7.
16 ibid.
17 *Hansard*, 1850, 3rd series, vol. 112, 444 (Palmerston); 586 (Gladstone).
18 G. Wilkinson 'Sources: Newspapers', *Modern History Review*, Nov. 1991.
19 *Leeds Mercury* June 1832.
20 *Poor Man's Guardian* no. 72, 27 October 1832.
21 Adelman *Gladstone, Disraeli and Later Victorian Politics*, op. cit., document 1.
22 *Fortnightly Review* 15, 1874.
23 *Fortnightly Review* 32, 1882.
24 *Annual Register*, 66, 1824.
25 B.R. Mitchell 'Sources: Statistics', *Modern History Review*, April 1993.
26 B. Disraeli *Coningsby* (1844), ch. 6.

SELECT BIBLIOGRAPHY

This section is intended to make a selection from the works used in compiling this book to introduce the reader to further study.

HISTORIOGRAPHY

This area really needs a separate list. As a basic introduction, however, the student of nineteenth-century British history will find much of interest in J. Gardiner (ed.) *What is History Today?* (Atlantic Highlands, NJ 1988). Standard works on historiography include A. Marwick *The Nature of History* (London 1970); E.H. Carr *What is History?* (London 1961); A.L. Rowse *The Use of History* (London 1946); G.R. Elton *The Practice of History* (London 1969); D.M. Sturley *The Study of History* (London 1969). These works will also provide further references to the 'Whig', 'Tory' and 'Marxist' theories of History. A more detailed analysis will be found in H. Butterfield *The Whig Interpretation of History* (London 1931); J. Hart 'Nineteenth-century Social Reform: a Tory Interpretation of History', in M.W. Flinn and T.C. Smout (eds) *Essays in Social History* (Oxford 1974); and K. Marx and F. Engels *Manifesto of the Communist Party* (1848).

GENERAL WORKS ON BRITAIN 1815–1914

The student approaching this period for the first time may want a simple introduction with a factual and narrative focus. This is provided in note form in N. Lowe *Mastering Modern British History* (London 1984); and in A. Wood *Nineteenth Century Britain 1815–1914* (London 1960). At a more advanced level is the classic work in six volumes by the French historian, E. Halévy *A History of the English People in the Nineteenth Century* (London 1924). Among the best of the more recent works are M. Bentley *Politics without Democracy* (London 1984) and J. Clarke *British Diplomacy and Foreign Policy 1782–1865* (London 1989) and N. McCord *British History 1815–1906* (Oxford 1991).

The period 1815–70 has a good range of general works. These include Sir L. Woodward *The Age of Reform* (Oxford 1938); A. Briggs *The Age of Improvement* (London 1959); D. Beales *From Castlereagh to Gladstone*

1815–1885 (London 1969); J.W. Hunt *Reaction and Reform 1815–1841* (London 1972); and K. Randell *Politics and the People* (London 1972). The pick of the range, however, are E.J. Evans *The Forging of the Modern State* (London 1983) and, in the same series, N. Gash *Aristocracy and People* (London 1979). The period 1870–1914 is best served by D. Read *England 1868–1914* (London 1979); E.J. Feuchtwanger *Democracy and Empire: Britain 1865–1914* (London 1985); R. Rhodes James *The British Revolution* (London 1976); B.H. Abbott *Gladstone and Disraeli* (London 1972); K.W.W. Aikin *The Last Years of Liberal England 1900–1914* (London 1972); and M. Pearce and G. Stewart *British Political History 1867–1990* (London 1992). One of the most literary works on the period is G.M. Young *Victorian England: Portrait of an Age* (London 1953).

The focus of N. Brasher *Arguments in History* (London 1968) and L.C.B. Seaman *Victorian England* (London 1973) is on interpretation, partly derivative, partly original. The aim of the present book is to continue this tradition.

SOCIAL AND ECONOMIC ISSUES

Although this book is concerned mainly with political developments, there are references throughout to economic and social issues. There are numerous general works on these. They include T. May *The Economy 1815–1914* (London 1972); R. Tames *Economy and Society in Nineteenth-Century Britain* (London 1972); P. Gregg *A Social and Economic History of Britain 1760–1970* (London 1950) – much stronger on the social side; J. Walker *British Economic and Social History 1700–1977* (London 1968); and P. Deane *The First Industrial Revolution* (Cambridge 1965). A lucid, readable but polemical synthesis between political, social and economic history can be seen in E. Hobsbawm *Industry and Empire* (London 1968). A. Briggs *Victorian People* (London 1954) provides an insight into classes, groups and individuals.

Free trade, agriculture and the repeal of the Corn Laws are covered in A.J. Taylor *Laissez-faire and State Intervention in Nineteenth-century Britain* (London 1972); J.D. Chambers and G.E. Mingay *The Agricultural Revolution 1750–1880* (London 1966); D.G. Barnes *A History of the English Corn Laws* (London 1930); and C.R. Fay *The Corn Laws and Social England* (Cambridge 1932). Working conditions are fully covered in E.P. Thompson *The Making of the English Working Class* (London 1963); J.L. and B. Hammond *The Town Labourer* (London 1917); and M.I. Thomis *The Town Labourer and the Industrial Revolution* (London 1974). Among the many books on social reform are U. Henriques *Before the Welfare State* (London 1979); E.C. Midwinter *Victorian Social Reform* (London 1968); J.R. Hay *The Development of the British Welfare State 1880–1975* (London 1978); and M. Bruce *The Coming of the Welfare State* (London 1961). Finally, the economy after 1870 is dealt with in W. Ashworth *An Economic History of England 1870–1939* (London 1960) and in S. Pollard *Britain's Prime and Britain's Decline. The British Economy 1870–1914* (London 1989).

RADICALISM AND WORKING-CLASS MOVEMENTS

These are given particular prominence in the early chapters of this book. Later radicalism converges with developments in the Liberal and Labour parties. Recommended general works are H.T. Dickinson *British Radicalism and the French Revolution* (Oxford 1985); M.I. Thomis and P. Holt *Threats of Revolution in Britain, 1789–1848* (London 1977); and J.T. Ward (ed.) *Popular Movements 1830–1850* (London 1970). More specifically, there has been a plethora of books on the Chartist movement. Among the earlier ones were J. West *A History of the Chartist Movement* (London 1920) and G.D.H. Cole *Chartist Portraits* (London 1941). More recent – and standard – works on the subject are A. Briggs *Chartist Studies* (London 1958); J. Epstein and D. Thompson (eds) *The Chartist Experience: Studies in Working-Class Radicalism and Culture, 1830–60* (London 1982); D. Thompson *The Chartists* (London 1984). A more detailed study is provided in D.J.V. Jones *The Last Rising: The Newport Insurrection of 1839* (Oxford 1985); and an interesting Hungarian perspective in E.H. Haraszti *Chartism* (Budapest 1978).

POLITICAL PARTIES

Political parties and their changing fortunes have a large place in this book. A good background can be found in B.W. Hill *British Parliamentary Parties 1742–1832* (London 1985); and in R. Stewart *Party and Politics* (London 1989). The Whigs are dealt with in A. Mitchell *The Whigs in Opposition 1815–1830* (Oxford 1967); E.A. Wasson *Whig Renaissance* (New York 1987); and, above all, in D. Southgate *The Passing of the Whigs 1832–1886* (London 1962). The Liberals are covered by J.R. Vincent *The Formation of the British Liberal Party 1857–1868* (London 1966); D.A. Hamer *Liberal Politics in the Age of Gladstone and Rosebery* (Oxford 1972); P.F. Clarke *Lancashire and the New Liberalism* (Cambridge 1971); and G.L. Bernstein *Liberalism and Liberal Politics in Edwardian England* (London 1986). The subsequent decline of the Liberal Party is interpreted in an original way by G. Dangerfield *Strange Death of Liberal England* (London 1936) and T. Wilson *Downfall of the Liberal Party* (London 1966).

There is also a wide range of works on the Tory and Conservative parties. Among the best are R. Stewart *The Foundation of the Conservative Party 1830–1867* (London 1978); P. Adelman *Peel and the Conservative Party 1830–1850* (London 1989); D. Southgate (ed.) *The Conservative Leadership 1832–1932* (London 1974); and R. Blake *The Conservative Party from Peel to Churchill* (London 1970). Recommended for the Labour movement and party are P. Adelman *The Rise of the Labour Party 1880–1945* (London 1972); H. Pelling *The Origins of the Labour Party, 1880–1900* (London 1965); and G. Phillips *The Rise of the Labour Party 1893–1931* (London 1992). Two books cut across party divisions: J. Belchem *Class, Party and the Political System in Britain 1867–1914* (Oxford 1990) and P. Thompson *Socialists, Liberals and Labour. The Struggle for London 1885–1914* (London 1967).

PARLIAMENTARY REFORM

D.G. Wright *Democracy and Reform 1815–1885* (London 1970) provides an excellent overall introduction and interpretation, as does chapter 5 of N. Gash *Pillars of Government and other Essays on State and Society c. 1770 – c. 1880* (London 1986). The 1832 Reform Act is included in A. Llewellyn *The Decade of Reform: The 1830s* (London 1972) and G.B. Finlayson *England in the Eighteen Thirties. Decade of Reform* (London 1969); it is explored briefly but lucidly in E.J. Evans *The Great Reform Act of 1832* (London 1983). Later developments are the focus of J.K. Walton *The Second Reform Act* (London 1987); M. Cowling *1867: Disraeli, Gladstone and Revolution* (Cambridge 1967); and W.A. Hayes *The Background and Passage of the Third Reform Act* (New York and London 1982).

INDIVIDUAL STATESMEN

The major political figures reappear constantly in all the chapters of this book. They also form a key part of all the works in this bibliography. Some titles can be singled out, however, for more explicit mention. A major earlier work was W.R. Brock *Lord Liverpool and Liberal Toryism 1820 to 1827* (Cambridge 1941), although some of the conclusions have been subject to reinterpretation, not least by J.E. Cookson *Lord Liverpool's Administration 1815–1822*. The main works on Liverpool's contemporaries are J.W. Derry *Castlereagh* (London 1976); W. Hinde *Castlereagh* (London 1981); P. Dixon *Canning* (London 1976); W. Hinde *George Canning* (London 1973); and Sir C. Petrie *George Canning* (London 1930).

N. Gash, the acknowledged expert on Peel, has written several major studies, including *Sir Robert Peel* (London 1972) and *The Age of Peel* (London 1968). A good introduction, with a selection of primary sources, is P. Adelman *Peel and the Conservative Party 1830–1850* (London 1989). Books on Palmerston include M.E. Chamberlain *Lord Palmerston* (Cardiff 1987); D. Southgate *The Most English Minister. The Policies and Politics of Palmerston* (New York 1966); D. Judd *Palmerston* (London 1975); W. Baring Pemberton *Lord Palmerston* (London 1954); J. Ridley *Lord Palmerston* (London 1970); and C.K. Webster *The Foreign Policy of Palmerston 1830–41* (London 1951).

P. Adelman provides an excellent introduction to the era after 1867 in *Gladstone, Disraeli and Later Victorian Politics* (London 1970). The original biography of Disraeli – W.F. Moneypenny and G.E. Buckle *The Life of Benjamin Disraeli* (London 1910–20) – is still worth looking at. More recent works include J.K. Walton *Disraeli* (London 1990); and R. Blake *Disraeli* (London 1966). Specific areas of Disraeli's policies are covered in P. Smith *Disraelian Conservatism and Social Reform* (London 1967).

The earliest biography of Gladstone was J. Morley *The Life of William Ewart Gladstone* (London 1908). Modern works include P. Magnus *Gladstone* (London 1954); A. Ramm *William Ewart Gladstone* (Cardiff 1989); and H.G. Matthew *Gladstone, 1809–1874* (London 1986). Examples of more detailed studies on Gladstone's policies are P. Stansky *Gladstone: A Progress in Politics* (Boston and Toronto 1979); P. Butler *Gladstone:*

Church, State and Tractarianism (Oxford 1982); J.L. Hammond *Gladstone and the Irish Nation* (London 1964); J. Vincent 'Gladstone and Ireland', *Proceedings of the British Academy* 63 (1977); and J. Loughlin *Gladstone, Home Rule and the Ulster Question 1882–93* (Dublin 1986).

The remaining statesmen of the nineteenth and early twentieth centuries are dealt with in R. Taylor *Salisbury* (London 1975); R. Rhodes James *Lord Randolph Churchill* (London 1959); R. Foster *Lord Randolph Churchill* (London 1982); P. Fraser *Joseph Chamberlain, Radicalism and Empire, 1868–1914* (London 1966); H. Browne *Joseph Chamberlain, Radical and Imperialist* (London 1974); R. Jay *Joseph Chamberlain* (London 1981); M. Balfour *Britain and Joseph Chamberlain* (London 1985); S. Constantine *Lloyd George* (London); K.O. Morgan *Lloyd George* (London 1974); C.L. Mowat *Lloyd George* (London 1964); R. Jenkins *Asquith* (London 1978); and S. Koss *Asquith* (London 1976).

FOREIGN AND IMPERIAL POLICY

There are substantial sections of foreign policy in the general works on the period or in the biographies covered above. Works more directly on foreign policy are D.R.Ward *Foreign Affairs 1815–1865* (London 1972); D. Beales *From Castlereagh to Gladstone* (London 1969); J. Clarke *British Diplomacy and Foreign Policy 1782–1865* (London 1989); M.E. Chamberlain *Pax Britannica? British Foreign Policy 1789–1914* (London and New York 1988); and M.C. Morgan *Foreign Affairs 1886–1914* (London 1973). More detailed studies include K.M. Wilson (ed.) *British Foreign Secretaries and Foreign Policy: From Crimean War to First World War* (London 1987); P. Knaplund *Gladstone's Foreign Policy* (London 1970); and R.W. Seton-Watson *Disraeli, Gladstone and the Eastern Question* (London 1962); C. Howard *Splendid Isolation* (London 1967); D. Dilks (ed.) *Retreat from Power. Studies in Britain's Foreign Policy of the Twentieth Century* (London 1981); P.M. Kennedy *The Rise of the Anglo-German Antagonism 1860–1914* (London 1980); F.H. Hinsley (ed.) *British Foreign Policy under Sir Edward Grey* (Cambridge 1977); and K.M. Wilson *The Policy of the Entente. Essays on the Determinants of British Foreign Policy 1904–1914* (Cambridge 1985).

Imperial expansion is the subject of J. Forbes Munro *Britain in Tropical Africa, 1880–1960. Economic Relationships and Impact* (London 1984); M.E. Chamberlain *The Scramble for Africa* (London 1974); J.M. Mackenzie *The Partition of Africa 1880–1900 and European Imperialism in the Nineteenth Century* (London 1983); R. Robinson and J. Gallagher *Africa and the Victorians* (London 1961).

The European diplomatic context for all these developments is best provided in R. Albrecht Carrié *A Diplomatic History of Europe since the Congress of Vienna* (London 1958); W.L. Langer *The European Alliances and Alignments 1871–1890* (New York 1931) and W.L. Langer *The Diplomacy of Imperialism* (New York and London 1935); A.J.P. Taylor *The Struggle for Mastery in Europe 1848–1918* (Oxford 1954); D. Thomson *Europe Since Napoleon* (London 1957); and R. Langhorne *The Collapse of the Concert of Europe; International Politics 1890–1914* (London 1981).

The best collection of diplomatic treaties is to be found in M. Hurst (ed.) *Key Treaties for the Great Powers 1814–1914* (London 1972).

IRELAND

Some of the works recommended for the study of Irish history have been included in the section on Gladstone. More general books include E. Norman *A History of Modern Ireland* (London 1971); J.C. Beckett *The Making of Modern Ireland, 1603–1923* (London 1969); and F.S.L. Lyons *Ireland Since the Famine* (London 1973). Specific episodes in the nineteenth century are covered in G.C. Bolton *The Passing of the Irish Act of Union* (Oxford 1966); D. Gwynn *Daniel O'Connell; The Irish Liberator* (London); G. Morton *Home Rule and the Irish Question* (London 1980); and M.J. Winstanley *Ireland and the Land Question 1800–1922*(London).

ARTICLES

Students may well find it rewarding to read articles from various journals kept in university and larger public libraries. Examples include the *Bulletin of the Institute of Historical Research, Economic History Review, English Historical Review, History, Historical Journal, History Today, Journal of Modern History, Past and Present, Proceedings of the British Academy* and *Victorian Studies*. These usually focus on the reinterpretation of widely accepted theories or provide a more detailed examination of a specific issue. In locating articles in these journals, the *Humanities Review* is an invaluable starting point.

INDEX